LLEDOTOY

A Collector's Guide with Values

Dr. Edward Force

77 Lower Valley Road, Atglen, PA 19310

ISBN: 0-7643-0013-X
Printed in China

Published by Schiffer Publishing Ltd.
77 Lower Valley Road
Atglen, PA 19310
Phone: (610) 593-1777
Fax: (610) 593-2002
Please write for a free catalog.
This book may be purchased from the publisher.
Please include $2.95 for shipping.
Try your bookstore first.

We are interested in hearing from authors
with book ideas on related subjects.

Title page: RPL 1003 set of gold DG 54002, 32008 and 53002.
Right: Souvenir of London set: 47-001 and 49-003.

Above: Rochdale set: 6-94-68 and M4.
Right: Dr. Oetker set: 72 and 73 Volkswagens plus 123 Mercedes van.

CONTENTS

Smarties Vintage Van box with 13-90-24.

The gray series, in numerical order, minus #15.

INTRODUCTION

Lledo has been with us for more than ten years now, and its products are numerous and interesting enough to fill a book - which I hope will please those who complained about my mixing two brands in *Matchbox and Lledo Toys* a few years ago. I hope too that our readers will be pleased to find Days Gone, Lledo Promotional and other lines of models separated - and Code 3 models not included at all - with a couple of possible exceptions about which I have doubts. The price guide probably will not please anybody, but that is to be expected.

The brand of Lledo was born when Jack Odell, once an executive of Lesney (the company that produced Matchbox toys for many years), founded a new firm and gave it his name spelled backward, continuing a personal tradition that dated from his service in World War II. The first six models, five of them horsedrawn, which appeared on the market in 1983, reminded us of the earlier Matchbox Models of Yesteryear that we collected in our younger days. They were followed by new models every year, mainly commercial vehicles that could be used with many different logo varieties. In recent years, such models have sold well and justified the cost of making the dies to cast them. But even so, the folks at Lledo did not anticipate the volume of business they would attract in terms of promotional models. The first few such orders appeared as Days Gone models along with the regular Lledo issues, but soon a separate category - and a different type of baseplate lettering - were created for the Lledo Promotionals.

Since then, various other lines of Lledo-built models have appeared, including: View Vans, made for sale as travel souvenirs; the Fantastic Set o' Wheels, made for sale in the United States; Tesco, made for sale in some European countries; and Marathons, an expansion of Lledo's own products offering a short series of modern vehicles. More recently, another series has appeared; Vanguards, a group of fifties and sixties vehicles, has joined the Premier Collection as part of the Days Gone family.

The basic Lledo models were numbered from the start, but it took some time before the world learned the real numbers of their individual versions. And then we were in for a

PM 122 Thrust SSC.

surprise. After listing the models in chronological order as they came on the market, we learned that Lledo had numbered them according to when they had planned or received an order for them, which was often quite different from the order of their issue. But at least it gives us a reliable, standard set of catalog numbers for all the individual Days Gone models, and since they are now made public and stamped on the boxes by Lledo, we can feel free to use them. This also applies to the PM 100 series numbers.

The story is quite different with the Lledo Promotional models. These have never been given official factory numbers, and while various organizations have numbered them, these numbering systems are copyrighted private property. The system I tried in *Matchbox and Lledo Toys* proved to be cumbersome, so it is gone. Instead, I shall alphabetize and number each year's promotional versions of each basic model. I hope this order will make it easier for the reader to locate a doubtful model, though, even then, one will have to look closely where the same business name has appeared on several versions of the same model, or where the model can be known, by two different names, such as Wakefield and Castrol, or Stapeley Water Gardens and The Palms. This is often true of bus models which bear both advertising and the name of the bus line; I usually alphabetize them by the advertising matter, but in the case of the 17 bus the name of the bus line is usually more dominant than what appears on the roof boards.

The Days Gone models will be described according to their cast metal and plastic parts, running gear and logo details - the main features by which a model can be identified, stressing the color and logo variations that matter to most collectors. Casting variations will be noted when the basic model is described, but not listed in individual variations unless they help to identify a particular variation. Collectors who want every detail can find further information in the pages of *Days Gone Collector.*

The Lledo Promotional models will be listed much more briefly, as there are so *&%$#@! many of them. Basic body colors will be noted, and if several models have appeared under the same name, I'll try to note the details by which you can tell them apart. Beyond that, if I have a specimen of the model, you will see it in the illustrations. If not, then I can't describe it very well. If you have such a model, I would be happy to receive a description of it. Perhaps it will be possible to publish an updated version of this book in the future.

As for colors, I have tried to describe the models as I see them, which may not be exactly as someone else sees them. Then too, the terminology I use is not identical to that used by, say, a cultivated European who knows one kind of wine from another. As I found while writing *Solido Toys,* claret and burgundy describe certain colors to some people, but not to me. If I read of such a color, I describe it as maroon and hope that will be close enough, unless I see the model and feel that dark red would be a better description. At least I have not found the term "marron" used to describe a chestnut brown - and sometimes confused with maroon - used in reference to Lledo models! As for shades of light brown, some people use tan and beige to describe two different shades, while I avoid beige (not to mention taupe and sandalwood) and call all sandy light browns tan and all un-sandy ones light brown. If you disagree with my color descriptions, please bear in mind that I am an unfashionable American who does not drink alcohol - and does most of his work by artificial light.

Shortly after I published *Matchbox and Lledo Toys,* I received a kind letter from an Englishman offering to send me descriptions of the models I lacked. Unfortunately, that letter seems to have vanished in the chaos of the next book I wrote. I would like to thank my unknown friend for his kind offer, which I would be only too happy to accept now.

Lledo collectors may subscribe to *Days Gone Collector* for information on the Days Gone models, and to *RDP Lledo Information Service* for data on the Lledo Promotionals. Both of these periodicals, as well as comprehensive yearly catalogs, are available from RDP Publications, P.O. Box 1946, Halesowen, West Midlands B63 3TS, England, or RDP Publications, P.O. Box 433, Sprowston, Norwich NR7 8RA, England. RDP is an excellent source of reliable information on all Lledo products. Some of the information in this book is based on that published in the RDP publications, which I am more than happy to acknowledge as a source of information. Many of the models in my collection have been obtained from Martin Cowlyn of Syston, Leicester, and I am happy to recommend his excellent service, and to thank him and the other dealers, named in *Matchbox and Lledo Toys,*

from whom I obtained the models in my collection. Hearty thanks also to Peter Schiffer, Doug Congdon-Martin and all their colleagues at Schiffer Publishing.

When it comes to collecting Lledo models, there are several possibilities. One can, of course, try to obtain every Days Gone and Lledo Promotional model, which is what I tried to do at first but soon found to be impossible. Even if my sources of supply had been able to supply every promotional model (and I must add that a few Days Gone issues are very hard to come by too), I could not have afforded them - and nowadays I collect practically nothing but Lledo actively. So the collector probably will find it necessary to set up some sort of limits: all the Days Gone models and nothing else; all the buses, emergency vehicles, newspaper vans, beer and soft-drink trucks, food product vehicles...; or even all the vehicles associated with television shows and cartoon characters. There are all sorts of possibilities, from Rolls-Royces to soccer team vans to military vehicles, to attract the collector. And if one likes to enjoy nostalgia, one can even collect the models that bring back fond memories of Dinky Toys or Models of Yesteryear. When a Lledo model reminds me of the models I collected when I first got into the hobby more than thirty years ago, I like it all the more, and I suspect I am not the only veteran collector who feels this way. I think this is why I still collect Lledo, and only Lledo, actively.

For the time being, though, my aim has been to collect all the Days Gone models (though I have not quite succeeded in this), plus a representative selection of Lledo Promotionals.

This is what you will see in the photographs, and if you should care to contribute information that I lack, please feel free to write.

Finally, my apologies for getting this book on the market a year later than planned. I had not expected to lose both my parents and have to administer their estates, a process that took up most of 1995 and left me far behind schedule in practically everything else. That is behind me now, and at last I have been able to finish this book, and even to add information on all 1995 Days Gone models I have seen or read of.

As a result of what I added, I had to subtract. To keep to the economically practical 96 color pages, I cut some of the early promotional models shown in *Matchbox and Lledo Toys*. These include all 1985 and 1986 LP issues of models 6, 13, 15, 16, 17 and 21, plus some 1987 LP 6 and all 1987 LP 17. In addition, the gray series, Fantastic Set o' Wheels, Tesco, and some Marathons will not be shown. I tried to use all the available width in each picture, sometimes fitting as many as seven models to one shelf. This in turn made the captions longer, and as the picture and caption have to fit onto a page of certain size, this meant making the captions as brief as possible, limiting each to the model number plus one or two key words to identify the model. For example, "News/World" refers to the British "News of the World" and "Rupert" refers to Rupert Bear, who appeared once in my handwritten notes as "Rupert Beer"! In the process, I created some abbreviations that may frustrate some readers. Sorry, but I wanted to give you all the data I could cram in.

Here I must add that I have tried to spell names correctly, even to using or not using an apostrophe, and to keep in mind, when naming and describing the models, that collectors in one part of the world may not be familiar with names and terms used elsewhere. For example, most Americans might not know that Hants is short for Hampshire, Aquascutum is a store, Boots is a firm, Fairy and Pears are soaps, a vesta is a match, and Crich is the site of a museum, and many Britons might not know that J.C. Penney gave his name - which has nothing to do with a British coin - to a chain of stores, or that Budweiser Beer is made by Anheuser, Busch & Company.

Anyway, the book is finished and in your hands. I hope you will find it informative and interesting. Constructive comments (not of the nit-picking kind) are welcome - and if you think you could have written a better book, go ahead and write it! Seriously, items such as bases, box types, certificates and figures could use more research. To contact me, since my address may change soon, please write to me via Schiffer Publishing Ltd., 77 Lower Valley Road, Atglen PA 19310 USA.

Row 1. 1000 **Westminster,** 1001 + 1002 **Main St.,** 1004 **Tram Museum.**
Row 2. 1005 **Downtown,** 1006 **Chocolate,** 1007 **DG Club,** 2000 **Express Dairy,** 2001 **Chambourcy.**
Row 3. 1-88-1 **Douglas,** 1-88-2 **Manx Telecom,** 1-88-3 **Manx PO,** 2003 **Clifford,** 2004 **Celtic.**
Row 4. 300 **Windmill,** 3001 **Coca-Cola,** 3002 **Fine Lady,** 3003 **Robertsons,** 3004 **Pepperidge.**

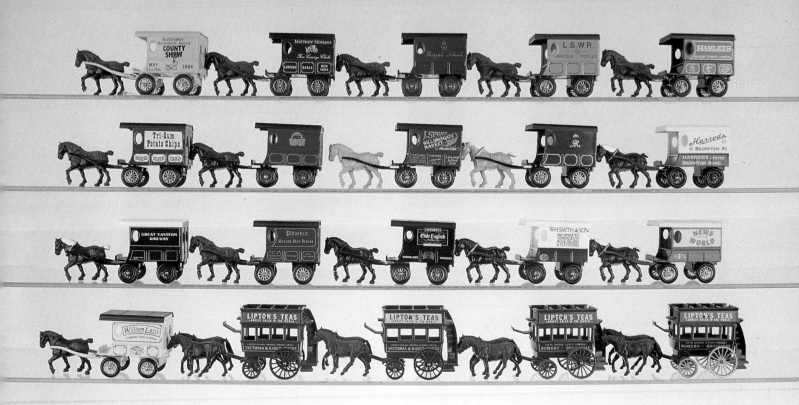

Row 1. 3005 **Stafford**, 3006 **Norman**, 3007 **Mail**, 3008 **LSWR**, 3009 **Hamleys**.
Row 2. 3010 **Tri-Sum**, 3011 **DG Club**, 3012 **Spratt**, 3013 **Mail**, 3014 **Harrods**.
Row 3. 3015 **Gt. Eastern**, 3-85-1 **Phoenix**, 3-88-1 **Chivers**, 3-92-2 **Smith**, 3-93-2 **News/World**.
Row 4. 3-93-5 **Lusty**, 4000 **Victoria**, 4001 + 4002 **Bowery**.

Row 1. 4003 **Oakey's**, 4004 **Mason's** x2, 4005 **Pears** x2.
Row 2. 4—6 4007 **Chapparal**, 4008 **Hamleys**, 4009 **Balmoral**, 4012 **Colman's**.
Row 3. 4010 **R.Times**, 4011 **News/World**, 4013 **Stone's**, 4014 **Oxo**, 4015 **Co-Op**.
Row 4. 4016 **Furness**, 4017 **Tussaud**, 4-85-1 **Bridlington**, 4-87-1 **Ex.& Mart**.

11

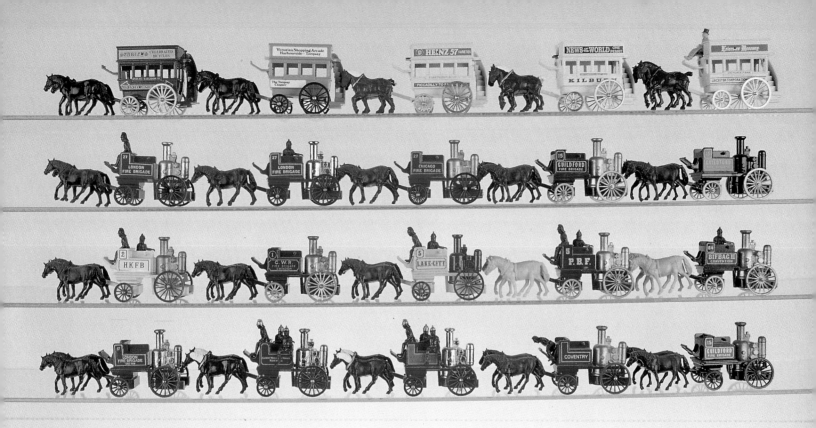

Row 1. 4-89-2 **Scarley's**, 4-89-4 **Torquay**, 4-92-2 **Heinz**, 4-93-1 **News/World**, 4-94-1 **Leicester**.
Row 2. 5000 **London** x2, 5001 **Chicago**, 5002 **Guildford** x2.
Row 3. 5003 **Hong Kong**, 5004 **GWR**, 5005 **Lake City**, 5006 **Philadelphia**, 5007 **BIFBAC**.
Row 4. 5008 **East Ham**, 5009 **Carrow**, 5010 **Metropolitan**, 5-86-1 **Coventry**, 5-86-2 **Guildford**.

Row 1. 5-86-3 **Hull,** 5-86-4 **Metropolitan,** 5-91-2 **Horsham,** 5-92-1 **Sheffield,** 5-92-2 **Shepshed.**
Row 2. 5-93-5 **Cleethorpe,** 5-93-6 **Nottingham,** 6000 **Ovaltine x2,** 6001 **Yorkshire,** 6002 **Cookie.**
Row 3. 6003 + 6005 **Br. Meat,** 6004 **Aeroplane,** 6006 **Marcol,** 6007 **Police,** 6008 **IPMS,** 6009 **Garden.**
Row 4. 6010 **Illinois,** 6011 **Stretton,** 6012 **Eve. post,** 6013 **DG Club,** 6014 **Bacon,** 6015 **Ramsden,** 6016 **Ovaltine 75.**

Row 1. 6017 **Dly.Express**, 6018 **Perrier**, 6019 **Home Ales**, 6020 + 6021 **Coca-Cola**, 6022 **Wonder**, 6023 **Railway Exp.**
Row 2. 6024 **Kodak**, 6025 **M & S**, 6026 **Marcol**, 6027 + 6028 **Philadelphia**, 6029 **Yorkshire**, 6030 **A.M.Ex.**
Row 3. 6031 **Echo**, 6032 **Stretton**, 6033 **Barclays**, 6034 **Magasin**, 6035 **Hamleys**, 6035 **Hamleys**, 6036 **Australia** x2.
Row 4. 6037 **Murphys**, 6038 **Wells**, 6039 **Woodwards**, 6040 **Lindt** x2, 6041 **Chronicle**, 6043 **Mail.**

14

Row 1. 6042 **Cwm Dale** x2, 6044 **Alton**, 6045 **Daily Mail**, 6046 **Cadburys** x2, 6047 **John Smith**.
Row 2. 6048 **Birdwood**, 6049 **Hardware**, 6050 **Toy Fairs** x4, 6051 **Cadburys**.
Row 3. 6053 **Tizer**, 6054 **Coca-Cola**, 6055 **Reese's**, 6056 **Hedges**, 6057 **Premium**, 6058 **Coca-Cola**, 6059 **Craft & Hobby**.
Row 4. 6060 **Wells**, 6061 **Fairy**, 6062 **Rose & Crown**, 6063 **RAF**, 6064 **Hamleys**, 6065 **St. Louis**, 6066 **DG Club**.

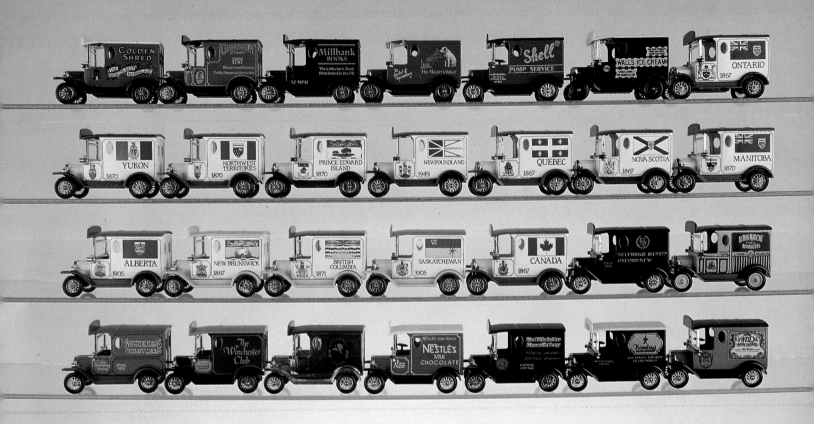

Row 1. 6068 **G.Shred**, 6069 **Charrington**, 6070 **Milbank**, 6071 **Master's**, 6072 **Shell**, 6073 **Wall's**, 6074 **Ontario**.
Row 2. 6075 **Yukon**, 6076 **Northwest**, 6077 **PE Island**, 6078 **Newfoundland**, 6079 **Quebec**, 6080 **Nova Scotia**, 6081 **Manitoba**.
Row 3. 6082 **Alberta**, 6083 **New Bruns.**, 6084 **Br. Columbia**, 6085 **Saskatchewan**, 6086 **Canada**, 6087 **Selfridges**, 6088 **Bon Marche**.
Row 4. 6089 **Schneider**, 6090 **Winchester**, 6091 **Britannia**, 6092 **Nestle**, 6093 **N.Yorkshire**, 6094 **Hamleys**, 6095 **4711**.

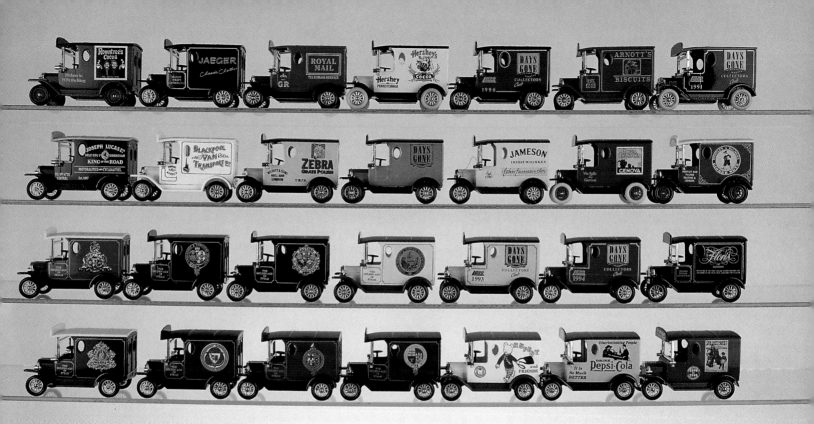

Row 1. 6096 **Rowntrees**, 6097 **Jaeger**, 6098 **Mail**, 6099 **Hershey**, 6100 **DG Club**, 6101 **Arnotts**, 6102 **DG Club**.
Row 2. 6103 **Lucas**, 6104 **Blackpool**, 6105 **Zebra**, 6106 **DG Club**, 6107 **Jameson**, 6108 **Columbia**, 6109 **Huntley**.
Row 3. 6110 **Midland**, 6111 **L & Y**, 6112 **N'eastern**, 6113 **LMS**, 6114 + 6115 **DG Club**, 6116 **Floris**.
Row 4. 6117 **LNWR**, 6119 **LSWR**, 6120 **Somerset**, 6121 **Rupert**, 6122 **Pepsi**, 6123 **SE Post**.

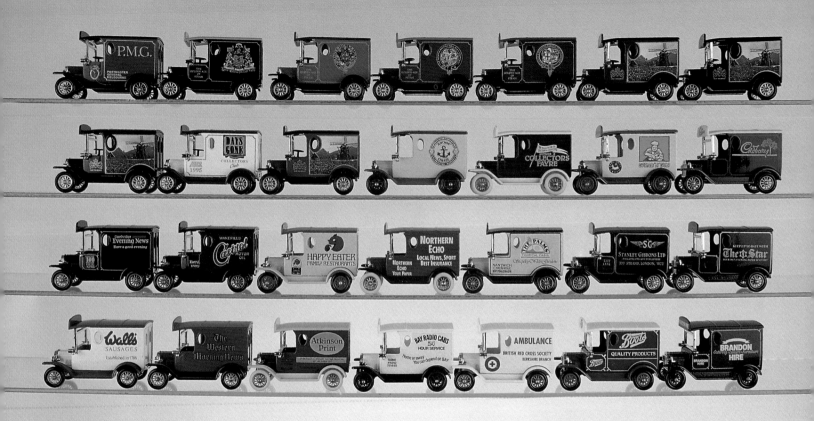

Row 1. 6124 **P.M.G.**, 6126 **Caledonian**, 6127 **Gt.Eastern**, 6128 **N.British**, 6129 **GWR**, 6130 + 6131 **Ten Bosch**.
Row 2. 6132 **Ten Bosch**, 6133 **DG Club**, 6135 **Ten Bosch**, 6-87-2 **Anchor**, 6-87-3 **Antique**, 6-87-8 **Bread &**, 6-87-8 **Cadbury**.
Row 3. 6-87-9 **Cambridge**, 6-87-11 **Castrol**, 6-87-26 **H.Eater**, 6-87-39 **N.Echo**, 6-87-42 **Palms**, 6-87-48 **Gibbons**, 6-87-52 **Star**.
Row 4. 6-87-59 **Wall's**, 6-87-63 **WM News**, 6-88-3 **Atkinson**, 6-88-8 **Bay Cabs**, 6-88-10 **Berkshire**, 6-88-11 **Boots**, 6-88-12 **Brandon**.

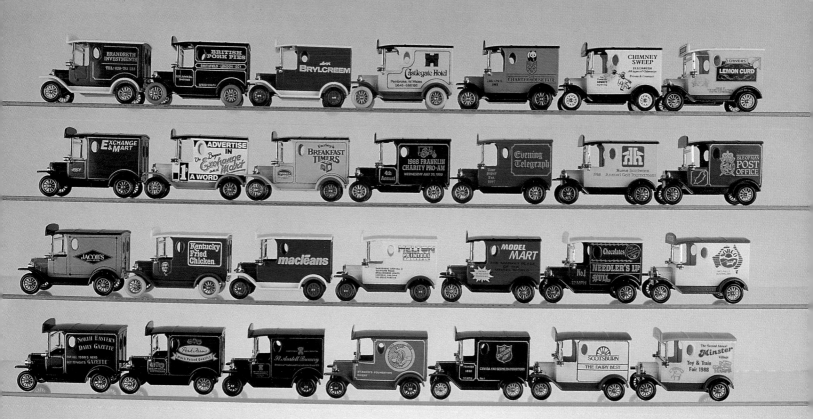

Row 1. 6-88-13 **Brandreth**, 6-88-14 **Br.Pork**, 6-88-16 **Brylcreem**, 6-88-19 **Castlegate**, 6-88-20 **Charterhouse**, 6-88-21 **Chimney**, 6-88-2 **Chivers**.
Row 2. 6-88-26+27 **Ex.& Mart**, 6-88-28 **Farley's**, 6-88-29 **Franklin**, 6-88-30 **Eve.Tele.**, 6-88-31 **Home Hdwe.**, 6-88-32 **I.O. Man**.
Row 3. 6-88-33 **Jacob's**, 6-88-34 **Ky.Fried**, 6-88-36 **Macleans**, 6-88-38 **Milton**, 6-88-39 **M.Mart**, 6-88-40 **Needler**, 6-88-41 **Norco**.
Row 4. 6-88-42 **NE Daily**, 6-88-44 **Pork Farms**, 6-88-46 **St.Austell**, 6-88-47 **St.David**, 6-88-48 **Salvation**, 6-88-49 **Scotsburn**, 6-88-50 **Minster**.

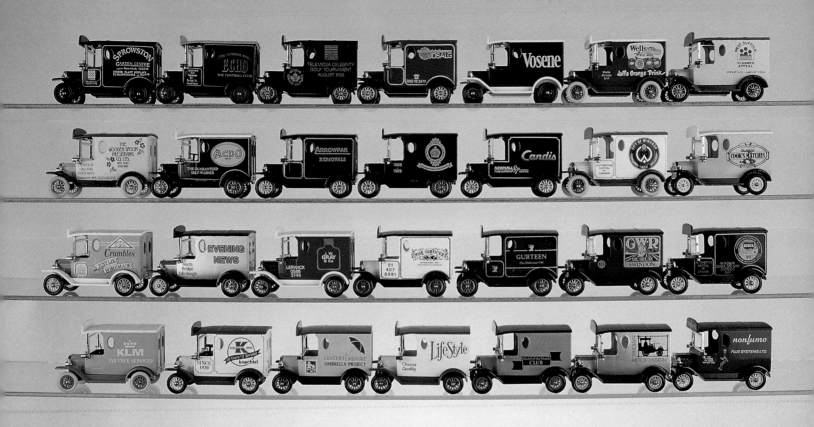

Row 1. 6-88-51 **Sprowston**, 6-88-53 **Sunderland**, 6-88-55 **Telemedia**, 6-88-57 **Udsalg**, 6-88-59 **Vosene**, 6-88-60 **Wells**, 6-88-61 **W.Suffolk.**
Row 2. 6-88-63 **W.Spoon**, 6-89-2 **ACDO**, 6-89-4 **Arrowpak**, 6-89-8 **Bolsover**, 6-89-10 **Candis**, 6-89-12 **Windsor**, 6-89-15 **Cook's.**
Row 3. 6-89-16 **Crumbles**, 6-89-19 **Eve.News**, 6-89-21 **Gray**, 6-89-22 **Grocer**, 6-89-23 **Gurteen**, 6-89-24 **GWR**, 6-89-27 **Intl.Plowing.**
Row 4. 6-89-30 **KLM**, 6-89-31 **Knechtel**, 6-89-32 **Leicester**, 6-89-34 **L.Style**, 6-89-36 **Lledo**, 6-89-41 **N.M.Museum**, 6-89-42 **Nonfumo.**

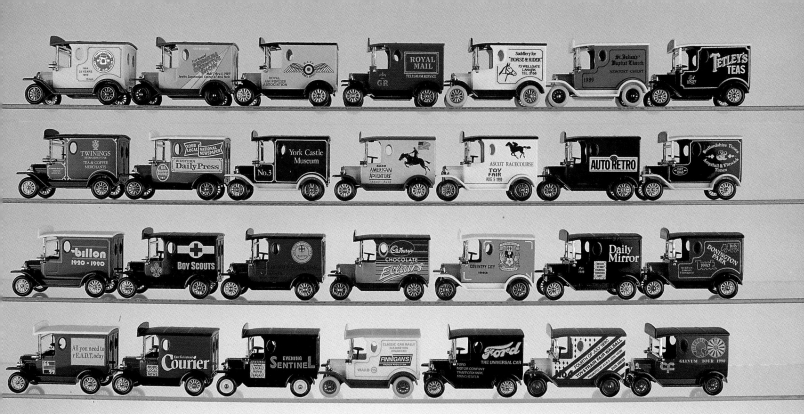

Row 1. 6-89-47 **Pembroke**, 6-89-40 **Premium**, 6-89-50 **RAFA**, 6-89-51 **Mail**, 6-89-52 **Saddlery**, 6-89-53 **St.Julian**, 6-89-58 **Tetley**.
Row 2. 6-89-59 **Twinings**, 6-89-62 **WD Press**, 6-89-63 **York**, 6-90-2 **American**, 6-90-4 **Ascot**, 6-90-6 **A.Retro**, 6-90-8 **Bedford**.
Row 3. 6-90-10 **Billon**, 6-90-14 **B.Scouts**, 6-90-15 **Buxton**, 6-90-16 **Cadburys**, 6-90-20 **Coventry**, 6-90-21 **D.Mirror**, 6-90-22 **Donington**.
Row 4. 6-90-24 **EADT**, 6-90-25 **Courier**, 6-90-27 **Sentinel**, 6-90-31 **Finnigans**, 6-90-32 **Ford**, 6-90-33 **4/July**, 6-90-34 **Glevum**.

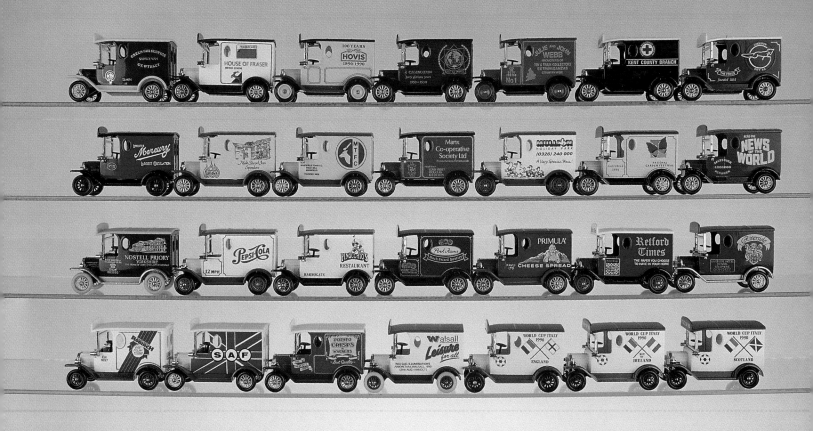

Row 1. 6-90-36 **Green Bus**, 6-90-42 **Fraser**, 6-90-43 **Hovis**, 6-90-44 **Police**, 6-90-46 **Webb**, 6-90-47 **Kent**, 6-90-49 **Leicester**.
Row 2. 6-90-50 **Mercury**, 6-90-54 **Malt Shovel**, 6-90-55 **Mansfield**, 6-90-56 **Manx**, 6-90-58 **Mullion**, 6-90-59 **Garden**, 6-90-60 **News/World**
Row 3. 6-90-61 **Nostell**, 6-90-64 **Pepsi**, 6-90-66 **Pinocchio**, 6-90-68 **Pork**, 6-90-69 **Primula**. 6-90-74 **Retford**, 6-90-75 **Riverside**.
Row 4. 6-90-76 **Robirch**, 6-90-79 **SAF**, 6-90-83 **Walkers**, 6-90-84 **Walsall**, 6-90-86,87,88 **World Cup**.

Row 1. 6-91-3 **Advertiser,** 6-91-11 **Beeston,** 6-91-20 **Chequers,** 6-91-22 **Cheshire,** 6-91-30 **Dundee,** 6-91-34 **Grampian,** 6-91-41 **Fraser.**
Row 2. 6-91-46 **Kent M,** 6-91-45 **Lincoln,** 6-91-50 **Meningitis,** 6-91-51 **Milton K,** 6-91-52 **Monk Bar,** 6-91-60 **PUP,** 6-91-65 **Portsmouth.**
Row 3. 6-91-69 **Ringtons,** 6-91-70 **ROSPA,** 6-91-71 **Mail,** 6-91-73 **Shipstones,** 6-91-75 **Smarties,** 6-91-77 **Somerset,** 6-91-78 **Southport.**
Row 4. 6-91-81 **S.Wales,** 6-91-82 **Sporting,** 6-91-87 **Trader,** 6-91-91 **Warburton,** 6-92-2 **Abbey,** 6-92-6 **Alton,** 6-92-16 **Baxter.**

Row 1. 6-92-21 **Branston**, 6-92-33 **Sumner**, 6-92-35 **Dentons**, 6-92-36 **Derby**, 6-92-37 **Derbyshire**, 6-92-38 **Digital**, 6-92-42 **Advertiser**.

Row 2. 6-92-46 **Grimsby**, 6-92-52 **Heinz**, 6-92-54 **Home Amb.x2**, 6-92-58 **J.West**, 6-92-59 **Jones**, 6-92-63 **Kleenex**.

Row 3. 6-92-68 **Telegraph**, 6-92-86 **Orchard**, 6-92-87 **Oxfam**, 6-92-94 **Powervacs**, 6-92-102 **ROSPA**, 6-92-104 **Mail**, 6-92-110 **Smith**.

Row 4. 6-92-113 **Spartan**, 6-92-120 **Trader**, 6-92-132 **Wiltshire**, 6-92-133 **Scouts**, 6-93-5 **Aspro**, 6-93-13 **Calkit**, 6-93-17 **S.Claus**.

Row 1. 6-93-20 **Coulters**, 6-93-29 **E.Midlands**, 6-93-32 **Ex.& Mart**, 6-93-34 **Finches**, 6-93-43 **Imperial**, 6-93-48 **Kent**, 6-93-57 **Midland**.
Row 2. 6-93-61 **N.Dairies**, 6-93-63 **Olive**, 6-93-67 **Penney**, 6-93-72 **Scollins**, 6-94-5 **Arjo**, 6-94-13 **Bilsthorpe**, 6-94-14 **Blobby**.
Row 3. 6-94-18 **British**, 6-94-24 **Crawley**, 6-94-30 **Eastwood**, 6-94-40 **Guinness**, 6-94-44 **Eliott**, 6-94-47 **Chronicle**, 6-94-49 **Lincoln**.
Row 4. 6-94-57 **Neptune**, 6-94-60 **Paynes**, 6-94-71 **Rupert**, 6-94-72 **St.Ivel**, 6-94-77 **Snodland**, 6-94-93 **York**, VV06-87-2 **Blackpool**.

25

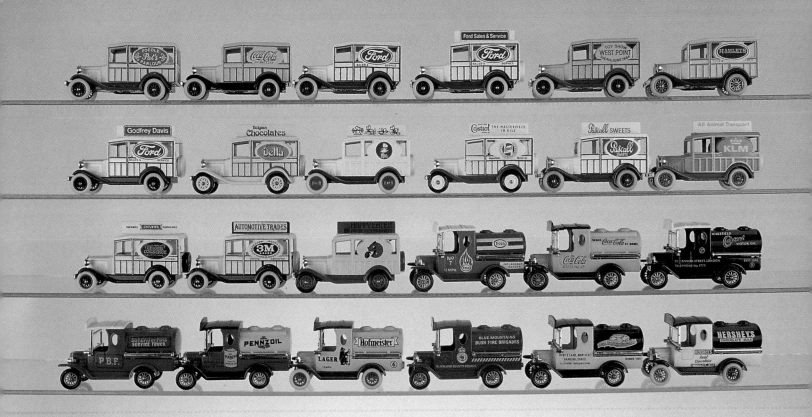

Row 1. 7000 **Poodle**, 7001 **Coca-Cola**, 7002 **Ford x2**, 7003 **West Point**, 7004 **Hamleys**.
Row 2. 7005 **G.Davis**, 7006 **Della**, 7007 **Comm.Games**, 7008 **Castrol**, 7009 **Pascall**, 7-87-1 **KLM**.
Row 3. 7-88-1 **Ginger**, 7-89-1 **3M**, 7-90-1 **H.Eater**, 8000 **Esso**, 8001 **Coca-Cola**, 8002 **Castrol**.
Row 4. 8003 **Philadelphia**, 8004 **Pennzoil**, 8005 **Hofmeister**, 8006 **Blue Mts.**, 8007 **Crow**, 8008 **Hershey**.

Row 1. 8009 **Water**, 8010 **Zerolene**, 8011 **Shell**, 8012 **Homepride**, 8013 **Duckhams**, 8014 **Shell-France**.
Row 2. 8015 **BP**, 8016 **Texaco**, 8017 **Army**, 8018 **Pratts**, 8019 **Mobilgas**, 8020 **ROP**.
Row 3. 8-85-1 **BP**, 8-86-1 **Bondy**, 8-86-2 **Marshall**, 8-86-3 **Midwest**, 8-86-4 **Shell-Mex**, 8-86-5 **Small Wheels**.
Row 4. 8-87-1 **BP Chem**, 8-87-2 **Castrol**, 8-87-4 **Cole's**, 8-87-5 **Milk**, 8-88-1 **Ampol**, 8-88-2 **KLM**.

Row 1. 8-88-4 **N.Smith**, 8-89-1 **Boehmers**, 8-89-3 **Unigate**, 8-90-1 **Bodygard**, 8-90-2 **Dairy Farm**, 8-91-6 **Walkers**.
Row 2. 8-93-2 **N.Dairies**, 8-93-6 **RAF**, 9000 **Police** x2, 9001 **NY-Rio**, 9002 **Philadelphia**.
Row 3. 9003 **15 Million**, 10000 **Brighton** x2, 10001 **Tillingbourne**, 10002 **Silver**, 10003 **S.Vectis**.
Row 4. 10004 **School**, 10005 **Potteries** x2, 10006 **GWR**, 10007 **Barton**, 10008 **London Country**.

Row 1. 10009 **Hamleys**, 10012 **Tartan**, 10013 **Trailways**, 10014 **Imperial**, 10015 **Redburns**, 10016 **Comm.Games.**
Row 2. 10017 **Hershey** x2, 10018 **Taylor**, 10019 **Coventry**, 10020 **BOAC**, 10021 **BEA.**
Row 3. 10-85-1 **C.Nederland**, 10-85-1 **LNER**, 10-85-3 **Tandhaus**, 10-85-4 **Thorpe**, 10-86-1 **Amsterdam** x2.
Row 4. 10-86-2 **Happy Days**, 10 86 3 **Ironbridge**, 10-87-1 **Dundee**, 10-87-2 **Glasgow**, 10-87-3 **GWR**, 10-87-4 **KLM.**

Row 1. 10-87-5 **Lakeside**, 10-87-6 **Lothian**, 10-87-7 **Maidstone**, 10-87-8 **Oxford**, 10-88-1 **Barclays**, 10-88-4 **Devon & Dorset**.
Row 2. 10-88-5 **Margham**, 10-88-6 **Manor H.**, 10-88-8 **Palms**, 10-88-9 **Stevenson**, 10-89-1 **Easter**, 10-90-1 **Ramsden**.
Row 3. 10-90-3 **Vectis**, 10-90-4 **Walsall**, 10-90-5 **W.Bromwich**, 11000 **Turnbull**, 11001 **Abels**.
Row 4. 11002 **Big Top**, 11003 **Stafford**, 11004 **Mail**, 11005 **Wms. Griffin**.

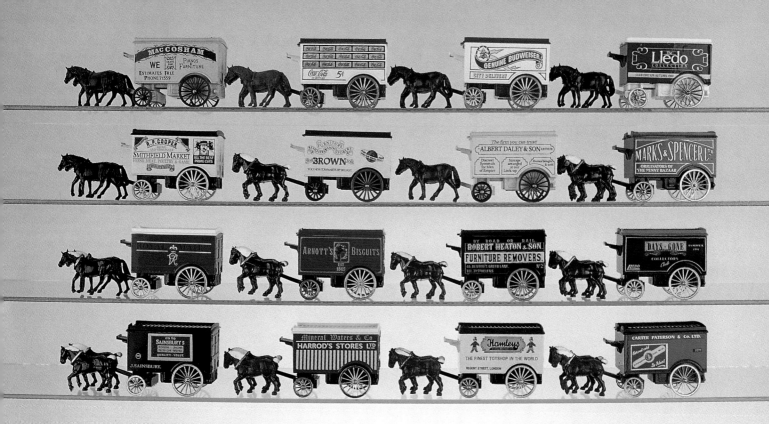

Row 1. 11006 **MacCoshan**, 11007 **Coca-Cola**, 11008 **Budweiser**, 11009 **DG Club**.
Row 2. 11010 **Cooper**, 11012 **Brown**, 11013 **Daley**, 11014 **Marks & S.**
Row 3. 11015 **Mail**, 11016 **Arnott's**, 11017 **Heaton**, 11018 **DG Club**.
Row 4. 11019 **Sainsbury**, 11020 **Harrods**, 11021 **Hamleys**, 11022 **Schweppes**.

31

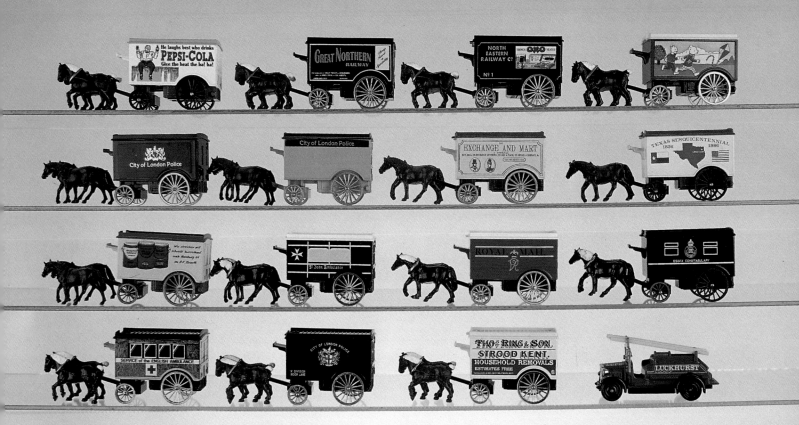

Row 1. 11023 **Pepsi**, 11024 **GNR**, 11025 **Oxo**, 11026 **Rupert**.
Row 2. 11-85-1 **London Police 7 Prison**, 11-86-1 **Ex.& Mart**, 11-86-2 **Texas**.
Row 3. 11-87-1 **Branth**, 11-88-1 **St.John**, 11-89-2 **Mail**, 11-90-1 **Essex**.
Row 4. 11-91-2 **Ambulance**, 11-92-1 **Police**, 11-93-2 **Ring**, 12000 **Luckhurst**.

Row 1. 12001 **Cardiff**, 12003 **Bermuda**, 21-85-2 **Surrey**, 12-86-1 **Borough Green**, 12-86-3 **Guildford**.
Row 2. 12004 **LCC**, 12005 **Chelmsford**, 12006 **Auxiliary**, 12007 **Essex**, 12008 **Ware**.
Row 3. 12009 **Windsor**, 12010 **Glasgow**, 12011 **Boston**, 12012 **Birmingham**, 12013 **Bradford**.
Row 4. 12014 **Hershey**, 12015 **Manchester**, 12016 **West Ham**, 12017 **Valletta**, 12018 **Hamleys**.

Row 1. 12-86-4 **J.Walker**, 12-86-6 **Milton**, 12-86-7 **National**, 12-88-4 **NSWales**, 12-89-2 **KLM**, 12-93-2 **Cleethorpes**.
Row 2. 12019 **London**, 12-86-2 **Chelmsford**, 12-86-5 **London**, 12-87-1 **Warringtons**, 12-88-1 **Chivers**.
Row 3. 12-88-3 **Invercargill**, 12-89-1 **Derby**, 12-89-3 **Sandringham**, 12-90-2 **Manch. Sq.**, 12-90-3 **Norfolk**.
Row 4. 12-91-1 **National**, 12-92-3 **Leicester**, 12-93-5 **Surrey**, 12-94-3 **Nottingham**, 12-94-5 **Blackwall**.

Row 1. 13000 **Camp**, 13001 **Eve.News**, 13002 **Tucher**, 13003 **Mitre 10**, 13004 **Hamleys**, 13005 **Michelin**.
Row 2. 13006 **Jersey**, 13007 **Mary Ann**, 13008 **Mail**, 13009 **Coca-Cola**, 13010 **Basildon**, 13011 **Ryder**.
Row 3. 13012 **Coca-Cola**, 13013 **Sentinel**, 13014 **Stroh's**, 13015 **Mail**, 13016 **Festival**, 13017 **Robinsons**.
Row 4. 13018 **Ever Ready**, 13019 **HP Sauce**, 13020 **F.D.B.**, 13021 **Coca-Cola**, 13023 + 13024 **Hershey's**.

Row 1. 13026 **Heinz**, 13027 **Tate**, 13028 **Ex.& Mart**, 13029 **E.Shaw**, 13030 **Oxydol**, 13031 **Aquascutum**.

Row 2. 13033 **Allenburys**, 13034 **Empire**, 13035 **Kleenex**, 13036 **A. Reed**, 13038 **Army**, 13039 **Persil**.

Row 3. 13040 **Tussaud**, 13041 **M & S**, 13042 **Mail**, 13043 **Hershey**, 13044 **N.Yorkshire**, 13045 **Arnott's**.

Row 4. 13046 **Rosella**, 13047 **Castrol**, 13048 **Hamleys**, 13049 **Rinso**, 13050 **Southern**, 13051 **Harrods**.

Row 1. 13052 **Qantas**, 13055 **G.Shred**, 13056 **Pepsi**, 13057 **M & S**, 13058 **G.Hotel**, 13059 **Carlsberg**.
Row 2. 13061 **Rupert**, 13062 **Dr.Pepper**, 13063 **SE Post**, 13064 **Ritter**, 13066 **D.Herald**, 13037/13-86-2 **BBC**.
Row 3. 13-87-2 **Bristol**, 13-87-3 **Chichester**, 13-87-4 **Coca-Cola**, 13-87-5 **Marocain**, 13-87-6 **Argus**, 13-87-7 **Telegraph**.
Row 4. 13-87-9 **Fotorama**, 13-87-10 **H & G**, 13-87-11 **Ramsden** x2, 13-87-13 **Holme**, 13-87-14 **Kellogg**.

Row 1. 13-87-15 **Kentish,** 13-87-16 **KLM,** 13-87-17 **Le Crunch,** 13-87-19 **Advertiser,** 13-87-20 **Roberts,** 13-87-21 **S.Essex.**
Row 2. 13-87-22 **Taylors,** 13-87-23 **T.Crier,** 13-87-25 **Victoria,** 13-88-4 **Barclays,** 13-88-5 **Beamish,** 13-88-6 **Bowers.**
Row 3. 13-88-7 **Bradford,** 13-88-8 **Broken Hill,** 13-88-9 **Chivers,** 13-88-10 **Covent G.,** 13-88-11 **Coventry,** 13-88-13 **Derby.**
Row 4. 13-88-14 **Dorset,** 13-88-15 **Glasgow,** 13-88-16 **Gloucester,** 13-88-17 **Hull,** 13-88-18 **Jersey,** 13-88-20 **Newcastle.**

Row 1. 13-88-22 **Oldham**, 13-88-23 **Optrex**, 13-88-24 **Orrey**, 13-88-25 **Outspan**, 13-88-26 **Palms**, 13-88-27 **Port Plumbing**.
Row 2. 13-88-28 **Potters**, 13-88-29 **Shell**, 13-88-30 **Showgard**, 13-88-31 **Thorntons**, 13-89-1 **Boots**, 13-89-2 **Chronicle**.
Row 3. 13-89-3 **Cumbria**, 13-89-4+5 **Dly.Express**, 13-89-7 **Edwards**, 13-89-8 **Emulsiderm**, 13-89-9 **Eve.Echo**.
Row 4. 13-89-10 **Eve.Gazette**, 13-89-12 **Guildford**, 13-89-13 **Hayes**, 13-89-14 **Jackson**, 13-89-15 **Mothers**, 13-89-16 **N.Echo**.

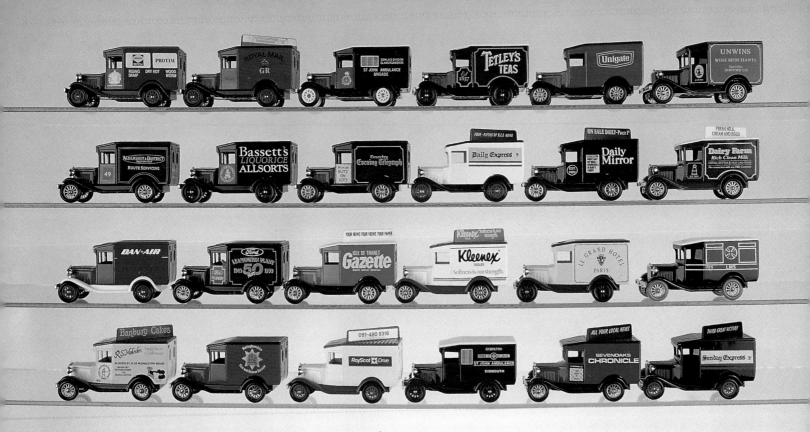

Row 1. 13-89-17 **Protim**, 13-89-19 **Mail**, 13-89-20 **St.John**, 13-89-21 **Tetley**, 13-89-22 **Unigate**, 13-89-23 **Unwins**.
Row 2. 13-90-2 **Aldershot**, 13-90-3 **Bassetts**, 13-90-7 **Coventry**, 13-90-8 **Dly.Express**, 13-90-9 **Dly.Mirror**, 13-90-10 **Dairy Farm**.
Row 3. 13-90-11 **Dan-Air**, 13-90-12 **Ford**, 13-90-13 **Thanet**, 13-90-15 **Kleenex**, 13-90-16 **Le Grand**, 13-90-17 **LMS**.
Row 4. 13-90-18 **Malcolm**, 13-90-19 **Nottingham**, 13-90-20 **Roy Scot**, 13-90-21 **St.John**, 13-90-23 **Sevenoaks**, 13-90-26 **Sunday Exp.**

40

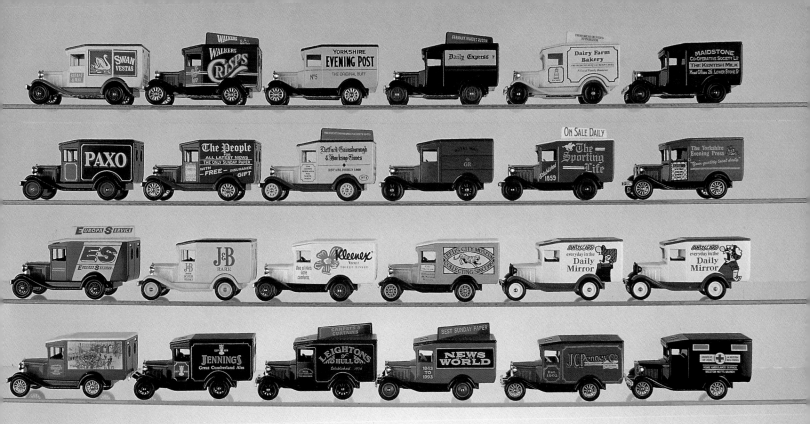

Row 1. 13-90-27 **Swan**, 13-90-30 **Walkers**, 13-90-31 **Yorkshire**, 13-91-1 **Dly.Express**, 13-91-2 **Dairy Farm**, 13-91-9 **Maidstone**.
Row 2. 13-91-11 **Paxo**, 13-91-12 **People**, 13-91-13 **Retford**, 13-91-14 **Mail**, 13-91-16 **Sporting**, 13-91-17 **Yorkshire**.
Row 3. 13-92-8 **Europa**, 13-92-9 **J & B**, 13-92-11 **Kleenex**, 13-92,19 **Leeds**, 13-93-5 **Dly.Mirror** x2.
Row 4. 13-93-8 **The Queen**, 13-93-11 **Jennings**, 13093-12 **Leightons**, 13-93-16 **News/World**, 13-93-17 **Penney**, 13-93-19 **St.John**.

Row 1. 13-93-12 **Schweppes**, 13-94-3 **AA**, 13-94-11 **Jersey**, 13-94-12 **Lilliput**, 13-94-16 **Radio Times**, 13-94-17 **Rupert**.
Row 2. 13-94-18 **St.John**, 14000 **San Diego**, 14001 **Taxi**, 14002 **Acme**, 14003 **Hamleys**, 14004 **Grand Hotel**.
Row 3. 14006 **State Pen**, 14007 **San Diego**, 14008 **Raleigh**, 14-86-1 **Metropolitan**, 14-86-2 **State Farm** x2.
Row 4. 14-86-3 **Taxi**, 14-87-1 **KLM**, 14-87-2 **Western**, 14-88-1 **H.Eater**, 14-88-2 **Ottawa**, VV13-89-51 **York**.

Row 1. 15000 **Hall's**, 15001 **Coca-Cola**, 15002 **Castlemaine**, 15003 **Hamleys**, 15004 **Liverpool**, 15005 **Cinzano**.
Row 2. 15006 **Eve.Argus**, 15007 **Halls + unpainted**, 15008 **Wedding**, 15009 **Tussaud**, 15010 **Swan**.
Row 3. 15011 **Caledonian**, 15012 **Heinz**, 15013 **Radio Times**, 15014 **TV Times**, 15015 **Hamleys**, 15016 **Birmingham**.
Row 4. 15017 **Golden Wonder**, 15018 **DG Club**, 15019 **Maples**, 15020 **Terry's**, 15021 **St.Ivel**, 15022 **Hamleys**.

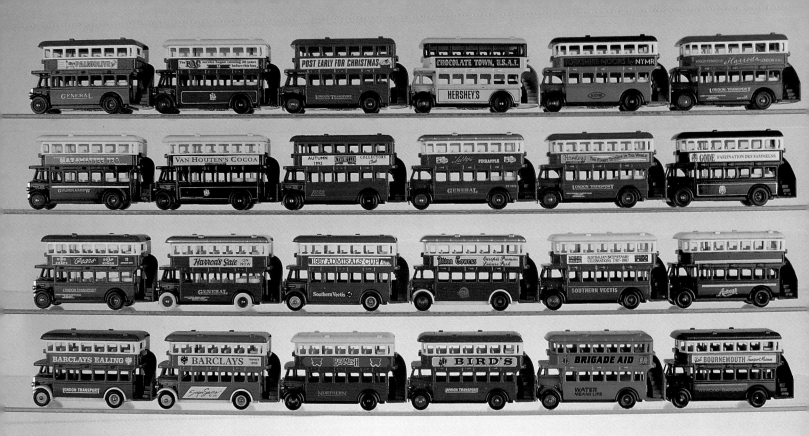

Row 1. 15023 **Palmolive**, 15024 **RAC**, 15025 **Mail**, 15026 **Hershey**, 15027 **N.Yorkshire**, 15028 **Harrods**.
Row 2. 15029 **Mazawattee**, 15030 **Van Houten**, 15031 **DG Club**, 15032 **Libby**, 15023 **Hamleys**, 15034 **Gode**.
Row 3. 15035 **Pears**, 15036 **Harrods**, 15-87-1 **Admirals**, 15-87-2 **Alton**, 15-87-3 **Australian**, 15-87-4 **Autocar**.
Row 4. 15-87-6 + 7 **Barclays**, 15-87-8 **Beamish**, 15-87-9 **Bird's**, 15-87-10 **Brigade Aid**, 15-87-12 **Bournemouth**.

Row 1. 15-87-15 **Castrol**, 15-87-16 **C. Cookson**, 15-87-17 **Butter**, 15-87-18 + 19 **Cowes**, 15-87-20 **Delaine**.

Row 2. 15-87-21 **Donington**, 15-87-22 **Essex**, 15-87-23 **Ex.& Mart**, 15-87-24 **Express & E**, 15-87-25 **Eve.Argus**, 15-87-26 **Eve.Telegraph**.

Row 3. 15-87-27 **I.O. Wight**, 15-87-28 **KLM**, 15-87-29 **Lambeth**, 15-87-30 **Gerson x2**, 15-87-34 **N.Dly.Mail**.

Row 4. 15-87-31 **Dundee**, 15-87-32 **Glasgow**, 15 87-33 **Lothian**, 15 87-35 **Persil**, 15-87-36 **Plymouth**, 25-87-37 **Stevenson's**.

Row 1. 15-87-31 **T.Crier**, 15-87-10 **United**, 15-87-41 **Visit**, 15-88-1 **Bassett's**, 15-88-2 **Bell Vue**, 15-88-3 **Bradford**.

Row 2. 15-88-4 + 5 **Canadian**, 15-88-6 **Sentinel**, 15-88-9 **Eve.Tele.**, 15-88-10 **Express**, 15-88-12 **Glamorgan**.

Row 3. 15-88-13 **Hornby**, 15-88-14 **Leicester**, 15-88-16 **Orange**, 15-88-17 **RDP**, 15-88-19 **Stapeley**, 15-88-20 **Sweetex**.

Row 4. 15-88-21 **Thanet**, 15-89-8 **Old Bank**, 15-89-10 **Post Early**, 15-89-11 **Potterton**, 15-89-12 **Robin Hood**, 15-89-14 **Sgt. Pepper**.

Row 1. 15-89-15 **Castrol**, 15-89-16 **Walsall**, 15-89-17 **WCDNT**, 15-90-2 **Advertiser**, 15-90-4 **Bowlers**, 15-90-6 **Children**.
Row 2. 15-90-8 **Clarendon**, 15-90-9 **Dan-Air**, 15-90-12 **Engineering**, 15-90-16 **Grocer**, 15-90-17 **Kleenex**, 15-90-18 **Lincoln**.
Row 3. 15-90-19 **Littlewoods**, 15-90-20 **Lytham**, 15-90-22 **Mornflakes**, 15-90-23 **Garden**, 15-90-27 **Sandown**, 15-90-28 **Standard**.
Row 4. 15-90-29 **Star**, 15-90-30 **Sutton**, 15-90-31 **Transport**, 15-90-33 **Ven**, 15-90-34 **Western**, 15-91-2 **Big Ben**.

47

Row 1. 15-91-3 **Blue Bus**, 15-91-4 **Clifford's**, 15-91-7 **Guide Dogs**, 15-91-10 **Nottingham**, 15-91-12 **St.David's**, 15-92-4 **Jubilee**.
Row 2. 15-92-6 **Lyons**, 15-92-9 **St.Ivel**, 15-92-11 **S.Wales**, 15-92-15 **Woodwards**, 15-93-6 **Langs**, VV15 **Specimen**.
Row 3. 16000 **Mayflower**, 16001 **Mail**, 16002 **Croft**, 16003 **Hamleys**, 16004 **Trebor**, 16005 **LNER**.
Row 4. 16006 **Kiwi**, 16007 **Bushells**, 16009 **Cadburys**, 16010 **Fyffes**, 16012 + 16013 **Hershey**.

Row 1. 16011 **Coca-Cola**, 16014 **Pickfords** x2, 16016 **Hamleys**, 16017 **Abels**, 16018 **Tussaud**.
Row 2. 16019 **Allied**, 16020 **Cosmos**, 16021 **Goodyear**, 16022 **Hamleys**, 16023 **Oxo**, 16024 **Mail**.
Row 3. 16025 **N.Yorkshire**, 16026 **Schweppes**, 16027 **Atora**, 16018 + 16029 **LNER**, 16030 **Tea Car**.
Row 4. 16031 Hudson's. 16032 **Tunnock**, 16033 **NAAFI**, 16034 **RAF**, 16036 **Bovril**, 16037 **Rupert**.

Row 1. **16038 DG Club**, **16039 Rupert**, 16-87-1 **Alton**, 16-87-3 **Brighton**, 16-87-4 **Br.Police**, 16-87-5 **Co-Op.**
Row 2. 16-87-7 **Jones**, 16-87-8 **Kleen-e-ze** x2, 16-87-9 **KLM**, 16-87-10 **Minster**, 16-87-11 **Natl.Fire.**
Row 3. 16-87-12 **Reading**, 16-87-13 **Sheltons**, 16-87-14 **Stoney**, 16-87-15 **Vernons**, 16-88-1 **Autobahn**, 16-88-4 **Barclays.**
Row 4. 16-88-6 **Be-Ro**, 16-88-8 **Demon T**, 16-88-11 **Farleys**, 16-88-12 **GWR**, 16-88-13 **Hadley**, 16-88-15 **Oven Fresh.**

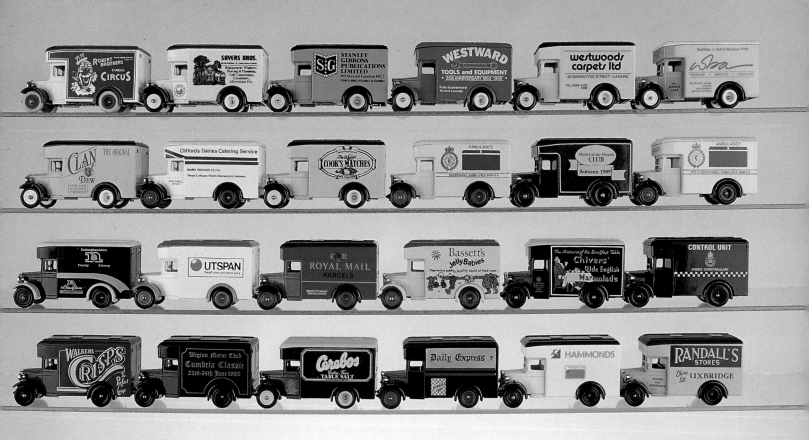

Row 1. 16-88-16 **Robert Bros.**, 16-88-18 **Sayers**, 16-88-19 **Gibbons**, 16-88-20 **Westward**, 16-88-21 **Westwoods**, 16-88-22 **WBA**.
Row 2. 16-89-1 **Clan Dew**, 16-89-2 **Clifford's**, 16-89-3 **Cook's**, 16-89-5 **Derbyshire**, 16-89-8 **Model/Month**, 16-89-9 **Nottingham Amb.**
Row 3. 16-89-10 **Nott.Library**, 16-89-12 **Outspan**, 16-89-13 **Mail**, 16-90-1 **Bassetts**, 16-90-2 **Chivers**, 16-90-4 **Essex**.
Row 4. 16-90-6 **Walkers**, 16-90-7 **Wigton**, 16-91-4 **Cerebos**, 16-91-5 **Dly.Express**, 16-91-7 **Hammonds**, 16-91-10 **Randall's**.

51

Row 1. 16-91-11 **Salvation**, 16-91-12 **Stokes**, 16-91-13 **Valor**, 16-92-2 **Broadway**, 16-92-4 **Gloucester**, 16-92-5 **London Police**.

Row 2. 16-92-6 **Dairy Farm**, 16-92-8 **Exp.Dairy**, 16-92-9 **Leicester**, 16-92-10 **Maynards**, 16-92-12 **Wall's**, 16-92-13 **Weetaflakes**.

Row 3. 16-93-3 **Grace**, 16-93-4 **Halford**, 16-93-7 **RNLI**, 16-93-9 **Tea Car**, 16-94-1 **Cardiff**, 16-94-4 **Wilts Dairies**.

Row 4. 17000 **Southend** x3, 17001 **Eurotour**, 17002 **BOAC**.

Row 1. 17003 **Hamleys**, 17004 **London**, 17005 **Morrell's**, 17006 **Comm.Games**, 17007 **Stratford**.
Row 2. 17008 **Burnley**, 17009 **Big Top**, 17010 **Pennine**, 17011 **RAF**, 17012 **Hamleys**.
Row 3. 17013 **Hants & D**, 17014 **Sutton's**, 17015 **Royal Blue**, 17016 **Colchester**, 17017 **Royal Navy**.
Row 4. 17018 **N.Yorkshire**, 17019 **Red & White**, 17020 **Buckland**, 17021 **S.Vectis**, 17022 **Green Line**.

Row 1. 17023 **Ovaltine,** 17024 **Red Cross,** 17-88-1 **Aldershot,** 17-88-2 **Clayton,** 17-88-3 **Exch.& Mart.**
Row 2. 17-88-4 **Leicester,** 17-88-5 **MacBraynes,** 17-88-7 **Merley,** 17-88-8 **Midland,** 17-88-10 **Norfolk.**
Row 3. 17-88-11 **Northern,** 17-88-12 **Oxford,** 17-88-13 **Royal Navy,** 17-88-15 **Thames V,** 17-88-17 **Time Machine.**
Row 4. 17-88-18 **Weald,** 17-89-1 **Advertiser,** 17-89-2 **Aldershot,** 17-89-3 **Belfast,** 17-89-4 **Boultons.**

Row 1. 17-89-5 **Buckland**, 17-89-6 **Burnley**, 17-89-7 **C T**, 17-89-8 **Coventry**, 17-89-9 **Dly.Independent.**

Row 2. 17-89-12 **Expr.& Star**, 17-89-14 + 15 **GWR**, 17-89-19 **Lincoln**, 17-89-20 **LMS.**

Row 3. 17-89-21 **LNER**, 17-89-23 **Stevenson's**, 17-89-24 **Twickenham**, 17-89-25 **Wolverhampton**, 17-90-5 **Bedworth Alms.**

Row 4. 17-90-1 + 2 **Aldershot**, 17-90-3 **Amersham**, 17-90-4 **Ash Green**, 17-90-6 **British Coal.**

Row 1. 17-90-8 **Burton**, 17-90-9 **Coventry**, 17-90-10 **Dan-Air**, 17-90-12 + 13 **Green Line** (13 = Jubilee).
Row 2. 17-90-11 **Friends of R.M.**, 17-90-14 **Hulley's**, 17-90-15 **LNER**, 17-90-16 **Metropolitan**, 17-90-17 **Midland Gen.**
Row 3. 17-90-18 **Midland red**, 17-90-22 **Southern**, 17-90-24 **Taunton**, 17-90-25 **Thames**, 17-90-26 **Trent.**
Row 4. 17-90-28 **Walsall**, 17-90-29 **W.M.News**, 17-90-31 **Worth**, 17-91-1 **Altonian**, 17-91-2 **Belle.**

Row 1. 17-91-7 **Gloucestershire,** 17-91-8 **Devon/Friends,** 17-91-11 **H.Eater,** 17-91-13 **Lamcote,** 17-91-16 **Majestic.**
Row 2. 17-91-18 **NCB,** 17-91-21 **Nottingham F,** 17-91-23 **St.John,** 17-91-24 **Scottish YH,** 17-91-27 **Walsall.**
Row 3. 17-91-29 **York,** 17-92-3 **BTS,** 17-92-5 **Bunty,** 17-92-9 **E.Yorkshire,** 17-92-13 **Halifax.**
Row 4. 17-92-14 **HB,** 17-92-15 + 16 **Hebble (15 = Webster's),** 17-92-20 **Heinz/SV,** 17-92-20 **Isle of Wight/SV.**

57

Row 1. 17-92-23 **Maidstone**, 17-92-29 **RHMS**, 17-92-32 **Smiths**, 17-92-34 **Trent**, 17-92-36 **Wiltshire.**
Row 2. 17-93-2 **Aldershot**, 17-93-9 **E.Kent**, 17-93-18 **Maplins**, 18000 + 18001 **Ambulances.**
Row 3. 18002 **Comm.Games**, 18003 **Rapid Cash**, 18004 **Firestone**, 18006 **White Star**, 18007 **Colman's.**
Row 4. 18008 **RAF**, 18009 **Peroni**, 18010 **NWBank**, 18011 **Fotorama**, 18012 **St.Ivel.**

Row 1. 18013 **Fortnum**, 18014 **B & C**, 18015 **St. Mary's**, 18016 **Leyland**, 18017 **Hamleys**.
Row 2. 18018 **Asprey**, 18019 **DG Club**, 18020 **McVitie**, 18021 **Camp**, 18022 **St. John**.
Row 3. 18023 **Ferodo**, 18024 **Imperial**, 18025 **Post**, no# **Camperdown**, 18-86-2 **Jon Acc**.
Row 4. 18-86-5 **St.John**, 18-86-7 **Western**, 18-87-1 **Exchange**, 18-88-3 **Mid-Sussex**, 18-88-4 **Strepsils**.

Row 1. 18-89-1 **Wetordry**, 18-89-2 **Cook's**, 18-89-3 **Vikki Harris**, 18-89-4 **W.M.News**, 18-89-5 **Windsor**.

Row 2. 18-90-2 **Cheshire**, 18-90-4 **Davis**, 18-90-6 **GWR**, 18-90-7 **Ramsden**, 18-90-8 **Portsmouth**.

Row 3. 18-91-1 **Atora**, 18-91-2 **Leprosy**, 18-91-3 **Northampton**, 18-91-4 **Walkers**, 18-92-1 **Standard**.

Row 4. 18-93-1 **Express**, 18-93-4 **Penney**, 18-94-1 **Haunted**, 18-94-2 **Co-Op**, 18-94-4 **Snickers**.

Row 1. no# **Cream**, 19000 **Burgundy**, 19001 **Yellow**, 19002 **Basket** x2, 19004 **Gold**.
Row 2. 19005 **Ruby Wedding**, 19006 **Coach Lines**, 19007 **Minder**, 19008 **DG Club**, 19009 **Staff Car**, 19010 **Black/Cream**.
Row 3. 19-86-1 **Blue/Red**, 19-86-2 **Wedding**, 19-86-3 **White**, 19-87-1 **Black**, 19-87-2 **Congrats**, 19-87-3 **Marilyn**.
Row 4 19-87-4 **Persil**, 19-91-1 **Anniversary**, 19-93-1 **Black**, 20000 **Eagle**, 20001 **Coca-Cola**, 18-? **Isle of Man**.

Row 1. 20002 **Stroh's**, 20003 **Whitbread**, 20004 **Goodrich**, 20005 **Auld Scotch**, 20006 **Uniroyal**, 20007 **Budweiser**.

Row 2. 20008 **Ind Coope**, 20009 **Watneys**, 20010 **Calor**, 20011 **HMS Rooke**, 20012 **Pirelli**, 20013 **Oxygen**.

Row 3. 20014 **Hershey's**, 20015 **RAF**, 20016 **Winn-Dixie**, 20017 **Dunlop**, 20018 **Goodyear**, 20019 **McDougall's**.

Row 4. 20020 **Nestle's**, 20021 **Dr.Pepper**, 20022 **Pennzoil**, 20-86-1 **BBC**, 20-86-2 **Burt's**, 20-86-3 **Laird's**.

Row 1. 20-86-4 **Lionel,** 20-87-1 **Lowcock** x2, 20-87-2 **Watneys** x2, 10-88-4 **Clifford's.**
Row 2. 20-88-6 **Pony,** 20-88-8 **Shell,** 20-89-2 **Forward,** 20-89-3 **KLM,** 20-90-1 **Atlas,** 20-90-2 **Gedling.**
Row 3. 20-91-1 **PG Tips,** 20-91-3 **Dairy Farm,** 20-91-4 **Hucknall,** 20-91-5 **Walker's,** 20-92-1 **Bilsthorpe,** 20-92-2 **Dunlop.**
Row 4. 20-92-4 **Sarsons,** 20-92-5 **Weston,** 20-93-1 **Abbott,** 20-93-3 **Bestwood,** 20-93-5 **Exp.Dairy,** 20-93-6 **J.Walker.**

Row 1. 20-93-7 **Lang,** 20-93-8 **N.Dairies,** 20-94-6 **Rufford,** 21000 **Sharp's,** 21001 **DG Club,** 21002 **Leicester.**
Row 2. 21003 **Hostess,** 21004 **Dr.Pepper,** 21005 **Coca-Cola,** 21007 **Hamleys,** 21008 **Budweiser,** 21009 **Bird's.**
Row 3. 21010 **Farrah's,** 21011 **Vita-Weat,** 21012 Simpson, 21013 **Benettons,** 21014 **Hershey's,** 21015 **Cherry.**
Row 4. 21016 **Majestic,** 21017 **Toy Fair,** 21018 **Reckitts,** 21019 **M & S,** 21020 **Liberty,** 21021 **DG Club.**

Row 1. 21022 **Bluebell**, 21023 **Bryant**, 21024 **Swan**, 21025 **Glory**, 21026 **Hamleys**, 21027 **Exide**.
Row 2. 21028 **Fairy**, 21029 **Bushells**, 21030 **Marine**, 21031 **Elliman's**, 21032 **Maggi's**, 21034 **LMS/LNER**.
Row 3. 21035 **Grand Hotel**, 21036 **LNER**, 21037 **Hamleys**, 21038 **Pepsi-Cola**, 21039 **Rose's**. 21041 **Henderson**.
Row 4. 21042 **World Cup**, 21043 **Post**, 21044 **Nivea**, 21045 **Rupert**, 21-87-1 **AACA**, 21-87-2 **ANC**.

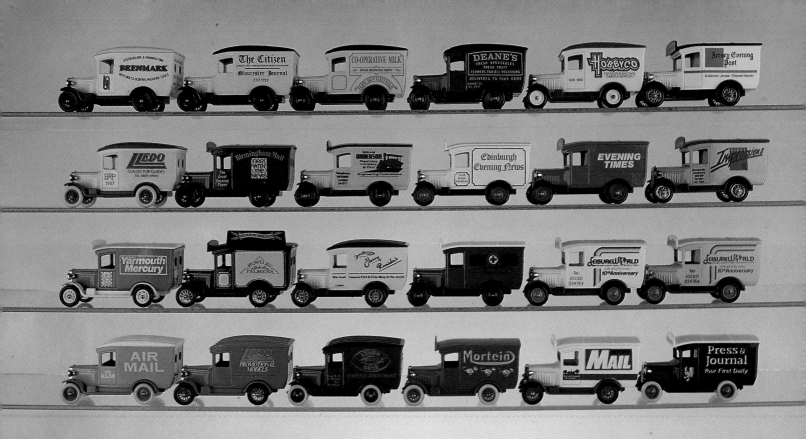

Row 1. 21-87-3 **Brenmark**, 21-87-4 **Citizen**, 21-87-5 **Co-Op**, 21-87-6 **Deane's**, 21-87-7 **Hobbyco**, 21-87-8 **Jersey**.

Row 2. 21-87-9 **RDP**, 21-88-1 **Birmingham**, 21-88-2 **Anderson**, 21-88-4 **Edinburgh**, 21-88-5 **Eve.Times**, 21-88-6 **Impressions**.

Row 3. 21-88-8 **Yarmouth**, 21-88-9 **Ramsden**, 21-88-11 **Huntley**, 21-88-12 **Kent**, 21-88-15 **Leisure World** x2.

Row 4. 21-88-13 **KLM**, 21-88-16 **Lledo**, 21-88-17 **Lower Deck**, 21-88-18 **Mortein**, 21-88-19 **Oxford**, 21-88-21 **Press & J.**

Row 1. 21-88-22 **Salvation**, 21-88-23 **S.Wales**, 21-88-24 **Sunlight**, 21-88-25 **Timbercraft**, 21-89-1 **Cordon Bleu**, 21-89-4 **PG Tips**.
Row 2. 21-89-5 **Clan Dew**, 21-89-6 **Derby**, 21-89-7 **Eastbourne**, 21-89-9 **Basildon Echo**, 21-89-10 **Dorset Echo**, 21-89-11 **Telegraph**.
Row 3. 21-89=12 **Fish.Friend**, 21-89-13 **Fox Talbot**, 21-89-14 **Glasgow**, 21-89-15 **Lincoln**, 21-89-16 **Malcolm**, 21-89-18 **Garden**.
Row 4. 21-89-22 **Torbay**, 21-89-23 **Van Dijk**, 21-90-2 **Bessetts**, 21-90-5 **Cadbury's**, 21-90-6 **Cleaning**, 21-90-7 **Dly.Herald**.

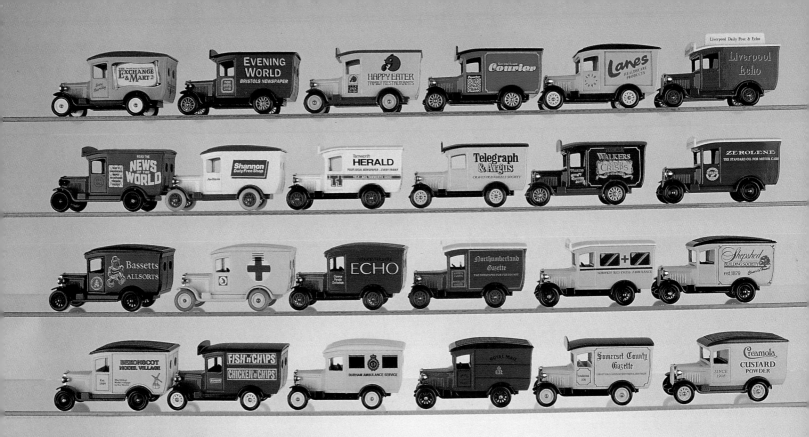

Row 1. 21-90-8 **Ex.& Mart**, 21-90-9 **Eve.World**, 21-90-10 **H.Eater**, 21-90-12 **K & S C**, 21-90-13 **Lanes**, 21-90-14 **Liverpool**.

Row 2. 21-90-15 **News/World**, 21-90-18 **Shannon**, 21-90-19 **Tamworth**, 21-90-20 **Tel/Argus**, 21-90-22 **Walkers**, 21-90-23 **Zerolene**.

Row 3. 21-91-1 **Bassetts**, 21-91-4 **Desert Rats**, 21-91-6 **Gloucester**, 21-91-8 **Northumberland**, 21-91-9 **Norwich**, 21-91-11 **Shepshed**.

Row 4. 21-92-2 **Bekonscot**, 21-92-4 **Fish'n'Chips**, 21-92-6 **Durham**, 21-92-11 **Mail**, 21-92-12 **Somerset**, 21-93-2 **Creamola**.

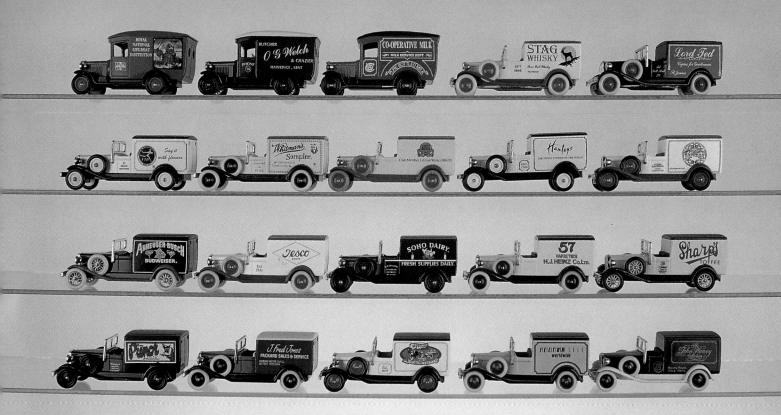

Row 1. 21-93-7 **RNLI**, 21-93-9 **Welch**, 21-94-2 **Co-Op**, 22000 **Stag**, 22001 **Lord Ted.**
Row 2. 22002 **FTD**, 22003 **Whitman**, 22004 **DG Club**, 12005 **Hamleys**, 22006 **Pizza.**
Row 3. 22007 **Budweiser**, 22008 **Tesco**, 22009 **Soho**, 22010 **Heinz**, 22011 **Sharps.**
Row 4. 22012 **Punch**, 22-86-1 **Jones**, 22-87-1 **Ex.& Mart**, 22-87-2 **Felton**, 22-87-3 **Harvey.**

Row 1. 22-87-4 **Telemedia**, 22-87-5 **West Point** x2, 22-88-2 **Showgard**, 22-89-1 **3M.**
Row 2. 22-89-2 **Eve.Herald**, 22-89-3 **Leicester**, 22-91.1 **E.Shaw**, 22-91-5 **Walkers**, 22-93-3 **Glengoyne.**
Row 3. 23000 **Greyhound**, 23001 **Golden West**, 23002 **Buffalo**, 23-87-1 **ARC**, 23-87-2 **B & A.**
Row 4. 23-87-3 **Töff Töff** x2, 23-88-1, 2 + 3 **Canadian blue, green, yellow.**

Row 1. 24000 **Yellow**, 24001 **Lilac**, 24003 **Red/White**, 24004 **Met.Green**, 24005 **Coach Lines.**
Row 2. 24-87-1 **Black**, 24-87-2 **Red/Green**, 24-89-1 **KLM**, 24-91-1 **Anniversary**, 25000 **Blue.**
Row 3. 25001 **Silver**, 25003 **White**, 25005 **Coach Lines**, 25-87-1 **Black**, 25-87-2 **Congrats.**
Row 4. 25-89-1 **KLM**, 26000 **Schweppes x2**, 26001 **DG Club**, 26002 **Coca-Cola.**

Row 1. 26003 **Budweiser**, 26004 **Barr's**, 26005 **Corona**, 26006 **Tizer**, 26007 **Canada Dry**, 26008 **Schweppes**.

Row 2. 26009 **Tennents**, 26010 **Bass**, 26011 **Fyffes**, 26012 **Pepsi**, 26013 **Perrier**, 26014 **Brooke Bond**.

Row 3. 26015 **Dr.Pepper**, 26016 **Beck's**, 26017 **7-Up**, 26-88-1 **Castrol**, 26-88-2 **Lowcock**, 26-89-1 **KLM**.

72 *Row 4.* 26-89-2 **Unigate**, 26-91-1 **Walkers**, 26-92-1 **Heinz**, 26-93-2 **Finches**, 26-93-3 **Schweppes**, 26-94-1 **Flowers**.

Row 1. 27000 **A-1,** 27001 **Hank's,** 27003 + 004 **Mobiloil** (004 **French**), 27005 **Daley.**
Row 2. 27006 **Army,** 27007 **LCC,** 27-88-1 **Bean St.,** 27-88-2 **Bournemouth,** 27-88-3 **KLM.**
Row 3. 27-92-1 **Brooklands,** 28000 **Ty-Phoo,** 28001 **Tate & Lyle,** 28002 **DG Club,** 28003 **Heinz.**
Row 4. 28004 **Dunlop,** 28006 **Navy,** 28007 **Stroh's,** 28008 **N.Yorkshire,** 28010 **Greene King.**

Row 1. 28011 **RAF**, 28013 **Hamleys**, 28014 **LNER**, 28015 **LMS**, 28016 **Army.**
Row 2. 28017 **Quartermaster**, 28019 **Marines**, 28020 **GWR**, 28021 **Hamleys**, 28022 **US Navy.**
Row 3. 28023 **Wincarnis**, 28024 **DG Club**, 28025 **Toy Fair**, 28026 **Navy**, 28027 **Marines.**
Row 4. 28028 **S.Region**, 28029 **Kaffee Hag**, 28030 **RAF**, 28031 **Model Show**, 28032 **Sainsbury.**

Row 1. 28033 **Pepsi,** 28034 **Dr.Pepper,** 28035 **Persil,** 28-88-1 **Bestwood,** 28-89-2 **Econofreight.**
Row 2. 28-88-4 **Ex.& Mart,** 28-88-5 **LMS,** 28-88-6 **LNER,** 28-88-7 **Moorgreen,** 28-88-8 **Southern.**
Row 3. 28-89-3 **Clan Dew,** 28-90-3 **Ex. & Mart,** 28-90-6 **Trebor,** 28-92-2 **N.Provision,** 28-92-3 **PO Phones.**
Row 4. 28-93-1 **Broadcasting,** 28-93-2 **Crinkley,** 28-93-3 **Finches,** 28-93-5 **It Ain't,** 28-93.6 **J.Walker.**

Row 1. 28-93-7 **Langs**, 28-93-9 **Massey Shaw**, 28-94-1 **NHS**, 29000 **US Army**, 29001 **RAF Aircrew**.
Row 2. 29002 **Texaco**, 29003 **US Army**, 29004 **BDS**, 29005 **Marines**, 29006 **Police**.
Row 3. 29007 **San Jose**, 29008 **Signals**, 29009 **Army Amb.**, 29-90-1 **Crew Transport**, 29-90-2 **Croydon/Sutton**.
Row 4. 29-9191 **Desert Rats**, 29-93-1 **Buds of May**, 29-93-4 **Transmitter**, 29-94-1 **Scouts**.

Row 1. 30001 **Fry's**, 30002 **Lipton's**, 30003 **DG Club**, 30004 **Hamleys**, 30005 **Spratts**.
Row 2. 30006 **Brooke Bond**, 30007 **Hershey**, 30008 **RAF**, 30009 **Nestle's**, 30010 **Golden Stream**.
Row 3. 30011 **Army Amb.**, 30012 **Surgical**, 30013 **US Navy**, 30014 **Stephens**, 30015 **Shell**.
Row 4. 30016 **Ransomes**, 30017 **Indian**, 30018 **7-Up**, 30-89-1 **3M**, 30-89-2 **Cowes Museum**.

Row 1. 30-90-2 **Ex.& Mart**, 30-90-3 **Fotorama**, 30-91-3 **Shields G**, 30-93-2 **Penney**, 31000 **Whitbread**.
Row 2. 31001 **Everard**, 31002 **Taunton**, 31003 **Greene**, 31004 **Truman**, 31005 **Courage**.
Row 3. 31006 **Worthington**, 31007 **Bass**, 31008 **Fuller's**, 31-88-1 **Burt's**, 31-92-1 **Fremlins**.
Row 4. 32000 **Silver**, 32001 **Coach Lines**, 32002 **Met.Green**, 32003 **DG Club Gold**, 32004 **Maroon**, 32005 **Blue**.

Row 1. 33000 **Black**, 33001 **Singer**, 33003 **Hershey**, 33004 **Gr.Hotel**, 33005 **H. de Paris**, 33006 **Gold**, 33007 **Pfaff.**
Row 2. 33009, 010, 011, 012 + 0__ **Ten Bosch**, 33-90-1 **Castrol**, 33-90-2 **Essex.**
Row 3. 33-94-2 **Grand Hotel**, 3309403 **Ramsden**, 34000 **Hovis**, 34001 **Smedley's**, 34002 **Hamleys**, 34003 **Cheddar.**
Row 4. 34004 **RAF**, 34005 **DG Club**, 34006 **Library**, 34007 **Harrods**, 34-89-1 **Finesse**, 34-89-2 **ADT.**

Row 1. 34-89-3 **Boots**, 34-89-5 **Showgard**, 34-89-6 **Tetley**, 34-90-3 **Ex.& Mart**, 34-90-4 **Isle of Man**, 34-90-6 **Walkers**.

Row 2. 34-91-2 **Dairy Farm**, 34-91-3 **Ramsden**, 34-93-2 **Finches**, 35000 **Edinburgh**, 35001 **PO Phones**, 35002 **RAF**.

Row 3. 35003 **Signals**, 35004 **NFS**, 35005 **BBC**, 35-89-1 **Isle of Wight**, 35-91-1 **BBC**, 35-93-1 **NTV**.

Row 4. 35-93-2 **Port of London**, 35-94-1 **London Fire**, 36000 **Buck & H**, 36001 **Cakebread**, 36002 **Avon**, 36003 **Explosives**.

Row 1. 36004 **Duckhams**, 36005 **Redex**, 36007 **Pennzoil**, 36008 **US Army**, 36009 **Dr.Pepper**.
Row 2. 36921 **Castrol**, 37000 **Canadian**, 37001 **Mr.Therm**, 37002 **Police**, 37003 **DG Club**, 37-91-1 **Champion**.
Row 3. 37-91-2 **News**, 37-91-4 **Halifax**, 37-92-1 **Exide**, 38000 **Coach Lines**, 38-90-1 **Queen Mother**, 38-91-1 **Anniversary**.
Row 4. 38-91-3 **Birthday**, 39000 **Ferrocrete**, 39001 **Ketton**, 39002 **Gas Light**, 39003 **Portland**.

Row 1. 39004 **Army**, 39-89-1 **Yorkshire**, 39-92-1 **Thwaite**, 40000 **Tarmac**, 40001 **Costain**.

Row 2. 40002 + 40003 **US Navy**, 40004 **RAF**, 41000 **Robin**, 41001 **Marks & S.**

Row 3. 41002 **Hamleys**, 41003 **Bisto**, 41004 **Bovril**, 41005 **N.Yorkshire**, 41006 **Saxa**.

Row 4. 41007 **Schweppes**, 41008 **Hamleys**, 41009 **Sun Maid**, 41010 **Crosse & B**, 41011 **Rowntree**.

Row 1. 41012 **Ten Bosch**, 41-90-6 **Ex.& Star**, 41-90-8 **Robin Hood**, 41-90-10 **Showgard**, 41-90-11 **Trebor**.
Row 2. 41-91-1 **80 Years**, 41-91-4 **Birm.Mail**, 41-91-5 **Birm.Post**, 41-91-10 **Cleethorpes**, 41-91-11 **Derbyshire**.
Row 3. 41-91-12 **Doncaster**, 41-91-15 **Chronicle**, 41-91-18 **Ramsden**, 41-91-20 **Leeds**, 41-91-21 **Lledo**.
Row 4. 41-91-24 **News/World**, 41-91-26 **Rotherham**, 41-91-29 **Sports Argus**, 41-92-3 **Beamish**, 41-92-7 **Clarendon**.

Row 1. 41-92-9 **Dove Holes,** 41-92-12 **Ex.& Mart,** 41-92-17 **Heinz,** 41-92-18 **Huddersfield,** 41-92-20 **Kleenex.**
Row 2. 41-92-26 **Nottingham,** 41-92-31 **St.George,** 41-92-34 **Scottish,** 41-92-36 **Telegraph,** 41-92-37 **Telephone.**
Row 3. 41-93-2 **Beamish,** 41-93-4 **Dairy Farm,** 41-93-8 **News/World,** 41-94-2 **ERA,** 41-94-3 **Miami Modes.**
Row 4. 41-94-4 **Radio Times,** 41-94-6 **Cobleigh,** 42000 **National,** 42001 **RAF,** 42002 **Regent.**

Row 1. 42003 **Air Corps**, 42004 **US Navy**, 42005 **Army**, 42007 **Pennzoil**, 42008 **Texaco**.
Row 2. 42-90-1 **Castrol**, 42-90-2 **Dan-Air**, 42-90-3 **Red Crown**, 42-91-1 **Dominion**, 42-91-2 **Food**.
Row 3. 42-92-1 **Exp.Dairy**, 42-92-2 **Shell**, 42-94-1 **Gunge**, 43000 **Weetabix**, 43001 **Chivers**.
Row 4. 43002 **Hamleys**, 43003 **DG Club**, 43004 **AC Plugs**, 43005 **LNER**, 43006 **Metropolitan**.

Row 1. 43007 **Bird's**, 43008 **Army Amb.**, 43010 **Home Guard**, 43011 **Hamleys**, 43012 **Ambrosia**.
Row 2. 43013 **Arnott's**, 43014 **GWR**, 43015 **Harrods**, 43017 **Tate**, 43018 **Brand's**.
Row 3. 43019 **Rupert red**, 43020 **Brasso**, 43021 **Rupert yellow**, 43-90-2 **Dairy Farm**, 43-90-3 **Danepak**.
Row 4. 43-90-5 **Lincolnshire**, 43-91-1 **Advertiser**, 43-91-2 **Anglian**, 43-91-5 **Kent**, 43-91-9 **Hemglas**.

Row 1. 43-91-10 **IPA Kent**, 43-91-11 **Jones**, 43-91-13 **Mail**, 43-91-14 **Saxa**, 43-91-16 **Tetley's**.
Row 2. 43-92-2 **Armley**, 43-92-6 **Carnation**, 43-92-7 **E.Shaw**, 43-92-8 **Ex.& Mart**, 43-92-9 **Exp.Dairy**.
Row 3. 43-92-14 **Kleenex**, 43-92-19 **Pork Farms**, 43-92-20 **Ringtons**, 43-92-21 **Worcester**, 43-92-22 **Smith**.
Row 4. 43-92-24 **Weetaflakes**, 43-92-25 **Wheelspin**, 43-92-26 **Wiltshire**, 43-93-3 **Police**, 43-93-6 **The Queen**.

Row 1. 43-93-9 **NSPCC**, 43-93-11 **Port of London**, 43093-13 **RNLI**, 43-94-9 **Crumpsall**, 43-94-13 **Lewis-DMR**.
Row 2. 44000 **Bisto**, 44001 **Tobler**, 44002 **Marmite**, 44003 **Fox's**, 44004 **N.Yorkshire**.
Row 3. 44005 **Rowntree's**, 44006 **McMullen**, 44007 **DG Club**, 44008 **Army**, 44010 **Tetley**.
Row 4. 44011 **Heinz**, 44012 **Carnation**, 44013 **US Army**, 44014 **Kronenbourg**, 44015 **Rupert**.

Row 1. 44016 **Smith's,** 55-90-1 **Kleenex,** 44-91-1 **Bisto,** 44-91-3 **Dairy Farm,** 44-91-6 **Malcolm.**
Row 2. 44-91-7 **Mail,** 41-91-9 **Vimto,** 41-92-3 **Sumner,** 41-92-5 **Ex.& Mart,** 41-92-12 **Weetaflakes.**
Row 3. 44-93-8 **The Queen,** 44-94-2 **Pork Pie,** 44-94-5 **Evans,** 44-94-8 **Garth,** 46000 **Bentley green.**
Row 4. 45000 **Met. Green,** 45001 **Red,** 45002 **Cream,** 45003 **Gold,** 45-94-1 **Eliott green,** 46001 **Bentley #1.**

Row 1. 46007 **Green #6**, 46006 **Black #7**, 46005 **Maroon #10**, 46004 **Cream**, 46003 **Green #2**, 46002 **Gold**.

Row 2. 46-92-1 **Green #85**, 47000 **Blue**, 47001 **Black**, 47002 + 47003 **Hamleys Blue + Maroon**, 47004 **Maroon**.

Row 3. 47-94-1 **Wait Till**, 47-94-2 **Mars**, 48001 **Cream/Green**, 48001 **DG Club**, 48002 **Cream/Maroon**, 48003 **Army**.

Row 4. 48004 **Yellow Cab**, 48005 **RAF**, 48006 **Highway**, 48007 **US Army**, 48008 **Staff Car**.

Row 1. 49000 **Cadburys**, 49001 **Rose's**, 49002 **Hamleys**, 49003 **Martini**, 49004 **Jantzen**.
Row 2. 49005 **Hamleys**, 49006 **DG Club**, 49007 **Harrods**, 49008 **Qantas**, 49009 **Pepsi**.
Row 3. 49010 **Hamleys**, 49011 **Littlewoods**, 49012 **St.Michael**, 49013 **Heinz**, 49014 **Swan**.
Row 4. 49015 **Ten Bosch**, 49016 **Shr.Wheat**, 49017 **Mars**, 49018 **Shamrock**, 49-91-1 **Coventry**.

Row 1. 49-92-1 **Toy & Train**, 41-92-4 **Bridlington**, 49-92-10 **Dairy Farm**, 49-92-11 **Derbyshire**, 49-92-12 **E.Lancs.**
Row 2. 49-92-18 **Leicester**, 49-92-21 **Mars**, 49-92-23 **Nottingham**, 49-92-24 **P & O**, 42-92-26 **Silver Queen.**
Row 3. 49-92-29 **United D.**, 49-93-3 **Castrol**, 49-93-5 **Ex.& Mart**, 49-93-8 **Northampton**, 49-94-1 **Nolan.**
Row 4. 50000 **Lyons**, 50001 **Bryant & May**, 50002 **Hamleys**, 50003 **Master's**, 50004 **DG Club**, 50005 **M & S.**

Row 1. 50006 **Raffles**, 50008 **Kiwi**, 50009 **Rupert**, 50010 **Pepsi**, 50011 **Harrods**, 50012 **Post**.
Row 2. 50013 **P.M.G.**, 50014 **Silver King**, 50-92-2 **Captain's**, 50-92-4 **Dairy Farm**, 50-92-6 **E.Yorks**, 50-92-7 **Telegraph**.
Row 3. 50-92-11 **Nestle's**, 50-92-12 **News/World**, 50-92-15 **Samuel**, 50-93-18 **B. Yeo**, 50-93-34 **Dennis**, 50-93-43 **Ex.& Mart**.
Row 4. 50-93-69 **Langs**, 50-93-71 **Leicester**, 50-93-82 **Lound Hall**, 50-93-100 **PAA**, 50-93-107 **Popeye**, 50-93-114 **Ripley**.

Row 1. 50-93-123 **Children**, 50-93-130 **Stokes**, 50-93-137 **Tetley's**, 50-94-4 **Nolan**, 50-94-7 **AA**, 50-94-23 **Bulmers**.
Row 2. 50-94-30 **Coventry**, 50-94-39 **Christmas**, 50-94-46 **GWR**, 50-94-57 **Kent**, 50-94-67 **Nat.Trust**, 50-94-89 **Rupert**.
Row 3. 50-94-90 **St.John**, 51000 **Tussaud**, 51001 **Start-Rite**, 51002 **Hovis**, 51003 **DG Club**, 51004 **M & S**.
Row 4. 51005 **Bushells**, 51007 **Army**, 51008 **Post**, 51009 **Hamleys**, 51010 **Rupert**, 51-93-1 **Glengoyne**.

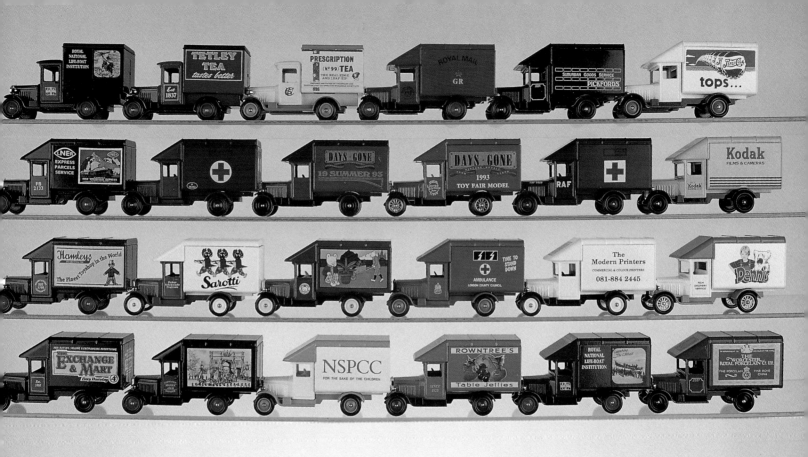

Row 1. 51-93-4 **RNLI**, 51-93-5 **Tetley**, 51-94-6 **Prescription**, 52000 **Mail**, 52001 **Pickfords**, 52002 **Pepsi**.
Row 2. 52003 **LNER**, 52004 **Army Amb.**, 52005 **DG Club**, 52006 **Toy Fair**, 52007 **RAF**, 52009 **Kodak**.
Row 3. 52011 **Hamleys**, 52012 **Sarotti**, 52013 **Rupert**, 52014 **Ambulance**, 52-92-1 **Mod.Printers**, 52093-3 **Dennis**.
Row 4. 52-93-4 **Ex.& Mart**, 52-93-5 **The Queen**, 52-93-7 **NSPCC**, 52-93-8 **Rowntree's**, 52-93-9 **RNLI**, 52-93-10 **Worcester**.

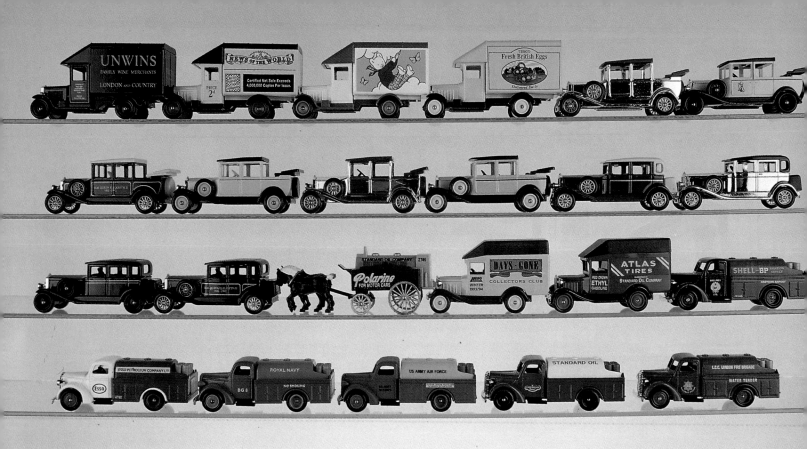

Row 1. 52-93-12 **Unwins**, 52-94-5 **News/World**, 52-94-8 **Rupert**, 52-94-10 **Tesco**, 53000 **Gold**, 53-92-2 **Buds of May.**
Row 2. 53-92-3 **The Queen**, 53-93-1 **Blue/Black**, 53-93-2 **Gold**, 53-94-1 **Gray**, 54000 **Blue/Cream**, 54001 **DG Club.**
Row 3. 54-92-1 **Scouts**, 54-92-2 **Queen E.**, 55-92-1 **Polarine**, 56000 **DG Club**, 56-92-1 **Atlas**, 57000 **Shell-BP.**
Row 4. 57001 **Esso**, 57002 **Navy**, 57003 **Air Force**, 57-93-1 **Standard**, 57-94-1 **London.**

Row 1. 58000 **PO Phones**, 58001 **Malvern**, 58002 **Mackenson**, 58003 **Mail**, 58004 **Gillette**, 58005 **Hamleys**.
Row 2. 58006 **Pepsi**, 58007 **DG Club**, 58009 **Singer**, 58010 **Railways**, 58012 **7-Up**, 58013 **Harrods**.
Row 3. 58-93-5 **Dairy Farm**, 58-93-7 **Hull**, 58-93-10 **Blobby**, 58-94-1 **Aidensfield**, 58-94-2 **Airborne**, 58-94-15 **Devon**.
Row 4. 58-94-19 **Gamma**, 58-94-22 **Ramsden**, 58-94-33 **Panasonic**, 58-94-39 **RSPCA**, 58-94-43 **Sports Merc.**, 58-94-49 **Winnie**.

Row 1. 59000 **Bird's**, 59001 **Canada Dry**, 59002 **Dunlopillo**, 59003 **Pepsi**, 59004 **Lucozade**.
Row 2. 59005 **Be-Ro**, 59006 **Hamleys**, 59007 **Pepsi**, 59008 **Weet-Bix**, 59011 **Arnotts**.
Row 3. 59012 **Oxydol**, 59013 **Railways**, 59015 **Rupert**, 59016 **7-Up**, 59017 **DG Club**.
Row 4. 59-93-1 **AA**, 59-93-5 **Exp.Dairy**, 59-93-8, 9 + 10 **Kleenex**.

Row 1. 59-93-6 **Hodges**, 59-93-13 **Museum**, 59-93-14 **News/World**, 59-93-16 **Samuel**, 59-93-19 **Unigate**.
Row 2. 59-94-2 **Dairy Farm**, 59-94-3 **Devon**, 59-94-8 **Giles**, 59-94-11 **London**, 59-94-14 **Police**.
Row 3. 59-94-17 **Rupert**, 60000 **Essex**, 60001 **Derbyshire**, 60002 **W.Area/Oban**, 60003 **W.Sussex**.
Row 4. 60004 **New Zealand**, 60005 **London**, 60006 **Harrods**, 60007 **London**, 60008 **C.Defence**.

Row 1. 60-94-2 **Nottingham**, 60-94-8 **Kent**, 60-94-9 **London**, 60-94-10 **N.Riding**, 60-94-12 **Rupert**.
Row 2. 61000 **Dr.Pepper red**, 61001 **Police**, 61002 **Ambulance**, 61004 **Pepsi**, 61005 **Excelsior**, 61006 **Dr.Pepper green**.
Row 3. 62000 **Regent**, 62002 **Fina**, 62-94-3 **Dairy Farm**, 63000 **Sainsbury**, 63001 **Penguin**.
Row 4. 63002 **Oxo**, 63003 **DG Club**, 63004 **Hamleys**, 63005 **Cerebos**, 63006 **Wall's**, 63008 **Rupert**.

Row 1. 63009 **Toy Fairs**, 63-94-1 **Nolan**, 63-94-2 **Ashfordly**, 63-94-4 **RDP Lledo**, 63-94-5 **EVRP**, 64000 **Kent**.
Row 2. 64001 **Durham**, 61002 **LCC**, 61003 **Army Med.**, 61004 **Railways**, 64-94-1 **Cheshire**, 64-94-5 **N.Riding**.
Row 3. 65000 **Green**, 65001 **White**, 65002 **Blue**, 65003 **Gray**, 65-94-1 **Dairy Farm**, 65-94-2 **Fire**.
Row 4. 65-94-4 **Vectis** x2, 65-94-5 **Swinley**, 69000 **Ever Ready**, 69001 **Currys**, 69002 **DG Club**.

Row 1. 66000 **Castrol**, 66001 **P.M.G.**, 66002 **Pepsi**, 66003 **Campbell**, 66004 **Harrods**, 66005 **DG Club**.
Row 2. 66-94-1 **Scouts**, 66-94-2 **We're Supporting**, 66-94-5 **RSPCA**, 66-94-6 **Samuel**, 72000 **Blue**, 72001 **Green**.
Row 3. 67000 **Dunlop**, 67001 **Circus**, 67002 **Lyons**, 67003 **DG Club**.
Row 4. 68000 **Duxford**, 68001 **DG Club**, 68002 **See London**, 68003 **Welsh Zoo**, 68004 **Victory**, 70000 **Anchor**.

Row 1. 71000 **Kodak**, 71001 **Wormwood**, 71002 **HP Sauce**, 71003 **DG Club**, 73000 **Cinzano**, 73001 **Bosch**.
Row 2. 74000 **Blue**, 74001 **Red**, 74002 **Police**, PM 100 **Tetley + Children**, PM 105 **Botham**.
Row 3. PM 101 **MG**, PM 102 **Aston Martin**, PM 103 **Sunbeam**, PM 104 **Alfa Romeo**, PM 106 **Zerolene**, PM 107 **Standard**.
Row 4. PM 108 **Ringtons + News/World**, PM 113 **Steptoe**, PM 116 **Lifeboat**, PM 120 **Fairclough + Heartbeat**.

Row 1. PM 109 **Spirit**, PM 110 **Railton**, PM 111 **Bluebird**, PM 112 **Thrust 2**.
Row 2. PM 118 **Promovers**, PM 119 **RDP**.
Row 3. M1 **Chronicle**, M2 **Pan Am + Ghana**, M3 **Speedlink & Gatwick**.
Row 4. M4 **Federal**, Beanz + Tetley, M5 **ARC**, M6 **Shell**.

104

LLEDO MODELS & VARIATIONS

1   HORSE DRAWN TRAM 118 mm 1983
Cast body, roof, domes, pillars and hitch, plastic seats and horse, small cream flanged plastic wheels, chassis bottom lettered "DAYS GONE DG 1 MADE IN ENGLAND by Lledo". Castings:
   A. Plain hitch and end panel.
   B. Hitch with horizontal bar, plain end panel.
   C. Hitch with horizontal bar, brace on end panel.
   D. Hitch with bar and angle brace, brace on end panel.

1000 WESTMINSTER 1983
Green body, light gray roof, gold domes and hitch, cream pillars, reddish seats, dark brown or black horse. Logo: red and green "Westminster" on light gray roof panels, crest on front and back body panels.
   1. Yellow crest.
   2. Cream crest.
   3. White crest.
   4. White crest, dark red seats, light cream pillars.

1001 MAIN STREET 1984
Light gray roof, gold domes and hitch, cream pillars, reddish seats, dark brown or black horse. Logo: red and green "Main Street" on white roof panels, white crest on front and back body panels.
   1. Green body.

1002 MAIN STREET 1984
Same as #1001 except:
   1. Brown body.

1003 (Not used)

1004 NATIONAL TRAMWAY MUSEUM 1984
Blue body, cream roof and pillars, gold domes and hitch, light brown seats, dark brown horse. Logo: red "The National Tramway Museum, Crich, Derbyshire, August 1984" on cream roof panels, plus white or cream "Grand Transport Extravaganza" on front and rear body panels.
   1. Cream front and rear logo.
   2. White front and rear logo.

1005 DOWNTOWN 1984
Cream body, red roof, gold domes and hitch, silver pillars, green seats, black horse. Logo: white or cream "3 Downtown 3" on roof panels, plus crest on front and back body panels.
   1. Cream main logo, red and gold crest.
   2. White main logo, red and gold crest.
   3. White main logo, all-red crest.

1006 HERSHEY CHOCOLATE TOWN 1990
Brown body and horse, green roof and seats, gold domes, pillars and hitch, white mane and tail. Logo: brown "Chocolate Town U.S.A. no. 3" on white roof panels, gold "Hershey PA" and designs on front and rear body panels. Special Hershey box.
   1. As above.

1007 DAYS GONE CLUB, SUMMER 1995 1995
White body, red roof, gold domes and hitch, dark brown horse, white mane and tail. Logo: black-outlined blue "Days Gone Collectors Club" on white panel, black "Summer Edition 1995". Special club model box.
   1. As above.

2   HORSE DRAWN MILK FLOAT 91 mm 1983
Cast body, chassis, hitch and axle mount, plastic roof and horse, 12-spoke hubs, "DG2-DG3" usually on bottom of hitch, "Made in England by Lledo" on axle mount. Castings:
   A. Horizontal rib across each side of body.
   2. No horizontal rib.

2000 EXPRESS DAIRY 1983
Dark blue body, white roof, blue chassis, hitch and mount, gold hubs, black tires, black or dark brown horse. Logo: white "Express Dairy 20" and frame.
   1. As above.

2001 CHAMBOURCY 1984
Cream body, light blue or turquoise roof, blue chassis, hitch and mount, gold hubs, white tires, black or dark brown horse. Logo: blue and green "Chambourcy" and design, red and green fruit, blue "real fruit yoghurt".
   1. Light blue roof.
   2. Turquoise roof.
   3. Darker blue chassis.

02002 (Not used)

2003 W. CLIFFORD & SONS 1984
Red body, white roof, yellow chassis, hitch and mount, gold wheels, black tires and horse. Logo: yellow "W. Clifford & Sons Dairymen, 31 Cross Lances Rd. Hounslow", horizontal line and phone number.
   1. As above.

2004 CELTIC DAIRIES 1984
Cream body, red roof, chassis, hitch and mount, gold hubs, white tires, tan horse. Logo: green "Celtic Dairies" above and below black and gold prince's plumes and "ich dien".
   1. As above.

3   HORSE DRAWN DELIVERY VAN 93 mm 1983
Cast body, chassis, hitch and axle mount, plastic roof and horse, usually 12-spoke hubs, usually "DG2-DG3" on bottom of hitch, "Days Gone" on chassis, "Made in England by Lledo" on mount. Variations of this lettering exist. Casting variations.
   A. Vertical ribs on body meet horizontal ribs.
   B. Vertical ribs shortened, don't meet horizontal ribs.

3000 WINDMILL BAKERY 1983
Medium, light or dark yellow body, light tan chassis, cream or light tan hitch, tan mount, light brown roof, gold hubs, black tires, tan, light brown or dark brown horse. Logo: brown "Windmill Bakery" and arc, tan windmill design on white semicircle with brown figures, brown frames on lower panels.
   1. Cream hitch, medium yellow body.

2. Tan hitch, medium yellow body.
3. Lighter yellow body.
4. Darker yellow body, no DG2-DG3 on hitch.

3001 COCA-COLA 1985
Dark yellow body, black roof, chassis, hitch and mount, gold hubs, black tires and horse. Logo: red "The Coca-Cola Co.", black frames.
1. As above.

3002 FINE LADY BAKERIES 1984
Light tan body, chassis, hitch and mount, light brown roof, gold hubs, black tires, dark brown horse. Logo: red "Fine Lady Bakeries Ltd.", brown figures and frame, red lettering in brown frames on lower panels.
1. As above.

3003 ROBERTSON'S SILVER SHRED 1984
Dark green body, cream or white chassis, hitch and mount, yellow roof, gold wheels, black tires, light or dark brown horse. Logo: yellow "Robertson's Silver Shred Marmalade" and lines, multicolored designs. Green logo color may be light or dark.
1. Cream chassis, hitch and mount.
2. White chassis, hitch and mount.

3004 PEPPERIDGE FARM 1983
White body, light tan chassis, hitch and mount, light brown roof, gold hubs, black tires, light or dark brown horse. Logo: white "Pepperidge Farm" in red-orange-black design, orange frames on lower panels.
1. As above.

3005 STAFFORDSHIRE COUNTY SHOW 1984
Pale or lime green body, light tan roof, chassis, hitch and mount, gold hubs, black tires, black horse. Logo: red "Staffordshire Agricultural Society", black "County Show", red wreath and date, black rope design.
1. Pale green body.
2. Lime green body.

3006 MATTHEW NORMAN 1984
Dark green body, chassis, hitch and mount, black roof, gold hubs, black tires and horse. Logo: yellow "Matthew Norman", carriage design, "fine carriage clocks", yellow lettering and frames on lower panels.
1. As above.

3007 ROYAL MAIL 1985
Red body, black roof, chassis, hitch and mount, red 6-bolt hubs, black tires and horse. Logo: black-outlined gold GR crest and "Royal Mail", black frames on lower panels. Special box.
1. As above.

3008 L.S.W.R. PARCELS 1984
Salmon body, dark brown roof, chassis, hitch and mount, gold hubs, black tires and horse. Logo: brown "L.S.W.R.", design, lines, "Parcels Ropley" and frames.
1. As above.

3009 HAMLEYS 1984
Dark blue body, chassis, hitch and mounts, black roof, gold hubs, black tires and horse. Logo: white "Hamleys", underline and "Regent Street, London", three white toy designs, gold frames.
1. As above.

3010 TRI-SUM POTATO CHIPS 1984
Red body, black roof, chassis, hitch and mount, gold wheels, black tires, brown or dark brown horse. Logo: red "Tri-Sum Potato Chips" on white panel, red lettering and scrolls on white panels.
1. As above.

3011 LLEDO CLUB 1987
Red body, black roof, chassis, hitch and mount, red 20-spoke hubs, black tires and horse. Logo: yellow and black Lledo emblem, black "Club Member Edition Spring 1987". Special box.
1. As above.

3012 J. SPRATT, BILLINGSGATE 1988
Dark blue body, black roof, chassis, hitch and mount, light gray horse. Logo: white "Billingsgate Market, fresh fish", gold design, "J. Spratt", etc., "Spratt Fresh Fish" on rear. Special Eastenders Collection box.
1. As above.

3013 ROYAL MAIL 1990
Red body, black roof, chassis, hitch and mount, gold hubs, black tires, light gray horse. Logo: black "Royal Mail", black and gold crown, gold monogram and frames. Special Royal Mail box.
1. As above.

3014 HARRODS 1992
Olive lower body, chassis and hitch, cream upper body and roof, green 20-spoke hubs, black tires, brown horse. Logo: black "Harrods Ltd, Brompton Road" on upper, same in gold on lower body. In set of four models.
1. As above.

3015 GREAT EASTERN RAILWAY 1993
Brown body, black chassis and hitch, white roof, brown horse and 20-spoke hubs, black tires. Logo: white "Great Eastern Railway" etc., "Great Eastern" on rear, gold frames. In set of three models.
1. As above.

4 HORSE DRAWN OMNIBUS 108 mm 1983
Cast body, steps and hitch, plastic upper floor and seats, two black or dark brown horses, spoked wheels, "DG4 Days Gone" usually on bottom of body, "Made in England" under rear platform. Castings:
A. Body notched sharply just above rear platform.
B. Notch filled in just above rear platform.
C. Notch filled in, signboards added under central windows.

4000 VICTORIA-KING'S CROSS 1983
Red body, steps and hitch, green or light brown seats, black wheels, dark brown or black horses. Logo: green or white "Lipton's Teas, largest sales in the world" on white, cream or green background above, yellow "London General Omnibus Company Limited, Victoria & King's Cross" in partial frame below.
1. Dark green seats, green-on-cream logo.
2. Dark green seats, green-on-white logo.
3. Dark green seats, white-on-green logo.
4. Bright green seats, white-on-green logo.
5. Light brown seats, white-on-green logo.
6. Reddish-brown seats, white-on-green logo.

4001 BOWERY-BROADWAY 1984
Red body, steps and hitch, green or light brown seats, black wheels, dark brown or black horses. Logo: same white-on-green Lipton's Tea logo as on #4000 above, yellow "Fifth Avenue Coach Company, Bowery-Broadway" below.
1. Green seats.
2. Light brown seats.
3. Reddish-brown seats.

4002 BOWERY-BROADWAY 1984
Green body (various shades), brown, orange-brown or gold wheels, otherwise as #4001.
1. Medium green body, green seats, brown sheels.
2. Medium green body, reddish-brown seats, brown wheels.
3. Medium green body, reddish-brown seats, orange-brown wheels.
4. Pale dark green body, light brown seats, gold wheels.
5. Dark green body, reddish-brown seats, gold wheels.
6. As type 5 plus "Fifth Avenue Coach Company" on new board.

4003 OAKEY'S, PUTNEY 1984
White body, steps and hitch, red seats and wheels, dark brown horses. Logo: blue-outlined cream "Oakey's",

white "Knife Polish" on blue panel above, white-outlined black "Putney" in frame below.
1. As above.
2. Extra decals on front, back and stairs. Not issued by Lledo.

4004 MASON'S PANTRY 1985
Dark brown body, steps and hitch, red seats, gold wheels, tan horses. Logo: brown-outlined yellow "Mason's Pantry" above, brown-outlined yellow "Mrs. Beaton's" and arched yellow "Foods of Character" below.
1. "Foods of Character" over rear wheels.
2. "Foods of Character" over front wheels.

4005 PEARS SOAP 1984
Light tan body, steps and hitch, red seats, red or black wheels, dark brown horses. Logo: red "King of Soaps, Pears, Soap of Kings" on yellow panel above, brown "London General Omnibus Company Limited" and either "Victoria and King's Cross" or just "Victoria" on new board below.
1. Red wheels, "Victoria & King's Cross".
2. Red wheels, "Victoria".
3. Black wheels, "Victoria".

4006 MADAME TUSSAUD'S 1984
Yellow body, steps and hitch, red seats, red or black wheels, dark brown or black horses. Logo: red "Madame Tussaud's Exhibition" above, green "London General Omnibus Company Limited" and green-outlined yellow "Favorite" in green partial frame.
1. Red wheels.
2. Red wheels, "Favorite" on new board.
3. Black wheels, "Favorite" on new board.

4007 HIGH CHAPPARAL 1986
Tan body, steps and hitch, red seats, gold wheels, black horses. Logo: red "High Chapparal" and multicolored figures on white backbround with red frame above, black "Vasternstaden" on white background on new board, red "Wilda Western I Sverige" and partial frame below.
1. As above.

4008 HAMLEYS 1984
Red body, steps and hitch, green seats, gold wheels, black horses. Logo: yellow "Hamleys" and underline on blue background above, white "The World's Finest Toyshop" and address below. In special box or gift set.

4009 BALMORAL TOURS 1987
Light orange body, steps and hitch, red seats, dark brown horses, gold wheels. Logo: red "Balmoral", green "Tours" above, orange "Aberdeen" on new board, green lines and lettering below. Special box, part of Ruby Wedding set.
1. As above.

4010 RADIO TIMES 1988
Dark green body, steps and hitch, cream seats, gold wheels, dark brown horses. Logo: red "The Radio Times", green "2d every week" on white panel above, green "Acton Vale-23-Barking" on new board, white lettering below. Special Eastenders Collection box.
1. "A million copies a week" lower logo.
2. "T. Tilling Ltd. Omnibuses" lower logo.

4011 NEWS OF THE WORLD 1988
Same as #4010, Type 2, but with red "News of the World" upper logo. "T. Tilling Ltd. Omnibuses" lower logo.
1. As above.

4012 COLMAN'S MUSTARD 1989
Yellow body, steps and hitch, red seats, gold wheels, brown horses. Logo: yellow "Colman's Mustard" etc. on blue panel on green band above, blue "Piccadilly Circus" on new board, green "Victoria & King's Cross"

and frame below. First #4 model with lower seats, painted manes, tails and collars.
1. As above.

4013 STONE'S GINGER WINE 1991
Cream body, steps and hitch, red seats, gold wheels, dark brown horses. Logo: cream "Stone's Ginger Wine" on green panel above, black "Victoria Station in frame on new board, cream "Walham Green via Victoria" on green panel below.
1. As above.

4014 OXO BEEF STOCK 1992 .
Red body, chassis and hitch, black seats, gold wheels, dark brown horses. Logo: white "OXO puts beef into you" on black upper panel, red "Barnes-Liverpool St." on white panel, gold destinations and frame below.
1. As above.

4015 COOPERATIVE TEA 1993
Yellow body, chassis and hitch, black seats, gold wheels, dark brown horses. Logo: red-yellow-green "Cooperative Tea" on upper panel, red "Edinburgh and District Tramways Company Limited" on panel below windows, black panel with gold lettering, black-red-gold emblem below.
1. As above.

4016 FURNESS RAILWAY 1993
Dark blue body, chassis and hitch, light blue seats, gold wheels, dark brown horses. Logo: white "Furness Railway" in red frame above, black "Coniston" on white board, red "new steam yacht 'Lady of the Lake'" on red-framed white panel below, white lettering on stairs. In set of three models.
1. As above.

4017 MADAME TUSSAUD'S 1994
Cream body, chassis and hitch, red seats, gold wheels, dark brown horses. Logo: black-outlined "Madame Tussaud's Exhibition" on red upper panel with gold and black frame, black "Marylebone - Station" on raised panel, blue-black-cream lettering below.
1. As above.

4018 HARRODS 1994
Red body, chassis and hitch, black seats, gold wheels, dark brown horses. No other data.
1. As above.

4019 MANN'S BEER 1995
Red body, chassis and hitch, black seats, gold wheels, dark brown horses. Logo: blue and red "Drink a Mann's Beer" on light blue upper panel, red "Shepherd's Bush" on white raised panel, gold lettering and frame.
1. As above

5 SHAND-MASON HORSE DRAWN FIRE ENGINE 106 mm 1983
Cast body, chassis, boiler and hitch, two plastic horses, spoked wheels, "DG5" on bottom of central chassis, "Made in" and "England" on rear sides, "Days Gone by Lledo" at rear. Early issues have three firemen figures fitting onto cast-in pins. Castings:
A. No braces.
B. Brace at base of footrest.
C. Braces at base of footrest and on bottom ahead of rivets.
D. No figure pins, otherwise as type C.

5000 LONDON FIRE BRIGADE 1983
Red body, chassis and hitch, gold or unpainted boiler, gunmetal wheels, black or dark brown horses. Logo: yellow "London Fire Brigade", number 27 and frame.
1. Gold boiler.
2. Unpainted boiler (sometimes called chromed).

5001 CHICAGO FIRE BRIGADE 1983
Red body, chassis and hitch, gold boiler, black or gunmetal wheels, black or dark brown horses. Logo: yellow "Chicago Fire Brigade", number 27 and frame.
1. As above.

5002 GUILDFORD FIRE BRIGADE 1983
Dark green body, chassis and hitch, gold or black boiler, gold wheels, black or dark brown horses. Logo: yellow "Guildford Fire Brigade", number 15 and frames. (Other colors are LP, not DG.)
1. Black boiler.
2. Gold boiler.

5003 HONG KONG FIRE BRIGADE 1984
Cream body, chassis and hitch, red or gold boiler, red wheels, black horses. Logo: red or maroon "HKFB", number 2 and frames.
1. Red boiler and logo.
2. Gold boiler, red logo.
3. Gold boiler, maroon logo.

5004 GREAT WESTERN RAILWAY 1984
Dark brown body, chassis and hitch, gold boiler, dark brown or gold wheels, tan or black horses. Logo: gold "G.W.R. Fire Brigade, Swindon" in frame, number 1 in circle. In regular box or on plinth in special box.
1. Brown wheels.
2. Gold wheels.

5005 LAKE CITY 1985
Dark yellow body, chassis and hitch, red boiler, red or black wheels, black horses. Logo: green "Lake City", number 5 and frames.
1. Red wheels.
2. Black wheels.

5006 PHILADELPHIA BUREAU OF FIRE 1984
Red body, chassis and hitch, gold boiler and wheels, tan horses. Logo: gold "P.B.F. and number 5, black frames. American and British issues said to be different shades of red.
1. As above.

5007 BIFBAC II CONVENTION 1984
Maroon body, chassis and hitch, gold boiler and wheels, tan horses. Logo: gold "BIFBAC II Convention", number 84 and frames.
1. As above.

5008 LONDON - EAST HAM 1988
Red body, chassis and hitch, copper boiler, black wheels, dark brown horses. Logo: yellow "17 London Fire Brigade, East Ham" and frame. Special Eastenders Collection box.
1. As above.

5009 CARROW WORKS, NORWICH 1989
Red body, chassis and hitch, gold (sometimes very glossy) boiler, black wheels and horses. Logo: yellow "Carrow Works Fire Brigade, Norwich" and frame.
1. As above.

5010 METROPOLITAN FIRE BRIGADE 1994
Red body, chassis and hitch, gold boiler, black wheels and horses. Logo: black-shadowed gold "62 Metropolitan Fire Brigade" on gold-bordered gray panel. In set of three models.
1. As above.

6   MODEL T FORD VAN 70 mm 1983
Cast body and chassis, plastic roof with header, silver or gold grille and windshield, 12-spoke metal or 20-spoke plastic wheels with tires. Base numbered DG6-DG, DG6-DG8, DG6-8, or DG6-8-33.
Castings have clear or unclear door lines, two header sizes, also vary internally in height of panel behind seat. Major variations:
1. Original castings.
2. Chassis modified to take plastic base, steering wheel and   textured roof pattern added.
3. Two tabs on upper rear to hold roof (either #1 or #2 casting).

6000 OVALTINE 1983
Orange body, light brown roof, brown chassis, gold or silver grille and windshield, 12-spoke gold hubs, black tires. Logo: blue "Ovaltine", orange and brown design on cream or yellow disc, black lettering. No header logo. (75 Years version is #6016.)
1. Gold grille and windshield.
2. Silver grille and windshield.

6001 YORKSHIRE POST 1983
Blue body, black roof and chassis, gold grille, windshield and 12-spoke hubs, black tires. Logo: yellow "Yorkshire Post Twixt Trent & Tweed", lines etc. No header logo.
1. As above.

6002 COOKIE COACH CO. 1984
Orange body, black roof and chassis, gold grille and 12-spoke hubs, black tires. Logo: yellow or white "Cookie Coach Company", gold or yellow ovals and frames.
1. Yellow lettering, gold frames.
2. White lettering, yellow frames.

6003 BRITISH MEAT 1984
Cream body, brown or black roof and chassis, gold grille, windshield and 12-spoke hubs, black tires. Logo: red and blue "British Meat" on blue design, blue "Smithfield, London", lettering and frames. No rear logo. Header: white "British Meat", two sizes of lettering.
1. Brown roof and chassis, small header.
2. Black roof and chassis, small header.
3. Brown roof, large header.

6004 AEROPLANE JELLY 1984
Blue body, white roof, red chassis, gold grille, windshield and 12-spoke hubs, black tires. Logo: yellow "Aeroplane Jelly Co.", red and white emblem, white music and frame, yellow lettering. Header: blue music and "Aeroplane Jelly Co."
1. As above.

6005 BRITISH MEAT 1984
Same as #6003, with brown roof and chassis, plus black "Prime tasty fresh beef, lamb, pork" and frames on rear doors.
1. As above.

6006 MARCOL 1984
Tan body, black roof, maroon chassis, gold grille, windshield and 12-spoke hubs, black tires. Logo: maroon emblem with red dragon, maroon-outlined tan "Marcol", maroon "Product" and other lettering, no rear logo. Header: gold "M. A. Rapport Co. Ltd."
1. As above.

6007 CITY OF LONDON POLICE 1984
Cream body, white roof, black chassis, gold grille, windshield and 12-spoke hubs, black tires. Logo: red cross, red and black coat of arms, black "City of London Police Ambulance" and other lettering, red crosses on rear. Header: red "Police Ambulance".
1. As above.

6008 I.P.M.S. 21ST ANNIVERSARY 1984
Cream body, blue roof and chassis, gold grille, windshield and 12-spoke hubs, black tires. Logo: blue globe, "21st Anniversary IPMS 1984", lettering and frames. Header: white "(U.K.) Region".
1. As above.

6009 INTERNATIONAL GARDEN FESTIVAL 1984
Cream body, green roof, black chassis, gold grille, windshield and 12-spoke hubs, black tires. Logo: black "2nd May, 14th Oct. International Garden Festival, Liverpool 84", green and black figures. Header: +/- white "Liverpool '84".
1. Header logo.
2. No header logo.

108

6010 ILLINOIS TOY SHOW 1984
Yellow body, light brown roof, dark brown chassis, gold grille, windshield and 12-spoke hubs, white tires. Logo: brown car design and "2nd. Illinois Miniature Toy Show". No header logo.
    1. As above.

6011 STRETTON SPRING WATER 1984
White body, roof and chassis, gold grille and windshield, black 12-spoke hubs, white tires. Logo: white "Stretton Spring Water" on blue ribbon, multicolored design, blue lettering, green frames. No header logo. (Green version is #6032.)
    1. As above.

6012 YORKSHIRE EVENING POST 1984
Yellow body, black roof and chassis, gold grille, windshield and 12-spoke hubs, black tires. Logo: black "Yorkshire Evening Post, the Original Buff" and lines. No header logo.
    1. As above.

6013 DAYS GONE COLLECTORS CLUB 1984
Black body, roof and chassis, gold grille, windshield and 12-spoke hubs, white tires. Logo: cream "Models of Days Gone Collectors Club", other lettering, gold frames. Header: cream "Beautiful Diecast Models".
    1. As above.

6014 BRITISH BACON 1984
Light blue body, blue roof, black chassis, gold grille, windshield and 12-spoke hubs, black tires. Logo: blue "British", stripe and "Bring home the best", red and white emblem, blue and white ribbon. Header: white "British Bacon".
    1. As above.

6015 HARRY RAMSDEN'S FISH AND CHIPS 1984
Cream body, red roof and chassis, gold grille, windshield and 12-spoke hubs, black tires. Logo: blue "Harry Ramsden's" and lines, black design and lettering. No header logo.
    1. As above.

6016 OVALTINE 75TH ANNIVERSARY 1985
Same as #6000, with blue "Ovaltine 75 Years" logo at bottom of disc. Sometimes in special box.
    1. As above.

6017 DAILY/SUNDAY EXPRESS 1985
Green body, black roof and chassis, gold grille, windshield and 12-spoke hubs, black tires. Logo: cream "Daily Express, Sunday Express" and line, black disc. No header logo. Collector Pack 1.
    1. As above.

6018 PERRIER-JOUET 1985
Ivory body, green roof, black chassis, gold grille, windshield and 12-volt hubs, white or black tires, or black wheels. Logo: flower design, green-outlined gold "Perrier-Jouet", gold "Champagne" and "Epernay". Header: gold "Perrier-Jouet".
    1. Lighter green roof, white tires.
    2. Darker green roof, white tires.
    3. Darker green roof, black tires.
    4. Darker green roof, black one-piece wheels.

6019 HOME ALES 1985
Green body and roof, black chassis, gold grille, windshield and 12-spoke hubs, black tires. Logo: green figure on white, black-outlined gold "Home Ales", gold lettering, black frames; green figure, white background and "Fine Ales: on rear. Header: gold "Home Ales".
    1. Darker green body and roof (both same shade).
    2. Lighter green roof and even lighter body.

6020 COCA COLA AT SODA FOUNTAINS 1984
Yellow-orange body, black roof and chassis, gold grille, windshield and 12-spoke hubs, black tires. Logo:

red "Coca-Cola at soda fountains". No header logo. (Code 2 model has lighter yellow body, smaller and lighter lettering.)
    1. As above.

6021 COCA-COLA EVERY BOTTLE STERILIZED 1984
Yellow-orange body, black roof and chassis, gold grille, windshield and 12-spoke hubs, black tires. Logo: red "The Coca-Cola Co.", black "every bottle sterilized" and frames. No header logo.
    1. As above.

6022 WONDER BREAD 1984
White body, light blue roof, blue chassis, gold grille, windshield and 12-spoke hubs, black tires. Logo: bread loaf design with red "Wonder", blue "Bread", blue and red "It's Slo-Baked". Header: white "Wonder Bread".
    1. As above.

6023 RAILWAY EXPRESS AGENCY 1984
Dark green body, black roof and chassis, gold grille, windshield and 12-spoke hubs, black tires. Logo: multicolored design with black "Railway Express for speedy service", white "Railway Express Agency" on black stripe, white emblem. No header logo.
    1. As above.

6024 KODAK FILM 1984
Orange body, black roof and chassis, gold grille and windshield, 12-spoke gold or 20-spoke white hubs, black tires. Logo: black-outlined red "Kodak", red "film", red and black design and frames. Header: yellow-outlined black "Kodak".
    1. As above.

6025 MARKS & SPENCER 1985
Dark green body, light green roof, black chassis, gold grille, windshield and 12-spoke hubs, black tires. Logo: black circles with "Marks & Spencer 1884-1984 centenary year" and design on gold background, gold lettering and frames, "Penny Bazaars" on rear. Header: black "Marks & Spencer".
    1. As above.

6026 MARCOL 1984
Same as #06006, but with yellow body, light brown roof, dark brown chassis, yellow header lettering, +/- red dragon and "Wales" on rear.
    1. No rear logo.
    2. Rear logo.

6027 PHILADELPHIA FIRE AMBULANCE 1984
Cream body and chassis, black roof, gold grille and 12-spoke hubs, black tires. Logo: gold "Bureau of Fire Ambulance", "P.B.F." and no. 3, black frames. No header logo.
    1. As above.

6028 PHILADELPHIA FIRE RESCUE 1984
Red body and chassis, black roof, gold grille, windshield and 12-spoke hubs, black tires. Logo: gold "Rescue Company, Philadelphia Bureau of Fire, no. 1, black frames. No header logo.
    1. As above.

6029 YORKSHIRE BISCUITS 1984
Brown body, black roof and chassis, gold grille, windshield and 12-spoke hubs, black tires. Logo: white or cream "Yorkshire Biscuits limited, Haworth Keighley", red lines, yellow emblem, design and frames. Header: white "Yorkshire Biscuits Ltd."
    1. White logo lettering.
    2. Cream logo lettering.

6030 AUTOMODEL EXCHANGE 1984
Maroon body, tan roof, black chassis, gold grille, windshield and 12-spoke hubs, black tires. Logo: gold "the Automodel Exchange", black and gold lettering, map and figure. Header: black "collect Lledo".
    1. As above.

6031 SOUTH WALES ECHO CENTENARY 1984
Cream body, blue roof and chassis, gold grille, windshield and 12-spoke hubs, white or black tires. Logo: black-outlined white "1884-1984", multicolored emblem with white "South Wales Echo", gold "Centenary", black lettering and frame. Header: white "South Wales Echo".
    1. As above.

6032 STRETTON SPRING WATER 1985
Same as #6011, but with green roof and chassis, gold hubs, black tires.
    1. As above.

6033 BARCLAY'S BANK 1985
Blue body, cream roof and chassis, gold or silver grille and windshield, black 12- or 20-spoke hubs, white tires. Logo: black eagle emblem, blue "Barclays" on white panels, white lettering, black frame. Header: blue or cream "Barclays" and eagle.
    1. Cream header lettering.
    2. Blue header lettering.

6034 MAGASIN DU NORD 1984
Green body, black roof and chassis, gold grille, windshield and 12-spoke hubs, black tires. Logo: gold "Magasin du Nord", "A/S Wessel & Vett" and frames. Header: gold or white "A/S Wessel & Vett".
    1. White header lettering.
    2. Gold header lettering.

6035 HAMLEYS 1984
Dark green body, light green roof, red chassis, gold grille, windshield and 12-spoke hubs, black tires. Logo: white "Hamleys" and underline, "Regent Street London, The World's Finest Toyshop", gold frames. Header: white "Hamleys" and underline. Special box.
    1. As above.

6036 AUSTRALIAN DAYS GONE CLUB 1985
Tan body, brown roof, dark brown chassis, gold grille, windshield and 12-spoke hubs, black tires. Logo: orange or dark red "Australian Collector's Club" and boomerang, brown and tan figures, brown frame. Header: pale green or dark brown boomerang with brown (roof color) "Founded 1984".
    1. Dark brown roof, dark red logo lettering, pale green header.
    2. Light brown roof, orange logo lettering, dark brown header.

6037 MURPHYS CRISPS 1984
Yellow-orange body, red roof and chassis, gold grille, windshield and 12-spoke hubs, black tires. Logo: red-outlined blue "Murphys" on blue background, blue "Crisps & Snacks" on white panel, white and blue border. Header: white "Murphys Crisps".
    1. As above.

6038 WELLS DRINKS 1985
Yellow body, brown roof and chassis, gold grille, windshield and 12-spoke hubs, black tires. Logo: multicolored fruit design with black-outlined yellow "Wells", orange "wonderful world", black "Wells Drinks", orange and green frames. Header: orange "Taste the goodness".
    1. As above.

6039 WOODWARD'S 1985
Blue body, roof and chassis, gold grille, windshield and 12-spoke hubs, black tires. Logo: white design and "get it at", blue-outlined white "Woodward's", white "we sell everything". Header: blue-outlined white "Woodward's".
    1. As above.

6040 CHOCOLAT LINDT 1985
Light blue body, blue or light blue roof, blue chassis, gold grille, windshield and 12-spoke hubs, white tires. Logo: gold and white emblem and "Chocolat Lindt", gold "Lindt of Switzerland Ltd." Header: gold "Lindt".
    1. Light blue roof (matches body).
    2. Blue roof (darker than body).

6041 EVENING CHRONICLE 1985
Red body, black roof and chassis, gold grille, windshield and 12-spoke hubs, black tires. Logo: emblem with black-outlined gold "1885-1985", black "Evening Chronicle", red "Centenary", cream panel with black "All the latest news" and frame. Emblem oval varies from off-white to light yellow.
    1. As above.

6042 CWM DALE SPRING 1986
White body and roof, blue or red chassis, gold grille and windshield, 12-spoke gold or 20-spoke black hubs, white or black tires. Logo: blue spring design, red "Cwm Dale Spring", blue "Wells Drinks Ltd.", red and blue frames. Header: red "Mineral Water".
    1. Blue chassis.
    2. Red chassis.

6043 ROYAL MAIL 350 YEARS 1985
Red body, black roof and chassis, gold grille, windshield and 12-spoke hubs, black tires. Logo: gold circular "Royal Mail, 350 years service to the public" and frames. No header logo. Special box.
    1. As above.

6044 ALTON TOWERS 1985
Dark brown body, cream roof and chassis, gold grille, windshield and 12-spoke hubs, black or white tires. Logo: off-white to light yellow "Alton Towers, Europe's Premier Leisure Park" and frame, gold and yellow emblem. Header: brown "Alton Towers". Special box.
    1. As above.

6045 NORTHERN DAILY MAIL 1985
Green body, tan roof, black chassis, gold grille, windshield and 12-spoke hubs, black tires. Logo: tan "The Northern Daily" on white, tan-outlined white "Mail", green "West Hartlepool" on white, white lettering, gold and tan frame. Header: green "The Northern Daily Mail".
    1. As above.

6046 CADBURYS BOURNVILLE 1986
Dark red or maroon body, cream roof and chassis, gold grille and windshield, red 20-spoke hubs, white tires. Logo: brown-outlined gold "Cadbury's", brown "Cocoa" on gold, white "Bournville" and design, gold frame. No header logo. Certificate.
    1. Dark red body, clear door lines.
    2. Maroon body, faint door lines.

6047 JOHN SMITH'S TADCASTER BREWERY 1986
Dark green body, light red roof, black chassis, gold grille, windshield and 12-spoke hubs, black tires. Logo: red-outlined yellow "John Smith's" and frames, red and white magnet, white "Tadcaster Brewery", etc. Header: yellow "Magnet Ales".
    1. Bright yellow logo color.
    2. Yellow-green logo color.
    3. "Shredded Wheat" on header (somebody goofed!).

6048 BAY TO BIRDWOOD RUN 1986
Black body, roof and chassis, gold grille, windshield and 12-spoke hubs, black tires. Logo: gold-outlined red "Bay to Birdwood Run", gold "Adelaide, Australia", designs and frame, black lettering on gold stripes. Header: gold "Bay to Birdwood Run".
    1. As above.

6049 AUSTRALIAN HARDWARE JOURNAL 1986
Dark blue body, cream roof, light cream chassis, gold grille, windshield and 12-spoke hubs, black tires. Logo: white "Australian Hardware Journal, "1886 1986" and frame, gold and black "100" emblem.
    1. As above.

6050 DAYS GONE TOY FAIRS 1986ff
Dark red body, cream roof and chassis, gold grille and windshield, 20-spoke black hubs, white tires. Logo: silver "Models of Days Gone, 1986 Toy Fairs", names of 8 locations, etc., gold frames. Header: red "Collect Lledo".

1. Misspelled "Harrowgate".
2. Correct "Harrogate".
3. 1987 Toy Fairs logo.
4. 1988 Toy Fairs logo.
5. 1989 Toy Fairs logo.

6051 CADBURY'S DRINKING CHOCOLATE 1986
Maroon body, cream roof and chassis, gold grille and windshield, gold 12-spoke or red 20-spoke hubs, white tires. Logo: gold and white "Cadbury's", gold "Drinking Chocolate" and frame, white cup. Header: cream "Cadbury" on dark red background. Special box.
1. Red wheels.
2. Darker body, lighter roof and chassis, gold wheels.

6052 (Not used)

6053 TIZER 1986
Yellow-orange body, black roof and chassis, gold grille, windshield and 12-spoke hubs, black tires. Logo: white "Tizer, the Appetizer" and red lettering on black and white panel, black "Tizer Limited" and address, red frames. No header logo.
1. 1. As above.

6054 COCA-COLA (green) 1986
Green body, roof and chassis, gold grille, windshield and 12-spoke hubs, white tires. Logo: white "Drink Coca-Cola, Delicious and Refreshing" on red panel, white lettering, yellow frames. Header: white "Coca-Cola".
1. As above.

6055 HERSHEY'S--REESE'S PIECES 1986
Orange body, dark brown roof, brown chassis, gold or silver grille and windshield, gold 12-spoke hubs, white tires. Logo: brown-outlined yellow "Reese's Pieces" and multicolored design in white frame, white "Hershey's" on brown background. Header: white "Hershey's" and frame.
1. As above.

6056 HEDGES & BUTLER 1987
Green body, tan roof, cream chassis, gold grille and windshield, 20-spoke black hubs, white tires. Logo: gold "Hedges & Butler Limited, Wine Merchants since 1667" and emblem. No header logo.
1. As above.

6057 CANADIAN PREMIUM INCENTIVE TRAVEL SHOW 1986
White body, orange roof and chassis, gold grille, windshield and 12-spoke hubs, white tires. Logo: black "Toronto", date, etc., orange "Canadian Premium Incentive Travel Show & Business Gift Exposition" and frame. Header: black "Metro Toronto Convention Centre".
1. As above.

6058 COCA-COLA (red) 1986
Tangerine red body, black roof and chassis, silver or gold grille and windshield, 20-spoke red hubs, white tires. Logo: yellow "Drink", white "Coca-Cola", yellow "in sterilized bottles", etc., and frame. Header: white "Coca-Cola".
1. As above.

6059 CRAFT & HOBBY SHOWCASE 1986
White body, blue roof and chassis, gold grille and windshield and 12-spoke hubs, black tires. Logo: blue maple leaf design, "Craft & Hobby Showcase", date, etc., and frame. Header" white "Collect Lledo".
1. As above.

6060 WELLS BLACK VELVIT 1987
Light rose body, black roof and chassis, gold grille and windshield and 12-spoke hubs, white tires. Logo: gold panel with black "Wells", black and gold design, black "Wonderful World" on ribbon, white panel with black "Blackcurrant Black Velvet", black "Wells Drinks Ltd." Header: white "Vitamin C".
1. As above (LP issue same except for LP base).

6061 FAIRY SOAP 1987
White body, light green roof, dark green chassis, gold grille, windshield and 12-spoke hubs, black tires. Logo: 2-tone green "Fairy" and design, red lettering and frame. No header logo.
1. As above.

6062 ROSE & CROWN 1987
Green body and chassis, white roof, gold grille, windshield and 12-spoke hubs, black tires. Logo: white "Rose & Crown" and "Fine Ales & Stouts", multicolored emblem, gold frame. Header: red "Rose & Crown".
1. As above.

6063 ROYAL AIR FORCE 1987
Pale gray body, dark blue chassis and roof, gold grille, windshield and 12-spoke hubs, black tires. Logo: "Royal Air Force" emblem, gold "216 Squadron Ground Electrics". Header: white "'C' Flight". In set of 3 RAF models with certificate.
1. As above.

6064 HAMLEYS 1988
Green body, black chassis and roof, gold grille, windshield and 12-spoke hubs, black tires. Logo: gold "Hamleys" etc. and frames. Header: gold "Est. 1760".
1. As above.

6065 ANHEISER-BUSCH (Budweiser) 1988
Cream body, brown chassis and roof, gold grille, windshield and 12-spoke hubs, white tires. Logo: red-gold-black "Anheuser-Busch St. Louis Beer" design, red lettering and frame. Header: white "King of Beers". Special Budweiser box.
1. As above.

6066 LLEDO COLLECTORS CLUB 1988
Dark green body, black chassis and roof, gold grille, windshield and 12-spoke hubs, black tires. Logo: White "The Lledo Collection Winter 1987-88", gold design and lines, similar rear logo. Header: white "Club Edition" and design. Special box.
1. As above.

6067 (Not used)

6068 GOLDEN SHRED 1988
Red body, green chassis, white roof, gold grille, windshield and 12-spoke hubs, black tires. Logo: black-outlined gold "Golden Shred", multicolored design with black "The World's Best Marmalade" on white ribbon, figure on door. Header: black "Robertson's".
1. As above.

6069 CHARRINGTON 1988
Red body, brown chassis and roof, gold grille, windshield and 12-spoke hubs, black tires. Logo: yellow and green "Charrington", yellow lettering and frames, multicolored emblem. Header: yellow "Charrington".
1. As above.

6070 SCHIFFER-MILLBANK 1988
Black body, chassis and roof, gold grille, windshield and 12-spoke hubs, black tires. Logo: gold "Millbank Books" on left, "Schiffer Publishing Ltd" on right. Header: gold "The Collector's Book".
1. As above.

6071 HIS MASTER'S VOICE 1990
Dark rose body, black chassis, cream roof, gold grille, windshield and 12-spoke hubs, black tires. Logo: brown and white figures, white "His Master's Voice" and "the Symbol of Supremacy". Header: red "His Master's Voice".
1. As above.

6072 SHELL PUMP SERVICE 1989
Red body, black chassis and roof, gold grille, windshield and 12-spoke hubs, black tires. Logo: yellow "Shell Pump Service" and emblem, white lettering and stripes. Header: yellow "Shell Motor Spirit".
1. As above.

111

6073 WALL'S ICE CREAM 1989
Black body and chassis, cream roof, silver grille and windshield, black 20-spoke hubs and tires. Logo: black "Walls Ice Cream" etc. and no. 99 on yellow panels. No header logo.
    1. As above.

6074-6086 CANADIAN SERIES 1988
The following models all have white body, gold grille, windshield and 12-spoke hubs, black tires. Logo includes name of province (also on header), flag, coat of arms, and year of joining Dominion of Canada. Special box.
    6074 ONTARIO Red roof and chassis.
    6075 YUKON Green roof, blue chassis.
    6076 NORTHWEST TERRITORIES Blue roof, red chassis.
    6077 PRINCE EDWARD ISLAND Red roof, green chassis.
    6078 NEWFOUNDLAND Red roof, blue chassis.
    6079 QUEBEC Blue roof, red chassis.
    6080 NOVA SCOTIA Red roof, blue chassis.
    6081 MANITOBA Red roof and chassis.
    6082 ALBERTA Blue roof and chassis.
    6083 NEW BRUNSWICK Yellow roof and chassis.
    6084 BRITISH COLUMBIA Blue roof, yellow chassis.
    6085 SASKATCHEWAN Green roof, yellow chassis.
    6086 CANADA Red roof and chassis.

6087 SELFRIDGES 1989
Green body, black chassis and roof, gold grille, windshield and 12-spoke hubs, black tires. Logo: gold emblem, "Selfridge & Co. Ltd.", address and date. No header logo. Sold singly or in set.
    1. As above.

6088 AU BON MARCHE 1989
Yellow body, black chassis and roof, gold grille and windshield, yellow disc hubs. Logo: gold-black-red "Au Bon Marche Paris Nouveautes" etc. Header: gold "Au Bon Marche".
    1. As above.

6089 SCHNEIDERS QUALITY MEATS 1989
Orange body, blue chassis and roof, gold grille, windshield and 12-spoke hubs, black tires. Logo: white-outlined blue "Schneiders Quality Meats" etc., blue frames. Header: orange "Schneiders".
    1. As above.

6090 WINCHESTER CLUB 1989
Green body, light green roof, black chassis, gold grille, windshield and 12-spoke hubs, black tires. Logo: gold "The Winchester Club", frames and door panel with green "Members Only". Header: light green "The Winchester Club" on black panel.
    1. As above.

6091 BRITANNIA FILMS 1989
Gold body and chassis, green roof, silver grille and windshield, gold 12-spoke hubs, black tires. Logo: multicolored "Britannia Films" emblem, black lettering and frames. In set of four models.
    1. As above.

6092 NESTLE'S MILK CHOCOLATE 1989
Light red body, black chassis, white roof, gold grille, windshield and 12-spoke hubs, black tires. Logo: white "Nestle's Milk Chocolate", lettering and frames. Header: black "Gold Medal Milk".
    1. As above.

6093 NORTH YORKSHIRE MOORS RAILWAY 1989
Dark blue body, black chassis and roof, gold grille, windshield and 12-spoke hubs, black tires. Logo: white "North Yorkshire Moors Railway", trim and "Express Cartage", gold emblem and 4 town names. Header: gold "NYMR" emblem. In set of three models.
    1. As above.

6094 HAMLEYS 1989
Dark blue body, cream roof, black chassis, gold grille, windshield and 12-spoke hubs, black tires. Logo: black-red-gold "Hamleys" design, gold "The Finest Toyshop in the World", and address. Header: gold "Hamleys" design. Special box.
    1. As above.

6095 4711 EAU DE COLOGNE 1990
Turquoise body, black roof and chassis, gold grille, windshield and 12-spoke hubs, black tires. Logo: gold-black-white "4711 Eau de Cologne" design, black and gold emblem. Header: gold "4711" design.
    1. As above.

6096 ROWNTREE'S COCOA 1990
Red body and chassis, black roof, gold grille and windshield, red disc hubs, black tires. Logo: multicolored "Rowntree's Cocoa" design, white frame, yellow lettering. Header: yellow "Rowntree's Cocoa".
    1. As above.

6097 JAEGER CLASSIC CLOTHES 1990
Navy body, chassis and roof, gold grille, windshield and 12-spoke hubs, black tires. Logo: gold "Jaeger Classic Clothes", address and frames. Header: gold "Jaeger". In set of four models.
    1. As above.

6098 ROYAL MAIL TELEGRAPH SERVICE 1990
Red body and roof, black chassis, gold grille, windshield and 12-spoke hubs, black tires. Logo: gold "Royal Mail" and monogram, white "Telegraph Service" and frames, gold and black crown. No header logo.
    1. As above.

6099 HERSHEY'S COCOA 1990
Cream body, brown roof and chassis, gold grille, windshield and 12-spoke hubs, white tires. Logo: multicolored "Hershey's Cocoa" design, brown "Hershey Pennsylvania". Header: gold "Hershey's". Special box.
    1. As above.

6100 DAYS GONE COLLECTORS CLUB 1990
Plum body, black roof and chassis, gold grille, windshield and 12-spoke hubs, black tires. Logo: black "Days Gone" on gold panel, gold "Vintage Models" on green ribbon, gold "Collectors Club, "Lledo 1990" and frames. No header logo.
    1. As above.

6101 ARNOTT'S BISCUITS 1990
Red body, chassis and roof, gold grille, windshield and 12-spoke hubs, black tires. Logo: black-outlined gold "Arnott's Biscuits", yellow-blue-red design, gold lettering and frames. Header: gold "Arnott's". In set of three models.
    1. As above.

6102 DAYS GONE COLLECTORS CLUB 1991
Dark blue body, green roof and chassis, gold grille, windshield and 12-spoke hubs, black tires. Logo: black "Days Gone" on gold panel, gold "Collectors Club, "Lledo 1991" and frame. No header logo.
    1. As above.

6103 JOSEPH LUCAS LTD. 1991
Dark green body, black chassis, light gray roof, gold grille, windshield and 12-spoke hubs, black tires. Logo: white "Joseph Lucas Ltd., Great King St. Birmingham, King of the Road", stripes and lettering, multicolored emblem. Header: black "Joseph Lucas Ltd."
    1. As above.

6104 BLACKPOOL VAN TRANSPORT 1991
White body, chassis and roof, gold grille, windshield and 12-spoke hubs, black tires. Logo: black-outlined red "Blackpool Van Transport", black designs, lettering and frames. Header: red "Cheswick and Wright Ltd."
    1. As above.

6105 ZEBRA GRATE POLISH 1991
Yellow-orange body, dark green roof, black chassis, gold grille, windshield and 12-spoke hubs, black tires.
Logo: black-outlined red "Zebra Grate Polish", black-white-green zebra design, black lettering. Header:
white "Reckitt & Sons".
   1. As above.
6106 DAYS GONE COLLECTORS CLUB 1992
Metallic green body, black roof and chassis, gold grille, windshield and 12-spoke hubs, black tires. Logo:
black-gold-green "Days Gone" emblem, gold lettering and frames. Header: gold "10th Anniversary".
   1. As above.
6107 JAMESON IRISH WHISKEY 1992
Cream body, red-brown roof, green chassis, gold grille, windshield and 12-spoke hubs, black tires. Logo:
brown "Jameson Irish Whiskey", date and lines, red "John Jameson & Son". Header: gold "Jameson".
   1. As above.
6108 HOTEL COLOMBIA 1992
Red body, black roof and chassis, gold grille and windshield, red 20-spoke hubs, white tires. Logo:
multicolored "Hotel Colombia, Genova" panel, yellow address. No header logo.
   1. As above.
6109 HUNTLEY & PALMER 1993
Green body, black chassis, cream roof, gold grille and windshield, red 20-spoke hubs, black tires. Logo:
multicolored "Huntley & Palmer Ginger Nuts" emblem, yellow frame and trim, white lettering. Header:
black "Huntley & Palmers".
   1. As above.
6110 MIDLAND RAILWAY 1993
Orange body, black chassis, cream roof, gold grille, windshield and 12-spoke hubs, black tires. Logo:
multicolored Midland coat of arms, gold "The Golden Age of Steam" and frames. Header: red "Midland
Railway". Special box.
   1. As above.
6111 LANCS & YORKS RAILWAY 1993
Green body and roof, black chassis, gold grille, windshield and 12-spoke hubs, black tires. Logo:
multicolored "Lancashire & Yorkshire Railway" emblem, gold crest, lettering and frames. Header" gold "L
Y R". Special box.
   1. As above.
6112 NORTH EASTERN RAILWAY 1993
Black body, chassis and roof, gold grille, windshield and 12-spoke hubs, black tires. Logo: multicolored
"North Eastern Railway" emblem, gold lettering and frames. Header: gold "North Eastern Rwy". Special
Golden Age of Steam box.
   1. As above.
6113 L M S RAILWAY 1993
Cream body, maroon chassis and roof, gold grille, windshield
and 12-spoke hubs, black tires. Logo: multicolored "London Midland and Scottish Railway Company"
emblem, maroon "The Golden Age of Steam" and frames. Header: gold "L M S". Special box.
   1. As above.
6114 DAYS GONE CLUB 1993 1993
Yellow body, black chassis and roof, gold grille, windshield and 12-spoke hubs, black tires. Logo: black and
gold "Days Gone" panel, black "Collectors Club" and "Lledo 1993", green trim and frame. Header: gold
"Lledo".
   1. As above.
6115 DAYS GONE CLUB 1994 1994
Red body, black chassis and roof, gold grille, windshield and 12-spoke hubs, black tires. Logo: black-gold-
green "Days Gone" design, gold "Collectors Club", "Lledo 1994" and frame. Header: gold "Lledo". Special
box.

   1. As above.
6116 FLORIS TOILETRIES 1994
Dark blue body, black chassis and roof, gold grille, windshield and 12-spoke hubs, black tires. Logo: gold "Floris
of London, Purveyors of the finest English flower perfumes and toiletries", etc. and frames, "Floris"
monogram also on header.
   1. As above.
6117 LONDON & NORTHWESTERN RAILWAY 1994
Maroon body, black chassis, cream roof, gold grille, windshield and 12-spoke hubs, black tires. Logo:
multicolored London & Northwestern emblem, gold lettering and frames. Header: black "LNWR". Special
box.
   1. As above.
6118 LONDON & SOUTHWESTERN RAILWAY 1994
Maroon body, brown chassis and roof, gold grille, windshield and 12-spoke hubs, black tires. Logo:
multicolored emblem, gold "The Golden Age of Steam" and frames. Header: gold "L & S W R". Special
box.
   1. As above.
6119 CAMBRIAN RAILWAY 1994
Green body, black chassis and roof, gold grille, windshield and 12-spoke hubs, black tires. Logo:
multicolored "Cambrian Railway" emblem, gold lettering and frames. Header: gold "Cambrian Railway".
Special box.
   1. As above.
6120 SOMERSET & DORSET RAILWAY 1994
Dark blue body, black chassis and roof, gold grille, windshield and 12-spoke hubs, black tires. Logo:
multicolored Somerset & Dorset Railway emblem, gold "The Golden Age of Steam" and frames. Special
box.
   1. As above.
6121 RUPERT BEAR 1994
White body, blue chassis and roof, gold grille, windshield and 12-spoke hubs, black tires. Logo:
multicolored "Rupert and Friends" design and emblem. Header: white-outlined "Rupert". Special box.
   1. As above.
6122 PEPSI-COLA 1994
Cream body, green chassis and roof, gold grille, windshield and 12-spoke hubs, black tires. Logo: black and
red design, black "Discriminating people drink" etc., red "Pepsi-Cola". Header: white "Pepsi-Cola". Special
box.
   1. As above.
6123 SATURDAY EVENING POST 1994
Red body, black chassis and roof, gold grille, windshield and 12-spoke hubs, black tires. Logo: Saturday
Evening Post design, white "Norman Rockwell 100th Anniversary" emblem. Special box.
   1. As above.
6124 AUSTRALIAN P.M.G. 1994
Red body, black chassis and roof, gold grille, windshield and 12-spoke hubs, black tires. Logo: black-
shadowed "P.M.G.", gold "Postmaster General Melbourne", multicolored coat of arms. Header: gold
"P.M.G.".
   1. As above.
6125 ANTHON BERG 1995
Maroon body, black chassis, gray roof, gold grille, windshield and 12-spoke hubs, black tires. Logo: gold
"Anthon Berg" etc., crown and frames, white "Chocolate" etc. Header: gold "Anthon Berg".
   1. As above.
6126 CALEDONIAN RAILWAY 1995
Dark blue body, black chassis, gray roof, gold grille, windshield and 12-spoke hubs, black tires. Logo:

Caledonian Railway emblem, gold lettering and frames. Header: black "Caledonian Railway". Special box.
  1. As above.

6127 GREAT EASTERN RAILWAY 1995
Tan body, black chassis, maroon roof, gold grille, windshield and 12-spoke hubs, black tires. Logo: Great Eastern Railway emblem, gold lettering and frames. Header: gold "Gt. Eastern Rly." Special box.
  1. As above.

6128 NORTH BRITISH RAILWAY 1995
Maroon body, black chassis, gray roof, gold grille, windshield and 12-spoke hubs, black tires. Logo: North British Railway Company emblem, gold lettering and frames. Header: red "North British Rly." Special box.
  1. As above.

6129 GREAT WESTERN RAILWAY 1995
Green body, black chassis, red roof, gold grille, windshield and 12-spoke hubs, black tires. Logo: Great Western Railway Company emblem, gold lettering and frames. Header: gold "Great Western Rly." Special box.
  1. As above.

6130-31-32 HUIS TEN BOSCH 1995
Black chassis and roof, gold grille, windshield and 12-spoke hubs, black tires. Logo: Windmill scene, gold Huis Ten Bosch emblem. Header" gold "Huis Ten Bosch".
  6130. Maroon body.
  6131. Dark blue body.
  6132. Dark green body.

6133 DAYS GONE CLUB 1995 1995
White body, maroon chassis and roof, gold grille, windshield and 12-spoke hubs, black tires. Logo: black "Days Gone" and frame on gold panel, green ribbon, gold "Lledo 1995" and "Collectors Club". Header: gold "Lledo". Special box.
  1. As above.

6135 HUIS TEN BOSCH 1995
Blue body, black chassis and roof, gold grille, windshield and 12-spoke hubs, black tires. Logo: same windmill scene and gold emblem as #6130.
  1. As above.

7 1934 MODEL A FORD WOODY WAGON 74 mm 1984
Cast body and chassis, plastic seats, grille, base, later roof blade and spare wheel. 12-spoke metal, 20-spoke or disc plastic hubs. Base originally DG7-DG9, then with DG13 and DG14 over front and rear axles, then DG7-9-13-14-37. Castings:
  A. Recessed body panel just under oval sign.
  B. Panel not recessed.
  C. Panel not recessed, rear spare and roof blade attachments.

7000 PAT'S POODLE PARLOUR 1984
Yellow body, brown trim, red chassis, cream interior, silver grille, 12-spoke hubs, white tires. Logo: white "Poodle Pat's Parlour" and designs.
  1. As above.

7001 COCA-COLA 1984
Light orange body, brown trim, black chassis, cream interior, silver grille, 12-spoke hubs, white tires. Logo: red "Drink Coca-Cola in bottles".

7002 FORD SALES & SERVICE 1984
White body, blue trim and chassis, cream interior, silver grille, 12-spoke hubs, white tires. Logo: white "Ford: on blue oval with white border, blue "Sales & Service" below.
  1. As above (no blade).
  2. Blade with white "Ford Sales & Service" on white-bordered blue   background; 1988 reissue.

7003 WEST POINT TOY SHOW 1984
Yellow body, green chassis and trim, cream interior, silver grille, 12-spoke hubs, white tires. Logo: blue "Toy Show, West Point" and date.
  1. As above.

7004 HAMLEYS 1984
Cream body, tan trim, red chassis, cream interior, silver or gold grille, 12-spoke gold hubs, white tires. Logo: tan "Hamleys" and underline on red oval, cream border, tan "Toys and Games".
  1. As above.

7005 GODFREY DAVIS FORD 1985
White body, blue chassis and trim, off-white roof blade, cream or white interior, cream or black spare, silver grille, 12- or 20-spoke hubs, white tires. Logo: white "Ford" on white-bordered blue oval. Blade: white "Godfrey Davis on white-bordered blue background.
  1. Cream interior and spare.
  2. Cream interior, black spare.
  3. White interior, ? spare.

7006 CHOCOLATES BY DELLA 1986
Cream body, chassis, blade, interior and spare, silver grille, cream 20-spoke hubs, black tires. Logo: brown "Chocolates by", brown-outlined cream "Della" on pink oval. Blade: brown "Belgian Chocolates".
  1. As above.

7007 COMMONWEALTH GAMES 1986
White body and blade, blue chassis, cream interior and spare, silver grille, red disc hubs, white tires. Logo: red disc with black border and "Commonwealth Games 1986", white "Mac" and underline, white and black dog figure. Blade: Black dog figures. Special box.

7008 CASTROL 1988
White and green body, green chassis and interior, white blade and spare, silver grille, white disc hubs, black tires. Logo: red-white-green "Castrol" emblem, gold wreath, green 'Wakefield Motor Oil". Blade: red "Wakefield Castrol Motor Oil, the Masterpiece in Oils".
  1. As above.

7009 PASCALL SWEETS 1990
White body, spare and blade, green chassis, interior, trim and 20-spoke hubs, silver grille, white tires. Logo: white "Pascall Sweets" on green oval. Blade: green "Pascall Sweets".
  1. As above.

8 MODEL T FORD TANKER 80 mm 1984
Cast body and chassis, plastic tank, roof, pipes, grille and windshield, 12-spoke metal or 20-spoke plastic hubs, tires. Base lettered DG6-DG8, then DG6-8, then DG6-8-33, with steering wheel added. Chassis modified to take plastic base.

8000 ESSO 1984
Light blue body, dark blue chassis, blue tank, white roof, gold grille, windshield and pipes, 12-spoke gold or 20-spoke white hubs, black tires. Logo: red "Esso" and stripes in blue oval on white background, red-white-blue "Esso" emblem, red "Inflamable Danger" or "Inflammable Danger" on white panel, white lettering. No header logo.
  1. Red chassis (a few factory specimens only).
  2. "Inflamable" misspelling.
  3. "Inflammable" correctly spelled.

8001 COCA-COLA 1984
Light orange body, dark yellow or light orange tank, black roof and chassis, gold grille, windshield, pipes and 12-spoke hubs, black tires. Logo: black "Serve" and "at home", red "Coca-Cola" and "The Coca-Cola Bottling Co.". No header logo.
  1. Dark yellow tank (lighter than body).
  2. Light orange tank (matches body).

8002 CASTROL 1985
Dark green body and tank, white roof, black chassis, gold grille, windshield, pipes and 12-spoke hubs, black tires. Logo: white-outlined red "Castrol", gold "Wakefield" and "Motor Oil", gold address, phone number, etc. No header logo.
1. As above.

8003 PHILADELPHIA BUREAU OF FIRE 1984
Red body, tank and chassis, black or white roof, gold grille, windshield, pipes and 12-spoke hubs, black tires. Logo: gold "Bureau of Fire Service Truck" and "P.B.F." in black frames. No header logo at first, then black "P.B.F." and frame.
1. Black roof, no header logo.
2. White roof, header logo (Code 3).

8004 PENNZOIL 1985
Red body, yellow tank, black roof and chassis, gold grille, windshield and pipes, 12-spoke gold or 20-spoke cream hubs, black tires. Logo: black "Pennzoil" across red Liberty Bell, black "Pennzoil Place, Houston, Texas", yellow-black-red "Pennzoil Motor Oil" design, black lettering and Liberty Bell on rear. No header logo.
1. As above.

8005 HOFMEISTER LAGER 1985
Yellow body and tank, brown chassis and roof, gold grille, windshield and pipes, 20-spoke red or 12-spoke gold hubs, white tires. Logo: black "Hofmeister: on black-bordered white ribbon, black bear figure and lettering (also on rear). No header logo.
1. Tank lighter yellow than body.
2. Tank matches body.
3. Purplish-brown chassis.

8006 BLUE MOUNTAINS BUSH FIRE BRIGADES 1986
Red body, chasiss, tank and roof, gold grille, windshield, pipes and 12-spoke hubs, black tires. Logo: yellow "Blue Mountains Bush Fire Brigades", lettering and lines, red-white-green emblem and yellow "Fire Tanker" on rear. Header: yellow "Fire Tanker".
1. As above.

8007 CROW CARRYING CO. 1987
Yellow body, black roof, tank and chassis, gold grille, windshield, pipes and 12-spoke hubs, black tires. Logo: red and white design and bird figure, red "as the crow flies", red-outlined white "Crow Carrying Company Ltd.", red address, phone number, etc. Header: white "Crow Carrying Co."
1. As above.

8008 HERSHEY'S CHOCOLATE MILK 1986
White body, brown chassis, tank and roof, gold grille, windshield, pipes and 12-spoke hubs, white tires. Logo: white "Hershey's", brown "Chocolate Milk" on white stripe, brown "Real Chocolate", white "Hershey's Chocolate Milk" on brown stripes. Header" white "Hershey's" and frame.
1. As above.
2. Darker brown chassis, lighter brown logo color.

8009 WATER WORKS 1987
Dark blue body and chassis, black roof and tank, gold grille, windshield, pipes and 12-spoke hubs, black tires. Logo: white "Water Works" on blue background, silver "Rutland District Emergency Service", white lettering on rear. No header logo.
1. As above.

8010 ZEROLENE 1987
Green body and tank, black chassis, white roof, gold grille, windshield, pipes and 12-spoke hubs, black tires. Logo: white "Zerolene Standard Oil for Motor Cars", "Standard Oil Company", etc. No header logo.
1. As above.
2. "Lubrication Specialists" lettering; 1988 issue.

8011 SHELL-MEX 1988
Red body and chassis, white roof, gold grille, windshield and pipes, gold 12-spoke or cream 20-spoke hubs, black tires. Logo: black-outlined yellow "Shell", yellow "Fuel Oil" and "Shell-Mex Ltd. fuel oil", etc. Header: red "Shell-Mex".
1. As above.

8012 HOMEPRIDE FLOUR 1988
White body, red chassis, blue tank and roof, gold grille, windshield, pipes and 12-spoke hubs, black tires. Logo: white "Homepride", black and white figure on white oval (also on rear). Header: white "Homepride".
1. As above.

8013 DUCKHAMS OILS 1988
Light gray body, black chassis, dark green roof, light gray tank, gold grille, windshield, pipes and 12-spoke hubs, black tires. Logo: dark green "Duckhams Oils" and "Perfection in Lubrication", green-gold-red emblems. Header: gold "Duckhams".
1. As above.

8014 SHELL-FRANCE 1989
Red body and tank, black chassis, white roof, gold grille, windshield, pipes and 12-spoke hubs, black tires. Logo: black-outlined yellow "Shell", yellow "Fuel Oil" and "Shell-France Fuel Oil", etc. Header: red "Shell-Mex".
1. As above.

8015 B.P. MOTOR SPIRIT 1989
Green body and tank, black chassis and roof, gold grille, windshield, pipes and 12-spoke hubs, black tires. Logo: black-outlined yellow "Motor B P Spirit" (also on rear) and other lettering. Header: yellow "Motor B P Spirit".
1. As above.

8016 TEXACO 1989
Red body and tank, black chassis and roof, gold grille, windshield, pipes and 12-spoke hubs, black tires. Logo: black-outlined white "Texaco", white "Petroleum Products" and other lettering, red-white-black emblems. Header: white "Texaco".
1. As above.

8017 ARMY WATER TANKER 1989
Olive body, chassis, tank, roof, pipes and disc hubs, black grille and tires. Logo: white "Water", other lettering, also on rear. Header: white "RASC". In boxed set of three models.
1. As above.

8018 PRATTS 1990
Green body, black chassis and roof, gold grille, windshield, pipes and 12-spoke hubs, black tires. Logo: white "Pratts", gold "Anglo-American Oil Co.", gold lettering on doors and rear. Header: white "Pratts".
1. As above.

8019 MOBILGAS 1991
Red body and tank, black chassis and roof, gold grille, windshield and pipes, red disc hubs, black tires. Logo: blue-outlined white "Mobilgas", red-white-blue "Mobiloil" emblem, white lettering, "Mobilgas" and emblem on rear. Header: white "Mobilgas".
1. As above.

8020 RUSSIAN OIL PRODUCTS 1993
Gray body, lighter gray tank and roof, red chassis, gold grille, windshield, pipes and 12-spoke hubs, black tires. Logo: black-shadowed red "R.O.P." and number, black-shadowed gold "Motor Spirit" and "Lamp Oil", gold and red lettering on side, black-shadowed gold "Motor Spirit R.O.P. Lamp Oil" on rear of tank. Header: red "R.O.P. Motor Spirit".
1. As above.

9   MODEL A FORD CAR   77 mm   1984
Cast body and chassis, plastic interior, grille, windshield and base, later spare wheel, 12- or 20-spoke hubs. Cream and black interiors and spare wheels may have been switched after models left factory. Base first DG7-DG9, then with DG13-DG14 added over axles, then DG7-9-13-14. Castings:
　A. No spare wheel mount.
　B. Spare wheel mount (interior component modified).
　C. Spare wheel mount, only front door outlines.

9000   POLICE   1984
Light or dark blue body, dark blue chassis, cream (or black?) interior, silver grille and windshield, 12- or 20-spoke hubs, white tires, +/- cream spare. Logo: white "Police", white door area with black and gold star, white no. 055.
　1. Light blue body, cream interior, no spare.
　2. Dark blue body, cream interior, no spare.
　3. Dark blue body, black interior, no spare.
　4. Medium blue body, cream interior and spare.
　5. Dark blue body, ? interior, tan spare, 20-spoke hubs.

9001   NEW YORK TO RIO   1984
Silver body, red chassis, black (or cream?) interior, silver grille and windshield, 12-spoke hubs, white tires. Logo: blue "New York-Rio", red-white-blue Union Jack, blue circled no. 3.
　1. Black interior.
　2. Cream interior (Code 3?).

9002   PHILADELPHIA BUREAU OF FIRE   1984
Red body and chassis, black (or cream?) interior, silver grille and windshield, gold 12-spoke hubs, black tires. Logo: gold disc with black "Battalion Chief 9 D.P.S. Bureau of Fire".
　1. Black interior.
　2. Cream interior (Code 3?).

9003   THE 15 MILLIONTH FORD   1985
Black body and chassis, black (or cream?) interior and spare, silver grille, silver or gold windshield, 12- or 20-spoke black hubs, white tires. Logo: white "The Fifteen Millionth Ford".
　1. Black interior and spare.
　2. Cream interior and spare (Code 3?).

10   ALBION SINGLE DECKER COACH   83 mm   1984
Cast body and chassis, plastic upper body/roof, interior, grille, base, hubs and tires. Base first DG10-12, then DG10-12-34-35. Each casting to 1989 exists with either thick or thin front fender ends. Castings:
　A. Original front end.
　B. Thickened front end to stabilize grille.
　C. Thickened front end, 2 holes under grille.
　D. Wide base tab slot, otherwise as type C.

10000   BRIGHTON BELLE   1984
Maroon body, green and yellow trim, green chassis, cream or tan roof, cream interior, silver or gold grille, green 6-bolt hubs, white tires. Logo: yellow "Brighton Belle", white "Hastings-Eastbourne-Worthing-Bognor". Header: black "Brighton".
　1. Tan roof, dark cream interior, silver or gold grille.
　2. Cream roof, dark cream interior, gold grille.
　3. Light cream roof and interior, gold grille.

10001   TILLINGBOURNE VALLEY   1984
Maroon body and roof, black chassis, cream interior, gold grille, dark red 6-bolt hubs, black tires. Logo: yellow "Tillingbourne Valley". Header: yellow "Peaslake" and frame.
　1. As above.

10002   SILVER SERVICE   1987
Silver body and chassis, red roof, white interior, silver grille, red 6-bolt hubs, black tires. Logo: black "Darley Dale & Matlock" in frame and "Silver Service". Header: white or silver "Matlock" and frame.
　1. Silver header, darker red roof.
　2. White header, lighter red roof, wide front slot.

10003   SOUTHERN VECTIS   1984
Green body, black chassis, cream roof and interior, gold grille, green 6-bolt or disc hubs, black tires. Logo: black-outlined yellow or white "Southern Vectis", address and stripe. Header: black "Newport" and frame. Boxed on plinth. Certificate. White logo lettering is probably faded yellow.
　1. Cream roof and interior, yellow logo.
　2. Light cream roof and interior, white logo?, wide slot.

10004   SCHOOL BUS   1984/1987
Yellow-orange body and roof, black chassis, cream or white interior, gold or silver grille, black 6-bolt hubs, white tires. Original logo: black "District 17, Union Free School", etc., and lines, white "School Bus". Header: black "School" amd frame.
　1. Original logo, cream interior, gold or silver grille.
　2. Black "Oakridge School District", red stripes, white interior.(Has DG base, wide slot, unlike FSW version.)

10005   POTTERIES   1984
Red body, black chassis, cream or red roof, cream interior, black grille, red 6-bolt hubs, black tires. Logo: black "Cheadle-Longton" on white panel, black stripe, black-outlined gold "Potteries", underline and no. 23. Header: black (on cream) or white (on red) "Longton" and frame.
　1. Cream roof, black header.
　2. Red roof, white header.

10006   GREAT WESTERN RAILWAY   1985
Brown body, black or purplish-brown chassis, cream roof, red interior, gold grille, brown 6-bolt hubs, white tires. Logo: red-outlined gold "G.W.R.", gold frames. Header: black "Station" and frame. Special box, sometimes plinth.
　1. Black chassis, dark cream roof.
　2. Purplish-brown chassis, light cream roof.

10007   BARTON   1985
Red body, magenta chassis, cream roof and interior, gold grille, dark red 6-bolt hubs, black tires. Logo: black-outlined gold "Barton", underline and no. 175, gold "T. H. Barton, Director, Beeston" and frame, black and cream or white stripes. Header: black "Nottingham" and frame.
　1. Cream stripe.
　2. White stripe.

10008   LONDON COUNTRY   1986
Green body, dark green or black chassis, cream roof and interior, gold or silver grille, dark green 6-bolt or disc hubs, black tires. Logo: yellow "London Country" and "30 M.P.H.". Header: black "Ongar" and frame.
　1. Dark cream roof, dark green chassis, gold or silver grille.
　2. Light cream roof, black chassis, gold grille.

10009   HAMLEYS   1984
Dark brown body, cream chassis, roof and interior, gold grille, cream 6-bolt hubs, black tires. Logo: white "Hamleys" and underline, yellow "The Finest Toyshop in the World" and address. Header: black "Regent Street" and frame. Special box.
　1. As above.

10010, 10011 (Not used)
10012   TARTAN TOURS   1985
Red body, cream chassis, roof and interior, gold grille, cream 6-bolt hubs, black tires. Logo: white

"Ecclefechan & Auchtermuchty Tartan Tours", green and white plaid design. Header: black "Perth" and frame.
  1. Dark cream roof and interior.
  2. Light cream roof and interior, thick front end with holes.

10013 TRAILWAYS 1985
White body, red chassis and interior, light cream roof, gold grille, red 6-bolt hubs, white tires. Logo: white "Trailways" and American flag on red stripe. Header: black "Dallas" and frame.
  1. As above.

10014 IMPERIAL AIRWAYS 1985
Cream body and interior, light blue chassis, dark blue or red roof, gold grille, cream 6-bolt or disc hubs, black tires. Logo: blue "London-Africa-India-Far East", red "Imperial Airways" and other lettering, red and blue emblem. Header: white "Croydon" and frame.
  1. Blue roof, 6-bolt or disc hubs.
  2. Red roof, ? hubs.
  3. Lighter cream body, ? roof, disc hubs.

10015 REDBURNS 1986
Red body and chassis, cream roof, cream or white interior, gold grille, red 6-bolt hubs, black tires. Logo: black-outlined gold "Redburns", gold "Motor Services Ltd.", address, etc. Header: black "South St." and frame.
  1. Cream interior.
  2. White interior.

10016 COMMONWEALTH GAMES 1986
White body, red chassis, blue roof, cream or white interior, gold grille, red 6-bolt hubs, white tires. Logo: blue-white-red "XIII", black "XIII Commonwealth Games, Scotland 1986" and "Courtesy Coach". No header logo. Special box.
  1. Cream interior.
  2. White interior.

10017 HERSHEY'S CHOCOLATE 1986
Brown body, cream or brown chassis, cream roof, cream or white interior, gold grille, cream 6-bolt or disc hubs, black tires. Logo: white and brown "Hershey's Milk Chocolate" panel, yellow "Express" and "Hershey PA". Header: "Hershey's". Special box.
  1. Cream chassis and interior.
  2. Brown chassis, cream interior.
  3. Purplish-brown chassis, cream interior, disc hubs.
  4. Purplish brown chassis, white interior.

10018 E. B. TAYLOR 1988
Red body and roof, cream interior and hood, black chassis, silver grille, red 6-bolt or disc hubs, black tires. Logo: black-bordered white stripe, gold "E. B. Taylor", black lettering, gold and red rear lettering. Header: gold "Taylor's" and frame.
  1. As above.

10019 CITY OF COVENTRY 1989
Magenta body and chassis, cream roof and seats, gold grille, plum disc hubs, black tires. Logo: black-shadowed gold "City of Coventry", gold lettering and frame, cream Lady Godiva figure. Header: black "Coventry" and frame.

10020 B. O. A. C. 1990
Black body and chassis, cream roof and interior, silver grille, black wheels. Logo: white "British Overseas Airways Corporation", gold emblem and "B.O.A.C." Header: black emblem and "B.O.A.C.".
  1. As above.

10021 BRITISH EUROPEAN AIRWAYS 1991
Gray body and chassis, cream roof and interior, silver grille, gray 8-lug hubs, black tires. Logo: gray "British European Airways" on white stripe, white "BEA" on red panel. Header: white "Amsterdam" on red panel.
  1. As above.

11 HORSE DRAWN REMOVAL VAN 109 mm 1984
Cast body, spoked wheels, plastic roof and two tan, light or dark brown or black horses. Only casting changes involve lettering on bottom of body (DG11 moved from front to rear) and modification of seat backrest.

11000 TURNBULL & CO. 1984
White body, red chassis and hitch, green roof, gold wheels, tan horses. Logo: green "Furniture Removers", red lines and stripe with gold "Turnbull & Co.", green address and no. 11.
  1. As above.

11001 ABELS OF EAST ANGLIA 1985
Light blue body, red chassis and hitch, dark blue roof, gold wheels, tan or dark brown horses. Logo: dark blue "Abels of East Anglia", light blue "World Wide Removals" on dark blue ribbon, red address, red, white and dark blue trim.
  1. As above.

11002 BIG TOP 1985
Cream body, red chassis and hitch, dark blue roof, gold wheels, dark brown or black horses. Logo: black "Big Top" on red-bordered yellow ribbon, blue trim, multicolored scenes.
  1. As above.

11003 STAFFORDSHIRE COUNTY SHOW 1985
Tan body, dark brown chassis, hitch and roof, gold wheels, dark brown horses. Logo: brown "Staffordshire Agricultural Society County Show", date and design.
  1. As above.

11004 ROYAL MAIL 1985
Red body, black chassis, hitch and roof, gold wheels, black horses. Logo: black-outlined gold "Royal Mail" and monogram, black and gold crown. Special box.
  1. As above.

11005 WILLIAMS GRIFFIN 1985
Dark green body, red chassis and hitch, tan roof, gold wheels, black horses. Logo: gold griffin, gold-outlined yellow "Williams Griffin", yellow "Department Store", address, etc.
  1. As above.

11006 MacCOSHAM 1985
Dark yellow body, chassis, hitch and roof, gunmetal wheels, dark brown horses. Logo: yellow "MacCosham: on dark green ribbon, dark green lettering.
  1. As above.

11007 COCA-COLA 1986
White body, red chassis, hitch and roof, gold wheels, light or dark brown horses. Logo: multicolored cases, red "Coca-Cola" and frame, black "In Bottles" and "5c". Special box.
  1. Lighter red roof.
  2. Darker red roof.

11008 BUDWEISER 1988
White body, red chassis, hitch and roof, gold wheels, dark brown horses. Logo: multicolored "Genuine Budweiser" design and "City Delivery", red frames. Special box.
  1. As above.

11009 LLEDO COLLECTION 1988
Blue body, white chassis, hitch and roof, gold wheels, black horses. Logo" silver "The Lledo Collection" and frame, blue lettering on white and silver stripe. Special box.
  1. As above.

11010 A. P. COOPER, SMITHFIELD MARKET 1988
Cream body, black chassis, hitch and roof, gold wheels, black horses. Logo: maroon and gold designs, maroon "A. P. Cooper", gold lettering, black "Smithfield Market" and lines, black and cream design. Eastenders Collection box.
    1. As above (maroon logo color).
    2. Red logo color.
11011 (Not used)
11012 JAMES BROWN & SONS 1989
Cream body, dark green chassis, hitch and roof, gunmetal wheels, dark brown horses. Logo: black "Furniture Removers and Storers James & Sons" and address, black-shadowed dark green "Brown", globe with lettering, ribbons.
    1. As above.
11013 ALBERT DALEY & SON 1989
Dark yellow body, chassis, hitch and roof, black wheels, dark brown horses. Logo: red "The Firm You Can Trust" and frames, black "Albert Daley & Son Arthur", etc.
    1. As above.
11014 MARKS & SPENCER 1990
Red body and roof, black chassis and hitch, gold wheels, dark brown horses. Logo: black-outlined white "Marks & Spencer Ltd.", white lettering and frames. Special box.
    1. As above.
11015 ROYAL MAIL 1990
Red body, black chassis and hitch, white roof, gold wheels, black horses. Logo: black "Royal Mail", white lines (not on #11004), black and gold crown, gold monogram. Special box.
    1. As above.
11016 ARNOTTS BISCUITS 1990
Red body and roof, black chassis and hitch, gold wheels, brown horses. Logo: black-outlined gold "Arnott's Biscuits", multicolored design, gold lettering and frame. In set of three models.
    1. As above.
11017 ROBERT HEATON & SON 1991
Black body, chassis and roof, gold wheels, dark brown horses. Logo: cream and blue "Robert Heaton & Son", black and blue "Furniture Removers" on cream panel, gold lettering and frames.
    1. As above.
11018 LLEDO COLLECTORS CLUB 1991
Dark brown body, chassis and hitch, tan roof, gold wheels, dark brown horses. Logo: black "Days Gone" on gold panel, gold and green ribbon with lettering, gold "Lledo Collectors Club, Summer 1991" and frame.
    1. As above.
11019 J. SAINSBURY 1992
Blue-black body, chassis, hitch and roof, gold hubs, dark brown horses. Logo: red and cream "Go to Sainsbury's" panel, gold "J. Sainsbury".
    1. As above.
11020 HARRODS 1992
Olive body, black chassis and hitch, cream roof, gold wheels, brown horses. Logo: gold "Mineral Waters & Co.", cream "Harrod's Stores Ltd." and stripes. In boxed set of two models.
    1. As above.
11021 HAMLEYS 1992
Cream body, black chassis, hitch and roof, gold wheels, brown horses. Logo: black and gold Hamleys emblem, red "the finest toyshop in the world", black address, red and black figures. In boxed set of four models.
    1. As above.

11022 CARTER PATERSON/SCHWEPPES TONIC 1993
Green body, red chassis and hitch, black roof, gold wheels, brown horses. Logo: white "Carter Paterson & Co. Ltd." on red stripe, Schweppes Tonic Water logo on white-framed red panel.
    1. As above.
11023 PEPSI-COLA 1993
White body, blue chassis and hitch, light blue roof, black wheels, brown horses. Logo: black-outlined red "Pepsi-Cola", black lettering, multicolored figure. Special Pepsi-Cola box.
    1. As above.
11024 GREAT NORTHERN RAILWAY 1993
Dark green body, black chassis, hitch and roof, gold wheels, dark brown horses. Logo: gold "Great Northern Railway", white panel with black lettering, white lettering and frame. In boxed set of three railway road vehicles.
    1. As above.
11025 NORTH EASTERN RAILWAY/OXO TRENCH HEATER 1994
Black body, chassis, hitch and roof, gold wheels, brown horses. Logo: gold "North Eastern Railway Co. No. 1" and frame, red-white-black "Oxo Trench Heater" design on white and gray panel.
    1. As above.
11026 RUPERT BEAR 1995
Red body, black chassis and hitch, cream roof, gold wheels, brown horses, tan driver. Logo: kite-flying scene. Special Rupert box.
12 DENNIS 1934 FIRE ENGINE 82/100 mm 1984
Cast body and chassis, plastic grille, windshield, floor, base, hubs and tires; either one ladder attached to truck, or wheeled escape ladder. Ladder rack above windshield exists with or without tongue. Chassis has same fender and front end variations as #10, and seats are with or without pins for figures. Base first DG10-12, then DG10-12-34-35.
12000 LUCKHURST COUNTY 1984
Red body, dark green chassis, black floor, cream ladder, gold grille and windshield, red or green 6-bolt hubs, black tires. Logo: yellow or white "Luckhurst County", frame and "L.C.F.B.".
    1. Yellow logo, red hubs.
    2. Yellow logo, green hubs.
    3. White logo?
    4. Reissued with escape ladder in 1989.
12001 CARDIFF CITY FIRE BRIGADE 1985
Red body, white chassis, black floor, light brown ladder, gold grille and windshield, 6-bolt red hubs, black tires. Logo: yellow "Cardiff City Fire Service 6" and "C.C.F.S.".
12002 (Not used)
12003 BERMUDA FIRE DEPARTMENT 1985
Dark blue body, cream chassis and ladder, cream or white floor, gold grille and windshield, 6 bolt red hubs, black tires. Logo: gold "Bermuda Fire Dept.", frame and "B.F.D.".
    1. Cream floor.
    2. White floor.
12004 LONDON FIRE BRIGADE 1986
Red body, black chassis and floor, cream escape ladder with light brown, black, gunmetal or gold wheels, gold or silver grille and windshield, red or green hubs, black tires. Logo: gold "L.C.C.", no. 52, "London Fire Brigade" and frames, red-white-blue shield.
    1. Cream ladder with light brown wheels, red 6-bolt hubs.
    2. With four ladder wheel colors, two grille colors, two colors   of 6-bolt or disc hubs, many other combinations may exist.

12005 CHELMSFORD TOWN FIRE BRIGADE 1986
Red body, black chassis and floor, light brown escape ladder with gold wheels, gold or silver grille and windshield, green 6-bolt hubs, black tires. Logo: gold "Chelmsford Town Fire Brigade" and frame, red-white-blue shield.
  1. Gold grille and windshield.
  2. Silver grille and windshield.
  3. Gold grille, silver windshield, or vice versa.
  4. Green disc hubs?

12006 AUXILIARY FIRE SERVICE 1987
Dark green body and chassis, black floor, cream escape ladder with gunmetal wheels, gold grille and windshield, 6-bolt green hubs, light gray tires. Logo: white shield, "Auxiliary Fire Service" and frame.
  1. As above.

12007 ESSEX COUNTY FIRE BRIGADE 1987
Red body, white chassis, off-white floor, dark cream escape ladder with gold wheels, gold grille and windshield, red 6-bolt hubs, black tires. Logo: gold "Essex County Fire Brigade" and shield.
  1. As above.

12008 WARE FIRE SERVICE 1987
Red body, black chassis and floor, brown escape ladder with gold wheels, gold grille and windshield, red 6-bolt hubs, black tires. Logo: gold "Ware Fire Service", emblem and "W.F.S.", white frame.
  1. As above.

12009 WINDSOR FIRE BRIGADE 1987
Red body and chassis, black floor, gold or silver grille and windshield, dark cream or brown escape ladder with gold wheels, black or red 6-bolt hubs, black tires or one-piece wheels. Logo: gold "Windsor Fire Brigade" and lines. Special Ruby Wedding box.
  1. Cream ladder, gold grille and windshield, black hubs.
  2. Brown ladder, silver grille and windshield, red hubs.
  3. Cream ladder, gold grille and windshield, black wheels.

12010 GLASGOW FIRE BRIGADE 1988
Red body and chassis, black floor, cream escape ladder with gold wheels, gold grille and windshield, red 6-bolt hubs, black tires. Logo: gold emblem and "Glasgow Fire Brigade".
  1. As above.

12011 BOSTON FIRE DEPARTMENT 1988
Red body and chassis, cream floor and escape ladder with black wheels, gold grille and windshield, red 6-bolt hubs, white tires. Logo: gold "Boston Fire Dept.", "B.F.D." and frame.
  1. As above.

12012 BIRMINGHAM FIRE BRIGADE 1989
Red body, black chassis and floor, brown escape ladder with gold wheels, silver grille and windshield, red 6-bolt hubs, black tires. Logo: white "Birmingham Fire Brigade" and "B.F.B.", white and gold coat of arms, gold frames.
  1. As above.

12013 BRADFORD CITY FIRE BRIGADE 1990
Red body, black chassis and floor, cream escape ladder with gold wheels, gold grille and windshield, red 6-bolt hubs, black tires. Logo: black and gold emblem, gold "Bradford City Fire Brigade", "B.C.F.B." and frames.
  1. As above.

12014 HERSHEY CHOCOLATE TOWN 1990
Red body, white chassis and floor, brown escape ladder with gold wheels, gold grille and windshield, red 6-bolt hubs, black tires. Logo: white "Chocolate Town U.S.A.", "Hershey PA", no. 5 and frame. Special box.
  1. As above.

12015 MANCHESTER FIRE BRIGADE 1991
Red body, black chassis and floor, tan escape ladder with gold wheels, gold grille and windshield, red 6-bolt hubs, black tires. Logo: gold "Manchester Fire Brigade", no. 12, "M.F.B." and frame.
  1. As above.

12016 WEST HAM FIRE BRIGADE 1992
Red body, black chassis and floor, cream escape ladder with gold wheels, gold grille and windshield, red 6-bolt hubs, black tires. Logo: gold "West Ham", emblem and frames.
  1. As above.

12017 VALLETTA FIRE BRIGADE 1992
Red body, black chassis and floor, tan escape ladder with gold wheels, gold grille and windshield, red 6-bolt hubs, black tires. Logo: black-outlined white "Valletta Fire Brigade" and Maltese cross, white number on fender. In boxed set of three models.
  1. As above.

12018 HAMLEYS 1994
Red body, black chassis and floor, tan escape ladder with gold wheels, gold grille and windshield, red 6-bolt hubs, black tires. Logo: blue "Hamleys", gold "Fire Brigade" and frame. In boxed set of two models.
  1. As above.

12019 LONDON FIRE BRIGADE 1994
Red body, black chassis and floor, tan ladder with gold wheels, gold grille and windshield, red 6-bolt hubs, black tires. Logo: white ":L.C.C. London Fire Brigade", black hood panel, gold frames. In boxed set of three models.
  1. As above.

13 MODEL A FORD 1934 VAN 77 mm 1984
Cast body and chassis, plastic roof, blade if any, grille and base, 12-spoke metal or 20-spoke plastic hubs, tires. Roofs with blades have transverse ridges; roofs without blades lack them. Seats and a steering wheel were added, and the body was lengthened. Base first DG7-9 with DG13 and DG14 over the axles, then DG7-9-13-14-, then DG7-9-13-14-37.

13000 CAMP COFFEE 1986
Dark cream body, black chassis, brown roof, gold grille, 20-spoke cream hubs, black tires. Logo: blue "Camp" and date, brown "Coffee" and trim, multicolored emblem with brown "R. Paterson & Sons Ltd." and cream "Glasgow".
  1. As above.

13001 EVENING NEWS 1984
Yellow-orange body, chassis, roof and blade, silver grille, gold 12-spoke hubs, black tires. Logo: red "Evening News", red shield with white "6:30". black and white newspaper rack design. Blade: black "First with the News".
  1. As above.

13002 TUCHER BRAU 1985
Turquoise body, blue chassis, black roof, gold grille, yellow-orange 20-spoke hubs, black tires. Logo: black and gold emblems, gold-outlined black "Tucher", black "Brau-Tradition seit 1672", gold and blue frames.
  1. As above.

13003 MITRE 10 1986
Light brown body, black chassis and roof, gold grille, 20-spoke yellow hubs, black tires. Logo: red-white-black figure, black-white-yellow "Mitre 10" emblems, black "Australia's Biggest Hardware Specialists".
  1. As above.

13004 HAMLEYS 1984
Yellow-orange body, chassis and roof, silver grille, gold 12-spoke hubs, black tires. Logo: white "Hamleys" and underline, address, red panel, black frames. In special box or set.
  1. As above.

13005 MICHELIN 1985
Yellow body, blue chassis and roof, gold or silver grille, gold 12-spoke or white or cream 20-spoke hubs, black tires. Logo: blue "Michelin" and stripe, black and white tire and figure, black frames.
    1. As above.

13006 JERSEY EVENING POST 1985
White body, black chassis, pink roof and blade, gold grille and 12-spoke hubs, black tires. Logo: black "Jersey Evening Post" and address, pink stripe. Blade: black "Reporting Island Life".
    1. As above.

13007 MARY ANN BREWERY 1985
Dark blue body and roof, white chassis, gold grille and 12-spoke hubs, black tires. Logo: white "Ann Street Brewery Co. Ltd." and address, blue and white arms and map, black "Mary Ann" and slogan.
    1. As above.

13008 ROYAL MAIL 1984
Red body, black chassis and roof, silver grille, 12-spoke gold hubs, black tires. Logo: black "Royal Mail" and round "Post Office" emblem, black and gold crown, gold monogram. Special box.
    1. As above.
    2. Longer body (1992).

13009 COCA-COLA (At Soda Fountains) 1985
Yellow-orange body, black chassis and roof, silver grille, gold 12-spoke hubs, black tires. Logo: red "Coca-Cola at Soda Fountains".

13010 BASILDON BOND 1985
White body, dark blue chassis, blue roof and blade, gold or silver grille, gold 12-spoke hubs, black tires. Logo: gold "Basildon Bond" on gold-rimmed blue panel, blue and black "DRG Stationery" and lines, black frames. Blade: gold "Britain's Most Popular Writing Paper".
    1. As above.

13011 RYDER TRUCK RENTAL 1986
Yellow-orange body and roof, black chassis, silver grille, cream 20-spoke hubs, black tires. Logo: black "Ryder" and "Truck Rental", red-white-black stripes and Ryder emblem.

13012 COCA-COLA (Every Bottle Sterilized) 1985
Yellow-orange body, chassis, roof and blade, gold or silver grille, red 20-spoke hubs, white tires. Logo: red "Drink Coca-Cola in Bottles" and "The Coca-Cola Bottling Co.", red-white-brown bottle, brown frame. Blade: black "Every Bottle Sterilized".
    1. As above.

13013 EVENING SENTINEL 1985
Navy blue body, black chassis and roof, silver grille, cream 20-spoke hubs, black tires. Logo: gold "Evening Sentinel", blue and white rack design.
    1. As above.

13014 STROH'S BEER 1985
Red body, black roof, silver or gold grille, gold 12-spoke hubs, white tires. Logo: gold and black emblem and "Stroh's Beer", white lettering and line, gold frames.
    1. As above.

13015 ROYAL MAIL 350 YEARS 1985
Red body, black chassis and roof, silver grille, red 20-spoke hubs, black tires. Logo: black "Royal Mail", black and gold crown, black-outlined gold monogram, black frame, round gold "350 Years" emblem. Special box.
    1. As above.

13016 FESTIVAL GARDENS 1985
Cream body, brown chassis and roof, gold grille, cream 20-spoke hubs, black tires. Logo: green-outlined cream "Festival", green "Gardens, Liverpool", black dates.

13017 ROBINSON'S SQUASHES 1986
Cream body and chassis, green roof, gold grille, cream 20-spoke hubs, black tires. Logo: black "Robinsons Original High Juice Squashes", green and black stripes and design, cream emblem, white lettering on black ribbon, black Robinsons emblem.
    1. As above.

13018 EVER READY 1988
Blue body and chassis, white roof, silver grille, black 20-spoke hubs and tires. Logo: orange-white-blue emblem with "Ever Ready" and "Made in Britain", white lettering.

13019 H. P. SAUCE 1987
Magenta body and chassis, white roof and blade, gold or silver grille, dark blue 20-spoke hubs, black tires. Logo: white "The One & Only H.P. Sauce" and stripes, dark blue panel. Blade: white "H.P." on blue background.
    1. As above.

13020 F. D. B. 1986
Gray body, black chassis and roof, gold or silver grille, gold 12-spoke hubs, black tires. Logo: blue dragon and "F.D.B."
    1. Light bluish-gray body.
    2. Darker greenish-gray body.

13021 COCA-COLA (Join the 7 Million) 1986
Yellow-orange body, roof and blade, black or yellow-orange chassis, silver or gold grille, yellow 20-spoke hubs, white tires. Logo: white "Drink Coca-Cola in Bottles", red panel with white border, brown and white hand holding bottle, red and brown lettering. Blade: brown "Join the seven million". Special box.
    1. Black chassis.
    2. Yellow-orange chassis.

13022 LYONS ICE CREAM 1988
Dark blue body and chassis, white roof, gold grille, blue 20-spoke hubs, black tires. Logo: blue "Lyons", "Bricks", etc., gold "Ice Cream" and "J. Lyons & Co. Ltd.", tan background, cream designs and frames.
    1. As above.

13023 HERSHEY'S KISSES 1986
Brown body, cream chassis and roof, gold grille, brown 20-spoke hubs, white tires. Logo: white "Hershey's Kisses", candy design, line and "Milk Chocolate Cocoa". Special box.
    1. As above.

13024 HERSHEY'S SWEETS AND TREATS 1986
Cream body, brown chassis, roof and blade, gold grille and 12-spoke hubs, white tires. Logo: cream 'Hershey's' on brown background, brown "Milk Chocolate" on cream panel, brown designs, red frames. Blade: white "Sweets and Treats". Special box.
    1. Chocolate brown chassis.
    2. Purplish brown chassis.

13025 ROYAL MAIL 1987
Same model as #13008, but with gold 20-spoke hubs (!), Ruby Wedding box.
    1. As above.

13026 HEINZ TOMATO SOUP 1988
Rose red body, black chassis, cream roof, black and 20-spoke hubs, black tires. Logo: white "Heinz Cream of Tomato Soup" on black and hold design, black-rimmed gold "57 Verieties". Blade: red "Heinz".
    1. As above.

13027 CHARLES TATE 1988
Brown body, black chassis, roof and blade, gold grille, white 20-spoke hubs, black tires. Logo: gold

"Charles Tate", etc., white "Tailors & Gents Outfitters", gold-black-white design, white "a stitch in time".
Blade: white "Tate", lettering and lines. Eastenders Collection box.
    1. As above.

13028 EXCHANGE & MART 1988
White body, black chassis, roof and blade, silver grille, red 20-spoke hubs, black tires. Logo: black-red-white "The Exchange & Mart" design, black and red lettering. Blade: "At your Newsagent 4d" on white background.
    1. As above.

13029 ELIZABETH SHAW 1988
Cream body, navy blue chassis, black roof, gold grille, navy blue 20-spoke hubs, black tires. Logo: gold coat of arms, lettering and line, blue "Elizabeth Shaw".
    1. As above.

13030 OXYDOL 1989
Light blue body, dark blue chassis and roof, silver grille, dark blue disc hubs, black tires. Logo: 2-tone blue and white design with "Oxydol", "for whiter whites", etc, and door emblem, white lettering.
    1. As above.

13031 AQUASCUTUM 1989
Gray body, dark blue chassis and roof, gold grille, black 20-spoke hubs and tires. Logo: gold "Aquascutum of London, makers of fine clothes since 1851" and coat of arms. In boxed set of four models.
    1. As above.

13032 (Not used)

13033 ALLENBURY'S DIET 1989
Magenta body, black chassis, cream roof, gold grille, maroon 20-spoke hubs, white tires. Logo: black-shadowed maroon "Allenbury's Diet", maroon lettering and black stripe on cream panel, cream lettering on door.

13034 EMPIRE FILMS 1989
Gold body and chassis, green roof, silver grille, gold 12-spoke hubs, black tires. Logo: red-white-black "Empire" emblem, black lettering and frames. In boxed set of four models.
    1. As above.

13035 KLEENEX 1989
White body, blue chassis, roof and blade, gold grille and 12-spoke hubs, black tires. Logo: black "Kleenex Tissues" and stripes, blue "Softness is our Strength" and stripe. Blade: white "Kleenex Tissues, Softness is our Strength" on one side.
    1. As above.

13036 AUSTIN REED 1990
Blue body, white roof, black chassis, silver grille, dark blue 20-spoke hubs, black tires. Logo: silver "Austin Reed of Regent Street" (also on rear), figure, address and frames. In boxed set of four models.
    1. As above.

13037 BBC TV 1989
Dark green body, black chassis, roof and blade, gold grille and 12-spoke hubs, black tires. Logo: gold "1936 BBC 1896", circla and "Fifty Years of Television". Blade: "Radio Times 2d".
    1. As above.

13038 BRITISH ARMY RECRUITMENT 1989
Olive body, chassis, roof, grille and disc hubs, black tires. Logo: black and red lettering on white panel, white line and lettering, red-white-black emblem. In boxed set of three models.
    1. As above.

13039 PERSIL SOAP 1990
Green body, black chassis and roof, silver grille, green disc hubs, black tires. Logo: multicolored "Persil das

sebstta"tige Waschmittel" design, white and red "Henkel" oval.
    1. As above.

13040 MADAME TUSSAUD'S 1990
Light blue body, dark blue chassis, white roof, silver grille, blue 20-spoke hubs, black tires. Logo: dark blue "Madame Tussaud's Exhibition", other lettering, dark blue and white figures.
    1. As above.

13041 MARKS & SPENCER 1990
White body, green chassis, roof and 20-spoke hubs, gold grille, black tires. Logo: red-white-blue "Marks & Spencer Ltd., the Originators of the Penny Bazaars" design, red date. Special box.
    1. As above.

13042 ROYAL MAIL 1990
Red body, black chassis, roof and blade, gold grille, red 20-spoke hubs, black tires. Logo: black "Royal Mail" and "No. 21", black and gold crown, gold monogram. Black lettering and design on white blade panel. Special box.
    1. As above.

13043 HERSHEY'S MILK CHOCOLATE 1990
Silver body, brown chassis, roof and blade, silver grille, black 20-spoke hubs and tires. Logo: silver and brown "Hershey's Milk Chocolate" and designs, red frames. Blade: white "Sweets and Treats". Special box.
    1. As above.

13044 NORTH YORKSHIRE MOORS RAILWAY 1990
Dark green body, black chassis, red roof and disc hubs, gold grille, black hubs. Logo: multicolored "Dine Well by NYMR" design, cream NYMR emblem. In set of three models.
    1. As above.

13045 ARNOTTS BISCUITS 1990
Red body, chassis and roof, gold grille, red 20-spoke hubs, black tires. Logo: black-outlined gold "Arnott's Biscuits", blue-yellow-red design, gold lettering and frames. In boxed set of three models with certificate.

13046 ROSELLA MARMALADE 1991
Yellow body and chassis, jade green roof, silver grille, yellow disc hubs, black tires. Logo: multicolored design with black "Rosella Preserving Co. Ltd," yellow "Marmalade", other lettering, horseshoe and bird emblem.

13047 CASTROL MOTOR OIL 1991
Red body and disc hubs, black chassis and roof, gold grille, red disc hubs, black tires. Logo: black-white-yellow "Wakefield Castrol Motor Oil" emblem, black lettering.

13048 HAMLEYS 1992
White body, black chassis and roof, gold grille, blue-black 20-spoke hubs, black tires. Logo: red "Hamleys Estd 1760", white "Hamley Brotyhers Ltd." on red ribbon, red-blue-black design, black lettering. Special box.

13049 RINSO 1992
Blue body, blue-black chassis and roof, gold grille, black disc hubs and tires. Logo: white and red "Rinso" emblem, white lettering (also on rear), red frames.
    1. As above.

13050 SOUTHERN RAILWAY 1992
Green body, black chassis, cream roof, silver grille, red 20-spoke hubs, black tires. Logo: pale yellow "Southern Railway", lettering and lines, yellow "Southern Railway" on rear. In set of three models with certificate.
    1. As above.

13051 HARRODS 1992
Olive body, black chassis, cream roof, silver grille, green disc hubs, black tires. Logo: gold-outlined "Harrods Ltd" on greenish cream panel, god lettering, red-on-white Toy Fair poster with black frame. In set of four models.
   1. As above.

13052 QANTAS CARGO HANDLING 1992
Cream body, green chassis, roof and disc hubs, gold grille, black tires. Logo: red and cream triangle, black "Qantas Cargo Handling", lettering and lines. In set of two models.
   1. As above.

13053 GODE 1992
No data.

13054 RAMA BUTTERFEIN 1992
No data.

13055 GOLDEN SHRED 1993
Red body, black chassis, cream roof, gold grille and 12-spoke hubs, black tires. Logo: gold "Golden Shred Marmalade" and frame, multicolored design, white lettering.
   1. As above.

13056 PEPSI-COLA 1993
Cream body, dark blue chassis and roof, silver grille, blue-balck 20-spoke hubs, black tires. Logo: blue and cream "Drink Pepsi-Cola" design, red "it PEPS you up!", cream 5c on red disc. In special Pepsi-Cola box.
   1. As above.

13057 MARKS & SPENCER 1993
Blue body, black chassis and roof, gold grille, blue 20-spoke hubs, black tires. Logo: gold "From Marks & Spencer Ltd", "original penny bazaars", "black hooks & eyes", etc, design and frame, plus door lettering. In set of four Marks & Spencer models.
   1. As above.

13058 GRAND HOTEL DE PEKIN 1993
Brown body and chassis, cream roof, gold grille, brown 20-spoke hubs, white tires. Logo: brown-white-yellow oval emblem with brown "Grand Hotel de Pekin, Peking, China: and frame, dark brown hotel name on doors. In set of three hotel vans.
   1. As above.

13059 CARLSBERG LAGER 1994
Cream body, green chassis and roof, gold grille and 12-spoke hubs, black tires. Logo: green "Carlsberg" and frames, red and gold crowns, similar logo on rear.
   1. As above.

13060 KODAK 1993
Yellow body, black chassis, red roof, gold grille, black 20-spoke hubs and tires. No other data. German issue.

13061 RUPERT BEAR 1994
Cream body, blue-black chassis and roof, gold grille and 12-spoke hubs, black tires. Logo: multicolored design and emblem. Special box.
   1. As above.

13062 DR. PEPPER 1994
Red body, black chassis and roof, silver grille, red disc hubs, black tires. Logo: black-outlined white "Drink Dr. Pepper", black "good for life" on white ribbon, white "3 A Day Keeps Energy Up!" on black stripe, white lettering, also on rear. Special box.
   1. As above.

13063 SATURDAY EVENING POST 1994
Black body and chassis, cream roof, gold grille and 12-spoke hubs, black tires. Logo: Saturday Evening Post design, white "Norman Rockwell 100th Anniversary" emblem, black "The Saturday Evening Post" on blade. Special box.
   1. As above.

13064 RITTER SCHOKOLADE 1995
Pale blue body, black chassis and roof, silver grille, gold 12-spoke hubs, black tires. Logo: gold-outlined dark blue "Ritters", two-tone blue and gold coat of arms, dark blue "Schokoladen Pralinen" etc.
   1. As above.

13065 7-UP 1995
Maroon body, black chassis and roof, silver grille, gold 12-spoke hubs, black tires. Logo: green-white-black "Drink 7-Up" emblem, red lettering on white panel, white "Fresh Up" on door. Special 7-Up box.
   1. As above.

13066 DAILY HERALD 1995
Green body, black chassis, cream roof and blade, black grille, green disc hubs, black tires. Logo: red "Daily Herald" on cream panel, "War is over" on blade, "Hitler dead" on door. In set of three VE-Day models.
   1. As above.

14 MODEL A FORD 1934 TOURER, TOP UP 78 mm 1985
Cast body and chassis, plastic top, interior, grille, windshield, spare wheel and base, 12-spoke metal or 20-spoke or disc plastic hubs, tires. Same basic model as DG9 plus raised top, which was first plain, then given a textured panel. Top of windshield frame +/- two pegs to hold roof, interior +/- holes for figure pegs. Base first DG7-DG9, then DG7-DG9 with DG13 and DG14 over axles, then DG7-9-13-14-37.

14000 SAN DIEGO FIRE CHIEF (yellow chassis) 1985
Red body, yellow chassis, tan top, interior and spare, gold grille and windshield, red 20-spoke hubs, white tires. Logo: black-outlined gold "San Diego" on gold-bordered white panel, gold or red "Fire Chief" on white panel, black lettering, black and white checkered stripes, white "Fire Dept. 1" on hood.
   1. Gold "Fire Chief".
   2. Red "Fire Chief".

14001 TAXI 1985
Yellow body and chassis, black top, interior and spare, gold grille and windshield, yellow 20-spoke hubs, black tires. Logo: black "Taxi", no. 57 and rate, black and white checkered stripes.
   1. As above.

14002 ACME OFFICE CLEANING 1985
Light cream body and chassis, cream top, interior and spare, silver grille and windshield, cream disc hubs, white tires. Logo: black "Acme Office Cleaning Co." and no. 17.
   1. As above.
   2. Black spare (1988 reissue).

14003 HAMLEYS 1986
Red body, black chassis, top and interior and spare, gold grille and windshield, red 20-spoke hubs, black tires. Logo: gold "Hamleys" and underline. Special box.
   1. As above.

14004 GRAND HOTEL 1986
Brown body, yellow or tan chassis, cream or tan top, interior and spare, gold grille and windshield, red disc hubs, white tires. Logo: gold "Grand Hotel, Brighton", no. 77 and "Courtesy Car".
   1. Cream top, yellow chassis.
   2. Tan top, darker tan chassis.

14005 (Not used)

14006 STATE PENITENTIARY 1987
Ivory body and chassis, black roof, interior and spare, silver grille and windshield, black 20-spoke hubs, white or black tires. Logo: black and red stripes, black "State Penitentiary", red-outlined shield and "R S B". Rarely found with wrong grille.
   1. As above.

14007 SAN DIEGO FIRE CHIEF (all red) 1988
Same model as #14000 but with red chassis.
   1. Red body and chassis.

14008 RALEIGH CYCLES 1990
Dark green body, black chassis, roof, interior and spare, gold grille and windshield, green 20-spoke hubs, black tires. Logo: gold "Raleigh Cycles" and frame.
   1. As above.

15 AEC DOUBLE DECKER BUS 86 mm 1985
Cast body, chassis, roof and stairs, plastic windows/upper deck, grille, 8-bolt or other hubs, tires. The very first roofs had smooth undersides, all others are ridged. Stairs are same color as body. The base was modified to take a DG or LP panel. Lower seats were added in 1989. This was the first model never sold with figures.

15000 HALL'S WINE/GENERAL (red) 1985
Red body and roof, black chassis, silver roof, cream windows, silver or gold grille, red hubs, black tires. Upper logo: black "Take", black-outlined red "Hall's Wine", black "and defy Influenza" on yellow background. Lower logo: black-outlined gold "General" and underline. Smooth or ridged underside of roof.
   1. As above.

15001 COCA-COLA/CHICAGO 1985
Red body and roof, black chassis, cream windows, silver grille, red hubs, black tires. Upper logo: brown and white "Drink" and "In Bottles", red "Coca-Cola" on tan panel. Lower logo: yellow "Chicago Transit" and underline.
   1. As above.

15002 CASTLEMAINE CORPORATION 1985
Red body, cream chassis, roof and windows, silver grille, red hubs, black tires. Upper logo: red "Castlemaine", black-outlined XXXX on yellow background. Lower logo: red "Corporation Transport" on yellow stripe.
   1. As above.

15003 HAMLEYS/LONDON TRANSPORT 1985
Red body and roof, black chassis, cream windows, silver grille, red hubs, black tires. Upper logo: yellow "Regent Street, Hamleys London W.1" and underline on blue panel. Lower logo: gold "London Transport". Special box.
   1. As above.

15004 LIVERPOOL FESTIVAL GARDENS 1985
Cream body and roof, brown chassis and windows, silver grille, cream hubs, black tires. Upper logo: green-outlined cream "Festival", green "Gardens", black "Liverpool" and date. Lower logo: green "Festival Transport" and underline.
   1. As above.

15005 CINZANO/LONDON TRANSPORT 1985
Red body and roof, black chassis, cream or ivory windows, gold or silver grille, red hubs, black tires. Upper logo: white "Vermouth Cinzano Vermouth" on red and blue background. Lower logo: white "London Transport" and underline.
   1. Cream windows, silver grille.
   2. Ivory windows, either grille. Also in 1993 Hamleys set.

15006 EVENING ARGUS/BRIGHTON HOVE 1986
Red body, black chassis, cream roof and windows, silver grille, black hubs and tires, or black wheels. Upper logo: black "Evening Argus" on cream panel. Lower logo: cream stripe, gold "Brighton Hove & District Transport" and underline.
   1. As above.

15007 HALL'S WINE/GENERAL (brick red) 1986
Brick red body, red chassis, blue-gray roof, cream windows, silver grille, light red hubs, white tires. Same

logo as #15000.
   1. As above.
   2. Unpainted model with cream windows, no logo.

15008 ROYAL WEDDING 1986
Blue body and windows, red chassis and roof, gold or silver grille, red hubs, black tires. Upper logo: gold "The royal Wedding", date and frame. Lower logo: gold "H.R.H. Prince Andrew, Miss Sarah Ferguson", line and frame. Not issued with rear label.
   1. As above.
   2. Gold "Westminster Abbey, London" on blue adhesive rear label.

15009 MADAME TUSSAUD'S/LONDON TRANSPORT 1987
Red body and roof, black chassis, cream windows, silver or gold grille, red hubs, black tires. Upper logo: blue "Madame Tussauds" on cream panel. Lower logo: yellow "London Transport" and underline.
   1. As above.

15010 SWAN VESTAS/SOUTHDOWN 1986
Light green body, dark green chassis and roof, cream or ivory windows, silver or gold grille, dark green hubs, black tires. Upper logo: black "Swan Vestas, British Made by Bryant & May", etc., and design. Lower logo: black-outlined gold "Southdown".
   1. Cream windows, silver grille.
   2. Ivory windows, gold grille.

15011 COMMONWEALTH GAMES 1986
Red body and roof, black chassis, cream windows, gold or silver grille, red hubs, black tires. Upper logo: white "British Caledonian Airways" and gold shield on blue panel. Lower logo: red-white-blue "XIII Commonwealth Games" emblem, white lettering. Special box.
   1. As above.

15012 HEINZ/THOMAS TILLING 1987
Red body and roof, black chassis, cream windows, silver or gold grille, red hubs, black tires. Upper logo: white "57 Heinz Tomato Ketchup 57" on light blue panel. Lower logo: white stripe and panel, gold "Thomas Tilling Limited" and underlines.
   1. As above.

15013 RADIO TIMES/STRATFORD BLUE 1987
Light blue body, blue chassis, silver gray roof, cream windows, silver grille, black wheels. Upper logo: red "Radio Times 2d", black or gold "Special Wedding Edition" on white panel. Lower logo: red-outlined gold "Stratford Blue" and underline, white lettering, gold frame. Special Ruby Wedding box; reissued 1988-89 in standard box.
   1. Black "Special Wedding Edition", Ruby Wedding box.
   2. Gold "Special Wedding Edition" on pale blue panel.

15014 TV TIMES/LONDON TRANSPORT 1987
Red body and roof, black chassis, cream windows, silver grille, red hubs, black tires. Upper logo: black-outlined red "TV Times" and emblem on white panel. Lower logo: white "London Transport" and underline.
   1. As above.

15015 HAMLEYS/LONDON TRANSPORT 1988
Red body, chassis, roof and windows, gold grille, red hubs, black tires. Upper logo: gold "Hamleys, the Finest Toyshop in the World" on black. Lower logo: gold "London Transport" and underline.
   1. As above.

15016 BIRMINGHAM MAIL 1988
Blue body and chassis, cream roof, white windows, silver grille, black wheels. Upper logo: dark blue "The Birmingham Mail, The Great Evening Paper, 1d" on bluish-white panel. Lower logo: coat of arms, gold frame.
   1. As above.

15017 GOLDEN WONDER CRISPS 1988
Light blue body, blue chassis, silver roof, cream windows, silver grille, orange hubs, black tires. Upper logo: orange "Golden Wonder, Britain's Noisiest Crisps!" on white panel. Lower logo: orange "Golden Wonder" and stripes, white trim.,
    1. As above.

15018 LLEDO COLLECTORS CLUB 1988
Red body and roof, black chassis, cream windows, red hubs, black tires. Upper logo: black and white "Start Your Lledo Collection Today", etc. Lower logo: black and gold "The Lledo Collection".
    1. As above.

15019 MAPLES PIANOS/THOMAS TILLING 1989
Red body, chassis and roof, cream windows, silver grille, red hubs, black tires. Upper logo: green-white-black "Maples Second Hand Pianos", etc. Lower logo: white stripe and panel, red "Thomas Tilling Ltd."
    1. As above.

15020 TERRY'S MOBILE GYMNASIUM 1989
Light blue body, cream chassis and windows, silver roof and grille, blue hubs, black tires. Upper logo: red and blue "Terry's Mobile Gymnasium" and lines. Lower logo: red "Fulham Garage".
    1. As above.

15021 ST. IVEL CHEESE/GENERAL 1990
Red body and chassis, cream roof and windows, silver grille, black wheels. Upper logo: black-outlined green "St. Ivel Cheese aids digestion" on yellow panel. Lower logo: gold "General" and underline.
    1. As above.

15022 HAMLEYS/LONDON TRANSPORT 1989
Red body and roof, black chassis, cream windows, silver grille, red hubs, black tires. Upper logo: black-on-gold Hamleys emblem, gold lettering and frame. Lower logo: white "London Transport" and underline. Special box.
    1. As above.

15023 PALMOLIVE SOAP 1990
Red body and roof, black chassis, cream windows, silver grille, red hubs, black tires. Upper logo: green-white-black Palmolive design. Lower logo: gold "General" and line.
    1. As above.

15024 ROYAL AUTO CLUB/BIRMINGHAM 1990
Blue body and chassis, cream roof and windows, silver grille, blue hubs, black tires. Upper logo: red-white-blue "The RAC service began running 26 years before this bus". Lower logo: coat of arms, gold frame.
    1. As above.

15025 ROYAL MAIL/LONDON TRANSPORT 1990
Red body, roof and hubs, black chassis, silver grille, red hubs, black tires. Upper logo: red "Post early for Christmas", red and black design on white panel. Lower logo: gold "London Transport" and line. Special box.
    1. Red seats.
    2. Cream seats.

15026 HERSHEY'S CHOCOLATE 1990
Cream body and roof, brown chassis and windows, gold grille, brown hubs, black tires. Upper logo: white "Chocolate Town U.S.A.!" on brown panel. Lower logo: brown "Hershey's" and frame. Special box.
    1. As above.

15027 NORTH YORKSHIRE MOORS RAILWAY 1990
Light green body, dark green chassis and roof, cream windows, gold grille, dark green hubs, black tires. Upper logo: red "Yorkshire Moors by", yellow "NYMR" on dark green panel. Lower logo: red NYMR emblem. In set of three models.
    1. As above.

15028 HARRODS 1992
Red body and roof, black chassis, cream windows, silver grille, red hubs, black tires. Upper logo: cream "Harrods", gold address on green panel. Lower: black-outlined gold "London Transport" and underline, white lettering. In set of two models.
    1. As above.

15029 MAZAWATTEE TEA 1993
Green body, black chassis, cream roof and windows, silver grille, red hubs, black tires. Upper logo: brown-cream "Mazawattee Tea" and white lettering on tan panel. Lower: white stripe, black-outlined gold "Golden Arrow" and underline.
    1. As above.

15030 VAN HOUTEN'S COCOA 1993
Navy blue body, black chassis, cream roof and windows, silver grille, dark blue hubs, black tires. Upper logo: red "Van Houten's Cocoa" on pale blue panel, white lettering on black stripe. Lower: multicolored coat of arms, gold "Birmingham City Transport" and frame.
    1. As above.

15031 DAYS GONE COLLECTORS CLUB 1993
Blue body, roof and hubs, black chassis, silver grille, black wheels. Upper logo: black and gold "Days Gone" emblem, black "Autumn 1993" and "Collectors Club" on white panel. Lower: gold "Lledo". White "Enfield" on black front board.
    1. As above.

15032 LIBBY'S PINEAPPLE 1994
Red body and hubs, black chassis and tires, cream windows, silver roof and grille. Upper logo: multicolored "Libby's pineapple" on blue panel. Lower: black-outlined gold "General" and underline. white "Woolwich 75" etc. on black front board.
    1. As above.

15033 HAMLEYS 1994
Red body and roof, black chassis, cream windows, silver grille, red hubs, black tires. Upper logo: red "Hamleys", blue "The Finest Toyshop in the World" on yellow panel. Lower: black-outlined gold "London Transport" and underline. In set of two models.
    1. As above.

15034 GODE 1994
Navy blue body, black chassis and roof, cream windows, silver grille, dark blue hubs, black tires. Upper logo: blue emblem and "Gode Faszination des Sammelns" on bluish-white panel. Lower: gold coat of arms and frame. White "Gode" on front board.
    1. As above.

15035 PEARS SOAP 1995
Red body and roof, black chassis, cream windows, silver grille, red hubs, black tires. Upper logo: multicolored "Pears, the king of soaps, the soap of kings" panel; lower: black-outlined gold "London Transport" and underline, white lettering. Destination 11, Shepherd's Bush.
    1. As above.

15036 HARRODS SALE 1994
Red body, black chassis, silver roof, cream windows, silver grille, red hubs, white tires. Upper logo: gold-shadowed "Harrods Sale", red "on now" on cream panel; lower: black-outlined "General" and underline. In boxed set of four models.
    1. As above.

16   DENNIS 1934 PARCELS VAN 82 mm 1985
Cast body and chassis, plastic roof, grille, base, 6-bolt or disc hubs and tires. Very slight lower body modification very early. Steering wheel and seat added later. Same chassis and base types as #010 and #012.

16000 MAYFLOWER 1985
Dark yellow body, black chassis, green roof, gold grille, cream 6-bolt hubs, black tires. Logo: black-outlined

red "Aero Mayflower Transit Co.", black lettering, no. 38, green design.
    1. As above.

16001 ROYAL MAIL 1985
Red body, black chassis and roof, gold grille, red 6-bolt hubs, black tires. Logo: black "Royal Mail" and frame, gold and black crown, black-outlined gold monogram. Special box.
    1. As above.

16002 CROFT ORIGINAL 1985
Cream body, black chassis, brown roof, gold grille, cream 6-bolt, cream or white disc hubs, black tires. Logo: white "Croft Original" on emblem, black "The Sherry of Distinction".
    1. As above.

16003 HAMLEYS TOYS 1986
black body, chassis, roof, 6-bolt hubs and tires, gold grille. Logo: gold "Hamleys, all the world's finest toys", design and frame. Special box.
    1. As above.

16004 TREBOR PEPPERMINTS 1986
Dark green body, black chassis, white roof, gold grille, green 6-bolt or disc hubs, black tires. Logo: dark green "Trebor" and "None so good" on white panels, white "extra strong peppermints" and line, light green stripes.
    1. As above.

16005 L.N.E.R. EXPRESS PARCELS 1986
Navy blue body, black chassis and roof, gold or black grille, cream 6-bolt hubs, black tires. Logo: white emblem and "L.N.E.R. Express Parcels Services", "L.N.E.R." on front and "London North Eastern Railway" on rear.
    1. As above.

16006 KIWI POLISHES 1986
Black body, chassis, roof, 6-bolt or disc hubs and tires, gold or silver grille. Logo: black-outlined gold "Kiwi Polishes", multicolored emblem, cream or light green frame.
    1. As above.

16007 BUSHELLS TEA 1985
Navy blue body, black chassis and roof, gold grille, cream, black or white 6-bolt or disc hubs, black tires. Logo: white-outlined tan "Bushells", tan "the Tea of Flavor", multicolored teacup design, yellow or orange "Bushells" on front.
    1. Light yellow front logo.
    2. Light orange front logo.

16008 (Not used)

16009 CADBURYS 1987
Purple body and chassis, white roof, gold or silver grille, white 6-bolt hubs, black tires. Logo: gold "Cadbury's", white design and "Dairy Milk Chocolate", white and gold stripes.
    1. As above.

16010 FYFFES 1987
Yellow-orange body, navy blue chassis, white roof, gold grille, yellow-orange or yellow 6-bolt or disc hubs, black tires. Logo: light blue "Blue Label Fyffes Brand" and trim on dark blue oval, light and dark blue stripes.
    1. As above.

16011 COCA-COLA 1986
Red body, black chassis and roof, gold grille, cream or black 6-bolt hubs, black or white tires. Logo: white stripes and "Drink Coca-Cola", same lettering in red on white circle on rear. Special box.
    1. As above.

16012 HERSHEY'S MR. GOODBAR 1986
Yellow body, brown chassis and roof, gold grille, brown 6-bolt or disc hubs, white tires. Logo: white

"Hershey's" on brown panel, red "mr. Goodbar", yellow "Peanuts in Milk Chocolate" on brown stripe. Special box.
    1. As above.

16013 HERSHEY'S KRACKEL 1986
Red body, brown chassis and roof, gold or silver grille, red 6-bolt hubs, white tires. Logo: white "Hershey's" on brown panel, white "krackel" with red line, yellow lettering. Special box.
    1. Chocolate brown chassis.
    2. Purplish brown chassis.

16014 PICKFORDS 1988
Blue body and chassis, white roof, gold grille, red 6-bolt or disc hubs, black tires. Logo: white "Pickfords Express Carriers-Removers-Storers" etc., red-white-blue emblem, white front and back lettering.
    1. Dull blue body.
    2. Dark blue body.

16015 LLEDO COLLECTORS CLUB 1987
Black body, chassis, roof, gold 6-bolt hubs and tirss, gold grille. Logo: gold Lledo emblem and "Club Member Autumn Edition 1987". Special box.
    1. As above.

16016 HAMLEYS 1988
Black body, chassisn roof, 6-bolt hubs and tires, gold grille. Logo: gold "Hamleys, the Finest Toyshop in the World" and date.
    1. As above.

16017 ABELS OF EAST ANGLIA 1988
Light blue body, navy blue chassis, black roof, silver grille, red 6-bolt hubs, black tires. Logo: blue and red "Abels of East Anglia", 2-tone blue "World Wide Removals", red lettering, blue and white design.
    1. As above.

16018 MADAME TUSSAUD'S 1990
Red body, black chassis and roof, silver grille, red 6-bolt hubs, black tires. Logo: multicolored design with white "Madame Tussaud's" and "Battle of Trafalgar".
    1. As above.

16019 ALLIED VAN LINES 1989
Orange body, black chassis, white roof, silver grille, white 6-bolt hubs, black tires. Logo: white "Allied, the Careful Movers" (also on front), multicolored highway design with no. 1.
    1. As above.

16020 COSMOS LAMPS 1989
White body and chassis, black roof, silver grille, white 6-bolt hubs and tires. Logo: multicolored "Cosmos Lamp, British Made" and designs, black MV monogram.
    1. As above.

16021 GOODYEAR TIRES 1989
Light blue body, black chassis, white roof, silver grille, black wheels. Logo: white-outlined black or all-white "Goodyear Tyres" and emblem, black lettering.
    1. White-outlined black "Goodyear".
    2. All-white "Goodyear".

16022 HAMLEYS 1989
Maroon body, black chassis, cream roof, gold grille, maroon 6-bolt hubs, black tires. Logo: multicolored "Hamleys" design, gold "The Finest Toyshop in the World" and frame, gold address, gold "Hamleys" design on front. Special box.
    1. As above.

16023 OXO/CITY & SUBURBAN 1990
Black body, chassis, roof, 6-bolt hubs and tires, silver grille. Logo: white "City & Suburban Carriers Ltd.", multicolored design with "I'm a pick-up like Oxo", white "City & Suburban" on front.
    1. As above.

16024 ROYAL MAIL 1990
Red body, black chassis and roof, gold grille, red 6-bolt hubs, black tires. Logo: gold "Royal Mail", line and monogram, black and gold crown, black "Parcels", white lettering. Special box.
    1. As above.

16025 NORTH YORKSHIRE MOORS RAILWAY 1990
Cream body, dark blue chassis and roof, gold grille, dark blue 6-bolt hubs, black tires. Logo: white "Yorkshire Moors by NYMR" on multicolored panel with design, blue and white emblem, blue "Yorkshire Moors" on front. In set of three models.
    1. As above.

16026 SCHWEPPES/CARTER PATERSON 1991
Dark blue body, chassis, roof and 6-bolt hubs, silver grille, black tires. Logo: white "Carter Paterson", multicolored "Schweppes Table Water" design, white frame, white "Express Carriers" on front.

16027 ATORA/CARTER PATERSON 1991
Green body and roof, black chassis, gold grille, red 6-bolt hubs, black tires. Logo: white "Carter Paterson" (also on front), multicolored Atora design.

16028 LNER EXPRESS PARCELS 1991
Dark blue body, black chassis and roof, silver grille, red disc hubs, black tires. Logo: white "LNER Express Parcels Services", multicolored "East Coast" poster. White "LNER" on front and back. In set of three models.
    1. As above.

16029 LNER EXPRESS PARCELS/SKEGNESS 1991
Same as #016028 except for multicolored Skegness poster on logo.
    1. As above.

16030 YMCA TEA CAR 1991
Olive body, chassis, roof, grille, and 6-bolt hubs, black tires. Logo: white "YMCA" on black stripe, "Tea Car", other lettering, black frame and lettering on black-framed white panel, YMCA emblem (also on back with white lettering), red "Tea Car" on front. In set of three models.
    1. As above.

16031 HUDSONS SOAP 1992
Blue body, black chassis and roof, silver grille, blue 6-bolt hubs, black tires. Logo: multicolored design, white "Hudson's Dry Soap", yellow and white lettering, yellow frame.
    1. As above.

16032 TUNNOCKS BAKERY 1993
Red body, black chassis and roof, gold grille, red 6-bolt hubs, black tires. Logo: cream oval with red "Uddingston & Bothwell T. Tunnock Bakery & Purveyor", cream lettering and emblems, cream "Tunnock" on front.
    1. As above.

16033 N A A F I REFRESHMENT VAN 1993
Olive body, chassis, roof, grille and 6-bolt hubs, black tires. Logo: black-bordered white N-A-A-F-I (also on rear), white NAAFI emblem and "Refreshment Van", multicolored design. In set of 3 Dambusters models.

16034 R A F RUNWAY CONTROL VAN 1993
Dull blue body, chassis, grille and 6-bolt hubs, black tires, black and white checkered roof and upper body. Logo: white RAF and numbers, red-white-blue roundel. In set of three Dambusters models.
    1. As above.

16035 KODAK 1993
Yellow-orange body and roof, black chassis, gold grille, black wheels. Logo: black-outlined red "Kodak", black "Films & Cameras" and trim, similar lettering on doors and front.
    1. As above.

16036 BOVRIL 1994
Dark blue body and chassis, black roof, silver grille, dark blue 6-bolt hubs, black tires. Logo: black and white figures, multicolored bottle, red-outlined yellow "Bovril", white "keeps you up to par".
    1. As above.

16037 RUPERT BEAR 1994
Dark yellow body, chassis, red roof and 6-bolt hubs, gold grille, black tires. Logo: multicolored design and emblem. Red-outlined "Rupert" on front. Special Rupert Collection box.
    1. As above.

16038 DAYS GONE CLUB, AUTUMN 1994 1994
Light gray body and chassis, white roof, silver grille, gray 6-bolt hubs, black tires. Logo: black "Days Gone" on black-framed gold panel, gold "Collectors Club" and "Lledo", black "Autumn 1994" on door. Special box.
    1. As above.

16039 RUPERT BEAR 1995
Blue body, black chassis, silver grille, red 6-bolt hubs, black tires. Logo: scene with policeman, The Rupert Collection emblem. Special Rupert box.
    1. As above.

17 HALF CAB SINGLEDECK BUS 92 mm 1985
Cast body, chassis and roof, plastic windows-interior, grille, base, hubs and tires, or one-piece wheels. The first few #17000 buses had a fuel filler cap cast in; this was soon eliminated, and all models since #17006 have a vertical bar in the center of the rear seat. A roof with signboards was introduced in 1988.

17000 SOUTHEND CORPORATION 1985
Blue, red or orange body, cream chassis and windows, blue or red roof, silver grille, light blue or red hubs, black or white tires. Logo: black "Southend Corporation" on yellow or orange stripe, black lettering, black and white coat of arms.
    1. Blue body and roof, light blue hubs, black tires, filler cap.
    2. Blue body and roof, light blue hubs, black tires.
    3. Orange body, blue roof, light blue hubs, black tires.
    4. Red body, roof and hubs, white tires.

17001 EUROTOUR CRUISES 1985
Green body, cream chassis, roof and windows, silver grille, cream hubs, black tires. Logo: white "Eurotour Cruises" and stripes, red-white-blue national flags.
    1. As above.

17002 BOAC CORPORATION TRANSPORT 1985
Yellow body, light gray chassis and roof, cream windows, silver grille, red hubs, white tires. Logo: red "Corporation Transport No. 37" on red-bordered white stripe, blue emblem and "Fly B.O.A.C." on white panel. Type with no white panel is not DG.
    1. As above.

17003 HAMLEYS 1986
Dark green body and roof, cream chassis and windows, gold grille, dark green hubs, black tires. Logo: cream "Hamleys World of Toys" etc. and underline. Special box.
    1. As above.

17004 LONDON TRANSPORT 1985
Red body and roof, black chassis, cream or white windows, silver grille, red hubs, black tires. Logo: gold "London Transport" etc. and underline.
    1. Cream windows.
    2. White windows?

17005 MORRELL'S/OXFORD 1986
Red body, black chassis, maroon roof and windows, silver grille, black hubs and tires or wheels. Logo: blue and gold emblems, blue "Morrell's Castle Ale, Morrell's Malt Stout" and lines on cream or white stripe,

black-outlined gold "Oxford" and underline.
1. Maroon roof and windows, cream logo stripe.
2. Darker maroon roof and windows, white logo stripe.

17006 COMMONWEALTH GAMES 1986
White body, chassis and roof, blue windows, silver grille, white hubs, black tires. Logo: blue and red "XIII" design, blue "XIII Commonwealth Games, Scotland 1986, red lettering, blue and white emblem. Special box.
1. As above.

17007 STRATFORD BLUE 1986
Light blue body, dark blue chassis, silver roof, white windows, silver or gold grille, blue hubs, gray tires. Logo: red-outlined gold "Stratford Blue" and underline, gold-bordered light blue stripe with white lettering.
1. As above.

17008 BURNLEY CORPORATION 1987
Navy blue body, white chassis and roof, blue windows, silver grille, navy blue hubs, black tires, or black wheels. Logo: navy blue "Burnley Corporation Tramways & Omnibus" on white stripe, white coat of arms.
1. As above.

17009 BIG TOP CIRCUS 1986
Cream body and roof, black chassis, red windows (two shades exist), silver grille, red hubs, black tires. Logo: multicolored design and ribbon with blue "Big Top".
1. As above.

17010 PENNINE 1987
Orange body, black chassis and roof, light gray windows, silver grille, black wheels. Logo: gold "Pennine", gold lettering on rear, destination Malham.
1. As above.

17011 ROYAL AIR FORCE 1987
Pale gray body, dark blue chassis, roof and windows, silver grille, yellow hubs, black tires. Logo: blue "Royal Air Force" on yellow stripe, blue and gold eagle; "216 Squadron" on front board. In set of three models.
1. As above.

17012 HAMLEYS 1988
Pale blue body, navy blue chassis and roof, white windows, gold grille, navy blue hubs, gray tires. Logo: navy blue "The Finest Toyshop in the World", "Hamleys" and frame.
1. As above.

17013 HANTS & DORSET 1988
Green body and roof with signboards, black chassis, cream windows, silver grille, black wheels. Logo: yellow "Hants & Dorset" and underline; red "Bognor" and white lettering on boards; destination "Fareham/Southampton 23".
1. As above.

17014 SUTTON'S 1988
Red body and roof with boards, light gray chassis, cream windows, silver grille, black wheels. Logo: black names on white stripe, black-outlined gold "Sutton's" (also on front board); gold lettering on boards.
1. As above.

17015 ROYAL BLUE COACH 1989
Dark blue body and roof with boards, black chassis, cream windows, silver grille, black wheels. Logo: yellow "Royal Blue" and emblem; yellow and black "Royal Blue Luxury Coach" on boards, yellow "Royal Blue" on front board.
1. As above.
2. Header with white background.

17016 COLCHESTER CORPORATION 1989
Dark red body and roof, black chassis, cream windows, silver grille, black wheels. Logo: gold "Colchester Corporation" and coat of arms, yellow stripe and frame.
1. As above.

17017 ROYAL NAVAL COLLEGE 1988
Navy blue body, chassis and windows, white roof, silver grille, black wheels. Logo: white "Britannia" and "Royal Naval College", multicolored emblem. Black "Dartmouth" on front board. In boxed set of three models with certificate.
1. As above.

17018 NORTH YORKSHIRE MOORS RAILWAY 1989
Dark blue body and roof with boards, black chassis, cream windows, gold grille, black wheels. Logo: white "North Yorkshire Moors Railway", trim and NYMR emblem, gold frame; white "Journeys across time" on boards, gold frame; destination Pickering. In set of three models.
1. As above.

17019 RED AND WHITE COACH 1990
Cream body, black chassis, red roof, windows and hubs, silver grille, black tires. Logo: black-outlined gold "Red & White and line; gold lettering and lines on boards, white "South Wales" on front board.
1. As above.

17020 BUCKLAND BUS CO. 1991
Red body and roof with boards, black chassis, cream roof with boards, silver grille, red hubs, black tires. Logo: black-outlined cream "Buckland Omnibus Co.", cream "East Anglia", stripes and frames; cream lettering on boards, cream "Suffolk Coast" on front board.
1. As above.

17021 SOUTHERN VECTIS 1992
Apple green body and roof with boards, dark green chassis, cream windows, silver grille, dark green hubs, black tires. Logo: gold "Southern Vectis", white lettering; "tonic water Schweppes ginger beer" on boards; destination Newport.
1. As above.

17022 GREEN LINE 1993
Green body, black chassis, light green windows, silver roof with boards and grille, green hubs, black tires. Logo: black-outlined yellow "Green Line" and underline, black stripes. Boards: white "J" and destinations on black panel. White "Reigate" and frame on black front board, +/- number on motor hood.
1. As above.

17023 OVALTINE 1995
Maroon lower body, cream roof and windows, silver grille, maroon hubs, black tires. Logo: black-outlined red "Ovaltine", black lettering on boards, gold "Sunderland Corporation" below.
1. As above.

17024 RED CROSS CLUBMOBILE 1995
Light gray body and roof, darker gray windows and grille, white chassis, gray hubs, black tires. Logo: red cross, red "It's over...over here!" on white panel, white "Clubmobile Texas", star, etc., "Clubmobile" on front board.
1. As above.

18 PACKARD VAN 90 mm 1985
Cast body and chassis, plastic roof, grille, base, hubs and tires, side spares. Several chassis variations exist, with different rear flange sizes and shapes. Models also exist with Rolls-Royce or Ford grilles. Base first DG18-19, then DG18-19-22, then DG18/19/22/24/25, then DG18/19-22-24-25-38.

18000 BRITISH AMBULANCE 1985
Cream body and roof, black chassis, silver or gold grille, green disc hubs, white tires. Logo: black "Ambulance: and windows, red crosses without circles (also on roof).

18001 AMERICAN AMBULANCE 1985
Same model as above, but with circled red crosses.
1. As above.

18002 COMMONWEALTH GAMES 1986
White body and chassis, blue roof, silver or gold grille, white disc hubs, black tires. Logo: blue and red XIII design, black "XIII Commonwealth Games, Scotland 1986" and "Services", multicolored emblem. Special box.
   1. As above.

18003 RAPID CASH TRANSPORT 1986
Green body, black chassis, cream roof, silver grille, green disc hubs, white tires. Logo: black-outlined white "Rapid Cash Transit", multicolored shield, white "Unit 6", black "Unit 6" on roof.
   1. As above.

18004 FIRESTONE 1986
White body, red chassis and roof, gold or silver grille, red disc hubs, white or gray tires. Logo: white "Firestone" on white-bordered red panel, red lines.
   1. Lighter red roof.
   2. Darker red roof.

18005 (Not used)

18006 WHITE STAR 1987
Red body and chassis, white roof, gold or silver grille, black disc hubs and tires. Logo: white-outlined yellow "White Star", black and white emblem, black "Steamship Co. Ltd." and lines.
   1. As above.

18007 COLMAN'S MUSTARD 1987
Yellow body and roof, black chassis, silver grille, red disc hubs, black tires. Logo: black-outlined red "Colman's Mustard", black design and date, black and red frame.
   1. As above.

18008 ROYAL AIR FORCE 1987
Pale gray body, dark blue chassis and roof, gold grille, white disc hubs, black tires. Logo: blue-white-red roundel, red cross on white disc, red "Ambulance"; white "Ambulance" on roof. In boxed set of three models with certificate.
   1. As above.

18009 PERONI 1988
White body and roof, blue chassis, silver grille, blue 20-spoke hubs, black tires. Logo: multicolored emblem with white "Peroni" and red "Nastro Azzuro", gold lines, blue emblem and lettering.
   1. As above.

18010 NATIONAL WESTMINSTER BANK 1988
Silver body, white chassis and roof, silver grille, black disc hubs, gray tires. Logo: black "National Westminster Bank" and emblem; black lettering and emblem on rear.
   1. As above.

18011 FOTORAMA 1988
Silver body, blue chassis and roof, gold or silver grille, blue disc hubs, white tires. Logo: blue-red-yellow "Fotorama", blue "A World of Colour" and frame, red F.
   1. As above.

18012 ST. IVEL CHEESE 1990
Yellow body, black chassis, green roof and disc hubs, gold grille, black tires. Logo: black "St. Ivel", lettering and lines, yellow "Cheese" and address on green panels.
   1. As above.

18013 FORTNUM & MASON 1989
Aqua body, magenta chassis, maroon roof, gold grille, maroon disc hubs, black tires. Logo: red-outlined gold "Fortnum & Mason Ltd" and address, dark red and gold designs; similar rear logo.
   1. As above.

18014 B & C FILMS 1989
Gold body and chassis, green roof, silver grille, gold 12-spoke hubs, black tires. Logo: red "B & C", red-

white-gold crown, black wreath, lettering and frames. In set of four models.
   1. As above.

18015 ST. MARY'S HOSPITAL 1988
White body, chassis, roof and disc hubs, silver grille, black tires. Logo: blue-orange-white emblem, blue "St. Mary's General Hospital, Kitchener, Ontario, Canada", red cross.
   1. As above.

18016 LEYLAND PAINTS 1989
Navy blue body, maroon chassis and roof (different shades), silver grille, black disc hubs and tires. Logo: white "Leyland quality paints and varnishes" etc., gold sun and rays, green panels and emblem.
   1. As above.

18017 HAMLEYS 1989
Cream body, dark blue chassis and roof, gold grille and 12-spoke hubs, black tires. Logo: black-red-gold "Hamleys" design, red "The Finest Toyshop in the World" and frame, gold address. Special box.
   1. As above.

18018 ASPREY 1990
Purple body, maroon chassis, black roof, gold grille and 12-spoke hubs, black tires. Logo: gold "Asprey Jewellers & Goldsmiths" and address. In boxed set of four models.
   1. As above.

18019 LLEDO COLLECTORS CLUB 1990
Yellow body, chassis and roof, silver grille, green disc hubs, white tires. Logo: black-gold-green "Days Gone" design, gold "Autumn 1990" and other lettering.
   1. As above.

18020 McVITIE & PRICE 1991
Maroon body, black chassis, cream roof, maroon disc hubs, white tires. Logo: yellow "McVitie & Price Digestive Biscuits", circled no. 145, multicolored design in yellow circle.
   1. As above.

18021 CAMP COFFEE 1992
Yellow body, brown chassis and roof, gold grille, yellow disc hubs, black tires. Logo: white "Drink Camp, it's the best" on black-framed red panel, black date.
   1. As above.

19022 ST. JOHN AMBULANCE 1992
Black body and chassis, cream roof, silver grille, dark blue disc hubs, black tires. Logo: blue "St. John Ambulance Brigade" on white panel, white and blue (also on rear) and red-white-blue emblems, white frames and "Valletta". In set of three models.
   1. As above.

18023 FERODO BRAKE LININGS 1993
Green body, black chassis and hubs, silver grille, green disc hubs, black tires. Logo: black "Ferodo" on black-framed gold panel, gold "Brake Linings" and other lettering, black stripe.
   1. As above.

18024 IMPERIAL HOTEL 1993
Cream body, maroon chassis and roof, gold grille, maroon 20-spoke hubs, white tires. Logo: maroon-green-cream-black rectangular design with cream "Imperial Hotel", green "Imperial Hotel, Tokyo, Japan" on doors. In set of three hotel vans.
   1. As above.

18025 SATURDAY EVENING POST 1994
Cream body, blue-black chassis and roof, gold grille and 12-spoke hubs, black tires. Logo: Saturday Evening Post design, black "Norman Rockwell 100th Anniversary" emblem. Special box.
   1. As above.

No # CAMPERDOWN HOSPITAL 1986
Light orange body, black chassis and roof, gold grille, orange disc hubs, black tires. Logo: black and red

"The Children's Hospital, Camperdown" emalem, red cross; white lettering and figure on roof.
1. As above.

19 ROLLS-ROYCE 1931 PHANTOM II 84 mm 1985
Cast body and chassis, plastic roof, interior-trunk, grille and base; cast 12-spoke or plastic 20-spoke or disc hubs, tires, two side spares. The chassis, shared with #018, has various flanges, and the same base types exist.

19000 BURGUNDY & BLACK 1985
1. Burgundy body, black chassis and roof, tan interior, silver grille, dark red disc hubs, white tires. Certificate sometimes.
1. As above.

19001 YELLOW WITH TAN ROOF 1986
Yellow body and chassis, dark tan roof and interior, silver or gold grille, dark tan disc hubs, black tires.
1. Dark tan roof, normal yellow body.
2. Dark tan roof, lighter yellow body.
3. White or ivory roof?

19002 OLIVE WITH BASKET WEAVE 1986
Light olive-tan body with tampo-printed red-brown wicker design, yellow-tan chassis, light tan or brown roof and interior, gold or silver grille, yellow disc hubs, white, gray or tan tires.
1. Brown roof, tan interior, gray tires.
2. Tan roof and interior, gray, tan or white tires.
3. Brown roof and interior, gray tires.
4. Lighter brown roof and interior, gray tires.

19003 SILVER GRAY & BLACK 1987
Silver gray body, black chassis and roof, cream interior, silver spoked hubs, black tires. Sold on plinth with #024 and #025.
1. As above.
2. Not on plinth, with no screw holes (unofficial).

19004 GOLD WITH WHITE ROOF 1987
Gold body and chassis, white roof and interior, gold grille and 12-spoke hubs, white tires.
1. As above.

19005 RUBY WEDDING 1987
Magenta body, black chassis, cream roof and interior, gold grille, magenta disc hubs, white tires. Logo: gold "H.M. Queen Elizabeth II, H.R.H. Prince Philip". Special Ruby Wedding box.
1. As above.

19006 GREEN & BLACK WITH COACH LINES 1989
Dark green body, black chassis, light tan roof and interior, gold grille, green disc hubs, white tires, gold coach lines.
1. As above.

19007 MINDER (GOLD & WHITE) 1988
Gold body, white chassis, roof and interior, gold grille and 12-spoke hubs, white tires. Logo: black "Minder Christmas Special 1988".
1. As above.

19008 LLEDO CLUB (SILVER & BLACK) 1989
Silver body, black chassis, white roof and interior, silver grille and 20-spoke hubs, gray tires. Logo: red stripes, black "Club Edition Winter 1988/89". Special box.
1. As above.

19009 ARMY STAFF CAR 1989
Olive body, chassis, roof, interior, grille and disc hubs, black tires. Red and gold lion emblems on doors and fenders. In boxed set of three models.
1. As above.

19010 BLACK WITH CREAM ROOF 1992
Black body and chassis, cream roof and interior, silver grille, black disc hubs and tires.
1. As above.

19011 SILVER WITH BLACK ROOF 1992
Silver body and chassis, black roof and interior, silver grille, gray hubs, black tires. German issue.
1. As above.

No # CREAM 1985
Cream body, chassis, roof, interior, hubs and tires, silver grille.
1. As above.

20 FORD STAKE TRUCK 90 mm 1986
Cast cab, rear body and chassis, plastic load, grille, base, 6-bolt hubs, tires. Same chassis and base types as #010, #012 and #016. Steering wheel and seat added in 1991. Loads include coal, barrels, tires, gas cylinders, flour sacks and milk churns.

20000 EAGLE ALE 1986
Yellow cab and body, black or brown chassis, dark brown barrels, black grille, red 6-bolt hubs, black tires. Logo: black-white-gold "Eagle Ale" on yellow panel, black and gold eagle on white disc, black lettering.
1. Dark yellow cab and body, black chassis.
2. Light yellow cab and body, purplish-brown chassis.

20001 COCA-COLA 1986
Dark yellow cab and body, black chassis, silver grille, dark brown or red barrels, red hubs, black tires. Logo: white "Coca-Cola Bottling Company" on white-bordered red panel, multicolored figure, black "drink", red "Coca-Cola" on red-bordered white panel, red lettering.
1. Dark brown barrels.
2. Red barrels.

20002 STROH'S BEER 1987
Red cab and body, black chassis, gold or silver grille, six black barrels, gold or silver grille, white 6-bolt hubs, black tires. Logo: black-outlined gold "Stroh's", white "America's only Fire-Brewed Beer", gold and black emblem, white and black lettering.
1. As above.

20003 WHITBREAD 1986
Brown cab and body, black chassis, six dark brown barrels, gold or silver grille, red 6-bolt hubs, black tires. Logo: gold "Whitbread" and "Brewers since 1742", red frames, gold lettering and design.
1. Brown cab and body.
2. Darker brown cab and body.
3. Purplish-brown cab and body.

20004 GOODRICH 1986
Off-white cab and body, navy blue chassis, black tire load, silver or gold grille, cream 6-bolt hubs, black tires. Logo: white "Goodrich" on white-bordered dark blue panel, multicolored figure, red and green emblem. Rarely found with Packard grille.
1. As above.

20005 AULD SCOTCH GINGER 1988
Dark blue cab, body and chassis, gold grille, white barrels and 6-bolt or cream disc hubs, black tires. Logo: multicolored "Barr's Auld Scotch Ginger", white "A-1" on red oval, gold lettering
1. White 6-bolt hubs.
2. Cream disc hubs.

20006 UNIROYAL 1987
Red cab and body, black chassis, black tire load, gold grille, red 6-bolt hubs, black tires. Logo: black "Uniroyal", black and white tread design on black-bordered panel, black lettering on white panel, black emblem and "Uniroyal". Rarely found with Packard grille.
1. As above.

129

20007 BUDWEISER 1988
White cab, body and chassis, gold grille, red barrels and 6-bolt hubs, black tires. Logo: white-on-red "Budweiser" and "Anheuser-Busch", red "King of Beers" and frames, multicolored emblem. Special box.
 1. As above.
20008 IND COOPE 1988
Green cab, and body, green or black chassis, brown barrels, gold grille, green 6-bolt hubs, black tires. Logo: gold "Ind Coope", lettering and emblem, gold and white frames.
 1. Green chassis.
 2. Black chassis.
20009 WATNEY'S BREWERY 1989
Green cab and body, black chassis, brown barrels, gold grille, green 6-bolt hubs, black tires. Logo: gold "Watneys" and other lettering, white frames.
 1. As above.
20010 CALOR GAS 1989
Orange cab, white body, green chassis, silver grille, orange load and 6-bolt hubs, black tires. Logo: orange-white-black "Calor Gas" and design, black lettering.
 1. As above.
20011 ROYAL NAVY 1988
Navy blue cab, body and chassis, dark brown barrels, silver grille, navy blue 6-bolt hubs, black tires. Logo: white "Royal Navy" and "H.M.S. Rooke, Gibraltar", gold-black-white emblem. In set of three models.
 1. As above.
20012 PIRELLI TIRES 1990
Yellow cab and body, black chassis and tire load, silver grille, yellow 6-bolt hubs, black tires. Logo: red "Pirelli" in black frame, red lettering, green design in black frames.
 1. As above.
20013 BRITISH OXYGEN 1990
Dark red cab and body, black chassis and load, gold grille, dark red 6-bolt hubs, black tires. Logo: gold "For Quality and Service" and "British Oxygen Co. Ltd.", emblem and "BOC".
 1. As above.
20014 HERSHEY'S CHOCOLATE 1990
Brown cab and barrels, cream body and chassis, gold grille, cream 6-bolt hubs, black tires. Logo: cream and brown "Hershey's Chocolate" design, white lettering and lines, multicolored design. Special box.
 1. As above.
20015 ROYAL AIR FORCE 1990
Dull blue body, cab, chassis, grille and 6-bolt hubs, black load and tires. Logo: white "RAF" and number, red-on-white danger sign, red-white-blue roundel. In set of three models.
 1. As above.
20016 WINN-DIXIE 1990
Black cab, light tan body and chassis, brown load, gold grille, cream 6-bolt hubs, black tires. Logo: black-white-red 'The Table Supply Stores" etc., white design and "Since 1925". Special box.
 1. As above.
20017 DUNLOP 1991
White cab and body, black chassis and tire load, silver grille, dark blue 6-bolt hubs, black tires. Logo: black "Dunlop" in blue frame, multicolored design, red "The World's Master Tyre".
 1. As above.
20018 GOODYEAR TIRES 1991
Dark blue cab and body, black chassis and tire load, gold grille, dark blue 6-bolt hubs, black tires. Logo: gold "Goodyear Tires" emblem, gold-white-blue flag, white lettering and frame.
 1. As above.

20019 McDOUGALL'S FLOUR 1993
Pale gray cab, dull blue body, black chassis, tan load, silver grille, light gray 6-bolt hubs, black tires. Logo: white "McDougall's", "Self Raising Flour", etc., multicolored design on body, black and white emblem, white lettering on doors.
 1. As above.
20020 NESTLE'S MILK 1994
Cream cab, blue body and chassis, gray load, silver grille, blue 6-bolt hubs, black tires. Logo: black-outlined white "Nestle's Milk" in oval, white lettering, Swiss flags on white discs, blue lettering on doors, name and flags on front.
 1. As above.
20021 DR. PEPPER 1994
Red cab and body, black chassis, brown load, silver grille, yellow 6-bolt hubs, black tires. Logo: black-outlined white "Dr. Pepper", figure in circle, white emblem on doors. Special box.
 1. As above.
20022 PENNZOIL 1995
Yellow cab and body, black chassis, tan load, silver grille, red 6-bolt hubs, black tires. Logo: black "Pennzoil" etc., red bell, red-yellow-black oilcan design.
 1. As above.
21 CHEVROLET 1934 VAN 80 mm 1986
Cast body and chassis, plastic roof, grille, base, 12-spoke metal, 20-spoke or disc hubs, tires. Steering wheel and seat have been added; roofs with header, or header plus blade, exist, and there was a small early change in the axle covers on the base, which was first lettered DG21, then DG21-26, then DG21-26-51.
21000 SHARP'S TOFFEE 1986
Cream body, brown chassis, tan roof, silver or gold grille, maroon disc hubs, white tires. Logo: brown "Sharp's" and emblem, name and address, orange "Super-Kreem Toffee", multicolored figure.
 1. Brown chassis, silver grille.
 2. Purplish brown chassis, silver grille.
 3. Dark cream-yellow body, dark maroon hubs, gold grille.
21001 LLEDO COLLECTORS CLUB 1986
Maroon body, black chassis, light tan roof, gold grille, maroon disc hubs, white tires. Logo: black "Models of" and "Lledo Original 1986", black-outlined gold "Days Gone" on gold and black emblem, gold "Club Member Edition Autumn 1986". Special box.
 1. As above.
 2. Black door lettering.
21002 LEICESTER MERCURY 1986
Blue body, black chassis and roof, gold grille, black 20-spoke hubs and tires. Logo: white "Leicester Mercury, Largest Circulation, Illustrated Chronicle" and circled no. 27.
 1. As above.
21003 HOSTESS CAKE 1986
White body, red chassis and roof, silver grille, red disc hubs, white tires. Logo: white "Hostess Cake" and stripes on blue ribbons, white silhouette on red heart, red "America's Favorite Quick Dessert".
 1. As above.
21004 DR. PEPPER 1987
Red body, black chassis, white roof with header, gold grille, red disc hubs, white tires. Logo: black-outlined white "Drink Dr. Pepper", black "good for life" on white background, white lettering; header: red "King of Beverages" and underline.
 1. As above.
21005 COCA-COLA 1986
Cream body, red chassis and roof, gold grille and 12-spoke hubs, white tires. Logo: red "Keep a Case Coca-Cola in your Home" on brown-bordered red oval on grid pattern, hand holding bottle, brown and red

lettering. Special box.
1. As above.
21006 (Not used)
21007 HAMLEYS 1988
Red body, cream chassis and roof, gold grille and 12-spoke hubs, black tires. Logo: gold "Hamleys, the finest toyshop in the world" and frames. Header: gold "Est. 1769".
1. As above.
21008 BUDWEISER 1988
Dark green body, black chassis and roof, gold grille and 12-spoke hubs, black tires. Logo: white "Anheuser-Busch" etc., designs and
frames, red-outlined white "Genuine Budweiser", red-white-brown emblem. Header: white "King of beers". Special box.
1. As above.
21009 BIRD'S CUSTARD 1988
Yellow bodsy, blue chassis, red roof, silver grille, blue disc hubs, white tires. Logo: white "Bird's" and emblem on red, blue "Custard Powder", white "Original Flavour" on blue, emblem on doors, yellow and blue "Bird's Custard Powder" on rear. Header: white "Bird's".
1. As above.
21010 FARRAH'S TOFFEE 1988
Metallic purple body and chassis, white roof, silver grille, white disc hubs, black tires. Logo: silver "Farrah's Original Harrogate Toffee" etc., emblem and trim. Header: purple "Farrah's".
1. As above.
21011 VITA-WEAT 1988
Tan body, dark brown chassis and roof, gold grille, brown disc hubs, black tires. Logo: orange "Vita-Weat", brown "The British Crispbread" etc., orange frames, brown "Peek Frean & Co. Ltd." on door. Header: cream "Peek Frean & Co. Ltd."
1. As above.
21012 SIMPSONS 1989
Black body, chassis and roof, gold grille and 12-spoke hubs, black tires. Logo: gold emblems, red-brown and pale yellow "DAKS Simpson" and lines, yellow lettering. In boxed set.
1. As above.
21013 BENETTON ANTHOLOGY 1989
Dark cream body, green chassis and roof, silver grille, cream 20-spoke hubs, black tires. Logo: red "Anthology", black "Benetton", lettering, trim and frame, green emblem.
1. As above.
21014 HERSHEY'S KISSES 1989
Brown body, yellow tan chassis, light tan roof, gold grille, brown 20-spoke hubs, white tires. Logo: white "Hershey's Kisses" design, "Milk Chocolate Cocoa". Special box.
1. As above.
21015 CHERRY BLOSSOM 1989
Dark blue body and chassis, white roof, silver grille, dark blue disc hubs, black tires. Logo: white-red-blue design with "Cherry Blossom Boot Polish", lettering and emblem.
1. As above.
21016 MAJESTIC PICTURES 1989
Gold body and chassis, green roof, gold grille and 12-spoke hubs, black tires. Logo: multicolored "Majestic Pictures" emblem, black lettering and frames. In boxed set of four models.
1. As above.
21017 DAYS GONE TOY FAIR 1990
Cream body, green chassis and roof, gold grille, green 20-spoke hubs, black tires. Logo: black-on-gold "Days Gone" and "Toy Fair Model", black lettering and "1990", green ribbon with cream lettering. Header:

gold "Toy Fair Model". Plain white box.
1. As above.
21018 RECKITTS BLUE 1990
Blue-black body, black chassis. dark blue roof, silver grille, dark blue disc hubs, black tires. Logo: two-tone blue and white design with "Reckitt's Blue . . . in the last rinse", white frame, white "Reckitt's Blue" on rear. Header: light blue "Reckitt's Blue".
1. As above.
21019 MARKS & SPENCER 1990
Dark cream body, green chassis and roof, gold grille, green 20-spoke hubs, black tires. Logo: cream "M&S" on black-rimmed green circle, black and gold emblem, black lettering. Special box.
1. As above.
21020 LIBERTY & CO. 1990
Dark purplish-blue body, black chassis and roof, silver grille, gold 12-spoke hubs, black tires. Logo: gold arms, "Liberty & Co. Ltd.", address and frames. In boxed set of four models.
1. As above.
21021 DAYS GONE COLLECTORS CLUB 1990
Blue body, cream chassis and roof, gold grille and 12-spoke hubs, white tires. Logo: black "Days Gone" on gold panel, gold "Vintage Models" on green ribbon, gold "Collectors Club", "Lledo", "Summer 1990", trim and frame.
21022 SCOTTISH BLUEBELL 1990
Cream body, dark blue chassis and roof, gold grille, dark blue disc hubs, white tires. Logo: Two-tone blue and white "Scottish Bluebell matches" design, white "Bryant & May Ltd." on blue door panel, blue lettering. In set of four models with next three.
1. As above.
21023 BRYANT & MAY 1990
Same model as #21022 except for logo: red-cream-blue "Celebrated Bryant & May's Wax Vestas" design, red "Bryant & May's" on door.
1. As above.
21024 SWAN VESTAS 1990
Same model as #21022 except for logo: red-green-cream "The Smoker's Match, Swan Vestas" design with swan figure, green "Bryant & May Ltd.", red lettering.
1. As above.
21025 ENGLAND'S GLORY 1990
Same model as #21022 except for logo: red-white-blue "England's Glory" design with ship, red-white-blue "S. J. Moreland & Sons Ltd., Gloucester" on doors.
1. As above.
21026 HAMLEYS 1990
Pale blue body, blue-black chassis and roof, gold grille, blue-black disc hubs, black tires. Logo: red "Hamleys" and "the finest toyshop in the world", white name on red ribbon, red-white-black design. Special box.
1. As above.
21027 EXIDE 1991
Cream body, dark green chassis and roof, silver grille, green 20-spoke hubs, black tires. Logo: black "Exide", red "the long life car battery" and frames, green lettering.
1. As above.
21028 FAIRY SOAP 1991
White body, green chassis and roof, gold grille, green disc hubs, black tires. Logo: black-outlined green "Fairy Soap", green figure and frame, black lettering.
1. As above.

21029 BUSHELLS COFFEE 1991
Tan body, dark blue chassis and roof, gold grille, dark blue 20-spoke hubs, white tires. Logo: cream "Bushells is delicious", orange "Coffee" and other lettering, orange-blue-tan design on blue panel and emblem on doors.
   1. As above.

21030 U.S. MARINE AMBULANCE 1991
Light gray body, chassis, roof, grille and disc hubs, black tires. Logo: red-on-white crosses, red-white-blue star and emblems, dark blue "U.S.M.C." and other lettering, red cross, emblem and "U.S.M.C." on rear. In boxed set of three models.
   1. As above.

21031 ELLIMAN'S EMBROCATION 1992
Red body, black chassis and roof, gold grille, black tires. Logo: multicolored design with white "Elliman's Embrocation". white lettering on doors.
   1. As above.

21032 MAGGI'S SOUP 1992
Dark blue body, black chassis, gray roof, silver grille, dark blue disc hubs, black tires. Logo: white-shadowed yellow "Maggi's", maroon circles with white lettering and rims, bottle with white outline, yellow frames.
   1. As above.

21033 SCRIBBAN'S PURITY BREAD 1991
Cream body, dark brown chassis and roof, gold grille, green disc hubs, black tires. Logo: brown "Scribban's Purity Bread" etc., brown panels, cream lettering.

21034 LMS & LNER PARCELS 1992
Gray body, chassis, roof, grille and disc hubs, black tires. Logo: white "Express Parcels Traffic", "LMS & LNER", other lettering and line (similar rear lettering), red-white-black panel. In set of three models.
   1. As above.

21035 GRAND HOTEL DE PARIS 1992
Dark blue body and chassis and roof, gold grille, dark blue 20-spoke hubs, white tires. Logo: multicolored "Grand Hotel de Paris, Monte Carlo" panel, light blue lettering. In set of three models.
   1. As above.

21036 LNER PARCELS 1992
Blue body, black chassis and roof, silver grille, red 20-spoke hubs, black tires. Logo: white "L N E R Country Motor Service", other lettering (also on rear), gold address. In set of three models.
   1. As above.

21037 HAMLEYS 1992
Green body, black chassis and roof, gold grille, green disc hubs, black tires. Logo: Black "Hamleys" etc. on gold panel with figure, gold "The Finest Toyshop in the World" etc. and frame. In set of four Hamleys models.
   1. As above.

21038 PEPSI-COLA 1993
Blue-black body, black chassis and roof, silver radiator, blue-black disc hubs, black tires. Logo: Light blue "Pepsi Cola" with blue black lettering, white "I love its flavor" and other lettering, multicolored figure. Special Pepsi-Cola box.
   1. As above.

21039 ROSE'S LIME JUICE 1994
Green body, chassis, roof and disc hubs, silver grille, black tires. Logo: black-outlined gold "Rose's Lime Juice", two-tone green design.
   1. As above.

21040 SPRENGEL SCHOKOLADE 1994
Light blue body, black chassis and roof, silver grille, black disc hubs and tires. Logo: brown "Sprengel Schokolade" and design on white-framed yellow panel, brown "Sprengel Schokolade" on door.
   1. As above.

21041 HENDERSON MOTORCYCLES 1994
Black body, chassis and roof, silver grille, red disc hubs, black tires. Logo: multicolored "Henderson Motorcycles" design, gold lettering, gold and red frames. In set of three models.
   1. As above.

21042 USA WORLD CUP 1994
White body, green chassis and roof, gold grille and 12-spoke hubs, black tires. Logo: multicolored flag design, red-shadowed blue "USA World Cup:, blue-shadowed red "'94", green "Good Luck Ireland!", green shamrock on doors.
   1. As above.

21043 SATURDAY EVENING POST 1994
Light blue body, navy blue chassis and roof, gold grille and 12-spoke hubs, black tires. Logo: Saturday Evening Post design, black "Norman Rockwell 100th Anniversary" emblem. Special box.
   1. As above.

21044 NIVEA CREME OIL 1995
Blue body, black chassis, white roof, silver grille, blue disc hubs, black tires. Logo: white "Nivea Creme Oil" and frame, multicolored designs.

21045 RUPERT BEAR 1995
Orange body, black chassis and roof, gold grille, orange disc hubs, black tires. Logo: scene of Rupert tipping hat, The Rupert Collection emblem. Special Rupert box.
   1. As above.

21046 GOLD CLUB 1995
No data.

22 PACKARD 1933 TOWN VAN 87 mm 1986
Cast body and chassis, plastic roof, seat, windshield, base, disc hubs, tires, two side spare wheels, same chassis as DG19, same base types as DG18 and DG19.

22000 STAG WHISKY 1986
Cream body, red chassis, roof and seat, silver grille and windshield, red disc hubs, white tires. Logo: orange-outlined brown "Stag Whisky", black and orange stag figure, black lettering. Has been found with Rolls-Royce grille.
   1. Lighter red roof, seat and hubs.
   2. Darker red roof, seat and hubs.

22001 LORD TED CIGARS 1986
Black body, chassis, roof and seat, gold grille and windshield, red disc hubs, white tires. Logo: gold "Lord Ted Cigars for Gentlemen, St. James", phone number and trim. Has been found with Rolls-Royce grille.
   1. As above.

22002 FLORISTS TRANSWORLD DELIVERY 1987
Cream body, black chassis, roof and seat, gold or silver grille and windshield, cream disc hubs, black tires. Logo: black and gold emblem with gold "FTD" and figure, black "Florists Transworld Delivery since 1910", red lettering. Has been found with Ford and Rolls-Royce grilles.
   1. As above.

22003 WHITMAN'S SAMPLER 1987
Yellow body, brown chassis, red roof and seat, gold or silver grille and windshield, brown disc hubs, white tires. Logo: green "Whitman's Sampler", green and red flowers, brown lettering and frame. Has been found with Rolls-Royce grille.
   1. As above.

132

22004 LLEDO CLUB MEMBER 1987
Yellow body, red chassis, roof and seat, gold grille and windshield, red disc hubs, gray tires. Logo: gold and black Lledo emblem, gold "Club Member Edition Winter 1986/87". Special box. Has been found with Rolls-Royce grille.
  1. As above.
22005 HAMLEYS 1988
Cream body, black chassis, roof and seat, gold grille and windshield, cream disc hubs, black tires. Logo: black "Hamleys, the finest toyshop in the world", date and frame.
  1. As above.
22006 PIZZA EXPRESS 1988
White body, red chassis, roof and seat, silver grille and windshield, red disc hubs, black tires. Logo: blue "Pizza Express" on red emblem, other blue lettering.
  1. As above.
22007 BUDWEISER 1988
Black body, red chassis, roof and seat, red chassis, gold grille, windshield and 12-spoke hubs, white tires. Logo: white "Anheuser-Busch Budweiser", designs and frame, red-white-brown emblem. Special box. Has been found with Rolls-Royce and Ford grilles.
  1. As above.
22008 TESCO 1988
White body, red chassis, roof and seat, silver grille and windshield, red disc hubs, white tires. Logo: red "Tesco Brand" in diamond (same on rear), date on door.
  1. As above.
22009 SOHO DAIRIES 1989
Brown or black body, roof and seat, black chassis, gold grille and windshield, black 20-spoke hubs and tires. Logo: white "Soho Dairy, fresh supplies daily" etc. and stripe, white-brown-green design. Has been found with Rolls-Royce grille.
  1. Black body.
  2. Dark brown body.
22010 HEINZ 57 VARIETIES 1990
Cream body, blue-black chassis, roof and seat, gold grille and windshield, black disc hubs, white tires. Logo: black-outlined red "57 Varieties, H. J. Heinz Co. Ltd."
  1. As above.
22011 SHARPS TOFFEE 1991
Cream body, brown chassis, roof and seat, gold grille, windshield and 12-spoke hubs, black tires. Logo: brown "Sharp's Toffee" etc.
  1. As above.
22012 PUNCH MAGAZINE 1992
Green body and roof, black chassis and seat, gold grille and windshield, green disc hubs, black tires. Logo: red-white-black "Punch" design, white lettering.
  1. As above.
23   SCENICRUISER 1954 109 mm 1987
Cast body and chassis, plastic windows, base and wheels. First Greyhound issues lacked triangular spacers on base. Front part of roof either plain or ridged.
23000 GREYHOUND 1987
Silver body, silver or black chassis. Logo: black-outlined silver greyhound figure and black "Greyhound" on white stripe.
  1. Unpainted metal chassis.
  2. Silver chassis.
  3. Black chassis.

23001 GOLDEN WEST TOURS 1987
Gold body, black chassis. Logo: red and gold "Golden West" and design, gold "Tours" on light blue stripe.
  1. As above.
23002 BUFFALO LUXURY TRAVEL 1987
Red body, black chassis. Logo: white "Buffalo" and black "Luxury Travel" on red and yellow stripe.
  1. As above.
24   ROLLS-ROYCE 1934 PLAYBOY 88 mm 1987
Cast body and chassis (second type DG18), plastic top, interior-trunk, grille and base, hubs and tires, two spare wheels. DG18-19-22 base first, later DG18/19/22/24/25, then 18-19-22-24-25-38.
24000 YELLOW AND BLACK 1987
Dark yellow body, black chassis, light brown top and interior, gold grille, yellow disc hubs, black or gray tires. Has been found with Packard grille.
  1. As above.
24001 LILAC AND PURPLE 1987
Metallic lilac body, dark purple chassis, white top and interior, silver grille, disc or 20-spoke hubs, gray or black tires. Has been found with Packard grille.
  1. Purple disc hubs.
  2. Purple disc hubs, darker lilac body.
  3. Black disc or 20-spoke hubs?
24002 METALLIC GRAY AND BLACK 1988
Metallic gray body, black chassis and top, cream interior, silver 20-spoke hubs, black tires. On plinth in set of three models.
  1. As above.
  2. Also exists without plinth or screw holes (unofficial).
24003 RED AND WHITE 1987
Red body, white chassis, top and interior, silver grille, red 20-spoke hubs, white tires.
  1. As above.
24004 METALLIC GREEN AND BLACK 1988
Metallic green body, black chassis, tan top and interior, silver grille, disc or 12-spoke hubs, white tires. Has been found with Packard grille.
  1. Dark green disc hubs.
  2. Gold 12-spoke hubs.
24005 GREEN WITH COACH LINES 1989
Dark green body with gold coach lines, black chassis, tan top and interior, silver grille, red 20-spoke hubs, white tires. Has been found with Ford grille.
no# GOLD 1992
Gold body and chassis, green roof, interior and trunk, gold radiator and 12-spoke hubs, black tires, mounted on plinth.
  1. As above.
25   ROLLS-ROYCE SILVER GHOST 1925 93 mm 1987
Cast body and chassis, plastic top, interior, grille and base, hubs and tires. Same details as DG24.
25000 DARK BLUE AND BLACK 1987
Navy blue body, black chassis, top and interior, gold or silver grille, black 20-spoke hubs and tires.
  1. Gold grille.
  2. Silver grille.
  3. Lighter (but still dark) blue body, gold grille.
25001 SILVER AND BLUE 1987
Silver body, blue chassis and top, cream or white interior, gold grille and 12-spoke hubs, white tires. Has

been found with Packard grille.
1. Cream interior.
2. White interior.

25002 METALLIC GRAY AND BLACK 1988
Metallic gray body, black chassis and top, tan interior, silver grille and 20-spoke hubs, black tires. On plinth in set of three models.
1. As above.
2. Also exists without plinth or screw holes (unofficial).

25003 WHITE 1987
White body and chassis, black or white top, cream or white interior, gold grille anbd 12-spoke hubs, black tires. Version with white top and interior is not a DG issue.
1. Cream interior, black top.
2. White interior and top (not DG).

25004 DARK BLUE AND BLACK 1989
Dark blue body, black chassis, tan roof, black interior, gold grille and 12-spoke hubs.
1. As above.

25005 GREEN WITH COACH LINES 1989
Dark green body with gold coach lines, black chassis, tan top and interior, gold grille, green disc hubs, white tires.
1. As above.

26 CHEVROLET 1934 BOTTLE TRUCK 82 mm 1987
Cast cab, body and chassis (same as DG21), plastic load, blade, grille and base, disc or 6-bolt hubs and tires or wheels. DG21-26 base first, later DG21-26-51. Two other box loads exist.

26000 SCHWEPPES 1987
Yellow cab, body and blade, red or black chassis, brown or black load, gold grille, red disc hubs, black or white tires. Logo: black "Schweppes" on blade, red and gold emblem on door, multicolored "Schweppes" emblem on rear.
1. Dark yellow cab, body and blade, red chassis, black load and tires.
2. Light yellow cab, body and blade, red chassis, light brown load, black or white tires.
3. Black chassis and load, other details not known.

26001 LLEDO CLUB 1987
White cab, body and blade, black chassis and load, silver grille, white disc or 6-bolt hubs, black tires. Logo: black "The Lledo Collection" and stripes on blade, emblem on rear, "Club Member Summer Edition 1987" on doors.
1. As above.

26002 COCA-COLA 1987
Yellow-orange cab and body, black chassis, red blade, tan load, gold or silver grille, red disc hubs, black tires. Logo: yellow "Coca-Cola" and "Every bottle sterilized" on blade, red "Serve Coca-Cola at home" and frame on rear, red "Enjoy Coca-Cola" and frame on doors.
1. As above.

26003 BUDWEISER 1988
Red cab, body and blade, black chassis, light tan load, silver grille, red disc hubs, white tires. Logo: white "Genuine Budweiser" on blade, "Anheuser-Busch" and multicolored emblem on doors. Special box.
1. As above.

26004 BARR'S IRN BRU 1988
Red cab, body and blade, black chassis, tan load, gold grille, red disc hubs, black tires. Logo: white "Barr's" on blade, multicolored "Irn Bru" emblem on rear, white name and black date on doors.
1. As above.

26005 CORONA FRUIT DRINKS 1988
Dark green cab, body and blade, black chassis, dark brown load, gold grille, dark green disc hubs, black tires. Logo: gold "Corona Drinks", "direct supply" and frame on blade, "Corona Fruit Drinks" and frame on rear and door, white lettering and gold frame on body.
1. As above.

26006 TIZER 1988
Red body, blue chassis, white blade, tan load, gold grille, white disc hubs, black tires. Logo: blue "Tizer" on blade, multicolored "Tizer the Appetizer" design on rear, white lettering on body.
1. As above.

26007 CANADA DRY 1989
White cab, body and blade, black chassis, brown load, silver grille, black wheels. Logo: green "drink", red "Canada Dry", multicolored bottle on blade, varying "Canada Dry" emblems on doors and rear.
1. As above.

26008 SCHWEPPES GINGER ALE 1990
Red cab, body and blade, black chassis, brown load, gold grille, red disc hubs, black tires. Logo: black-outlined white "Schweppes", white "dry ginger ale" on blade, white "Schweppes dry Ginger Ale" on rear and doors.
1. As above.

26009 J. R. TENNENT ALES 1991
Green cab, body and blade, black chassis, brown load, gold grille, green disc hubs, black tires. Logo: red-outlined gold "J. P. Tennent Ltd.", gold lettering and frames on blade, similar lettering and frames on rear with red-gold-black emblem, similar emblem on doors, gold lettering and frame on body.
1. As above.

26010 BASS ALES 1992
Blue cab, body and blade, black chassis, brown load, silver grille, blue disc hubs, black tires. Logo: red-shadowed gold "Bass" on blade, red and gold logo on body and doors.
1. As above.

26011 FYFFES BANANAS 1992
Yellow cab and body, green chassis, silver grille, green disc hubs, black tires. Logo: black "Fyffes Bananas Bristol" etc. on body, two-tone blue emblems and black "are best bananas" on doors and rear, emblems on cases. No blade.
1. As above.
2. Logo reversed, with number in front.

26012 PEPSI-COLA 1993
Blue cab, body and blade, black chassis, cream load, silver grille, blue disc hubs, black tires. Logo: red "Pepsi-Cola" on blade and cases, white "double size" on blade, white lettering and trim on doors and sides. In special Pepsi-Cola box.
1. As above.

26013 PERRIER WATER 1993
Green cab, body and blade, black chassis, tan load, silver grille, green disc hubs, black tires. Logo: white "Perrier", yellow "Source France" and frame on blade, yellow lettering and frame on body, yellow and white emblem on rear, yellow and white emblem on door, green "Perrier" on load.
1. As above.

26014 BROOKE BOND TEA 1993
Red cab and body, black chassis, tan load, silver grille, red disc hubs, black tires. Logo: black-outlined "Brooke Bond Tea" on sides and back of body, same in red on cases. No blade.
1. As above.

26015 DR. PEPPER 1994
Red cab and body, black chassis, silver grille, yellow disc hubs, black tires. Logo: white "Drink", black-outlined white "Dr. Pepper" etc. on blade, white lettering on body and doors, red "Dr. Pepper" on cases, "Dr. Pepper" logo on rear. Special box.
1. As above.

26016 BECK'S BEER 1995
Green cab, body and blade, black chassis, tan load, gold grille, red disc hubs, black tires. Logo: white "Beck's", "Beck & Co.", frames, etc., multicolored emblems, green "Beck & Co." on load.
   1. As above.
26017 7-UP 1995
Green cab and body, black chassis, red blade, tan load, silver grille, green disc hubs, black tires. Logo: black-outlined green "7-Up", white lettering, red 7-Up emblems on load. Special box.
   1. As above.
27   MACK 1934 BREAKDOWN TRUCK 100 mm 1987
Cast body, chassis and boom, plastic rear bed, hook, grille, base, hubs, tires. DG27/28/ base first, later DG27/28/39/40. then with 42 added. Steering wheel from 27006 on..
27000 A1 RECOVERY 1987
Orange body, black chassis, white boom, black rear bed, hook, grille, 6-bolt hubs and tires. Logo: red circle, "A1" and "24 Hour Recovery", yellow stripes.
   1. As above.
27001 HANK'S AUTO SERVICE 1988
Green body and chassis, yellow boom, charcoal bed and hook, gold grille, yellow 6-bolt hubs, black tires. Logo: yellow "Hank's Auto Services", black stripes.
   1. As above.
27002 (Not used)
27003 MOBILOIL 1988
White body and boom, blue chassis, black bed and hook, silver grille, orange 6-bolt hubs, black tires. Logo: blue "Mobiloil" and "Cargoyle", orange figure, emblem and "a grade for each type of motor".
   1. As above.
27004 MOBILOIL-FRANCE 1989
White body and boom, blue chassis, black bed and hook, silver grille, orange 6-bolt hubs, black tires. Logo: blue "Mobiloil" and "Cargoyle", orange figure, emblem and "Le sommet pour chaque voiture". Identical to #27003 except for French lettering.
   1. As above.
27005 ARTHUR DALEY 1988
Red body, black chassis, boom, bed and hook, gold grille, red 6-bolt hubs, black tires. Logo: black "Arthur Daley breakdowns" etc., gold stripes and lettering.
   1. As above.
27006 U. S. ARMY 1991
Olive body, chassis, boom and grille, black hook, olive 6-bolt hubs, black tires. Logo: red-white-blue star, white and light blue lettering. In set of three models.
   1. As above.
27007 L.C.C. SUPPLIES DEPT. 1992
Green body and boom, black chassis, bed and hook, silver grille, green 6-bolt hubs, black tires. Logo: white "L.C.C. Supplies Dept.", other lettering and emblem.
   1. As above.
28   MACK 1934 CANVAS BACK TRUCK 97 mm 1988
Cast body and chassis (same as 28), plastic cover, grille, base, hubs, tires. Steering wheel added. DG27/28/ base first, then DG27/28/39/40, then DG27 28 39 40 42. Casting variations: plain front and rear corners of bed, then reinforced rear corners, then reinforced front and rear corners.
28000 TY-PHOO TEA 1988
Red body, black chassis, tan cover, silver grille, red 6-bolt hubs, black tires. Logo: tea leaves, white and black "Ty-Phoo", white "quality leaf tea" and stripes.
   1. Green and white tea leaves.
   2. Black and white tea leaves.

28001 TATE & LYLE 1988
Blue body, blue or cream chassis, tan cover, gold or silver grille, light blue or brown 6-bolt hubs, black tires. Logo: blue and gold "Tate & Lyle's" and design, blue lettering, white "Pure British Refined".
   1. Blue chassis, light blue hubs, gold or silver grille.
   2. Cream chassis, brown hubs, gold? grille.
28002 LLEDO COLLECTION 1988
Brown body, cream chassis, tan cover, gold grille, brown 6-bolt or disc hubs, black tires. Logo: brown "The Lledo Collection" and design, cream "Club Edition Spring 1988" and stripes.
   1. As above.
28003 HEINZ BAKED BEANS 1988
Turquoise body, black chassis, cream cover, gold or silver grille, black 6-bolt hubs, white tires. Logo: black-white-gold designs with white "Heinz Baked Beans", gold lettering, white "Heinz" and lines.
   1. As above.
28004 DUNLOP TYRES 1989
Blue body, black chassis, white cover, silver grille, blue 6-bolt hubs, black tires. Logo: blue "Dunlop" and panel, black tire, red-white-blue flag, white lettering.
   1. As above.
28005 (Not used)
28006 ROYAL NAVY FIELD GUN CREW 1989
Navy blue body and chassis, tan cover, silver grille, navy blue 6-bolt hubs, black tires. Logo: navy blue "Devon Port Command Field Gun Crew" and "Royal Tournament", white "Royal Navy". In set of three models.
   1. As above.
28007 STROH'S BEER 1990
Dark blue body, black chassis, blue cover, gold grille, black 6-bolt hubs and tires. Logo: white "Stroh's", red-white-blue emblem, gold "America's fire-brewed beer" and "since 1775".
   1. As above.
28008 NORTH YORKSHIRE MOORS RAILWAY 1990
Dark blue body, black chassis, tan cover, gold grille, black wheels. Logo: blue "North Yorkshire Moors Railway" and destinations, gold and blue emblem, white "Express Parcels Service" in gold frame. In set of three models.
28009 COCA-COLA (not issued)
28010 GREENE KING BEER 1991
Green body, black chassis, green cover, gold grille, green 6-bolt hubs, black tires. Logo: yellow "Greene King" and multicolored emblem, yellow "Beer is best" and lines.
   1. As above.
28011 ROYAL AIR FORCE 1990
Blue body, chassis, cover, grille and 6-bolt hubs, black tires. Logo: white "RAF", round emblem and other lettering, red-white-blue roundel, other markings. In set of three models.
   1. As above.
28012 WINN-DIXIE 1990
Red body, black chassis, white cover, gold grille, red hubs, black tires. No other data.
28013 HAMLEYS 1990
Dark blue body and cover, black chassis, gold grille, blue 6-bolt hubs, black tires. Logo: gold "Hamleys, the finest toyshop in the world", other lettering, design and lines, blue "Hamley Brothers Ltd." on gold ribbon, Special box.
   1. As above.
28014 LNER EXPRESS PARCELS 1991
Dark blue body, black chassis and cover, silver grille, red 6-bolt hubs, black tires. Logo: white LNER

Express Parcels Service", multicolored poster, white "London & North Eastern Railway" and "LNER". In set of three models.

    1. As above.

28015 LMS EXPRESS PARCELS 1991
Maroon body, black chassis and cover, silver grille, maroon 6-bolt hubs, black tires. Logo: white "L M S Express Parcels Traffic" and other lettering, multicolored "Family Health Soap" poster. In set of three models.

    1. As above.

28016 8TH ARMY TRUCK 1991
Tan body, chassis, cover, grille and 6-bolt hubs, black tires. Logo: white "3481 LST IV", black panel with white lettering and frame, red-white-blue roundel, red and white emblems, brown number. Special box.

    1. As above.

28017 QUARTERMASTER CORPS 1991
Olive body, chassis, cover, grille and 6-bolt hubs, black tires. Logo: white "Quartermaster Corps", light blue numbers, emblems. In set of three models.

    1. As above.

28018 REVELL--DAYS GONE 1991
Dark blue body and chassis, cream cover, gold grille, dark blue hubs, black tires. No other data.

28019 U.S. MARINE CORPS 1991
Gray body, chassis, cover, grille and 6-bolt hubs, black tires. Logo: blue "U.S. Marine Corps" and other lettering, star, emblems. In set of three models.

    1. As above.

28020 GREAT WESTERN RAILWAY 1992
Dark brown body, black chassis and cover, silver grille, brown disc hubs, black tires. Logo: white GWR emblem, "Express Cartage Service", multicolored panel, brown "Great Western Railway" on cream panel. cream and white lettering. In set of three models.

    1. As above.

28021 HAMLEYS 1992
Maroon body, black chassis, cream cover, gold grille, maroon 6-bolt hubs, black tires. Logo: red "Hamleys", white "Hamley Brothers Ltd." on red ribbon, red lettering, red-white-black design, gold lettering and frames. Special box.

    1. As above.

28022 U.S. NAVY TORPEDO BOAT SQUAD 1991
Light gray body, chassis, cover, grille and 6-bolt hubs, black tires. Logo: white "Black Jack", dark blue "U.S. Navy", white "MTB Squadron 1", red-white-blue star, other markings. In set of three models.

28023 WINCARNIS TONIC 1992
Maroon body and cover, black chassis, silver grille, maroon 6-bolt hubs, black tires. Logo: black and white "Wincarnis" with figures and lettering on white panel, gold "Wincarnis", "The World's Greatest Tonic & Restorative" and frames.

28024 LLEDO COLLECTORS CLUB 1992
Maroon body, black chassis and cover, gold grille, black 6-bolt hubs and tires. Logo: black "Days Gone" on gold and black panel, gold lettering on green and black ribbon, gold "Lledo Collectors Club" and "Winter 1991". Special box.

    1. As above.

28025 DAYS GONE TOY FAIRS 1992
Dark blue body, black chassis, cream cover, silver grille, dark blue 6-bolt hubs, black tires. Logo: gold "Toy Fair model" and frame, white lettering, gold "1992", gold panel with black "Days Gone" and frame, blue "Limited Edition", black lettering on green ribbon. Plain white box.

    1. As above.

28026 ROYAL NAVY 1992
Gray body and chassis, darker gray cover, grille and 6-bolt hubs, black tires. Logo: white "Royal Navy" and numbers. In set of three models.

    1. As above.

28027 U.S. MARINE CORPS 1992
Olive body and chassis, darker olive cover and grille, olive 6-bolt hubs, black tires. Logo: white "US Marine Corps" and other lettering, red-white-blue emblems. In set of three models.

28028 SOUTHERN RAILWAY 1992
Green body and cover, black chassis, silver grille, red 6-bolt hubs, black tires. Logo: white-framed "Hastings" poster, yellow "S R Express Parcels Service" and other lettering, yellow "Southern Railway". In set of three models.

    1. As above.

28029 KAFFEE HAG 1993
Red body, black chassis and cover, silver grille, red 6-bolt hubs, black tires. Logo: black "Kaffee Hag schont Ihr Herz", red heart, red-white-black design on cover, black "Kaffee Hag", red hearts, red-white-black design on white panel on body.

    1. As above.

28030 ROYAL AIR FORCE 1993
Dull blue body, black chassis, cover, grille and 6-bolt hubs. Logo: white "RAF", "G for George" and numbers, red-white-blue roundel.

In set of three Dambusters models.

28031 DAYS GONE WROUGHTON SHOW 1993
Maroon body, black chassis, cream cover, silver grille, maroon 6-bolt hubs, black tires. Logo: black "Days Gone" on black-framed gold panel, green ribbon with black border, black "Limited Edition" on cover, gold "International Model Show and Auction", frames and date on body, including "Made at Wroughton" on rear.

    1. As above.

`28032 SAINSBURY'S LAMB 1994
Maroon body, black chassis and cover, silver grille, maroon 6-bolt hubs, black tires. Logo: gold "J. Sainsbury" and frames on body, multicolored "For Whitsun, J. Sainsbury's Delicious Lamb" on cover.

28033 PEPSI-COLA 1994
Maroon body, black chassis, white top, silver grille, maroon 6-bolt hubs, black tires. Logo: black "drink", red "Pepsi-Cola" (also on front), blue figures on top, white lettering on rear body, maroon and white emblem on doors. Special Pepsi-Cola box.

    1. As above.

28034 DR. PEPPER 1994
Red body, black chassis, cream top, silver grille, red 6-bolt hubs, black tires. Logo: black-outlined white "Dr. Pepper" on maroon panel, figure with bottle, black lettering on top, "Drink Dr. Pepper" on front of cover and rear sides, emblem on doors. Special box.

    1. As above.

28035 PERSIL 1995
Dark green body, black chassis, cream top, silver grille, green 6-bolt hubs, black tires. Logo: multicolored design, black-outlined white "Persil", white lettering and frame.

    1. As above.

29 DODGE 4X4 1942 85 mm 1988
Cast body and chassis, plastic DG29 base, wheels and spare. A minor change improved the spare wheel mount.

29000 U.S. ARMY AMBULANCE 1988
Dark green body and chassis, black wheels. Logo: red-on-white cross and caduceus panels, white lettering and stars. No cross on back doors (specimens with it are not original).
   1. As above.
29001 R.A.F. AIRCREW 1989
Pale blue body and chassis, black wheels. Logo: red-white-blue roundels, white "Aircrew Transport" and other lettering.
   1. As above.
29002 TEXACO 1991
Red body, black chassis and wheels. Logo: black-outlined white "Texaco", white "Marfak specialized cleaner lubrication" and roof lettering, red-white-black Texaco emblem.
   1. As above.
29003 U.S. ARMY AMBULANCE 1991
Olive body and chassis, black wheels. Logo: white "Ambulance" and stars, red-on-white crosses, blue and white lettering.
   1. As above.
29004 BOMB DISPOSAL 1992
Olive body, red chassis, black wheels. Logo: red "Bomb Disposal" on white roof panel, white "Bomb Disposal", "BDS" and numbers, emblems.
   1. As above.
29005 U.S. MARINE CORPS 1992
Olive body and chassis, black wheels. Logo: red-on-white crosses, red-white-blue star emblem, blue "Ambulance: and emblem, white lettering. In set of three models.
   1. As above.
29006 POLICE EMERGENCY VAN 1993
Blue-black body and chassis, black wheels. Logo" white "Police Emergency Response Unit", emblem on doors, "Police" on rear and roof.
   1. As above.
29007 SAN JOSE FIRE DEPARTMENT 1994
Yellow-orange body, white chassis, black wheels and spare.Logo: red "San Jose Fire Dept." and "Airport", multicolored emblem.
   1. As above.
29008 CANADIAN ARMY AMBULANCE 1994
Khaki body and chassis, black wheels and spare. In set.
   1. As above.
29009 U S ARMY SIGNALS VAN 1994
Olive body, chassis and grille, black wheels and spare. Logo: white "US Army Signals" etc., star emblems. In D-Day set
   1. As above.
30 CHEVROLET 1939 PANEL VAN 92 mm 1989
Cast body and chassis, plastic interior, grille-lights-front bumper, rear bumper, base (first DG30, later DG30/36), with hubs and tires or black wheels.
30000 JOHN BULL TYRES 1989
Red body, black chassis, cream interior, silver grille and bumpers, black wheels or 6-bolt hubs and tires. Logo: black-outlined white "John Bull Tyres", black and white design and lettering.
   1. As above.
30001 FRY'S COCOA 1989
Dark brown body and chassis, cream interior, silver grille and bumpers, black wheels. Logo: cream "Fry's Cocoa", no. 49 and "Edinburgh Depot".
   1. As above.

30002 LIPTON'S TEA 1989
Green body, chassis, cream interior, silver grille and bumpers, black wheels. Logo: black-shadowed yellow "Lipton's Tea", yellow lettering.
   1. As above.
30003 LLEDO COLLECTORS CLUB 1989
Black body, silver chassis, white interior, silver grille and bumpers, red disc hubs, gray tires. Logo: white "Club Edition, Spring 1989", silver "The Lledo Collection".
   1. As above.
30004 HAMLEYS 1989
Magenta body and chassis, cream interior, silver grille and bumpers, black wheels. Logo: gold "Hamleys" design, "The Finest Toyshop in the World" and address, red-black-gold figure. Special box.
   1. As above.
30005 SPRATTS DOG FOOD 1990
Cream body and chassis, cream interior, silver grille and bumpers, brown disc hubs, black tires. Logo: brown "Spratts" design, "Spratts Bonio, Ovals and Dog Cakes".
   1. As above.
30006 BROOKE BOND TEA 1990
Red body and chassis, cream interior, silver grille and bumpers, red disc hubs, black tires. Logo: black-outlined white "Brooke Bond Tea".
   1. As above.
30007 HERSHEY'S MILK CHOCOLATE 1990
Brown body and chassis, cream interior, silver grille and bumpers, brown disc hubs, black tires. Logo: brown and cream design on blue panel, cream "Hershey PA" and "Hershey's Milk Chocolate Kisses" and designs. Special box.
   1. As above.
30008 ROYAL AIR FORCE 1990
Blue body, chassis, interior, grille, bumpers and disc hubs, black tires. Logo: red-on-white crosses, white "RAF" and other lettering, red-white-blue roundel. In set of three models.
   1. As above.
30009 NESTLE'S 1991
Maroon body and chassis, cream interior, gold grille and bumpers, maroon disc hubs, black tires. Logo: gold "Nestle's" and "Nestle's Sales Service".
   1. As above.
30010 GOLDEN STREAM TEA 1991
Gold body, black chassis, cream interior, silver grille and bumpers, black disc hubs and tires. Logo: black-outlined red "Golden Stream Tea", black lettering.
   1. As above.
30011 LIGHT ARMY AMBULANCE 1991
Olive body and chassis, black interior, olive grille, bumpers and disc hubs, black tires. Logo: red and white crosses in circles, white markings. Special box.
   1. As above.
30012 U.S. ARMY SURGICAL UNIT 1991
Olive body and chassis, black interior, olive grille, bumpers and disc hubs, black tires. Logo: white "Surgical Unit" on dark red stripe, white "Medical Unit US Army", red-on-white caduceus, light blue and white lettering, emblems. In set of three models.
   1. As above.
30013 U.S. NAVY AERONAUTICS 1991
Gray body and chassis, black interior, gray grille, bumpers and disc hubs, black tires. Logo: blue "U.S. Navy Bureau of Aeronautics, Hawaii", star on hood. In set of three models.
   1. As above.

30014 STEPHENS' INKS 1992
Light blue body, dark blue chassis, cream interior, silver grille and bumpers, dark blue disc hubs, black tires. Logo: blue "Stephens' Inks", white "Inks" on blue blot, red-white-blue design.
    1. As above.

30015 SHELL-BP PUMP SERVICE 1993
Dark yellow body and chassis, black interior, gold grille and bumpers, yellow disc hubs, black tires. Logo: black-outlined red "Shell "BP" Pump Service" and number 798.
    1. As above.

30016 RANSOMES LAWN MOWERS 1994
Green body and chassis, silver grille and bumpers, cream interior and disc hubs, black tires. Logo: Red "Ransomes", black "Quality Lawn Mowers" on cream panels, white "Lawn Mowers" etc.
    1. As above.

30017 INDIAN MOTORCYCLES 1994
Rust-red body and chassis, gold grille, white tires. Logo: black-outlined gold "Indian", gold "Motorcycles" etc., multicolored emblem. In set of three motorcycle vans.

30018 7-UP 1995
Yellow body, green chassis, silver grille, green disc hubs, black tires. Logo: black-outlined green "7-Up", bottle design, red and black discs. In special 7-Up box.
    1. As above.

31 HORSE DRAWN BREWER'S DRAY 98 mm 1988
Cast body, hitch and spoked wheels, plastic barrel load, seat with sign, driver and horses. Driver's hat, horses' manes, tails and collars painted. Hitch casting has either lugs on transverse bar ends or raised circle at base of tongue.

31000 WHITBREAD 1988
Brown body and hitch, tan driver and seat, dark tan or brown barrels, gray horses, gold wheels. Logo: gold "Whitbread" and frame, brown "London Stout" and line on sign.
    1. Tan barrels.
    2. Brown barrels?

31001 EVERARD 1988
Green body, hitch and seat, brown barrels and horses, tan driver, red wheels. Logo: black-outlined gold "Everards" and "Everards Brewery", black and gold design.
    1. As above.

31002 TAUNTON CIDER 1989
Red body, hitch and seat, brown barrels and horses, tan driver, gold wheels. Logo: white "Taunton Cider" and lines, black and gold "Dry Blackthorn" emblem.
    1. As above.
    2. Tampo print reversed (lettering behind rear wheels).

31003 GREENE KING 1989
Green body, hitch and seat, brown barrels and horses, tan driver, gold hubs. Logo: gold "Greene King fine ales", emblem and frame.
    1. As above.
    2. Tampo print reversed (lettering behind rear wheels).

31004 TRUMAN 1989
Red body, hitch and seat, brown barrels and horses, tan driver, gold wheels. Logo: black-shadowed gold "Truman", black and gold emblems, gold "Truman" and frame.
    1. As above.

31005 COURAGE ALES 1991
Blue body and hitch, black seat, brown barrels and horses, tan driver, gold wheels. Logo: gold "Courage Est. 1787", emblems and frame, gold "Courage Fine Ales".
    1. As above.

31006 WORTHINGTON 1992
Dark blue body and hitch, black seat and horses, brown barrels, tan driver, gold wheels. Logo: white "Worthington & Co. Limited, Burton on Trent", red and white emblems, gold frame.
    1. As above.

31007 BASS ALES 1993
Dark blue body and hitch, black seat, brown barrels and horses, tan driver, gold wheels. Logo: red-outlined white "Bass", white "Brewers since 1777", white and red triangle and frame, similar designs on rear and sign.
    1. As above.

31008 FULLER'S ALES 1994
Dark green body, hitch and seat, brown barrels, black horses, tan driver, gold wheels. Logo: multicolored Fuller's emblem, gold "Award winning ales" etc., similar logo on rear and sign.
    1. As above.

32 ROLLS-ROYCE 1907 SILVER GHOST 79 mm 1988
Cast open body, hood, chassis and windshield, plastic interior, steering wheel and grille, spoked hubs, tires, spare wheel. DG32 base at first, then DG32-45.

32000 SILVER 1988
Silver body, hood, chassis and windshield, maroon interior, gold grille, silver 12-spoke hubs, gray tires.
    1. As above.

32001 GREEN WITH COACH LINES 1989
Olive green body, chassis, hood and windshield, gold coach lines, tan interior, silver grille, green 20-spoke hubs, white tires.
    1. As above.

32002 METALLIC GREEN 1990
Metallic green body, hood, chassis, windshield and 20-spoke hubs, black interior, gold grille, gray tires.
    1. As above.

32003 LLEDO COLLECTORS CLUB 1990
Gold body, hood, chassis, windshield and 12-spoke hubs, maroon interior, gray tires. No logo. Special box.
    1. As above.

32004 DARK RED 1991
Dark red body, hood, chassis, windshield and 12-spoke hubs, gold grille, black interior and tires.
    1. As above.

32005 BLUE 1992
Blue body, hood, chassis and windshield, maroon interior, gold grille, blue 12-spoke hubs, black tires.
    1. As above.

32006 BRONZE 1992
Bronze body, hood and chassis, black seats and tires. No other data. German issue.

32007 GOLD 1992
Gold body, hood and chassis, black seats and tires. No other data. German issue.

32008 GOLD 1995
Gold body, chassis, grille, windshield and 12-spoke hubs, black seats and tires. No logo. In set of three Rolls-Royce models.

33 MODEL T FORD 1920 74 mm 1989
Cast body and chassis, plastic roof, interior, steering wheel, grille, windshield and DG6-8-33 base, spoked hubs, tires, two spares.

33000 BLACK 1989
Black body, chassis and roof, maroon interior, gold grille, windshield and 12-spoke hubs, black tires.
    1. As above.

33001 SINGER SEWING MACHINE CO. 1989
Dark green body, black chassis and roof, maroon or black interior, gold grille, windshield and 12-spoke hubs, black tires. Logo: white "Singer Sewing Machine Co. Ltd." and S emblem.
  1. Maroon interior.
  2. Black interior.
33002 (Not used)
33003 HERSHEY'S TAXI 1990
Brown body, cream chassis, roof and interior, gold grille and windshield, cream 20-spoke hubs, black tires. Logo: white "Chocolate Town U.S.A. Taxi", checker pattern and "Hershey PA". Special box.
  1. As above.
33004 GRAND HOTEL 1991
Dark red body, black chassis and roof, cream interior, gold grille, windshield and 12-spoke hubs, black tires. Logo: gold "Grand Hotel at the Opera--Paris" and lines.
  1. As above.
33005 HOTEL DE PARIS 1992
Yellow body, green chassis and roof, cream interior, gold grille and windshield, green 20-spoke hubs, white tires. Logo: multicolored "Hotel de Paris, Monte Carlo" emblem, brown address. In set of three models.
  1. As above.
33006 GOLD 1994
Gold body, chassis, grille, windshield and 12-spoke hubs, green roof and interior, black tires and spares. No logo.
  1. As above.
33007 PFAFF SEWING MACHINES 1993
Cream body, maroon chassis and roof, black seats, gold grille, windshield and 12-spoke hubs, white tires and spares. Logo: maroon-cream-black design, black "G. M. Pfaff A.G." etc.
  1. As above.
33008 EXCHANGE & MART 1993
Black body, chassis, roof, interior, grille, wheels and tires. No other data.
33009-10-11 HUIS TEN BOSCH 1994
Black chassis, cream seats, gold grille and 12-spoke hubs, black tires. Logo: gold emblem and "Huis Ten Bosch".
  009. Maroon body, black roof.
  010. Green body, black roof.
  011. Blue-black body, gray roof.
33012 HUIS TEN BOSCH 1994
As 33009 except black seats, white tires, maroon logo, and:
1 Cream body, maroon chassis and roof.
33022 HUIS TEN BOSCH 1995
Dark blue body, black chassis, cream roof and seats, gold grille, windshield and 12-spoke hubs, white tires. Logo same as 33009.
  1. As above.
34 DENNIS 1932 DELIVERY VAN 82 mm 1989
Cast body and chassis (same as DG10), plastic upper body-roof, interior, grille and base, hubs and tires or wheels. Usually DG10-12-34-35 base, sometimes DG10-12 type.
34000 HOVIS 1989
Tan body and chassis, light tan roof and interior, gold grille, black wheels. Logo: golden brown "Hovis" (also on header) and bread design, black "For Tea" and hand, brown door lettering.
  1. As above.
34001 SMEDLEY'S CANNED FRUITS 1989
Green body, chassis and roof, cream interior, gold grille, green 6-bolt hubs, black tires. Logo: gold

"Smedley's Canned Garden Fruits" and frame, multicolored design. Header: gold "Smedley's".
  1. As above.
34002 HAMLEYS 1989
Dark green body and roof, black chassis, dark green interior, gold grille, green 6-bolt hubs, black tires. Logo: red-black-gold "Hamleys" design, gold "The Finest Toyshop in the World" and address. Special box.
  1. As above.
34003 CHEDDAR CHEESE STRAWS 1990
Yellow body and roof, cream interior, silver grille, green 6-bolt hubs, black tires. Logo: green "Cheddar Cheese Straws", brown lettering, green and brown design. Header: green "Cheddar Cheese Straws".
  1. As above.
34004 R.A.F. RECRUITMENT 1990
Blue body and chassis and grille, blue interior and 6-bolt hubs, black tires. Logo: multicolored coat of arms, gold "Royal Air Force Mobile Recruitment Office", white lettering. Header: gold "Royal Air Force". In set of three models.
  1. As above.
34005 LLEDO COLLECTORS CLUB 1991
Green body, chassis and roof, cream interior, silver grille, green 6-bolt hubs, black tires. Logo: black "Days Gone" on gold panel, gold "Collectors Club", "Lledo Spring 1991", etc. Header: gold "Lledo". Special box.
  1. As above.
34006 WARTIME TRAVELLING LIBRARY 1992
Green body and roof, black chassis, cream interior, silver grille, green 6-bolt hubs, black tires. Logo: red-white-black Kent emblem, white "Kent County War Time Travelling Library" and other lettering. Header: white "Travelling Library".
  1. As above.
34007 HARRODS 1994
Olive body, black chassis, cream roof and interior, gold grille, green 6-bolt hubs, white tires. Logo: gold-outlined olive "Harrods", gold "special Bread delivery" and number; header: olive "Harrods". In set of four models.
35 DENNIS 1932 LIMOUSINE 82 mm 1989
Cast body and chassis, plastic upper body-roof, ladder, interior, grille and base, hubs, tires. Roof and ladder differ from #34, other components same, including base.
35000 EDINBURGH FIRE BRIGADE 1989
Red body, chassis and roof, tan interior and ladder, gold grille, red 6-bolt hubs, black tires. Logo: gold "Edinburgh Fire Brigade 1932" and "E.F.B." No header logo.
  1. As above.
35001 POST OFFICE TELEPHONES 1990
Green body, chassis and roof, cream interior and ladder, gold grille, green 6-bolt hubs, black tires. Logo: Gold crest, "GR", "Post Office Telephones" and other lettering. No header logo.
  1. As above.
35002 ROYAL AIR FORCE 1990
Blue body, roof and interior, black chassis and grille, blue 6-bolt hubs, black tires. Logo: white "RAF" and other lettering, red-white-blue roundel, yellow oval. Header: white triangle and "Workshop". In set of three models.
35003 HQ SIGNALS 1991
Olive and brown body and roof, olive chassis, black interior, olive grille and 6-bolt hubs, black ladder and tires. Logo: white "HQ Signals" (also on header) and number. Special box.
  1. As above.
35004 NATIONAL FIRE SERVICE 1991
Gray body, chassis and roof, black interior, gray grille and 6-bolt hubs, black ladder and tires. Logo: white

NFS emblem, white numbers on black panel, black emblem and numbers, white triangle emblem. In set of three models.

    1. As above.

35005 BBC OUTSIDE BROADCASTS 1992
Olive body, chassis and roof, cream interior, tan ladder, gold grille, olive 6-bolt hubs, black tires. Logo: gold "War Time Outside Broadcasts", BBC emblem, crest and other lettering.

    1. As above.

36 CHEVROLET 1938 PICK-UP TRUCK 90 mm 1989
Cast body and chassis, plastic interior, grille-lights-front bumper, rear bumper and base, hubs and tires or wheels. All components except body same as #30, including DG30-36 base. Several models have a load of oil drums.

36000 BUCK & HICKMAN 1989
Dark green body, black chassis, cream interior, silver grille and bumpers, black wheels. Logo: white "Buck & Hickman Ltd. London E.1."

    1. As above.

36001 CAKEBREAD, ROBEY & CO. 1990
Red body and chassis, white interior, silver grille and bumpers, red disc hubs, black tires. Logo: white "Cakebread, Robey & Co. Ltd." and other lettering (also on rear).

    1. As above.

36002 AVON TYRES 1991
Dark blue body and chassis, cream interior, gold grille and bumpers, dark green disc hubs, black tires. Logo: gold-outlined blue "Avon", gold "Tyres", other lettering and trim.

    1. As above.

36003 U.S. ARMY EXPLOSIVES 1991
Olive body and chassis, black interior, red bumpers, olive grille and 6-bolt hubs, black tires. Logo: white "Explosives" on red panels, white and blue lettering, emblems. In set of three models.

    1. As above.

36004 DUCKHAMS OILS 1992
Gray body, black chassis, black interior, green barrels, silver grille and bumpers, pale gray disc hubs, black tires. Logo: white "Duckhams Oils: etc. (also on barrels), multicolored emblems.

    1. Light gray body.
    2. Medium gray body.

36005 REDEX FUEL ADDITIVES 1993
Red body, black chassis and interior, gray barrels, silver grille and bumpers, red disc hubs, black tires. Logo: red-white-black Redex emblem (also on rear), black-outlined white lettering, red X and "Redex" on barrel tops.

    1. As above.

36006 GODE 1993
Dark blue body and chassis, cream seats, bold radiator, dark blue hubs, black tires. German issue. No other data.

36007 PENNZOIL 1993
Yellow body, black chassis, light brown barrels, silver grille and bumpers, yellow disc hubs, black tires. Logo: red-yellow-black Pennzoil can, black "Pennzoil Place, Houston, Texas" etc., Pennzoil emblem on rear.

    1. As above.

36008 U. S. ARMY TRUCK 1994
Olive body, chassis, bumpers, grille and disc hubs, black and yellow barrels, black tires. Logo: white star emblems and numbers. In set of three D-Day models.

    1. As above.

36009 DR. PEPPER 1994
Green body, black chassis, silver grille and bumpers, green disc hubs, black tires. Logo: black-outlined "Dr. Pepper" on doors and rear, white "Take Home A Carton" and design on sides. Special box.

    1. As above.

37 MODEL A FORD 1930 PANEL VAN 78 mm 1990
Cast body and chassis, plastic upper body-roof, interior, grille and base, hubs, tires, spare. Castings based on #9; DG7-9-13-14 base, soon replaced by DG7-9-13-14-37.

37000 CANADIAN CLUB 1990
Tan body and roof, black chassis, tan interior, gold grille and 12-spoke hubs, black tires. Logo: cream "Canadian Club Whisky" and frames. Header: cream "Canadian Club".

    1. As above.

37001 MR. THERM 1990
Green body, chassis and roof, cream interior, silver grille, green disc hubs, black tires. Logo: gold "The Gas Light & Coke Co." (also on header), "Mr. Therm burns to serve you", number and frame, gold and white figure.

    1. As above.

37002 CHIEF OF POLICE 1991
Black body, chassis, roof and interior, silver grille, black 20-spoke hubs and tires. Logo: white "Police" (also on header), gold and blue "Chief of Police. Ardmore I.T." badge.

37003 DAYS GONE COLLECTORS CLUB 1992
Cream body and roof, black chassis and interior, gold grille and 12-spoke hubs, black tires. Logo: black and gold "Days Gone" emblem on upper body, black "Collectors Club" and "1992" on body. Header: black "Autumn". Unnumbered DG box.

    1. As above.

38 ROLLS-ROYCE 1925 SILVER GHOST SALOON 1989
Cast body and chassis (same as #25), plastic roof, seats, base, grille, hubs and tires. DG18/19/22/24/25 base at first, later 18-19-22-24-25-38.

38000 GREEN WITH COACH LINES 1989
Green body and chassis, tan roof and seats, gold grille, green disc hubs, white tires, two spares, gold coach lines.

39 MACK 1934 OPEN TRUCK 97 mm 1989
Cast body and chassis (same as #28), plastic load, grille and base, hubs and tires or wheels, steering wheel added later. DG27/28/ base at first, then DG27/28/39/40, then DG27 28 39 40 42.

39000 FERROCRETE CEMENT 1990
Yellow body, blue chassis, light gray load, silver grille, yellow 6-bolt hubs, black tires. Logo: blue "use Ferrocrete and save time", "Cement Marketing Company" and lines, blue and white Portland Cement emblem.

    1. As above.

39001 KETTON CEMENT 1991
Yellow body, black chassis, gray load, silver grille, cream 6-bolt hubs, black tires. Logo: black "Ketton Cement", other lettering and emblems.

39002 GAS LIGHT & COKE CO. 1989
Black body and chassis, gray load, silver grille, black wheels. Logo: white "The Gas Light & Coke Co.", "Coke for central heating" and lines.

    1. As above.

39003 BEST PORTLAND CEMENT 1992
Yellow body, blue chassis, gray load, silver grille, yellow 6-bolt hubs, black tires. Logo: blue "Best Portland Cement", other lettering and emblem (emblems also on sacks).
   1. As above.

39004 ARMY SANDBAG TRUCK 1992
Olive body, chassis and grille, brown load, olive 6-bolt hubs, black tires and camouflage paint. Logo: white numbers, various emblems. Special box.
   1. As above.

40 MACK 1934 CRANE TRUCK 100 mm 1990
Cast body, chassis (same as #27) and boom, plastic rear bed, hook, base, seat, hubs and tires, steering wheel added later. Same base lettering types as #39.

40000 TARMAC 1990
Black body, red chassis, white boom, silver grille, red 6-bolt hubs, black tires and hook. Logo: gold "Tarmac".
   1. As above.

40001 RICHARD COSTAIN 1991
Light gray body and boom, black chassis, rear bed and hook, silver grille, black 6-bolt hubs and tires. Logo: white "Transport Service Crane" and "Richard Costain Limited" on dark blue panels with white frames.
   1. As above.

40002 U.S. NAVY AMMUNITION DEPOT 1991
Light gray body, chassis, boom, grille and 6-bolt hubs, black tires and hook. Logo: dark blue "U.S. Navy" and other lettering, red-white-blue star. In set of three Pearl Harbor models.
   1. As above.

40003 U.S. NAVY 1992
Olive body, chassis and boom, dark olive grille and rear bed, olive 6-bolt hubs, black tires and hook. Logo: white "U.S. Navy" and other lettering, red-white-blue emblems. In set of three Guadalcanal models.
   1. As above.

40004 ROYAL AIR FORCE 1993
Dull blue body, chassis, grille and 6-bolt hubs, yellow rear bed, black crane and tires. Logo: white "RAF" and numbers, red-white-blue roundel. In set of three Dambusters models.
   1. As above.

41 KARRIER 1928 E6 TROLLEY BUS 93 mm 1990
Cast body, chassis and roof, plastic windows, interior, poles, base, hubs and tires. DG41 base at first, later DG41-49. Slight changes to front vents (filled in) and roof-to-base rivet.

41000 ROBIN STARCH 1990
Maroon body, chassis and roof, cream windows and interior, maroon hubs, black tires and poles. Upper logo: white "Robin the new Starch" and multicolored figures on red panel. Lower: gold "County Borough of Doncaster", arms and frame, gold arms.

41001 MARKS & SPENCER 1990
Dark green body, chassis and roof, cream windows and interior, dark green hubs, black tires and poles. Upper logo: black and gold "Marks & Spencer Ltd." and emblems, black lettering on maroon panel. Lower: gold "City of Nottingham", other lettering, emblem and frame. Special box.
   1. As above.

41002 HAMLEYS 1990
Red body and roof, cream windows and interior, red hubs, black tires and poles. Upper logo: black-red-white "Hamleys, the finest toyshop in the world", gold and black airplanes. Lower: black-outlined gold "London Transport", gold frames. Special box.
   1. As above.

41003 BISTO 1991
Red body and roof, cream windows and interior, red hubs, black tires and poles. Upper logo: multicolored "Ah! Bisto for all meat dishes" on tan panel. Lower: black-outlined gold "London Transport" and underline, gold frames.
   1. As above.

41004 BOVRIL 1991
Red body and roof, cream windows and interior, red hubs, black tires and poles. Upper logo: yellow "Bovril prevents that sinking feeling" and red-white-blue design on blue panel. Lower: black-outlined gold "London Transport", gold lettering and lines.
   1. As above.

41005 NORTH YORKSHIRE MOORS RAILWAY 1991
Red body and roof, white windows and interior, red hubs, black tires and poles. Upper logo: black "Visit the North Yorkshire Moors Railway" and multicolored design on gray panel. Lower: gold "Scarborough and District", emblem and frame. White "Pickering" on black boards. In set of two models.

41006 SAXA SALT 1992
Red body and roof, cream windows and interior, red hubs, black tires and poles. Upper logo: black-outlined red "Saxa Salt", black "the best packet", on yellow panel. Lower: black-outlined gold "London Transport", gold underline, white lettering. White "12 South Croydon" on black front board.
   1. As above.

41007 SCHWEPPES LIME JUICE 1992
Green body and chassis, cream windows and interior, green hubs, black tires and poles. Upper logo: gold-outlined yellow "Schweppes", white "Lime Juice", on light green panel, multicolored emblems, white squares. Lower: gold "City of Nottingham", other lettering, crest and frames.
   1. As above.

41008 HAMLEYS 1992
Red body and roof, cream windows and interior, red hubs, black tires and poles. Upper logo: red "Hamleys", black "the finest toyshop in the world" and address on black-framed gold panels, red and black figures, on white panel. Lower: black-outlined gold "London Transport", white lettering. In set of four models.
   1. As above.

41009 SUN-MAID RAISINS 1992
Red body and roof, cream windows and interior, red hubs, black tires and poles. Upper logo: brown "Sun-Maid Raisins and other lettering, multicolored design, on white panel. Lower: black-outlined "General" and underline, white lettering. White "11A Strand Aldwych" on black front board.
   1. As above.

41010 CROSSE & BLACKWELL 1994
Yellow body, brown chassis and hubs, cream roof, windows and interior, black tires and poles. Upper logo: yellow and 2-tone blue "Crosse & Blackwell" etc., lower: gold "Newcastle Corporation Transport" on brown stripe. Light blue "31, "Gosport" on dark blue boards.

41011 ROWNTREE PASTILLES 1994
Red body and roof, black chassis, cream windows and interior, red hubs, black tires and poles. Upper logo: yellow "Rowntree" etc., multicolored design on green panel; lower: black-outlined gold "London Transport" and underline. #604, "Wimbledon" etc. on boards.
   1. As above.

41012 HUIS TEN BOSCH 1994
Red body and roof, black chassis, cream windows and interior, red hubs, black tires and poles. Upper logo: red "Huis Ten Bosch" and black emblem on tan panel. Lower: gold "Huis Ten Bosch", emblem and frame.
   1. As above.

42   MACK TANK TRUCK   90 mm   1990

Cast body and chassis (same as #27), plastic tank, grille, base, hubs and tires. Steering wheel added later. DG27/28/39/40 base at first, then DG27 28 39 40 42.

42000   NATIONAL BENZOLE   1990

Yellow body and tank, black chassis, silver grille, yellow 6-bolt hubs, black tires. Logo: blue "National Benzole Mixture" (also on rear) and frame.

1. As above.

42001   ROYAL AIR FORCE   1990

Blue body, chassis, tank, grille and 6-bolt hubs, black tires. Logo: white "RAF", other lettering, red-on-white warning sign, red-white-blue roundel, yellow oval. In set of three models.

1. As above.

42002   REGENT PETROLEUM   1991

Blue body, black chassis, red tank, silver grille, red 6-bolt hubs, black tires. Logo: yellow "Regent" and stripe, cream "Petroleum Mixture", blue "Highly Inflammable" on cream stripe.

1. As above.

42003   U.S. ARMY AIR CORPS   1991

Olive body, chassis, tank, grille and 6-bolt hubs, black tires. Logo: white "Air Corps U S Army", white and blue lettering, red-white-blue star, other emblems. In set of three models.

1. As above.

42004   U.S. NAVAL AIR STATION HAWAII   1991

Gray body, chassis, tank, grille and 6-bolt hubs, black tires. Logo: blue "U.S. Navy", "U.S. Naval Air Station Hawaii", star emblem. In set of three Pearl Harbor models.

1. As above.

42005   ARMY WATER TANKER   1992

Tan body and chassis, light tan tank, grille and 6-bolt hubs, black tires. Logo: red-white-blue roundels, emblems, black numbers. In set of three El Alamein models.

1. As above.

42006   SHELL   1992

Red body and tank, black chassis, silver grille, red 6-bolt hubs, black tires. Logo: black-shadowed yellow "Shell", yellow "Fuel Oil", etc.

1. As above.

42007   PENNZOIL   1993

Dark yellow body, black chassis, yellow tank, gold grille, red 6-bolt hubs, black tires. Logo: black "Pennzoil", red Liberty Bell on tank, red-white-black design and black "Safe Lubrication" on sides, black oval emblem on rear.

1. As above.

42008   TEXACO   1994

Red body and tank, black chassis, silver grille, red 6-bolt hubs, black tires. Logo: blue-outlined white "Texaco", red-white-blue emblems, white lettering (latter two also on rear).

1. No rear logo.
2. Rear logo.

43   MORRIS 1931 VAN   91 mm   1990

Cast body, chassis and roof, plastic seat, grille, DG43 base, hubs and tires.

43000   WEETABIX   1990

Yellow body, chassis and roof, gold grille, yellow disc hubs, black tires. Logo: black-outlined red "Weetabix", black lettering.

1. As above.

43001   CHIVERS   1990

Cream body and roof, green chassis, gold grille, green disc hubs, black tires. Logo: two-tone blue "Chivers & Sons Ltd.", green panel with gold lettering.

1. As above.

43002   HAMLEYS   1990

Dark green body and roof, black chassis, gold grille, dark green disc hubs, black tires. Logo: gold "Hamleys", red-gold-green design, red "the finest toyshop in the world", good address. Special box.

1. As above.

43003   LLEDO COLLECTORS CLUB   1991

Magenta body, black chassis and roof, gold grille and 12-spoke hubs, white tires. Logo: black "Days Gone" and frame on gold panel, gold "Collectors Club", "Lledo", "Winter 1990" and frames. Special box.

1. As above.

43004   AC SPARK PLUGS   1991

Dark yellow body, dark blue chassis and roof, gold grille, yellow disc hubs, black tires. Logo: black-outlined red "AC" with yellow lines, red "Oil filters" and "Plugs", black and white spark plug design.

1. As above.

43005   LNER EXPRESS PARCELS   1991

Dark red body, black chassis and roof, silver grille, red disc hubs, black tires. Logo: white "LNER Express Parcels Services" and "LNER", multicolored poster. In set of three models.

1. As above.

43006   METROPOLITAN RAILWAY   1991

Cream body and roof, black chassis, gold grille, maroon 6-bolt hubs, black tires. Logo: maroon-shadowed gold "Metropolitan Railway", black-shadowed gold "Express Parcels Service", gold lines, emblem and white lettering on maroon panel, "Met. Rwy." In set of three models.

1. As above.

43007   BIRD'S CUSTARD   1991

Dark blue body, black chassis, cream roof, gold grille, blue-black disc hubs, black tires. Logo: white "Bird's", white-outlined blue "Custard" on yellow panel, white lettering and frames, brown and yellow design.

1. As above.

43008   ARMY AMBULANCE   1991

Tan body, chassis, roof, grille and disc hubs, black tires. Logo: white panels with red crosses, black numbers, red and white emblems. Special box.

1. As above.

43009   LLEDO TOY FAIRS   1991

Light yellow body and roof, green chassis, gold grille, green disc hubs, black tires. Logo: black "Days Gone" and frame on gold panel, green ribbon and "1991 Toy Fair Model".

1. As above (no door lettering).
2. Green list of sites on door.

43010   CORNWALL HOME GUARD   1991

Olive and brown body and roof, olive chassis, grille and disc hubs, black tires. Logo: white "12th BN Home Guard", "HQ COY", red and black emblem. In boxed set of three models.

1. As above.

43011   HAMLEYS   1992

Yellow body, dark green chassis and roof, gold grille, dark green disc hubs, black tires. Logo: gray "Hamleys", white and red lettering, red white black figures. Special box.

1. As above.

43012   AMBROSIA DEVON CREAM   1992

Green body and roof, black chassis, gold grille, green disc hubs, black tires. Logo: white "Lifton & Lapford Dairies, Devon" and lines, multicolored "Ambrosia Devon Cream" design.

43013   ARNOTTS BISCUITS   1992

Red body, chassis and roof, gold grille, red disc hubs, black tires. Logo: black-outlined gold "Arnott's Biscuits" and "Arnott's famous biscuits", gold panel with black-outlined red "Monte Carlo", multicolored

designs, gold lettering.
1. As above.

43014 GWR EXPRESS CARTAGE 1992
Brown body, black chassis, cream roof and side panels, silver grille, brown disc hubs, black tires. Logo: white-framed "London Pride" picture, brown "Express Cartage Services", brown and yellow GWR emblems, white number. In set of three models.
1. Posters to front on both sides.
2. Posters at left on both sides.

43015 HARRODS 1992
Olive body, black chassis, cream roof, gold grille, green disc hubs, black tires. Logo: gold "Harrods Ltd, black-shadowed gold "Brompton Road, London". In set of four models.
1. As above.

43016 SUNLICHT SEIFE 1992
Dark blue body and roof, black chassis, gold grille, dark blue disc hubs, black tires. Logo: white "Sunlicht" and frame, black "Seife" on yellow arc, black "schont die Wasche" on white panel, package design on door.
1. As above.

43017 TATE SUGAR 1993
Blue-black body, black chassis, cream roof and seat, gold grille, dark blue disc hubs, black tires. Logo: cream "British refined Tate Sugars", other lettering and diamond, multicolored designs.
1. As above.

43018 BRAND'S CALF'S FOOT JELLY 1994
Dark maroon body, black chassis, cream roof, gold grille, maroon disc hubs, black tires. Logo: white "Brand's Calf's Foot Jelly and Turtle Soup" etc., bottle designs on white panels.
1. As above.

43019 RUPERT BEAR 1994
Red body, black chassis, cream roof, gold grille and 12-spoke hubs, black tires. Logo: multicolored driving scene and emblem. Special Rupert box.
1. As above.

43020 BRASSO 1994
Light orange body, dark blue chassis and roof, gold grille, dark blue hubs, black tires. Logo: black-outlined red "Brasso" and "Polish", red "Metal", multicolored can design, black lettering.
1. As above.

43021 RUPERT BEAR 1995
Yellow body, green chassis and roof, gold grille and 12-spoke hubs, black tires. Logo: multicolored scene with mailman, The rupert Collection emblem. In set of three Rupert Bear models.
1. As above.

44 SCAMMELL 1937 SIX-WHEELER 106 mm 1990
Cast body and chassis, plastic roof, seat, grille, DG44 base, hubs and tires.

44000 BISTO 1990
Brown body, black chassis, cream roof, gold grille, brown hubs, black tires. Logo: blue "Bisto for all meat dishes" and design on multicolored panel.
1. As above.

44001 TOBLERONE 1990
Tan body, green chassis and roof, gold grille, green hubs, black tires. Logo: red "Chocolat Tobler", "Toblerone" and other lettering, multicolored design, black lettering.
1. As above.

44002 MARMITE 1991
Green body and roof, black chassis, gold grille, green 6-bolt hubs, black tires. Logo: cream-framed blue panel with dark blue-shadowed yellow "Marmite", cream "The Great Yeast Food", other lettering, multicolored emblem and design.
1. As above.

44003 FOX'S GLACIER MINTS 1991
Navy blue body, black chassis, light gray roof, silver grille, navy blue 6-bolt hubs, black tires. Logo: three-panel navy blue-light blue-white designs with "Fox's Glacier Mints" emblem in center, white lettering.
1. As above.

44004 NORTH YORKSHIRE MOORS RAILWAY 1991
Dark blue body, black chassis, gray roof, silver grille, dark blue 6-bolt hubs, black tires. Logo: white "North Yorkshire Moors Railway" and "Express Parcels", poster. In set of two models.
1. As above.

44005 ROWNTREES PASTILLES 1992
Light gray body, dark blue chassis and roof, silver grille, black wheels. Logo: blue-yellow-white design with white "Rowntrees Pastilles", white "Rowntrees" and other lettering.
1. As above.

44006 McMULLEN & SONS ALES 1992
Brown body and roof, black chassis, silver grille, green hubs, black tires. Logo: brown "McMullen & Sons Ltd., the Hertford Brewery" on cream panel, gold "Brilliant AK Ales", trim and lettering.
1. As above.

44007 LLEDO COLLECTORS CLUB 1992
Turquoise body, black chassis and roof, gold grille, black wheels. Logo: dark blue "the collectors club", black "Days Gone" on black-framed gold panel, green ribbon, gold "Spring 1992".
1. As above.

44008 BRITISH ARMY TRUCK 1992
Tan body and chassis, light tan roof, grille and hubs, black tires. Logo: red-white-blue roundel, black details and numbers, emblems. In set of three El Alamein models.
1. As above.

44009 BERLINER KINDL 1993
Gray body, navy blue chassis and roof, silver grille, navy blue hubs, black tires. No other data. German issue.

44010 TETLEY FINE ALES 1993
Blue-black body, black chassis, dark blue roof, silver grille, dark blue hubs, black tires. Logo: gold "Tetley Fine Ales" etc., gold firm name on rear, multicolored design on white oval with gold and black frame, emblem and gold lettering on doors.
1. As above.

44011 HEINZ FOOD PRODUCTS 1994
Cream body, green chassis and roof, silver grille, red hubs, black tires. Logo: multicolored Heinz emblem, black-outlined red "Pickles, Euchred Figs, Onions, Etc." etc.
1. As above.

44012 CARNATION FARM PRODUCTS 1994
White body, chassis and hubs, red top, silver grille, black tires. Logo: white "Carnation farm products" on red panel, black lettering, multicolored design.
1. As above.

44013 ARMY TRUCK 1994
Olive body, chassis, roof, grille and hubs, black tires. Logo: white stars, blue and white coat of arms. In D-Day set.
1. As above.

44014 KRONENBOURG 1995
Red body, blue chassis, white roof, silver grille, red hubs, black tires. Logo: white "Kronenbourg Biere d'Alsace", multicolored emblem.
1. As above.

44015 RUPERT BEAR 1995
Blue body, white chassis and roof, silver grille, blue hubs, black tires. Logo: multicolored scene with

sailboats, The Rupert Collection emblem. Special Rupert box.
   1. As above.

44016 JOHN SMITH'S ALE 1995
Green body and chassis, cream roof, silver grille, red hubs, black tires. Logo: white "Celebrate with" etc., yellow "John Smith's Victory Ale", red and white magnets and letters. In set of three VE-Day models.
   1. As above.

45 ROLLS-ROYCE 1908 SILVER GHOST COUPE 78 mm 1991
Open two-seater with cast body parts and chassis, plastic interior, grille, DG32 base, later DG32-45, spoked hubs, tires, spare wheel.

45000 METALLIC GREEN 1992
Metallic green body and chassis, black interior, gold grille, metallic green 12-spoke hubs, gray tires. No logo.
   1. As above.

45001 MAROON 1991
Maroon body and chassis, black interior, gold grille, maroon 12-spoke hubs, black tires. No logo.
   1. As above.

45002 CREAM 1993
Cream body and chassis, black interior, gold grille, cream 12-spoke hubs, black tires. No logo.
   1. As above.

45003 GOLD 1994
Gold body and chassis, green interior, gold grille and 12-spoke hubs, gray tires. No logo. Days Gone Collector box.
   1. As above.

46 BENTLEY 1930 4.5 LITER BLOWER 83 mm 1990
Cast body and chassis, plastic interior, grille, lights and windshield, spoked hubs, tires, spare wheel.

46000 GREEN (TV Times) 1990
Green body and chassis, cream interior, silver grille and windshield, green 20-spoke hubs, black tires. Logo: Union Jack and number disc. Special TV Times box.
   1. As above.

46001 DARK BLUE #1 1991
Dark blue body and chassis, black interior, silver grille and windshield, dark blue 20-spoke hubs, black tires. Logo: Union Jack, black #1 in white disc.
   1. As above.

46002 LLEDO COLLECTORS CLUB 1991
Gold body, chassis, grille and windshield, black interior, gold 20-spoke hubs, black tires. No logo. Special box.
   1. As above.

46003 GREEN #2 1992
Green body and chassis, cream interior, silver grille and windshield, green 20-spoke hubs, black tires. Logo: Union Jack, black #2 on white disc.
   1. As above.

46004 CREAM #18 1992
Cream body and chassis, silver grille and windshield, brown interior and 20-spoke hubs, black tires. Logo: Union Jack, white #18 in black disc.
   1. As above.

46005 MAROON #10 1993
Maroon body and chassis, black interior, silver grille and windshield, black 20-spoke hubs and tires. Logo: Union Jack, black #10 on white disc.
   1. As above.

46006 BLACK #7 1994
Black body, chassis and interior, silver grille, black 20-spoke hubs and tires. Logo: Union Jack, black #7 on white disc.
   1. As above.

46007 DARK GREEN 1994
Dark green body and chassis, cream interior, silver grille and windshield, black hubs and tires.
   1. As above.

47 AUSTIN 1933 TAXI 78 mm 1991
Cast body and chassis, plastic roof with sign, interior, grille, bumpers and base, spoked hubs, tires, spare wheel.

47000 BLUE AND BLACK 1991
Dark blue body, black chassis and roof, red interior, silver grille, blue 12-spoke hubs, black tires, white "Taxi" on sign.
   1. As above.

47001 BLACK 1992
Black body, chassis and roof, red interior, silver grille, black-gold 12-spoke hubs, black tires, white "Taxi" on sign.
   1. As above.

47002 BLUE HAMLEYS 1992
Blue body, black chassis and roof, red interior, silver grille, black 12-spoke hubs and tires. Logo: gold "Hamleys" and frame, design and lettering, white "Taxi" on sign. In set of two models.
   1. As above.

47003 MAROON HAMLEYS 1992
Maroon body, black chassis and roof, silver grille, black interior, 12-spoke hubs and tires. Logo: gold "Hamleys" and frame, figure, white "Taxi" on sign. In set of four models.
   1. As above.

47004 MAROON 1993
Maroon body, black chassis and roof, silver grille, black interior, 12-spoke hubs and tires, white "Taxi" on sign.
   1. As above.

48 CHEVROLET 1939 CAR 92 mm 1991
Cast body and chassis (latter same as #30-36), plastic interior, grille-front-bumper-headlights, rear bumper, DG30-36 base, hubs and tires, or wheels.

48000 CREAM & GREEN 1991
Cream body, green chassis, black interior, silver grille and bumpers, cream disc hubs, black tires. No logo.
   1. As above.

48001 DAYS GONE CLUB 1991
Gold body, black chassis, silver grille and bumpers, black interior and wheels. Logo: Days Gone emblem, black "Collectors Club" and "Lledo Autumn 1991".
   1. As above.

48002 CREAM AND MAROON 1992
Cream body, maroon chassis, cream interior, gold grille and bumpers, maroon disc hubs, black tires. No logo.
   1. As above.

48003 ARMY STAFF CAR 1992
Tan body, light tan grille, bumpers and disc hubs, black interior and tires. Logo: red-white-blue roundel, black numbers and lettering, various emblems. In set of three El Alamein models.
   1. As above.

48004 YELLOW CAB 1993
Yellow body and chassis, silver grille and bumpers, yellow disc hubs, black tires. Logo: red "Yellow Cabs"

on roof, red emblem and lettering on rear, black-shadowed gray "Yellow Cabs", red emblem and lettering on sides, Alberta license plates.

1. As above.

48005 RAF STAFF CAR 1993
Dull blue body, chassis, grille and disc hubs, black tires. Logo: white "RAF" and numbers, red-white-blue roundel. In set of three Dambusters models.

1. As above.

48006 HIGHWAY PATROL 1994
Black body and chassis, silver bumpers and grille, black disc hubs and tires. Logo: black "Highway Patrol", black and yellow badge on white panels, white "Police" on roof.

1. As above.

48007 U S ARMY STAFF CAR 1994
Olive body, chassis, grille and disc hubs, black tires. Logo: white lettering and star emblems, red-white-blue "A" emblem, other emblems. In set of three D-Day models.

1. As above.

48008 GHQ STAFF CAR 1994
Olive body, chassis, grille and hubs, black tires. Logo: Shield emblem on doors, front fender and trunk, white star and numbers on hood and trunk. In set of three models.

1. As above.

48009 BOOMERANG TAXIS 1995
Maroon body and chassis, silver grille and lights, maroon disc hubs, white tires. Logo: white "Boomerang Taxi" design (also on rear), "Taxi" on roof.

1. As above.

49 AEC RENOWN 1931 DOUBLE DECK BUS 92 mm 1991
Cast body, chassis and roof, plastic windows, interior, grille, DG41 base, almost immediately changed to DG41-49, hubs and tires. Some parts common to #41. Lugs added to steady grille, roof-to-base rivet modified.

49000 CADBURY'S BOURN-VITA 1991
Red body, black chassis, silver roof and grille, cream windows and interior, red hubs, black tires. Upper logo: brown "Cadbury's Bourn-Vita" on tan panel. Lower: black-bordered gold "General" and underline, white lettering. Front board: Shepherds Bush.

1. As above.

49001 ROSE'S LIME JUICE 1991
Red body and roof, black chassis, cream windows and interior, silver grille, red hubs, black tires. Upper logo: black-outlined gold "Rose's Lime Juice Cordial" and multicolored design on white panel, white "Liverpool St. 9" on black (latter also on front and back). Lower: black-shadowed gold "London Transport" and underline, white lettering.

1. As above.

49002 HAMLEYS 1992
Red body, red or black chassis, cream windows and interior, silver roof and grille, red hubs, black tires. Upper logo: red "Hamleys", red and white ribbon, black "the finest toyshop in the world", figure. Lower: black-outlined gold "General", white lettering. White "184A London Bridge Station" on boards. Special Hamleys box.

1. Black chassis.
2. Red chassis.

49003 MARTINI 1992
Red body, black chassis, cream windows and interior, silver roof and grille, red hubs, black tires. Upper logo: multicolored panel with Heinz, Martini and Hudson's Soap advertisements. Lower: gold "General". White "108 Crystal Palace" on front board.

1. As above.

49004 JANTZEN SWIMWEAR 1992
Red body, black chassis, cream windows and interior, silver roof and grille, red hubs, black tires. Upper logo: multicolored "Swim in a Jantzen swimming suit" panel. Lower: black-outlined gold "General", white lettering. White "18 London Bdg Stn" on front board.

1. As above.

49005 HAMLEYS 1992
Red body and roof, black chassis, cream windows and interior, silver grille, red hubs, black tires. Upper logo: gold and black "Hamleys" emblem, figures, red "The Finest Toy Shop in the World" on white panel. Lower: black-shadowed gold "London Transport", white lettering. White "West Hampstead" on front board. In set of two models.

1. As above.

49006 LLEDO COLLECTORS CLUB 1992
Red body, black chassis, cream windows and interior, silver roof and grille, red hubs, black tires. Upper logo: gold and black "Days Gone" emblems and black "Collectors Club" on white panel. Lower: black-outlined gold "Summer 1992" and line, gold Lledo emblem, white lettering. White "Enfield" on front board.

1. As above.

49007 HARRODS 1992
Red body and roof, black chassis, cream windows and interior, silver grille, red hubs, black tires. Upper logo: green "Harrods" and red "Sale" on cream panels, gold address on green panel, black frame. Lower: black-outlined gold "London Transport" and underline, white lettering. In set of four models.

1. As above.

49008 QANTAS 1992
Red body and roof, black chassis, cream windows and interior, silver grille, red hubs, black tires. Upper logo: red emblem, black "The Spirit of Australia" on whitish panel; lower: gold emblem, "Qantas" and lines. In set of two models.

1. As above.

49009 PEPSI-COLA 1993
Red body and roof, black chassis, silver roof, cream windows and interior, silver grille, red hubs, black tires. Upper logo: red-outlined blue "Drink Delicious" on yellow panel, white "Pepsi-Cola" on blue panel, bottle designs, tan frame. Lower: black-outlined gold "General", white lettering. White "88A Acton Green" on front board. Special Pepsi-Cola box.

1. As above.

49010 HAMLEYS 1993
Red body and roof, black chassis, cream windows and interior, gold grille, red hubs, black tires. Upper logo: cream-outlined red "The finest toyshop in the world", red and black figures, on white-framed gray panel. Lower: gold "London Transport", white lettering. White "Hamleys, Regent St." on front board. Special Hamleys box.

1. As above.

49011 LITTLEWOODS 1993
Green body and roof, black chassis, cream windows and interior, silver grille, green hubs, black tires. Upper logo: yellow-brown-white "Millions more prefer Littlewoods", white "5c Penny Lane" on black. Lower: gold arms, white "Liverpool Tramways" etc.

1. As above.

49012 ST. MICHAEL TEA 1993
Green body and roof, black chassis, cream windows, silver grille, green hubs, black tires. Upper logo: white-framed red panel with black-on-white "St. Michael" and white "Fine Quality Tea", etc. Lower: black-outlined yellow "Green Line". White "Hitchin" on black front board. In set of four Marks & Spencer models.

1. As above.

49013 HEINZ SPAGHETTI 1994
Blue body, black chassis, cream roof and windows, silver grille, blue hubs, black tires. Upper logo: black-shadowed white "Heinz Spaghetti", green "57" etc on gold-edged yellow panel. Lower: gold "Birmingham City Transport", emblem and frame. White "9 Quinton" on front board.
   1. As above.

49014 SWAN VESTAS 1994
Red body, black chassis and roof, cream windows, black grille, red hubs, black tires. Upper logo: red-yellow-green "Swan Vestas" etc. on light blue panel. Lower: black-outlined gold "London Transport", white lettering. White "38 Victoria" on boards.
   1. As above.

49015 HUIS TEN BOSCH 1994
Cream body, chassis, roof, windows and interior, gold grille, red hubs, black tires. Upper logo: gold "Huis Ten Bosch" and emblem on maroon panel. Lower: black "Huis Ten Bosch" and emblem, gold frame.
   1. As above.

49016 SHREDDED WHEAT 1995
Red body, black chassis, silver roof, cream windows, silver grille, red hubs, black tires. Upper logo: yellow "Shredded Wheat", white lettering etc. on blue panel; lower: black-outlined gold "London Transport", white lettering. White "53 Borstall Wood" on front board.
   1. As above.

49017 MARS 1995
Red body, black chassis and roof, cream windows, black grille, red hubs, black tires. Upper logo: red "Victory will be sweeter with", red and white "Mars", brown design on blue panel; lower: black-outlined gold "London Transport", white lettering. White "16 Victoria Stn." on front board.
   1. As above.

49018 SHAMROCK HERITAGE 1995
Green body and roof, black chassis, cream windows, silver grille, green hubs, black tires. Upper logo: orange-bordered green "Cead Mile Failte", designs; lower: white emblem, gold lettering. Special Shamrock Heritage Collection box.
   1. As above.

50 MORRIS 1926 BULL NOSE VAN 80 mm 1992
Cast body and chassis, plastic roof, interior, grille, windshield, DG50 base, hubs and tires.

50000 LYONS' TEA 1992
Dark blue body and chassis, white roof and seat, gold grille, dark blue disc hubs, black tires. Logo: white-outlined gray "Lyons' Tea", white-outlined blue "J. Lyons & Co. Ltd.", white and black lettering on gray panels, white frames, emblems.
   1. As above.

50001 BRYANT & MAY MATCHES 1992
Maroon body, black chassis, cream roof and seat, gold grille and 12-spoke hubs, black tires. Logo: cream and black design with black "British Made Brymay Special Safety Match", cream "Bryant & May's" on black ribbon, cream "Bryant & May Ltd." etc.
   1. As above.

50002 HAMLEYS 1993
Blue body, black chassis, gray roof, gold grille and windshield, gray 20-spoke hubs, black tires. Logo: white-shadowed red "Hamleys", white lettering, gold lines, figure. Special box.
   1. As above.

50003 MILLER & SON PIANOS 1993
Green body, black chassis, cream roof, gold grille, windshield and 12-spoke hubs, black tires. Logo: gold "His Master's voice" etc. and stripes, gold-outlined red "Miller & Son", red "Pianos", emblem.
   1. As above.

50004 DAYS GONE CLUB 1993
Red body and chassis, black roof and seat, gold grille, windshield and 12-spoke hubs, black tires. Logo: black "Days Gone" on black-framed gold plaque, green ribbon with gold lettering, gold "Spring 1993", "Lledo" and frames.
   1. As above.

50005 MARKS & SPENCER 1993
Cream body, black chassis, white roof, gold grille, windshield and 12-spoke hubs, black tires. Logo: purple "Marks & Spencer's original Penny Bazaar", etc., figure and trim. In set of four Marks & Spencer models.
   1. As above.

50006 RAFFLES HOTEL 1993
Dark green body, black chassis, white roof, cream seat, gold grille and windshield, green 20-spoke hubs, black tires. Logo: multicolored oval emblem with "Raffles Hotel, Singapore", same lettering in cream on doors. In set of three hotel vans.
   1. As above.

50007 KODAK 1994
Light orange body, black chassis, red roof, gold grille, windshield and 20-spoke hubs, black tires. Logo: black-outlined red "Kodak", black lettering, red-yellow-black box design.
   1. As above.

50008 KIWI BOOT POLISH 1994
Blue body, black chassis, cream roof, gold grille, red 20-spoke hubs, black tires. Logo: multicolored "Kiwi Boot Polish" design.
   1. As above.

50009 RUPERT BEAR 1994
Blue body, black chassis and roof, cream seat, gold grille, 12-spoke hubs, black tires. Logo: pet-feeding design and emblem. Special Rupert box.
   1. As above.

50010 PEPSI-COLA 1994
Dark yellow body, blue chassis and roof, gold grille, windshield and 12-spoke hubs, black tires. Logo: white "Drink Pepsi-Cola" etc. on blue panel, black lettering, red "Pepsi-Cola", design. Special Pepsi-Cola box.
   1. As above.

50011 HARRODS 1994
Olive body, black chassis, cream roof, gold grille and 12-spoke hubs, black tires. Logo: cream "Harrods Ltd., Brompton Road, London" and lines, emblem on door. In set of two models.
   1. As above.

50012 SATURDAY EVENING POST 1994
Green body, dark green chassis, cream roof, gold grille and 12-spoke hubs, black tires. Logo: Saturday Evening Post design, white "Norman Rockwell 100th Anniversary" emblem. Special box.
   1. As above.

50013 AUSTRALIAN P.M.G. 1994
Red body, black chassis and roof, gold grille and 12-spoke hubs, black tires. Logo: black-shadowed gold "P.M.G.", gold "Delivery Service", multicolored emblem, black lines.
   1. As above.

50014 SILVER KING 1995
Maroon body, black chassis, gray roof, gold grille, maroon 12-spoked hubs, black tires. Logo: multicolored "Silver King Golf Balls" design, white lettering and frames.
   1. As above.

51 CHEVROLET 1928 BOX VAN 82 mm 1992
Cast body (same as #26) and box, plastic roof, grille-lights, DG21 26 51 base, hubs and tires.

51000 MADAME TUSSAUD'S 1992
Black cab, box and roof, gold grille, red disc hubs, black tires. Logo: black-outlined gold "Madame

Tussaud's Exhibition" on red panel with gold frame, gold "Baker St. London".
1. As above.

51001 START-RITE SHOES 1992
White cab and box, black chassis, roof and seat, silver grille, dark blue disc hubs, black tires. Logo: multicolored figures, yellow and black Start-Rite emblems, black lettering.
1. As above.

51002 HOVIS BREAD 1993
Cream cab, box, roof and seat, brown chassis, gold grille, brown disc hubs, black tires. Logo: brown "Hovis", black "for tea", black and brown design on sides, similar logo on rear, brown-outlined cream "Hovis" on front of box, brown emblem on doors.
1. As above.

51003 DAYS GONE CLUB 1993
Black cab, box and chassis, gold grille, green disc hubs, black tires. Logo: black and gold "Days Gone" panel, green ribbon, gold "Collectors Club" and "Lledo", gold "Winter 1993" on front of box.
1. As above.

51004 MARKS & SPENCER 1993
White cab, box, chassis, roof and disc hubs, silver grille, black tires. Logo: multicolored panel with red "Marks & Soencer's", black-outlined white "Grand Annual", black "Summer Number", etc., and frame. In set of four Marks & Spencer models.
1. As above.

51005 BUSHELLS TEA 1994
Blue-black body and box, black chassis and roof, silver grille, cream disc hubs, black tires. Logo: white-outlined yellow "Bushells", yellow "The Tea of Flavor", red and white figure, yellow and black oval on door.
1. As above.

51006 ERDAL 1994
Dark green body, box and roof, black chassis, silver grille, green disc hubs, black tires. Logo: black "Erdal mit dem Rotfrosch" and brown and white frog figure on yellow panel, yellow lettering.
1. As above.

51007 ARMY RADIO TRUCK 1994
Olive body, chassis, box, roof, grille and disc hubs, black tires. Logo: white stars, numbers and "SIGINT" lettering, blue and white emblems. In set of three D-Day models.
1. As above.

51008 SATURDAY EVENING POST 1994
Yellow body and box, brown chassis and roof, gold grille and 12-spoke hubs, black tires. Logo: Saturday Evening Post design, black "The Saturday Evening Post", brown "Norman Rockwell 100th Anniversary" emblem on doors. Special box.
1. As above.

51009 HAMLEYS 1995
Cream body and box, dark blue chassis and roof, gold grille, dark blue disc hubs, black tires. Logo: gold-outlined red "Hamleys" and ribbon, gold and red lettering, figure, blue frame. Special Hamleys box.
1. As above.

51010 RUPERT BEAR 1995
Light orange body and box, black chassis, red roof, gold grille, red disc hubs, black tires. Logo: scene with jester, The Rupert Collection emblem. Special Rupert box.
1. As above.

52 MORRIS 1935 PARCELS VAN 102 mm 1992
Cast cab, body, roof and chassis, plastic grille, steering wheel, seat, DG52 base, hubs and tires.

52000 ROYAL MAIL 1992
Red cab, body and roof, black chassis and seat, gold grille, red disc hubs, black tires. Logo: black "Royal Mail" and Post Office emblem, black and gold crown, gold GR monogram.
1. As above.

52001 PICKFORDS 1992
Navy blue cab, body and roof, black chassis and seat, silver grille, navy blue disc hubs, black tires. Logo: white "Suburban Goods Service", "Pickfords", number and frames.
1. "Pickfords" at rear of logo.
2. "Pickfords" at front of logo.

52002 PEPSI-COLA 1993
White cab, body and roof, red chassis, silver grille, gray disc hubs, black tires. Logo: multicolored bottle-cap design, black "tops..." Special Pepsi-Cola box.
1. As above.

52003 LNER EXPRESS PARCELS 1993
Dark blue cab, body and roof, black chassis, silver grille, red disc hubs, black tires. Logo: white LNER emblem (also on roof), "Express Parcels Service" and number, multicolored design.
1. As above.

52004 43RD DIVISION AMBULANCE 1993
Olive cab, body, chassis, roof, grille and disc hubs, black tires. Logo: red crosses on white discs, white number in oval. Special Military Collection box.
1. As above.

52005 DAYS GONE CLUB SUMMER 1993 1993
Light green cab and nody, dark green roof, black chassis, gold grille, black wheels. Logo: black "Days Gone" on black-framed gold panel, green ribbon, gold "19 Summer 93", black and gold trim.
1. As above.

52006 1993 TOY FAIR MODEL 1993
Green cab, body and roof, black chassis, gold grille and 12-spoke hubs, black tires. Logo: black and gold "Days Gone", olive ribbon with gold lettering, white "1993 Toy Fair Model" and emblem, white names on rear. Plain white box.
1. As above.

52007 RAF AMBULANCE 1993
Dull blue cab, body, chassis, roof, grille and disc hubs, black tires. Logo: red crosses on white panels (also on roof and rear), white "RAF" and number, red-white-blue roundel. In set of three Dambusters models.
1. As above.

52008 NEW YORK TOY FAIR 1993
Dark blue cab, body and roof, black chassis, silver grille, dark blue disc hubs, black tires. Logo: black "Days Gone" and frame on yellow panel, green ribbon, white "1993 New York Toy Fair", white "Limited Edition" emblem on door.
1. As above.

52009 KODAK FILMS & CAMERAS 1994
Light orange cab, box and roof, black chassis, gold grille, black disc hubs and tires. Logo: black-outlined red "Kodak", black "Films & Cameras"; also on roof, similar logo on doors.
1. As above.

52010 HARRODS 1994
Olive cab, cream box, black chassis, gold grille, green hubs, black tires. No other data.

52011 HAMLEYS 1995
Dark green cab, box and roof, black chassis, gold grille, red disc hubs, black tires. Logo: red "Hamleys", black lettering, figure on cream panel, white lettering. Special Hamleys box.
1. As above.

52012 SAROTTI CHOCOLATES 1995
Blue cab and chassis, white box and roof, silver grille, white disc hubs, black tires. Logo: multicolored

figures, black "Sarotti", black and white lettering.
1. As above.

52013 RUPERT BEAR 1995
Green cab, box and roof, black chassis, gold grille, cream disc hubs, black tires. Logo: gardening scene, The Rupert Collection emblem. Special Rupert box.
1. As above.

52014 LONDON COUNTY AMBULANCE 1995
Gray cab, box, and chassis, black grille, gray disc hubs, black tires. Logo: red cross, white "Ambulance", "London County Council", emblem, etc., black and white windows. In set of three VE-Day models.
1. As above.

53   ROLLS-ROYCE 1926 LANDAULET 85 mm 1992
Cast body and chassis, plastic roof, interior, grille, 18-19-22-24-25-38 base, hubs and tires.

53000 DAYS GONE COLLECTORS CLUB 1992
Gold body and chassis, maroon roof and interior, gold grille and 12-spoke hubs, black tires. No logo. Exclusive Edition box.
1. As above.

53001 GOLD AND MAROON 1993
Gold body and chassis, maroon roof and interior, gold grille and 12-spoke hubs, black tires, no logo.
1. As above.

53002 GOLD 1995
Gold body, chassis and grille, black roof and folded top, gold 12-spoke hubs, black tires, side spare. No logo. In set of three Rolls-Royce models.
1. As above.

54   ROLLS-ROYCE 1929 D-BACK 82 mm 1993
Cast body and chassis (same as #19), plastic roof, interior, trunk, grille, base, hubs and tires.

54000 BLUE & CREAM 1993
Blue body and chassis, cream top, interior and trunk, gold grille and 12-spoke hubs, black tires, side spare. No logo.
1. As above.

54001 DAYS GONE COLLECTORS CLUB 1993
Gold body, chassis, grille and 12-spoke hubs, black top, trunk, seats and tires. In Days Gone Collector box.
1. As above.

54002 GOLD 1995
Gold body, chassis and grille, black roof and trunk, gold 12-spoke hubs, black tires. No logo. In set of three Rolls-Royce models.
1. As above.

54003 GOLD 1995
Gold body and chassis, dark blue roof and trunk, gold grille and 12-spoke hubs, black tires. No logo. German issue.
1. As above.

55   HORSE DRAWN TANKER 111 mm 1993
Not used for Days Gone models.

56   MODEL A FORD 1930 RAISED-ROOF VAN 82 mm 1993
Cast body and chassis (same as long-body #13), plastic roof, grille, seats, DG7-9-13-14-37 base, hubs and tires.

56000 DAYS GONE CLUB 1994
Cream body, brown chassis and roof, gold grille, cream disc hubs, black tires. Logo: brown-gold-green "Days Gone" design, brown "Collectors Club" and "Lledo Winter 1993/94. Special box.
1. As above.

57   FORD 1939 TANK TRUCK 94 mm 1993
Cast body, plastic tank, drums, grille-lights-bumper, interior, base with running boards (no #), hubs and tires.

57000 SHELL-BP AVIATION SERVICE 1993
Dark green body, red tank, gray drums, silver grille, dark green 6-bolt hubs, black tires. Logo: black-outlined yellow and white "Shell and BP Aviation Service" on tank, yellow-black-white emblem, white "Shell Mex Ltd." and "Croydon Airport".

57001 ESSO PETROLEUM 1994
White cab, red rear, gray drums, silver grille, red 6-bolt hubs, black tires. Logo: blue "Esso Petroleum Company Ltd." on white stripe, red-white-blue Esso emblem on door and rear.
1. As above.

57002 ROYAL NAVY 1994
Gray cab and rear, lighter gray tank, grille and hubs, black tires. Logo: white "Royal Navy" and other lettering. In set of three D-Day models.
1. As above.

57003 U S ARMY AIR FORCE 1994
Olive cab, rear, grille, tanks and 6-bolt hubs, yellow tank, black tires. Logo: black "US Army Air Force" on tank, red lettering on white panel, black lettering on door. In set of three D-Day models.

57004 GULF GASOLINE 1994
Blue cab and rear, red tank, silver grille, red 6-bolt hubs, black tires. Logo: white-outlined blue "That Good Gulf Gasoline", red lettering on white panel, blue and orange Gulf emblem and white "Refining Company" on doors.
1. As above.

58   MORRIS 1993 Z VAN 82 mm 1993
Cast body and chassis, black plastic roof panel, interior, grille, lights, base, 20-spoke hubs and tires.

58000 POST OFFICE TELEPHONES 1993
Dark olive body, black chassis, roof panel, hood, grille, 20-spoke hubs and tires. Logo: multicolored crown, white "Post Office Telephones" etc.
1. As above.

58001 SCHWEPPES MALVERN 1993
White body, all other parts black. Logo: blue "Schweppes Malvern" etc., red and gold emblem, red lettering.
1. As above.

58002 MACKESON STOUT 1993
Light gray body, black chassis, roof panel and grille, light gray 20-spoke hubs, black tires. Logo: white-outlined black "Mackeson". red "display service" and "Glasgow", red-white-black emblem on doors.
1. As above.

58003 ROYAL MAIL 1994
Red body, black chassis, roof, hood, grille, seats, 12-spoke hubs and tires. Logo: gold "Royal Mail and coat of arms, black "Post Office" emblem.
1. As above.

58004 BLUE GILLETTE BLADES 1994
Pale blue body, dark blue chassis, black roof and grille, dark blue 20-spoke hubs, black tires. Logo: blue "Blue Gillette", red "Slotted Blades" (also in back), silver blade design.
1. As above.

58005 HAMLEYS 1994
Green body and 20-spoke hubs, black chassis, roof, grille and tires. Logo: black "Hamleys" etc. on gold panel, red-white-black figure, gold lettering. Hamleys box.
1. As above.

58006 PEPSI-COLA 1994
Yellow body, blue chassis, black roof panel, grille, interior and tires, yellow 20-spoke hubs. Logo: red-white-blue "say Pepsi, please"! and Pepsi-Cola bottle cap. Special Pepsi-Cola box.
    1. **As above.**

58007 DAYS GONE CLUB 1994
Dark blue body, black chassis, roof panel, grille, 12-spoke hubs and tires. Logo: black "Days Gone" on black-framed gold panel with ribbon below, gold Lledo Collectors Club Spring 1994.
    1. **As above.**

58008 DAYS GONE GOLD CLUB 1994
Gold body and chassis, black roof and grille, gold 12-spoke hubs and tires. No other data.

58009 SINGER 1995
Green body, black chassis, roof and grille, red spoked hubs, black tires. Logo: white-outlined red "Singer", white "Na"*hmaschinen", multicolored Singer emblem.
    1. **As above.**

58010 BRITISH RAILWAYS 1995
Maroon body, black chassis, roof and grille, maroon disc hubs, black tires. Logo: yellow "British Railways advertising Service" etc. In set of three British Railways models.
    1. **As above.**

58012 7-UP 1995
Red body, black chassis and roof, silver grille, green disc hubs, black tires. Logo: black-shadowed red "Fresh Up", black "with", black-outlined green "7-Up", white lettering and figure. Special 7-Up box.
    1. **As above.**

58013 HARRODS 1994
Olive body, black chassis and roof panel, gold grille, green disc hubs, black tires. Logo: black-outlined gold "Harrods", gold "Knightsbridge" and emblem. In set of four models.
    1. **As above.**

59 BEDFORD 1950 30 CWT TRUCK 94 mm 1993
Cast cab, box and chassis, plastic grille-lights, steering wheel, base, hubs and tires.

59000 BIRD'S CUSTARD 1993
Dark blue cab and box, black chassis and grille, dark blue 6-bolt hubs, black tires. Logo: blue-orange-cream design with cream "Bird's Custard and Jellies" on orange-framed blue panel, cream frame, light orange "Bird's Custard" on front of body.
    1. **As above.**

59001 CANADA DRY GINGER ALE 1993
Turquoise cab and box, black chassis and grille, red 6-bolt hubs, black tires. Logo: black-outlined "Carter Paterson" on gold-framed red stripe, Canada Dry emblem, white lettering, white "Express Carriers" on front, "Carter Paterson" on rear of body.
    1. **As above.**

59002 DUNLOPILLO 1993
Cream cab and box, brown chassis, grille and roof, cream 6-bolt hubs, black tires. Logo: brown "Dunlopillo" (also on front of body) etc., black-white-pink design.
    1. **As above.**

59003 PEPSI-COLA 1993
Red cab and roof, white box, black chassis and grille, red 6-bolt hubs, black tires. Logo: Santa Claus design, blue "Merry Christmas", red "Pepsi-Cola", last also on front of body, white lettering on door. Special Pepsi-Cola box.
    1. **As above.**

59004 LUCOZADE 1994
Light orange cab, box and chassis, red top, black grille, 6-bolt hubs and tires. Logo: orange "Lucozade" on red ribbon (also on front of body), red lettering.
    1. **As above.**

59005 BE-RO FLOUR 1994
Maroon cab and box, black chassis, cream roof, black grille, maroon 6-bolt hubs, black tires. Logo: cream "Be-Ro for all home baking" etc., maroon "self raising Flour" on cream panel, cream "Be-Ro" on front of body.
    1. **As above.**

59006 HAMLEYS 1993
Maroon cab and box, black chassis and grille, cream roof and interior, maroon 6-bolt hubs, black tires. Logo: red-black-gold "Hamleys; design, gold lettering. Special Hamleys box.
    1. **As above.**

59007 PEPSI-COLA 1994
Cream cab and box, black chassis, grille, roof and interior, red 6-bolt hubs, black tires. Logo: design of woman with bottle, bottle cap, black and red "The Light Refreshment", red "Refresh without filling", Pepsi-Cola monogram, (also on front of body). Special Pepsi-Cola box.
    1. **As above.**

59008 WEET-BIX 1994
Yellow cab, box and roof, dark blue chassis and 6-bolt hubs, black grille and tires. Logo: blue "Renew your" and "each day", red "Energy", design, yellow and red "Weet-Bix", etc. on blue panel, emblem and lettering on door, red "Weet-Bix" on front and back of body.
    1. **As above.**

59009 DAYS GONE TOY FAIRS 1994
Light blue cab and box, blue chassis and grille, cream roof, blue 6-bolt hubs, black tires. Logo: black "Days Gone" and frame on gold panel, green ribbon, white-outlined red "1994", black "Toy Fair Model", lines, and door lettering.
    1. **As above.**

59010 DAYS GONE NEW YORK TOY FAIR 1994
Cream cab and box, black chassis, roof and grille, red 6-bolt hubs, black tires. Logo: black "Days Gone" and frame on gold panel, green ribbon, black "New York Toy Fair 1991" and door lettering.
    1. **As above.**

59011 ARNOTT'S BISCUITS 1995
Red cab, box and grille, black chassis, cream roof, red 6-bolt hubs, black tires. Logo: black-outlined gold "Arnott's Biscuits", multicolored emblem, white and black lettering.
    1. **As above.**

59012 OXYDOL 1995
Dark blue can and box, black chassis, cream roof, black grille, dark blue 6-bolt hubs, black tires. Logo: white-outlined red "Oxydol", white lettering, multicolored design.
    1. **As above.**

59013 BRITISH RAILWAYS 1995
Maroon cab, cream box and roof, black chassis and grille, cream 6-bolt hubs, black tires. Logo: maroon and yellow British Railways emblem and lettering, maroon panels. In set of three British Railways models.
    1. **As above.**

59015 RUPERT BEAR 1995
Maroon cab and box, green chassis and roof, maroon grille, cream 6-bolt hubs, black tires. Logo: birthday cake scene, The Rupert Collection emblem. In set of three Rupert models.
    1. **As above.**

59016 7-UP 1995
White cab and box, green chassis and roof, white grille and 6-bolt hubs, black tires. Logo: black-outlined green "&-Up", red and black discs, red lettering, black bubbles. Special 7-Up box.
    1. **As above.**

59017 DAYS GONE CLUB AUTUMN 1995 1995
Orange cab, box and roof, black chassis and grille, orange 6-bolt hubs, black tires. Logo: black "Days Gone"

on black-framed gold panel, green ribbon, black "Collectors Club", "Autumn 1995" and frame. Special Club Model box.

1. As above.

60   DENNIS F8 1955 FIRE ENGINE   92 mm   1993

Cast body and chassis, plastic roof, lights, ladder, rear panel, grille-headlights, base-bumper, hubs and tires.

60000   ESSEX   1993

Red body, black chassis and roof, silver grille, silver gray rear, tan ladder, red 6-bolt hubs, black tires. Logo: gold "Essex County Fire Brigade", white emblems.

1. As above.

60001   DERBYSHIRE   1993

Silver body, black chassis, roof, grille and hose, tan ladder and interior, red front panel and 6-bolt hubs, black tires. Logo: white "Derbyshire Fire Service" on red arc, coat of arms.

1. As above.

60002   WESTERN AREA--OBAN   1993

Red body, black chassis and roof, silver grille, silver gray hose, tan ladder, red 6-bolt hubs, black tires. Logo: red-white-blue emblem, gold "Western Area Fire Brigade" and "Oban".

1. As above.

60003   CRAWLEY WEST SUSSEX   1994

Yellow body, black roof, light brown ladder, silver gray hose, silver grille, yellow 6-bolt hubs, black tires. Logo: black "Crawley West Sussex Fire Brigade", multicolored emblem.

1. As above.

60004   NEW ZEALAND FIRE SERVICE   1994

Red body, black chassis and roof, light brown ladder, silver gray hose, silver grille, cream 6-bolt hubs, black tires. Logo: multicolored emblem, gold "New Zealand Fire Service".

1. As above.

60005   LONDON FIRE BRIGADE   1994

Red body and roof, black chassis, tan ladder, silver gray hose, silver grille, red 6-bolt hubs, black tires. Logo: white "L.C.C." and "London Fire Brigade", multicolored coat of arms, silver "Fire" on front. In set of three models.

1. As above.

60006   HARRODS SPECIAL FIRE SERVICE   1994

Red body, black chassis, cream roof, brown ladder, silver grille, cream disc hubs, black tires. Logo: yellow "Special Fire Service, Harrods, Knightsbridge" and coat of arms. In set of two models.

1. As above.

60007   LONDON FIRE BRIGADE   1995

Red body, black chassis and roof, brown ladder, silver grille, red 6-bolt hubs, black tires. Logo: white "London Fire Brigade", "L C C", etc., multicolored emblem.

1. As above.

60008   CIVIL DEFENCE CORPS   1995

Olive body and roof, black chassis, brown ladder, silver grille, olive 6-bolt hubs, black tires. Logo: white "Civil Defence Corps" and numbers, gold and red emblem.

1. As above.

61   PONTIAC 1953 DELIVERY VAN   88 mm   1993

Cast body and black chassis, plastic interior, front bumper-grille, rear bumper, headlights, hubs and tires.

61000   DR. PEPPER (red)   1993

Red body and disc hubs, cream interior, silver grille and bumpers, black tires. Logo: black-outlined white "Drink Dr. Pepper" design and emblem.

1. As above.

61001   DETROIT POLICE   1993

Dark blue body and disc hubs, cream interior, silver grille and bumpers, black tires. Logo: white "Detroit Police" and trim on sides and rear, "Police" on roof.

1. As above.

61002   MILWAUKEE AMBULANCE   1993

Cream body, silver grille and bumpers, red interior and disc hubs, black tires. Logo: black panel with silver and red cross, silver "Ambulance" and stripes, red "Ambulance" (also on roof and rear), "Milwaukee County Institutions No. 9".

1. As above.

61003   TWA AIRPORT SERVICES   (not made)

61004   PEPSI-COLA   1994

Light blue body, silver grille and bumpers, white disc hubs, black interior and tires. Logo: red "Drink Pepsi" on black-framed white panel, bottle cap, white lettering. Special Pepsi-Cola box.

1. As above.

61005   EXCELSIOR   1994

Metallic blue body, silver grille, bumpers and hubs, black tires. Logo: multicolored "Excelsior Auto Cycle" emblem, yellow lettering. In set of three motorcycle vans.

1. As above.

61006   DR. PEPPER (green)   1994

Green body, silver grille and bumpers, green disc hubs, black tires. Logo: white-outlined black "Drink Dr. Pepper" and underline with black lettering, black and white emblem on doors, white lettering on rear. Special box.

1. As above.

61007   AGFA PHOTO   1995

Red body, silver grille and bumpers, white disc hubs, black tires. Logo: white and black "Agfa" emblem, white "Photo-Artikel" and number.

1. As above.

61008   7-UP   1995

White body, silver bumpers, green disc hubs, black tires. Logo: multicolored 7-Up designs, red lettering.

1. As above.

62   FORD 1935 ARTICULATED TANKER   118 mm   1994

Cast cab, cab chassis and semi chassis, plastic tank, cab interior, grille-lights-bumper, hubs and tires.

62000   REGENT PETROLEUM   1994

Dark blue cab, red tank, black chassis, silver grille, red 6-bolt hubs, black tires. Logo: black-outlined gold "Regent", black lettering, cream stripes, white lettering on cab.

1. As above.

62002   FINA   1995

Light blue cab, dark blue tank, black chassis, silver grille, dark blue 6-bolt hubs, black tires. Logo: white "Fina Fuel Oil", blue and white Fina emblem on door.

1. As above.

63   BEDFORD 1950 30 CWT DELIVERY VAN   88 mm   1994

Cast body and chassis, plastic interior, grille-lights-bumper, hubs and tires.

63000   SAINSBURY'S   1994

Maroon body, black chassis and grille, maroon 6-bolt hubs, black tires. Logo: cream "Sainsbury's for your provisions" and frame on red panel, black-outlined cream "J. Sainsbury" (also on front).

1. As above.

63001   PENGUIN BOOKS   1994

Orange body and grille, black chassis, 6-bolt hubs and tires. Logo: silver "Penguin Books" (also on rear), black-white emblem, same lettering and emblem on front of roof.

1. As above.

63002   OXO   1994

Red body and 6-bolt hubs, black chassis, grille and tires. Logo: black-shadowed white "Oxo" (also on front

and back), white design.
1. As above.

63003 DAYS GONE CLUB 1994
Green body, black chassis and grille, green 6-bolt hubs, black tires. Logo: black "Days Gone" on black-framed gold panel, gold "Collectors Club", "Summer 1994" and "Lledo". Special club box.
1. As above.

63004 HAMLEYS 1995
Dark red body, black chassis and grille, red 6-bolt hubs, black tires. Logo: red "Hamleys" and ribbon, multicolored figure on cream panel, white lettering. Special Hamleys box.
1. As above.

63005 CEREBOS SALT 1995
Dark blue body, black chassis and grille, dark blue 6-bolt hubs, black tires. Logo: gold emblem and lettering, gold-outlined white "Cerebos", white "salt" etc.
1. As above.

63006 WALL'S SAUSAGES 1995
Cream body, dark blue chassis, cream grille, dark blue 6-bolt hubs, black tires. Logo: two-tone blue "Wall's", blue "Sausages & Pies", red and white Wall's emblem, gold coat of arms.
1. As above.

63008 RUPERT BEAR 1995
Blue body, black chassis, blue grille, red 6-bolt hubs, black tires. Logo: multicolored scene with model airplane, The Rupert Collection emblem. In set of three Rupert models.
1. As above.

63009 TOY FAIR MODEL 1995
Dark purple body, black chassis and grille, purple 6-bolt hubs, black tires. Logo: black "Days Gone" on black-framed gold panel, green ribbon, gold "1995 Toy Fair Model", white lettering. In plain white box.
1. As above.

63010 NEW YORK TOY FAIR 1995
Light orange body, black chassis and grille, red 6-bolt hubs, black tires. Logo: Same "Days Gone" panel as 63009, red lettering. Probably in plain white box.
1. As above.

64 BEDFORD 1950 AMBULANCE 88 mm 1994
Same parts as #63, but body has two rear windows on each side.

64000 KENT COUNTY AMBULANCE 1994
Light cream body, black chassis, 6-bolt hubs and tires. Logo: red "Kent County Council Health Dept.", emblem, black lattering, black "Ambulance" and frame on front, red "Ambulance" on rear.
1. As above.

64001 DURHAM COUNTY AMBULANCE 1994
Dark blue body. black chassis, grille, 6-bolt hubs and tires. Logo: white "Durham County Ambulance Service" and stripe, "Ambulance" on front and rear, blue-gold emblem.
1. As above.

64002 L C C AMBULANCE 1995
White body, chassis and grille, black 6-bolt hubs and tires. Logo: multicolored coat of arms, black-outlined gold "L C C Ambulance 1135".
1. As above.

64003 ARMY MEDICAL SERVICES 1995
Olive body, chassis, grille and 6-bolt hubs. Logo: red cross, white "Army Medical Services" etc.
1. As above.

64004 BRITISH RAILWAYS 1995
Cream body, black chassis, grille, 6-bolt hubs and tires. Logo: yellow and maroon British Railways emblem, cream lettering, maroon panels. In set of three British Railways models.

1. As above.

65 MORRIS 1960 TRAVELLER 88 mm 1994
Cast body and chassis, brown plastic woodwork, interior, windows, grille, headlights, bumpers, hubs and tires.

65000 GREEN 1994
Dull green body, gray interior, silver bumpers and lights, cream grille and disc hubs, black tires. No logo.
1. As above.

65001 CREAM 1994
Cream body, red interior, silver bumpers and lights, cream grille and disc hubs, black tires. No logo.
1. As above.

65002 BLUE 1995
Dark blue body, silver bumpers and lights, cream grille, silver gray disc hubs, black tires.
1. As above.

65003 GRAY 1995
Light gray body, silver bumpers and lights, cream grille and disc hubs, black tires.
1. As above.

65004 DAYS GONE CLUB 1995
Gold body and bumpers, black chassis, cream grille and disc hubs, black tires. No logo. Special Days Gone Collector box.

66 DENNIS 1926 DELIVERY VAN 84 mm 1994
Cast cab, box body and chassis, plastic roof, seat, steering wheel, grille-headlights, base, hubs and tires.

66000 WAKEFIELD CASTROL 1994
Dark green cab and box, black chassis, cream roof, silver grille, green disc hubs, white tires. Logo: white-outlined red "Castrol", gold "Wakefield Motor Oil Estd. 1899, gold #31 and green lettering on cream panel on cab.
1. As above.

66001 (Not yet used)
66002 PEPSI-COLA CHRISTMAS 1994
Blue cab and box, black chassis, cream roof, silver grille, red disc hubs, black tires. Logo: black "Drink" etc., red "Pepsi-Cola", Santa Claus and bottle figures. Special Pepsi-Cola box.
1. As above.

66001 AUSTRALIAN P.M.G. 1994
Red cab and box, black chassis and roof, gold grille, red disc hubs, black tires. Logo: black-shadowed gold "P.M.G.", multicolored emblem, gold "Express Deliveries".
1. As above.

66002 PEPSI-COLA 1994
Blue cab and box, black chassis, cream roof, silver grille, red disc hubs, black tires. Logo: Santa Claus figure, black "Drink" etc., red "Pepsi-Cola" and underline, gold "Season's Greetings", red-white-black bottle design. Special Pepsi-Cola box.
1. As above.

66003 CAMPBELL'S SOUPS 1995
White cab and roof, red box, black chassis, silver grille, red disc hubs, black tires. Logo: black-shadowed white "Campbell's". black and gold emblem, white and red lettering.
1. As above.

66004 HARRODS 1994
Olive cab and box, black chassis, cream roof, gold grille and 12-spoke hubs, black tires. Logo: gold-outlined olive "Harrods Ltd, gold and black coat of arms, etc., on cream panel, gold "London SW1" etc. Header: gold "Harrods". In set of four models.
1. As above.

151

66005   DAYS GONE CLUB WINTER 1994-95   1995
Red cab, box and chassis, cream roof, gold grille, red disc hubs, black tires. Logo: black "Days Gone" and frame on gold panel, green ribbon, black "Collectors Club", gold "Lledo" and "Winter 1994-95". Special box.
    1. As above.
67   FORD 3-TON ARTICULATED TRUCK   117 mm   1994
Cast cab, chassis and semi body, plastic semi roof, cab interior, grille-lights-bumper, cab base, hubs and tires.
67000   DUNLOP   1994
Blue cab, black chassis, white semi and roof, silver grille, blue 6-bolt hubs, black tires. Logo: orange-blue-white "Dunlop Fort" design, similar design on front and back, white "Dunlop" etc. on blue panel, white lettering on cab.
    1. As above.
67001   ROBERT BROTHERS CIRCUS   1994
Red cab, semi and roof, black cab chassis, silver grille, black 6-bolt hubs and tires.. Logo: white-outlined "Robert Brothers Circus", gray elephant figures, yellow background, white name.
    1. As above.
67002   LYONS SWISS ROLLS   1995
Dark blue cab and semi, white roof, black chassis, silver grille, dark blue 6-bolt hubs, black tires. Logo: white-outlined gray "Lyons Swiss Rolls", white-outlined blue "J. Lyons & Co." on gray panel, white lettering and frames.
    1. As above.
67003   DAYS GONE CLUB SUMMER 1995   1995
Light orange cab, semi and roof, black chassis, gold grille, orange 6-bolt hubs, black tires. Logo: black "Days Gone" and frame on gold panel, green ribbon, orange "Collectors Club" on red stripe, black "Summer 95". Special Club Model Box.
    1. As above.
68   OPEN TOP BUS   86 mm   1994
Cast body and chassis (same as #15, DG15 on base), plastic upper and lower seats, grille, hubs and tires.
68000   IMPERIAL WAR MUSEUM, DUXFORD   1994
Blue-gray body, chassis and grille, cream seats, blue hubs, black tires. Upper logo: red "Imperial War Museum, etc., blue "Duxford" and "Lledo", on white panel. Lower: white "RAF" and number. White Limited Edition emblem on rear, white "Museum Tour" on front board.
    1. As above.
68001   DAYS GONE CLUB SUMMER 1994   1994
Yellow-orange body, red chassis and hubs, cream seats, silver grille, black tires. Upper logo: black-outlined "Days Gone Collectors Club" and white "Summer Edition 1994" on red panel. Lower: black "General" and underline. Black "Enfield" on front board. Special box.
    1. As above.
68002   SEE LONDON AT ITS BEST   1995
Red body, black chassis, cream seats, silver grille, red hubs, black tires. Upper logo: red "See London at its best", black lettering and designs, on white panel; lower: black-outlined gold "London Transport" and underline, white lettering.
    1. As above.
68003   WELSH MOUNTAIN ZOO   1995
Green body, black chassis, cream seats, silver grille, green hubs, black tires. Upper logo: yellow "Welsh Mountain", white "Zoo", brown figures on blue panel; lower: yellow "Crosville".
    1. As above.
68004   VICTORY IN EUROPE   1995
Red body, black chassis, cream seats, silver grille, red hubs, black tires. Upper logo: black-outlined red

"Victory in Europe" on white panel; lower: black-outlined gold "London Transport" and underline, white lettering. In set of three VE-Day models.
    1. As above.
69   MORRIS MINOR 1960 VAN   85 mm   1995
Cast body and chassis-base, plastic interior, windows, grille, bumper, lights, hubs and tires.
69000   EVER READY BATTERIES   1995
Blue body, cream grille, silver bumper, silver gray disc hubs, black tires. Logo: orange-blue-white Ever Ready emblem, orange and white lettering.
    1. As above.
69001   CURRYS   1995
Red body, cream grille, silver bumper, silver gray disc hubs, black tires. Logo: red "Currys" and ribbon on white panel, white lettering.
    1. As above.
69002   DAYS GONE CLUB SPRING 1995   1995
Light blue body, black grille, silver bumper, black disc hubs and tires. Logo: black "Days Gone" and frame on gold panel, green ribbon, black and gold lettering. Special box.
    1. As above.
70   FORD 1939 CANVAS BACK TRUCK   90 mm   1995
Cast body and rear, plastic chassis-base, cover, interior, grille-lights-bumper, hubs and tires.
70000   ANCHOR BEER   1995
Red body and rear, black chassis, cream cover, silver grille, cream 6-bolt hubs, black tires. Logo: "Anchor Beer" flag and emblem, cream "Archipelago Brewery Company" and monograms.
71   MORRIS 1959 LD 150 VAN   84 mm   1995
Cast body and chassis-base, plastic interior, windows, lights, bumpers and wheels, or hubs and tires.
71000   KODAK FILM   1995
Yellow-orange body, silver bumpers, black wheels. Logo: black-white-gold coat of arms, black-outlined red "Kodak", black trim.
    1. As above.
71001   WORMWOOD SCRUBS   1995
Dark blue body, silver bumpers, black wheels. Logo: white "H.M. Prisons, Wormwood Scrubs" etc., gold-black-white coat of arms.
    1. As above.
71002   H. P. SAUCE   1995
Cream body, silver bumpers, black wheels. Logo: white "H.P." and frame, red "Sauce" etc., light and dark blue panels, maroon trim, gold coat of arms.
    1. As above.
71003   INTERNATIONAL MODEL SHOW   1995
Cream body, silver bumpers, red hubs, black tires. Logo: red "International Model Show", red-white-blue flag, black "Lledo", white "Duxford" and date on dark blue panel, blue lettering.
    1. As above.
72   VOLKSWAGEN 1952 BEETLE   94 mm   1995
Cast body and fenders, plastic base, interior, windows, lights, bumpers, wheels and hubcaps.
72000   BLUE BEETLE   1995
Dark blue body, silver bumpers and hubs, black wheels. No logo.
72001   PASTEL GREEN BEETLE   1995
Light green body, silver bumpers and hubs, black wheels. No logo.
    1. As above.

73 VOLKSWAGEN 1955 KOMBI VAN 86 mm 1995
Cast body and chassis-base, plastic interior, windows, lights, wheels and hubcaps.
73000 CINZANO 1995
Blue body, gray chassis, silver hubs, black wheels. Logo: white "Cinzano" on gold-framed red and blue panel, gold "Vermouth", white lettering.
    1. As above.
73001 BOSCH 1995
Yellow body, gray chassis, silver hubs, black wheels. Logo: red "Bosch", white "Bosch Auto Electrical" on red stripe, red-white-blue emblem, red lettering.
    1. As above.
73002 PEPSI-COLA 1995
Light blue body, white chassis, silver lights and hubs, black wheels. Logo: multicolored Pepsi bottle cap, wreath with red "Your Good old friend," Santa holding Pepsi bottle. Special Pepsi-Cola box.
    1. As above.
74 AUSTIN 7 1959 MINI 71 mm 1995
Cast body, chassis-base, plastic interior, windows, grille, lights, bumpers, wheels and hubcaps.
74000 PALE BLUE MINI 1995
Pale blue body, silver bumpers and hubs, black wheels. No logo.
    1. As above.
74001 DARK RED MINI 1995
Dark red body, silver bumpers and hubs, black tires. No logo.
    1. As above.
74002 POLICE MINI 1995
White body and roof sign, blue roof light, silver bumpers and hubs, black tires. Logo: black "Police" on body, white "Police" on black panel on roof sign.
    1. As above.
75 BRISTOL 1957 LODEKKA BUS 94 mm 1995
Cast upper and lower body and chassis, plastic interior, divider, windows, grille, hubs and tires or wheels.
75000 DULUX PAINT 1995
Red upper and lower body, cream divider, brown seats, black chassis and wheels. Upper logo: white "Dulux", multicolored design on black panel; lower: "Thames Valley".
    1. As above.
75001 WESTON'S BISCUITS 1995
Green upper and lower body, cream divider, brown seats, black chassis, green hubs, black tires. Upper logo: red "Weston's" blue "Quality Biscuits" etc. on cream panel; lower: gold "Eastern National".
    1. As above.
75002 DAYS GONE CLUB 1995
Red upper and lower body, cream divider and seats, black chassis and wheels. Upper logo: black "Days Gone Collectors Club", red and green ornaments on white panel; lower: "Days Gone" emblem, white "Christmas Edition 1995."
    1.As above.

OTHER SERIES

    The **"Fantastic Set o' Wheels"** series, comprising eight models, was marketed in the United States by Hartoy Inc. in 1985. The bases were usually lettered "Made in England by Lledo," though a few appeared with Days Gone bases. All were sold in blister packs. They had their own numbers, which will be followed here by the number of the basic model used.

FSW1-06 MALIBU OR BUST 1985
Yellow body, dark brown chassis, light brown roof, "Malibu or Bust!" logo with desert scene, "Gone Fishing" sign, fishing rod and tackle box. No header lettering.
FSW2-07 FORD TRI-STATE DEALER 1985
White body, blue chassis and trim, off-white roof blade, cream interior and spare, Ford emblem logo with "Sales & Service", "Tri-State Dealer" on blade.
FSW3-08 LIQUID BUBBLE 1985
Light blue body, pink chassis, white roof and tank, red hubs, white tires. "Liquid Bubble" logo with bubble design and "world's best bubbles", no header lettering.
FSW4-10 OAKRIDGE SCHOOL 1985
Yellow-orange body and roof, cream interior, black chassis and hubs, white tires. "Oakridge School District" logo with "School Bus", "15 MPH" and "No. 7". (Reissued with changes as DG model with DG base.)
FSW5-12 BOSTON FIRE DEPARTMENT 1985
Red body and chassis, cream floor and ladder, red hubs, white tires, "Boston Fire Dept." logo with "B.F.D." on hood.
FSW6-13 JOLLY TIME ICE CREAM 1985
Cream body, pink chassis, roof and blade, red hubs, white tires. "Jolly Time Ice Cream" logo with "42 Varieties", "Treat Time" and musical notes on blade.
FSW7-14 POLICE CAR 1985
Black body, chassis, top. interior and spare, black 12- or 20-spoke hubs, white tires. "Police" logo with "055" and star badge.
FSW8-14 SAN DIEGO FIRE CHIEF 1985
Red body and chassis, black top, interior and spare, black hubs, white tires. "San Diego Fire Chief" logo with "No. 1 Company" and checkered stripes, "Fire Dept. 1" on hood.

    The **EDOCAR** series, also of eight models, was marketed in Europe in 1986 by Edor BV of the Netherlands. The bases usually bore the Edocar name and catalog number, prefixed by the letter A. The models were sold in cardboard boxes with cellophane windows, and with the numbers prefixed by EA. Again, the casting number will be added here to identify the basic model.

A1-08 RED/ESSO 1986
Red or blue body, yellow-orange tank.
1. Red body, black chassis and roof, no logo.
2. Blue body, dark blue chassis, white roof, Esso logo.
A2-12 RED 1986
Red body and chassis, cream ladder, no logo.
1. White floor.
2. Black floor.
A3-14 TAXI 1986
Yellow body and chassis, black top, interior and spare, Taxi logo.
A4-16 HUMBROL 1986
Green body, white chassis and roof, Humbrol logo with "The Image of Perfection" and "Airfix".
A5-17 WHITE 1986
White body, chassis and roof, blue windows, no logo.
A6-18 AMBULANCE 1986
White body, chassis and roof, "Ambulance" logo with red crosses.
A7-19 SILVER 1986
Silver body, black chassis, roof, interior and trunk, no logo.
1. White tires.
2. Black tires.
A8-21 EDOCAR 1986
Blue body, black chassis, white roof, "Edocar Finest Diecast Miniatures" logo.

Plain gray versions of most of the models then in production were made in 1986 for use as samples to be shown to purchasers of promotional models. Not one has a logo, and there are scarcely any variations among them.

02 MILK FLOAT 1986
Gray body, chassis, hitch and axle mount, light blue load, black horse.
03 DELIVERY VAN 1986
Gray body, chassis, hitch and axle mount, black roof and horse.
04 OMNIBUS 1986
Gray body, steps and hitch, red seats, gold wheels, tan horses.
05 FIRE ENGINE 1986
Gray body, chassis and hitch, bronze boiler, tan horses.
1. Gold wheels.
2. Black wheels.
06 MODEL T FORD VAN 1986
Gray body and chassis, cream roof.
07 FORD WOODY WAGON 1986
Gray body and chassis, cream blade and interior. DG or LP base.

08 MODEL T FORD TANKER 1986
Gray body and chassis, dark green tank, white roof.
10 DENNIS BUS 1986
Gray body and chassis, cream interior.
1. Red roof.
2. Yellow roof.
11 LARGE VAN 1986
Gray body, chassis and hitch, blue roof, gold wheels, tan horses. DG or LP base.
12 FIRE ENGINE 1986
Gray body and chassis, white floor, brown ladder, white tires.
13 MODEL A FORD VAN 1986
Gray body and chassis, white roof (other colors?).
14 MODEL A FORD 1986
Gray body and chassis, cream top and interior, DG or LP base.
15 DOUBLE DECK BUS 1986
Gray body, chassis and roof.
1. Yellow windows.
2. Yellow-orange windows.
16 HEAVY GOODS VAN 1986
Gray body and chassis, cream roof, white tires.
17 LONG DISTANCE COACH 1986
Gray body, chassis and roof, white windows.
18 PACKARD VAN 1986
Gray body and chassis, light brown roof, white tires.
19 ROLLS-ROYCE 1986
Gray body and chassis, black roof, light brown interior and trunk, tan hubs and tires.

LLEDO PROMOTIONAL MODELS

It was not long before numerous commercial firms, charitable organizations, collectors' clubs and the like discovered that they could promote their activities with Lledo models. Only in 1985, though, did these promotional models become a separate series, usually fitted with baseplates that bore the words "Lledo Promotional." Since then there have been hundreds of promotional models and they have not always been easy to list, let alone obtain. At first I tried to get them all, but after the first few years I realized that I simply could not afford them all, even if they were all available to me, which they often were not. This is why you will not see pictures, or read all the details, of many models listed in this section of the book.

The listings, as you will see, are brief, to save space. Only major variations (the colors of components, etc.) have been listed. Minor variations, such as wheel types and colors or minor casting changes, usually occurred only in early models, and you may find more detailed information in *Matchbox and Lledo Toys*. I have tried to provide enough information to distinguish the model in question from any other. When I have not seen a model, I cannot describe it at all and have to rely on the RDP listings to know that it exists and what its one or two main colors are. For this I am extremely grateful to RDP.

While the fact that a certain model exists, has a certain logo, and is a certain color are public knowledge, the RDP system of listing and numbering the Lledo Promotional models is copyrighted and cannot be used here. Thus I have developed a different system, that of listing and numbering each year's issues in alphabetical order. This will, I hope, allow the collector to look for a model without scanning the entire list, as one need only look for the name of the model alphabetically in each year's listing until one finds it.

In recent years, RDP has listed those promotional models with adhesive labels separately as the SP series. This system is also copyrighted and will not be used in this book, nor do I feel that there is any need to separate these models from those with a tampo-printed logo. All promotional models issued in a given year will be listed together, alphabetically by name.

As for the names, I have tried to base the listed names on the actual lettering on the model. At times someone who knows the background information (such as what organization ordered the model) may refer to it by a name that does not occur prominently, if at all, on the model. Since not everyone will know all of this background information, I have used the actual logo as the basis for listing the model.

Many of the bus models have destination or other lettering on their front (and sometimes rear) boards (blinds), and I have listed these whenever possible, including the two or three variations found on some models. I must add that, while listed here as "destination", some of them, such as "excursion", "private" and "relief", to say nothing of "Hi-de-ho", are clearly not destinations. So please regard the "destination" listing as short for "the name on the destination blind", or whatever it is called in American English, the language in which, for the most part, this book is written (which is why "gray" is not spelled "grey" unless it refers to a hound).

I might add that I have numerous models that have Lledo Promotional baseplates but have not appeared in the RDP listing. They, I presume, may be properly classified as Code 3 models.

There are cases in which, thanks to RDP, I know the main colors of a model but cannot be sure just which colors appear on which parts of the body. In such cases I at first tried to make studied guesses, and probably guessed wrong several times, before I gave up and resorted to Using "..." to indicate that I simply do not know the rest of the story. Any information that anyone would care to send would be much appreciated and will find a happy home on my computer, and perhaps in a later edition of this book.

And now let's get on to the Lledo Promotional models.

1 HORSE DRAWN TRAM 1983
1-88-1 ISLE OF MAN: DOUGLAS 1988
Red body, white roof, "Douglas, Isle of Man" logo.
1-88-2 ISLE OF MAN: MANX TELECOM 1988
Red body, white roof, "Manx Telecom" logo.
1-88-3 ISLE OF MAN: POST OFFICE 1988
Red body, black roof, "Manx Post Office" logo.
2 HORSE DRAWN MILK FLOAT 1983
2-89-1 MILK INDUSTRY 1989
Red body, white chassis and roof, Milk Industry logo.
2-91-1 EXPRESS DAIRY 1991
Black body, white . . .
3 HORSE DRAWN DELIVERY VAN 1983
3-85-1 PHOENIX STEAM DYE HOUSE 1985
Dark blue body, black chassis and roof, "Phoenix Steam Dye House" logo.
3-88-1 CHIVERS OLD ENGLISH MARMALADE 1988
Black body, chassis and roof, "Chivers Olde English" logo.
3-88-2 EXCHANGE AND MART 1988
Light blue body, blue . . .
3-89-1 ROYAL MAIL 1989
Red body, black chassis and roof, "Royal Mail" logo.
3-90-1 SCHNEIDER MEATS 1990
Orange body, blue . . .

3-92-1 P. D. S. A. 1992
White body, blue chassis and roof, The Incredible Journey logo.
3-92-2 W. H. SMITH & SON 1992
White body and roof, red lower panels and chassis, W. H. Smith & Son logo.
3-93-1 HENRY ADLAM 1993
Cream body, black . . .
3-93-2 NEWS OF THE WORLD 1993
Blue body and chassis, cream roof, News of the World logo.
3-93-3 UNWINS 1993
Green body and roof, black chassis, Unwins Wine Marchants Since 1843 logo.
3-93-4 WARBURTON DIAMOND JUBILEE 1993
Maroon body, black chassis and roof, H. Warburton Diamond Jubilee Bakery logo.
3-93-5 WILLIAM LUSTY 1993
Cream body and chassis, brown roof, William Lusty logo.
3-94-1 BUSHELLS TEA 1994
Navy blue body, roof . . .
3-94-2 GURTEEN 1994
No data.
3-94-3 PETERBOROUGH CO-OP BAKERY 1994
Maroon body, cream . . .
4 HORSE DRAWN OMNIBUS 1983

4-85-1 BRIDLINGTON 1985
Red body, green seats, "Bridlington" logo.
  1. Orange logo.
  2. Green logo.
4-87-1 EXCHANGE AND MART 1987
Dark green body, red seats, "Exchange and Mart" logo.
4-89-1 BASSETTS 1989
Black body and seats, "Bassetts Allsorts Liquorice: logo.
4-89-2 COVENTRY--SCARLEYS 1989
Maroon body, cream seats, "Scarley's Celebrated Omnibuses" logo.
4-89-3 OLD BEN 1989
Blue body . . .
4-89-4 TORQUAY CLOPPER 1989
Light blue body, cream seats, "Victorian Shopping Arcade" and "The Torquay Clopper: logo.
4-92-1 GUILD 92 1992
White body . . .
4-92-2 HEINZ 57 VARIETIES 1992
Cream body and chassis, red seats, "Heinz 57 Varieties" logo.
4-93-1 NEWS OF THE WORLD 1993
Cream body, black seats, "News of the World, one penny" logo.
4-93-2 TELEGRAPH AND STAR 1993
Tan body and chassis . . ., Telegraph & Star upper logo.

4-94-1 LEICESTER MERCURY 1994
Cream body and chassis, black seats, Leicester Mercury, Victoria Park, and Leicester Corporation Tramways logo.
4-94-2 TEESIDE EVENING GAZETTE 1994
Maroon body . . .
4-94-3 WESTERN MAIL 1994
No data.
5 HORSE DRAWN FIRE ENGINE 1983
5-86-1 COVENTRY 1986
Red body, gold boiler, "Coventry" logo.
5-86-2 GUILDFORD FIRE BRIGADE 1986
Dark green body, black chassis, gold boiler, "Guildford Fire Brigade" logo, #15.
5-86-3 HULL POLICE FIRE BRIGADE 1986
Blue body, gold boiler, "Hull Police Fire Brigade" logo.
5-86-4 METROPOLITAN FIRE BRIGADE 1986
Red body, copper boiler, "Metropolitan Fire Brigade" logo.
5-91-1 DOUGLAS CORPORATION 1991
Red body . . .
5-91-2 HORSHAM FIRE ENGINE 1991
Red body and chassis, gold boiler, Horsham Fire Engine logo.
5-92-1 SHEFFIELD FIRE SERVICE 1992
Red body, gold boiler, royal crest logo, no lettering, Sheffield Fire Museum certificate.
5-92-2 SHEPSHED 1992
Red body, gold boiler, Shepshed logo. In Leicestershire set.
5-93-1 ALTON FIRE BRIGADE 1993
Red body . . .
5-93-2 BOURNE U. D. C. 1993
No data.
5-93-3 BURTON UPON TRENT 1993
Maroon body . . .
5-93-4 F. S. P. G. CHASEWATER 1993
Red body, gold boiler, F.S.P.G. Chasewater logo.
5-93-5 CLEETHORPE DISTRICT 1993
Red body, gold boiler, Cleethorpe District Council logo.
5-93-6 NOTTINGHAM 1993
Red body, gold boiler, City of Nottingham logo.
6 MODEL T FORD VAN 1983
6-85-1 AVON ROAD RESCUE 1985
Dark blue body.
6-85-2 BEAULIEU MOTOR MUSEUM 1985
Dark yellow body, black chassis and roof, Beaulieu, The National Motor Museum logo.
6-85-3 BRIDLINGTON 1985
Blue body and chassis, white roof, Bridlington For Funshine Holidays logo.
6-85-4 FARNHAM MALTINGS 1985
Black body, chassis and roof, Farnham Maltings 10th March 1985 logo.

6-85-5 FISHERMAN'S FRIEND 1985
Tan body, brown chassis and roof, Lofthouse's Original Fisherman's Friend logo.
6-85-6 FOTORAMA 1985
White body, red chassis and roof, red and blue Fotorama, a World of Colour logo.
6-85-7 GARDNER MERCHANT CATERING 1985
Tan body, dark brown chassis, light or reddish brown roof, Gardner Merchant, A Century of Catering Services logo.
   1. Light brown roof.
   2. Reddish brown roof.
6-85-8 GARDNER MERCHANT SITE SERVICES 1985
Tan body, dark brown chassis, light or reddish brown roof, logo presumably includes "site services".
   1. Light brown roof.
   2. Reddish brown roof.
6-85-9 W. HAYDON 1985
Black body, roof and chassis, W. Haydon Furnishing, Ironmonger logo. In box or on plinth.
6-85-10 HENDY MOTOR ENGINEERS 1985
Dark green body, black chassis and roof, Hendy Motor Engineers logo.
6-85-11 HORNBY RAILWAYS 1985
Dark red body, black chassis and roof, Hornby Railways logo.
6-85-12 LANCASHIRE EVENING POST 1985
Brown or magenta body, black chassis and roof, Lancashire Evening Post, Established 1886 logo.
   1. Brown body.
   2. Magenta body.
6-85-13 LEGAL & GENERAL 1985
White body, red chassis, yellow roof, Legal & General logo.
6-85-14 MILTON KEYNES DIGITAL TYPE 1985
White body, blue chassis and roof, Digital Type Suppliers Milton Keynes logo. (also known as Varityper)
6-85-15 MITRE 10 1985
Light brown body, black chassis and roof, Mitre 10, The Mighty Australians logo.
6-85-16 NATIONAL CHILDREN'S HOME 1985
White body, red chassis and roof, National Children's Home 1911-1986 logo.
6-85-17 SALTERNS/OVERDRIVE 1985
White body, green chassis and roof, Salterns, The World's Finest Transport Operation logo.
6-85-18 SALVATION ARMY 1985
Black body, chassis and roof, The Salvation Army Men's Social Services logo.
6-85-19 SCOTCH CORNER--THE SWAPMEET 1985
Silver body, black chassis and roof, Scotch Corner--The Swapmeet logo.

6-86-1 ANDERSON & McAULEY 1986
Maroon body, black chassis and roof, Anderson & McAuley logo.
6-86-2 AUTOMOTIVE COMMERCIAL 1986
No data.
6-86-3 BRIT TYRES 1986
Red body, black chassis and roof, Brit Tyres Quality tyre fitting service logo.
6-86-4 BRITISH HOVERCRAFT 1986
Ivory body, blue chassis, red roof, British Hovercraft Corporation Going Places logo.
6-86-5 CADA TOYS 1986
Light orange body, black chassis and roof, Cada Toys 1965-1986 logo.
6-86-6 CHANNEL 4 (4-TEL) 1986
Blue body and chassis, light blue roof.
6-86-7 CLARKSON PUCKLE 1986
Red body and chassis, black roof, Clarkson Puckle for Agreed Value Insurance logo.
6-86-8 CONESTOGA COUNTRY CLUB 1986
White body, green chassis and roof, Conestoga Country Club logo.
6-86-9 DH--TRANS BV 1986
Cream body, black chassis and roof, DH-Trans BV 24 Uur Service logo.
6-86-10 EPSOM STAMP COMPANY 1986
Cream body, brown chassis and roof, Epsom Stamp Co. logo.
6-86-11 EXCHANGE & MART (red) 1986
Red body and chassis, black roof, Exchange & Mart 1986 Motoring Events, Hagley Hall logo.
6-86-12 EXCHANGE & MART (tan) 1986
Tan body, brown chassis and roof, The Bazaar Exchange & Mart Journal of the Household logo.
6-86-13 FAMOUS MENSWEAR/BOYSWEAR 1986
Dark brown body, black chassis and roof, The Famous of Cheltenham Menswear Boyswear logo.
6-86-14 FRANKLIN CHARITY PRO-AM 1986
Maroon body, black chassis and roof, 1986 Franklin Charity Pro-Am logo.
6-86-15 HERITAGE HOMES 1986
Dark brown body and roof, black chassis, Heritage Homes in a class by themselves logo.
6-86-16 KOYANAGI--GERSON 1986
White body, light green chassis and roof, green and gold Japanese logo with blue phone number, gold header lettering.
6-86-17 MILLER OF NOTTINGHAM 1986
Dark yellow body, black chassis and roof, Miller of Nottingham Limited Nationwide Painting Contractors logo.
6-86-18 NATIONAL COAL BOARD 1986
Dark blue body.

6-86-19 NATIONAL GARDEN FESTIVAL 1986
Green body, red chassis, white roof, National Garden Festival, Stoke-on-Trent 1986 logo.

6-86-20 N. C. JEWELLERY 1986
Black body, roof and chassis, N C Jewellery Pty. Ltd. Sydney logo.

6-86-21 NEWBURY STEAM LAUNDRY 1986
Red body, black chassis and roof, Newbury Sanitary Steam Laundry logo.

6-86-22 SERVICE OFFSET SUPPLIES 1986
Tan body.

6-86-23 SHIPSTONES 1986
Red body, black chassis and roof, Shipstones Traditional Fine Ales logo, with or without Brit Tyres header lettering.
  1. No header lettering (correct form).
  2. Brit Tyres Sales logo (error).

6-86-24 SHREDDED WHEAT 1986
Yellow body, black chassis and roof, Nabisco Shredded Wheat logo. Wheels, grille and casting may vary.

6-86-25 TALYLLYN RAILWAY 1986
Dark green body, black chassis, red roof, The First Preserved Railway, Talyllyn Railway logo.

6-86-26 TAYLOR'S OF GLOUCESTER 1986
White body, blue chassis and roof, Taylor's of Gloucester 1925 1985 logo.

6-86-27 TERRY PRINTING GROUP 1986
Black body.

6-86-28 THRUWAY MUFFLER CENTRE 1986
Whitoe body, black chassis and roof, Thruway Muffler Centre left, Centre du Silencieux Autoroute right logo.

6-86-29 WAKEFIELD CASTROL 1986
Dark green body, black chassis, black or white roof, Wakefield Castrol Motor Oil logo.
  1. White roof.
  2. Black roof.

6-86-30 WHITBREAD 1986
Brown body and chassis, dark brown roof, Whitbread Blackburn Estd 1742 logo.

6-87-1 A E I CABLES 150 YEARS 1987
Black body.

6-87-2 ANCHOR CHEESE 1987
Yellow body, green chassis and roof, Anchor Cheese emblem logo.

6-87-3 ANTIQUE & COLLECTORS FAYRE 1987
Maroon body, cream chassis and roof, Antique & Collectors Fayre logo.

6-87-4 ARKLEY LABELS 1987
Yellow or black body
  1. Yellow body.
  2. Black body.

6-87-5 BASSETTS ALLSORTS LIQUORICE 1987
Black body, chassis and roof, Bassetts Allsorts Liquorice logo.

6-87-6 BEAMISH MUSEUM 1987
Plum body, cream chassis and roof, B.E.A.M.I.S.H. The Great Northern Experience logo.

6-87-7 BREAD 'N' BUN 1987
Cream body, blue chassis and roof, Bread 'n' Bun real dairy cream logo.

6-87-8 CADBURY 1987
Purple body, maroon chassis, cream roof, Cadbury logo with tree.

6-87-9 CAMBRIDGE EVENING NEWS 1987
Black body, chassis and roof, Cambridge Evening News logo.

6-87-10 CANADIAN PREMIUM INCENTIVE SHOW 1987
White body, orange chassis and roof, 14th Annual Canadian Premium Incentive Travel Show . . . September 9, 10, 11 1987.

6-87-11 CASTROL WORLD RALLY 1987
Dark green body, black chassis and roof, Castrol and Wakefield Motor Oil, Est'd 1899 logo, model sold in World Rally box.

6-87-12 CHAMPION SPARK PLUGS 1987
Yellow-orange body, black roof and chassis, Champion Double Ribbed Spark Plugs logo.

6-87-13 W. CLIFFORD DAIRYMEN 1987
Tangerine red body, black chassis, white roof, W. Clifford & Sons Dairymen logo.

6-87-14 COOK & HICKMAN 1987
Red body, black chassis and roof, Cook & Hickman Solicitors logo.

6-87-15 COUNTRY LIFE/BETTER BIT OF BUTTER 1987
Cream body, brown chassis and roof, You'll never put a better bit of butter on your knife logo, Country Life English Butter header.

6-87-16 COUTURE DESIGNER 1987
White body, black . . .

6-87-17 CUMBERLAND NEWS 1987
Red body and roof, black chassis, Cumberland News logo.

6-87-18 DELTIC PRESERVATION SOCIETY 1987
Dark blue body, black chassis, yellow-orange roof, Deltic Preservation Society 1977-10th Anniversary-1987 logo.

6-87-19 EASTERN DAILY PRESS 1987
Yellow body, black chassis and roof, Eastern Daily Press logo.

6-87-20 ELMIRA MAPLE SYRUP FESTIVAL 1987
White body, blue . . .

6-87-21 FAMOUS MENSWEAR 1987
Green body, black . . .

6-87-22 FARNHAM MALTINGS 1987 1987
Yellow body, black chassis and roof, presumably Farnham Maltings 1987 logo.

6-87-23 FOTORAMA 1987
Silver body, red chassis and roof, red-yellow-blue Fotorama, a World of Colour logo, red spoked hubs.

6-87-24 FRANKLIN CHARITY PRO-AM 1987 1987
Dark green body, black chassis and roof, 1987 Franklin Charity Pro-Am logo.

6-87-25 FURNISS OF TRURO 1987
Yellow body, black chassis and roof, Furniss of Truro, Established 1886, Famous for Biscuits and Fudge logo.

6-87-26 HAPPY EATER 1987
Yellow body and chassis, red roof, Happy Eater Family Restaurants logo.

6-87-27 HATFIELDS FURNISHERS 1987
White body, black chassis and roof, Hatfields Furnishers of Distinction logo.

6-87-28 HUDDERSFIELD DAILY EXAMINER 1987
Orange or yellow body, black chassis and roof, Huddersfield Daily Examiner, Your Local Paper logo.
  1. Orange body.
  2. Yellow body.

6-87-29 HUMI SERV 1987
Dark green body, black chassis and roof, Humi Serv logo.

6-87-30 T. JONES 1987
Green body, black chassis and roof, T. Jones, The Finest Quality Meats, Family Butcher logo.

6-87-31 JUWELIER WAGNER MADLER 1987
Magenta body, black chassis and roof, Juwelier Wagner Madler logo.

6-87-32 KIT KAT (50 Years) 1987
Red body, white chassis and roof, KitKat 1937-1987 50 Years logo.

6-87-33 KIT KAT (Have a Break) 1987
Red body, white chassis and roof, logo includes "Have a break".

6-87-34 KRONDORF AUSTRALIAN WINE 1987
Yellow-orange body, black chassis and roof, Krondorf Premium Australian Wines logo.

6-87-35 LINCOLNSHIRE ECHO 1987
Red body, black chassis and roof.

6-87-36 MASTIFF ASSOCIATION 1987
Black body, brown chassis, light brown roof, Mastiff Association logo.

6-87-37 MOORSIDE SCHOOL 1987
Yellow-orange body, black chassis and roof, Moorside School Staffordshire logo.

6-87-38 THE MUSTARD SHOP 1987
Tan body, dark brown chassis and roof, The mustard Shop logo.

6-87-39 NORTHERN ECHO 1987
Red body and roof, black chassis, Northern Echo logo.

6-87-40 ODD FELLOWS 1987
Maroon body, black chassis and roof, Independent Order of Odd Fellows logo.

6-87-41 OTTAWA CITIZEN 1987
Yellow body, black chassis and roof, The Ottawa Citizen Since 1843 logo.

6-87-42 THE PALMS (Stepeley Water Gardens) 1987
Yellow body, black chassis and roof, The Palms Tropical Oasis logo.

6-87-43 PERSIL 1987
Dark green body, black chassis, red roof, Persil Washes Whiter logo.

6-87-44 REDDICAP HEATH SCHOOL 1987
Blue body, yellow chassis and roof, Reddicap Heath First School
logo.
6-87-45 ROUND TABLE DIAMOND JUBILEE 1987
Cream body, red chassis and roof, Round Table Diamond Jubilee
1927-1987 logo.
6-87-46 ST. JOHN PARTY/AMBULANCE 1987
White body and chassis, black roof, Great St. John Party 20th June
1987 logo, Ambulance on header.
6-87-47 SCHWEPPES 1987
Dark yellow body, black chassis and roof, Schweppes logo.
6-87-48 STANLEY GIBBONS LTD. 1987
Dark green body and roof, black chassis, Stanley Gibbons Ltd.
Philatelists and Publishers logo.
6-87-49 SPRING GARDEN SHOW 1987
Ivory body, orange chassis and roof, The Spring Garden Show May 2-
4th 1987 logo.
6-87-50 STAFFORDSHIRE COUNTY SHOW 1987
Blue body, orange chassis and roof, Staffordshire County Show,
Staffordshire Agricultural Society logo.
6-87-51 STAFFORDSHIRE POLICE ORCHESTRA 1987
Dark green body, blue chassis, light blue roof, Staffordshire Police
Dance Orchestra logo.
6-87-52 THE STAR 1987
Brownish maroon body, black chassis and roof, Keep up to date with
the Star logo. (Has been listed as Sheffield Star.)
6-87-53 STRAND GIFT SHOPS 1987
White body and roof, black chassis, Strand and envelope design logo.
6-87-54 STUTTGART 1987
Cream body, red . . ., black . . .
6-87-55 TELEMEDIA CELEBRITY GOLF 1987
Black body, chassis and roof, Telemedia Celebrity Gold Tournament
September 1987 logo.
6-87-56 TENNENT'S LAGER 1987
Green body and chassis, black roof, Tennent's Lager, Brewers of Ales
& Stouts Since 1556 logo.
6-87-57 TRUE VALUE HARDWARE 1987
Black body, chassis and roof, True Value Hardware logo.
6-87-58 UNWINS WINE MERCHANTS 1987
Dark green body, black chassis, brown, black or green roof, Unwins
Wine Merchants logo. Wheel types and colors vary.
  1. Brown roof.
  2. Black roof.
  3. Green roof.
6-87-59 WALL'S SAUSAGES 1987
White body, blue chassis and roof, Wall's Sausages, Established in
1786 logo.
6-87-60 WELLS BLACK VELVIT 1987
Light rose body, black chassis and roof, Wells Blackcurrant Black
Velvit logo.

6-87-61 WERRINGTON PATISSERIE 1987
Tan body, brown chassis and roof, The Werrington Patisserie Ltd.
logo.
6-87-62 WESTERN AUTO SUPPLY 1987
Red body, black chassis and roof, Western Auto Supply Co. logo.
**6-87-63 WESTERN MORNING NEWS/EVENING HERALD
1987**
Red body and roof, black chassis, The Western Morning News logo
on left side, Western Evening Herald on right.
6-87-64 WORFIELD GARAGE 1987
Red or black body and chassis, black roof, Worfield Garage logo.
  1. Red body and chassis.
  2. Black body and chassis.
6-87-65 YORK CASTLE MUSEUM 1987
Dark green body, cream chassis, black roof, York Castle Museum
logo.
6-88-1 ABERDEEN BEEF 1988
White body, red . . .
6-88-2 AIR CALL MEDICAL SERVICES 1988
White body, red chassis and roof.
6-88-3 ATKINSON PRINT 1988
Blue body, yellow-orange chassis and roof, Atkinson Print logo.
6-88-4 AUTODROP 1988
White body, black . . .
6-88-5 BARCLAYS 1988
Blue body, green . . .
6-88-6 BARCLAYS GRACECHURCH STREET 1988
Black body.
6-88-7 BASS WINDOWS 1988
Maroon body, white . . .
6-88-8 BAY RADIO CABS 1988
White body and roof, black chassis, Bay Radio Cabs 24 Hour Service
logo.
6-88-9 BEAMISH OPEN-AIR MUSEUM 1988
Maroon body, white . . .
6-88-10 BERKSHIRE BRANCH 1988
White body, chassis and roof, British Red Cross Society, Berkshire
Branch logo
6-88-11 BOOTS QUALITY PRODUCTS 1988
Blue body and chassis, white roof, Boots Quality Products logo.
6-88-12 BRANDON HIRE 1988
Magenta body, black chassis and roof, Brandon Hire logo.
6-88-13 BRANDRETH INVESTMENTS 1988
Maroon body, white chassis and roof, Brandreth investments logo.
6-88-14 BRITISH PORK PIES 1988
Maroon body and chassis, black roof, British Pork Pies logo.
6-88-15 BRITISH SAUSAGES 1988
Blue body . . .
6-88-16 BRYLCREEM 1988
Red body, white chassis and roof, Brylcreem logo.

6-88-17 BURNHAM COURIER SERVICE 1988
White body, chassis and roof.
6-88-18 CARLSBERG 1988
White body, green . . .
6-88-19 CASTLEGATE HOTEL/RUMOUR BISTRO 1988
Cream body, red chassis, black roof, Castlegate Hotel left, Rumour
Bistro right logo.
6-88-20 CHARTERHOUSE FAIR 1988
Light green body, black chassis and roof, The Charterhouse Fair logo.
6-88-21 CHIMNEY SWEEP 1988
White body, black chassis and roof, Chimney Sweep logo.
6-88-22 CHIVERS LEMON CURD 1988
Yellow body, black chassis, white roof, Chivers Lemon Curd logo.
6-88-23 COTSWOLD DAIRY 1988
Cream body, green . . .
6-88-24 COVENTRY EVENING TELEGRAPH 1988
Black body, roof and chassis . . .
6-88-25 ELM FARM DAIRIES 1988
White body, cream . . .
6-88-26 EXCHANGE AND MART ANNIVERSARY 1988
Red body, black chassis and roof, Exchange & Mart 120th
Anniversary logo.
6-88-27 EXCHANGE & MART BAZAAR 1988
White body, light green chassis, black roof, Advertise in the Bazaar
Exchange and Mart logo.
6-88-28 FARLEY'S BREAKFAST TIMERS 1988
Cream body and chassis, brown roof, Farley's Breakfast Timers/
Crookes Healthcare logo.
6-88-29 FRANKLIN CHARITY PRO-AM 1988 1988
Black body, chassis and roof, 1988 Franklin Charity Pro-Am logo.
6-88-30 GRIMSBY EVENING TELEGRAPH 1988
Red body and roof, black chassis, Evening Telegraph logo.
6-88-31 HOME HARDWARE GOLF 1988 1988
Yellow body, black chassis and roof, Home Hardware 1988 Annual
Golf Tournament logo.
6-88-32 ISLE OF MAN POST OFFICE 1988
Red body, black chassis and roof, Isle of Man Post Office logo.
6-88-33 JACOB'S CREAM CRACKERS 1988
Orange body, black roof and chassis, Jacob's Cream Crackers logo.
6-88-34 KENTUCKY FRIED CHICKEN 1988
Red body and chassis, white roof, Kentucky Fried Chicken logo.
6-88-35 V. LEONARD & CO. 1988
Blue body, yellow . . .
6-88-36 MACLEANS 1988
Blue body, white chassis and roof, Macleans logo.
6-88-37 McCULLOUGHS 1988
Green body, black . . .
6-88-38 MELTON PRINTERS 1988
White body and roof, blue chassis, Melton Printers of Lincoln logo.

6-88-39 MODEL MART 1988
Red body, black chassis and roof, Model Mart logo.
6-88-40 NEEDLER'S CHOCOLATES 1988
Brown body, black chassis, cream roof, Needler's Ltd. Chocolates logo.
6-88-41 NORCO 1988
White body, blue chassis, red roof, Norco Naturally Australian logo.
6-88-42 NORTH EASTERN DAILY GAZETTE 1988
Maroon body and roof, black chassis, North Eastern Daily Gazette logo.
6-88-43 NOTTINGHAM EVENING POST 1988
Dark blue body . . .
6-88-44 PORK FARMS 1988
Dark green body, black chassis and roof, Pork Farms much prized quality logo.
6-88-45 PORK FARMS PIES & SAUSAGES 1988
Dark green body, black . . .
6-88-46 ST. AUSTELL BREWERY 1988
Dark blue body, black chassis and roof, St. Austell Brewery logo.
6-88-47 ST. DAVID'S FOUNDATION 1988
Orange body, green chassis and roof, St. David's Foundation, Gwent logo.
6-88-48 SALVATION ARMY 1988
Navy blue body, black roof and chassis, The Salvation Army logo.
6-88-49 SCOTSBURN 1988
White body, blue chassis and roof, Scotsburn, the dairy best logo.
6-88-50 SECOND MINSTER TOY FAIR 1988
White body, dark blue chassis, light blue roof, The second annual Minster Village Toy & Train Fair 1988 logo.
6-88-51 SPROWSTON GARDEN CENTRE 1988
Dark green body, black chassis and roof, Sprowston Garden Centre logo.
6-88-52 STANDARD LIFE 1988
White body, blue . . .
6-88-53 SUNDERLAND ECHO 1988
Black body, dark gray chassis, light gray roof, The Sunderland Echo logo.
6-88-54 SUSSEX EXPRESS 1987-88
Red body, black chassis and roof . . .
6-88-55 TELEMEDIA CELEBRITY GOLF 1988
Maroon body, black roof and chassis, Telemedia Celebrity Golf Tournament, August 1988 logo.
6-88-56 TWININGS TEA 1988
Black body, chassis and roof . . .
6-88-57 UDSALG 1988
Red body and roof, black chassis, traevarefabrikernes Udsalg logo.
6-88-58 UNION OF DEMOCRATIC MINEWORKERS 1988
Red body, white . . .
6-88-59 VOSENE 1988
Green body, white chassis and roof, Vosene logo.

6-88-60 WELLS JAFFA ORANGE DRINK 1988
Blue body and chassis, white roof, Wells Jaffa Orange Drink logo.
6-88-61 WEST SUFFOLK SCANNER APPEAL 1988
Cream body, blue chassis and roof, West Suffolk Scanner Appeal logo.
6-88-62 WIGAN PIER 1988
Dark green body, black chassis and roof . . .
6-88-63 WOODEN SPOON PRESERVING CO. 1988
Cream body, black chassis, green roof, The Wooden Spoon Preserving Co. Ltd. logo.
6-89-1 3M SUPER SEAM SEALER 1989
Green body, black . . .
6-89-2 ACDO 1989
Green body and chassis, white roof, ACDO, The Guaranteed Self-Washer logo.
6-89-3 ANGILLEY YATES 1989
White body, blue . . .
6-89-4 ARROWPAK REMOVALS 1989
Green body, black roof and chassis, Arrowpak Removals logo.
6-89-5 AUSTIN TRUMANNS STEEL 1989
White body, black . . .
6-89-6 BENSON & HEDGES 1989
Yellow body, black . . .
6-89-7 BICC CABLES 1989
White body, orange . . .
6-89-8 BOLSOVER COLLIERY 1989
Blue-black body, black chassis and roof, The Bolsover Colliery Company Limited Foundation Centenary logo.
6-89-9 BOOTS 1989
Blue body, white . . .
6-89-10 CANDIS 1989
Black body, chassis and roof, Candis and Newhall Publications Limited logo.
6-89-11 CARMARTHEN JOURNAL 1989
Yellow body, white . . .
6-89-12 CITY OF WINDSOR 1989
White body, blue chassis and roof, City of Windsor 1854 logo.
6-89-13 CLAYTON LTD. 1989
White body and roof, black chassis . . .
6-89-14 COCA-COLA (ULSTER) 1989
Red body, black . . .
6-89-15 COOK'S MATCHES 1989
Tan body, black chassis, white roof, Cook's Matches logo.
6-89-16 CRUMBLES 1989
Light blue body, white chassis and roof, Crumbles logo with Huntley & Palmers emblem.
6-89-17 DAIRY FARM HAMPERS 1989
Cream body, blue . . .
6-89-18 DUERRS 1989
Green body, black . . .

6-89-19 EDINBURGH EVENING NEWS 1989
Silver body, black roof and chassis, Evening News, North Bridge, Edinburgh logo.
6-89-20 ENSORS CENTENARY 1989
Pink body, black . . .
6-89-21 J. W. GRAY & CO. 1989
Blue body, white chassis and roof, J. W. Gray & Co. logo.
6-89-22 THE GROCER NEWSPAPER 1989
White body, black chassis and roof, The Grocer logo.
6-89-23 GURTEEN 1989
Dark blue body, black chassis and roof, Gurteen logo.
6-89-24 G.W.R. MUSEUM, SWINDON 1989
Maroon body, black chassis and roof, G. W. R. Museum, Swindon, No. 3 logo.
6-89-25 HAMPSHIRE CHRONICLE 1989
Black body, chassis and roof . . .
6-89-26 INSURANCE & BANKING PHILATELIC SOCIETY 1989
Dark blue body, cream . . .
6-89-27 INTERNATIONAL PLOWING FESTIVAL 1989
Black body, chassis and roof, International Plowing Festival, Windsor, Essex County, Ontario 1989 logo.
6-89-28 JERSEY EVENING POST 1989
Pink body, black . . .
6-89-29 JIM BEAM 1989
Red body, white . . .
6-89-30 KLM TAX-FREE SERVICES 1989
Light blue body, blue chassis, white roof, KLM Tax Free Services logo.
6-89-31 KNECHTEL 60 YEARS 1989
White body, blue chassis and roof, Knechtel 1930, 1990, 60 Years of Service logo.
6-89-32 LEICESTERSHIRE UMBRELLA PROJECT 1989
Yellow body, black chassis, red roof, Leicestershire Umbrella Project logo.
6-89-33 C. & E. LEIGHTON & SONS 1989
White body, green . . .
6-89-34 LIFE STYLE 1989
White body, red chassis and roof, Life Style and Choose Quality logo.
6-89-35 LIVERPOOL ECHO 1989
Blue body, black . . .
6-89-36 LLEDO MODEL OF THE MONTH CLUB 1989
Light blue body, black chassis and roof, Lledo 1989 Model of the Month Club logo.
6-89-37 LONDON BOROUGH OF SUTTON 1989
Green body, black . . .
6-89-38 MARIE CURIE 1989
Blue body, white . . .
6-89-39 MAXWELL HOUSE 1989
White body, red . . .

6-89-40 MURRAY FARM PUBLIC SCHOOL 1989
Dark blue body, red . . .
6-89-41 NATIONAL MOTOR MUSEUM 1989
Silver body, black chassis and roof, National Motor Museum logo.
6-89-42 NONFUMO FLUE SYSTEMS 1989
Blue body, black chassis and roof, Nonfumo Flue Ststems Ltd. logo.
6-89-43 NOTTINGHAM FOREST F. C. 1989
Red body, white . . .
6-89-44 NOTTINGHAMSHIRE CONSTABULARY 1989
White body, black . . .
6-89-45 NOTTS COUNTY F. C. 1989
White body, black . . .
6-89-46 OVENFRESH EASTBOURNE 1989
Yellow body, brown . . .
6-89-47 PEMBROKE VINTAGE CAR CLUB 1989
Ivory body, blue chassis and roof, 1964 PVCC 1989 logo.
6-89-48 PREMIUM INCENTIVE SHOW 1989
Light blue body, blue chassis and roof, 51st Annual Premium
Incentive Show logo.
6-89-49 PUSSERS RUM 1989
Dark blue body, chassis and roof . . .
6-89-50 RAFA WINGS APPEAL 1989
Light gray body, black chassis and roof, RAFA Wings Appeal and
Royal Air Force Association logo.
6-89-51 ROYAL MAIL TELEGRAM SERVICE 1989
Red body and roof, black chassis, Royal Mail Telegram Service logo.
6-89-52 SADDLERY 1989
White body, dark brown chassis and roof, Saddlery for Horse and
Rider logo.
6-89-53 ST. JULIAN'S BAPTIST CHURCH 1989
Blue body, white chassis and roof, St. Julian's Baptist Church,
Newport-Gwent logo.
6-89-54 SCOTTS CHINA & GLASS 1989
Brown body, black . . .
6-89-55 STA'UBLI UNIMATION 1989
Gray body, white . . .
6-89-56 STOKE MANDEVILLE HOSPITAL 1989
White body, blue . . .
6-89-57 SURREY ADVERTISER 1989
White body, black . . .
6-89-58 TETLEY'S TEAS 1989
Dark blue body, black chassis, white roof, Tetley's Teas logo.
6-89-59 TWININGS TEA CADDY 1989
Olive body, black chassis and roof, Twinings Established 1706 Tea &
Coffee Merchants logo.
6-89-60 VINTAGE CAR CLUB 1989
Tan body, black . . .
6-89-61 WALKERS FOODS 1989
Red body . . .

6-89-62 WESTERN DAILY PRESS 1989
Blue body, black chassis, white roof, Your Local National
Newspaper, Western Daily Press logo.
6-89-63 YORK CASTLE MUSEUM 1989
Dark green body, cream chassis, black roof, York Castle museum No.
3 logo.
6-90-1 ABERDEEN PRESS & JOURNAL 1990
White body and roof . . .
6-90-2 THE AMERICAN ADVENTURE 1990
Yellow body, blue chassis and roof, The American Adventure Theme
Park logo.
6-90-3 ANDERTON CIRCLIPS 1990
Blue body, black . . .
6-90-4 ASCOT RACECOURSE TOY FAIR 1990
White body and chassis, black roof, Ascot Racecourse Toy Fair, Aug.
5, 1990 logo.
6-90-5 AUTO CLUB USA 1990
Blue body, white . . .
6-90-6 AUTO RETRO 1990
Green body and chassis, black roof, Auto Retro logo.
6-90-7 BARCLAYS WEST KENSINGTON 1990
Light blue body, white . . .
6-90-8 BEDFORDSHIRE TIMES 1990
Navy blue body, cream chassis and roof, Bedfordshire Times logo.
6-90-9 BIG JIGS 1990
Yellow body, red . . .
6-90-10 BILLON 1920-1990 1990
Blue body, black chassis, white roof, Billon 1920-1990 logo.
6-90-11 BLACKPOOL PLEASURE BEACH 1990
White body, light blue . . .
6-90-12 A. BOLTON & SON 1990
Green body, white . . .
6-90-13 BOOTS 150 PHOTO 1990
Blue body, white . . .
6-90-14 BOY SCOUTS AMBULANCE 1990
Green body, chassis and roof, Boy Scouts and red cross logo.
6-90-15 BUXTON MOUNTAIN RESCUE 1990
Blue body, black chassis and roof, Buxton Mountain Rescue Team
logo.
6-90-16 CADBURY'S CHOCOLATE ECLAIRS 1990
Lilac body, dark purple chassis, black roof, Cadbury's Chocolate
Eclairs logo.
6-90-17 CHESHAM GLASS CO. 1990
Red body, black . . .
6-90-18 CLIFFORD DAIRIES 1990
White body, red . . .
6-90-19 COCA-COLA 1990
Black body, chassis and roof . . .
6-90-20 COVENTRY CITY FOOTBALL CLUB 1990
Light blue body, white chassis and roof, Coventry City 1983 logo.

6-90-21 DAILY MIRROR 1990
Black body, chassis and roof, tampo or label Daily Mirror Est. 1903
logo.
6-90-22 DONINGTON PARK 1990
Red body, black chassis and roof, Donington Park, July 1990 logo.
6-90-23 DRY SACK SHERRY 1990
Tan body and roof . . .
6-90-24 EAST ANGLIAN DAILY TIMES 1990
Blue body, black chassis, white roof, All you need to rE.A.D.T.oday
logo.
6-90-25 EAST GRIMSTEAD COURIER 1990
Red body, black chassis and roof, East Grimstead Courier logo.
6-90-26 EPWORTH BELLS 1990
White body, black . . .
6-90-27 EVENING SENTINEL 1990
Dark blue body, black chassis and roof, Evening Sentinel logo.
6-90-28 EXXON CHEMICALS 1990
White body, blue . . .
6-90-29 FARNHAM HERALD 1990
Blue body, chassis and roof . . .
6-90-30 FELLOWS 1990
White body, green . . .
6-90-31 FINNIGAN'S PAINTS 1990
White body, red chassis, yellow roof, Finnigan's proven protection
and Classic Car Rally logo.
6-90-32 FORD MOTOR COMPANY 1990
Black body, chassis and roof, Ford, the universal car logo.
6-90-33 FOURTH OF JULY TOY & TRAIN FAIR 1990
White body, red chassis, blue roof, Fourth of July 1990 Toy & Train
Fair Walsall logo.
6-90-34 GLEVUM TOUR 1990 1990
Red body, black chassis and roof, Glevum Tour 1990 logo.
6-90-35 GLOS WARKS RAILWAY 1990
Green body, black . . .
6-90-36 GREEN BUS LINES 1990
Green body, yellow chassis, cream roof, Green Bus Lines logo.
6-90-37 HAMMONDS OF HULL 1990
White body, green . . .
6-90-38 HANOVIA LAMPS 1990
Blue body, red . . .
6-90-39 HARRY HUSSMAN 1990
Blue body, black . . .
6-90-40 HARRY RAMSDEN 1990
Green body and roof . . .
6-90-41 THE HERALD 1990
Blue body and roof . . .
6-90-42 HOUSE OF FRASER 1990
White body, green chassis and roof, House of Fraser and Frasercard
logo.

6-90-43 HOVIS 100 YEARS 1990
Yellow body, brick red chassis, brown roof, Hovis emblem and 100 years 1890-1990 logo.
6-90-44 INTERNATIONAL POLICE ASSOCIATION 1990
Maroon body, black chassis and roof, International Police Association logo.
6-90-45 IRONBRIDGE GORGE MUSEUM 1990
Maroon body, gray . . .
6-90-46 JULIE & JOHN WEBB 1990
Red body, black chassis, green roof, Julie and John Webb Promoters logo.
6-90-47 KENT COUNTY BRANCH 1990
Navy blue body, black chassis, cream roof, Kent County Branch, British Red Cross Society logo.
6-90-48 LAUBERS 1990
Tan body, brown . . .
6-90-49 LEICESTER CITY F. C. 1990
Blue body and chassis, white roof, Leicester City F. C. logo.
6-90-50 LEICESTER MERCURY 1990
Blue body, black chassis and roof, Leicester Mercury, Largest Circulation logo.
6-90-51 LENNOX 1990
White body, chassis and roof . . .
6-90-52 LEX VEHICLE HIRE 1990
White body, blue . . .
6-90-53 LIFESTYLE 1990
Yellow body and roof . . .
6-90-54 MALT SHOVEL INN 1990
Cream body, red chassis and roof, Malt Shovel Inn, Spondon logo.
6-90-55 MANSFIELD TOWN FOOTBALL CLUB 1990
Yellow body, blue chassis and roof, MTFC logo.
6-90-56 MANX COOPERATIVE 1990
Red body, black chassis and roof, Manx Co-operative Society Ltd. logo.
6-90-57 MORRISONS 1990
Red body, yellow . . .
6-90-58 MULLION HOLIDAY PARK 1990
White body, blue chassis, red roof, Mullion Holiday Park logo.
6-90-59 NATIONAL GARDEN FESTIVAL 1990
Cream body, black chassis, green roof, National Garden Festival, Gateshead 1990 logo.
6-90-60 NEWS OF THE WORLD 1990
Red body and roof, black chassis, News of the World logo.
6-90-61 NOSTELL PRIORY 1990
Dark green body, tan chassis and roof, Nostell Priory, Yorkshire logo.
6-90-62 ORPHEE BEINOGLOU 1990
White body, brown chassis and roof, Orphee Beinoglou logo.
6-90-63 PEARSON CANDY 1990
Red body . . .
6-90-64 PEPSI-COLA 1990
White body, blue chassisn red roof, Pepsi-Cola logo.

6-90-65 PILGRIM HOSPITAL 1990
White body, chassis and roof . . .
6-90-66 PINOCCHIO'S RESTAURANT 1990
White body, black chassis, red roof, Linnochio's Restaurant, Harrogate logo, Harrogate Swapmeet 1990 on rear.
6-90-67 PLANTERS PEANUTS 1990
Blue body, black . . .
6-90-68 PORK FARMS (Queens Drive) 1990
Dark green body, black chassis and roof, Pork Farms much prized quality logo.
6-90-69 PRIMULA CHEESE 1990
Blue body, chassis and roof, Primula Cheese Spread logo.
6-90-70 PUSSERS RUM 1990
Blue body, chassis and roof . . .
6-90-71 RAINBOW CHILDRENS WARD 1990
White body, yellow . . .
6-90-72 RAWLEIGH 1990
Yellow body, black . . .
6-90-73 REDPATH SUGAR 1990
White body, dark blue . . .
6-90-74 RETFORD TIMES 1990
Blue body, black chassis, white roof, Retford Times logo.
6-90-75 RIVERSIDE HOTEL 1990
Blue body and roof, gold chassis, Riverside logo.
6-90-76 ROBIRCH FOODS 1990
White body and roof, maroon chassis, Robirch Fine Fresh Foods logo.
6-90-77 RODDAS CREAM MAKERS 1990
Cream body, chassis and roof . . .
6-90-78 ROYS 1990
White body, light brown . . .
6-90-79 SPORTS AID FOUNDATION 1990
White body and roof, blue chassis, Union Jack design with S A F logo.
6-90-80 SURCLIFFE CATERING 1990
Red body, black . . .
6-90-81 VICTOR ARTS 1990
Blue body, chassis and roof . . .
6-90-82 WAITS 1990
Green body, black . . .
6-90-83 WALKERS POTATO CRISPS 1990
Red body, green chassis, white roof, Potato Crisps by Walkers logo.
6-90-84 WALSALL ILLUMINATIONS 1990
White body, green chassis, red roof, Walsall Illuminations '90 logo.
6-90-85 WORKSOP TRADER 1990
Dark green body, white . . .
6-90-86 WORLD CUP 90 ENGLAND 1990
White body, red chassis and roof, World Cup 1990 and England logo.
6-90-87 WORLD CUP 90 IRELAND 1990
White body, green chassis and roof, World Cup 1990 and Ireland logo.

6-90-88 WORLD CUP 90 SCOTLAND 1990
White body, blue chassis and roof, World Cup 1990 and Scotland logo.
6-91-1 21 YEARS PATROL 1991
Black body, chassis and roof . . .
6-91-2 3M AUTO MASKING TAPE 1991
Dark green body, black . . .
6-91-3 ADVERTISER GROUP 1991
Blue body and roof, black chassis, Advertiser Group Newspapers logo.
6-91-4 ALARM EXPRESS 1991
Black body, chassis and roof . . .
6-91-5 ALCA 1991
Blue body, white . . .
6-91-6 ARROW FORD 1991
Blue body, white . . .
6-91-7 AVON & SOMEREST POLICE 1991
Navy boue body, white . . .
6-91-8 BARCLAYS BANK 1991
Blue body, cream . . ., thick black line in logo.
6-91-9 BEAMISH MUSEUM 1991
Maroon body, cream . . .
6-91-10 BEAULIEU 1991 1991
Blue body, black . . .
6-91-11 BEESTON AMBULANCE STATION 1991
Light blue body and roof, black chassis, 1949 Beeston Ambulance Station 1986 logo.
6-91-12 BIGGLESWADE CHRONICLE 1991
Dark green body, cream . . .
6-91-13 BIRMINGHAM CITY POLICE 1991
Navy blue body, black . . .
6-91-14 BOOTS DRUGS & GIFTS 1991
Blue body and roof . . .
6-91-15 BRADFORD TELEGRAPH 1991
Yellow body, black . . .
6-91-16 BRITISH LEGION 1991
Navy blue body, tan . . .
6-91-17 BRITISH RED CROSS--SOUTH YORKS 1991
White body, chassis and roof . . .
6-91-18 CARLTON TV 1991
White body and roof . . .
6-91-19 CHATHAM CITADEL 1991
Red body, blue . . .
6-91-20 CHEQUERS 1991
White body, black chassis and roof, Chequers logo.
6-91-21 CHESHIRE FOLDING CARTONS 1991
Cream body, brown . . .
6-91-22 CHESHIRE CONSTABULARY 1991
Blue body, black chassis, white roof, Cheshire Constabulary emblem, Cheshire Cathedral logo.

6-91-23 CORNISH SEAL SANCTUARY 1991
White body, green . . .
6-91-24 CORNWALL AMBULANCE SERVICE 1991
White body and roof . . .
6-91-25 COUNTY DAIRIES 1991
White body, green . . .
6-91-26 COVENT GARDEN GENERAL STORES 1991
Green body and roof . . .
6-91-27 CUMBRIA CLASSIC 1991
Green body, black . . .
6-91-28 DEL MONTE 1991
Green body and roof . . .
6-91-29 DERBY RENTAL SERVICE 1991
Red body, white . . .
6-91-30 DUNDEE MARMALADE 1991
Cream body, black chassis, orange roof, Dundee Orange Marmalade logo.
6-91-31 EXPRESS DAIRIES 1991
Black body, white . . .
6-91-32 FORD MOTOR CO. 1991
Black body, chassis and roof, red Ford logo.
6-91-33 GLO-WHITE 1991
White body, green . . .
6-91-34 GRAMPIAN POLICE 1991
White body, black chassis and roof, Grampian Police Diced Cap Appeal logo.
6-91-35 GRANNIES FUDGE SHOP 1991
Pink body, black . . .
6-91-36 GRATE EXPECTATIONS 1991
Black body, chassis and roof . . .
6-91-37 GWALIA SUPPLY CO. 1991
Dark green body, black . . .
6-91-38 HAYES GARDEN WORLD 1991
Green body, white . . .
6-91-39 HOMETUNE 1991
White body, blue . . .
6-91-40 HORNSEA POTTERY 1991
Red body, cream . . .
6-91-41 HOUSE OF FRASER 1991
Dark green body, black chassis and roof, Expect the Best, House of Fraser logo.
6-91-42 IRONBRIDGE GORGE MUSEUM 1991
Red body, gray . . .
6-91-43 JOE LONGTHORNE APPEAL 1991
Black body, chassis and roof, circled Joe Longthorne Appeal logo.
6-91-44 JOHN JOYCE & SON 1991
Yellow body, green . . .
6-91-45 KENDALS 1991
White body, green . . .
6-91-46 KENT MESSENGER 1991
Yellow body, black chassis and roof, Kent Messenger logo.

6-91-47 LAX & SHAW 1991
Black body, chassis and roof . . .
6-91-48 LINCOLNSHIRE CONSTABULARY 1991
White body, black chassis and roof, Lincolnshire Constabulary Headquarters Church Lane lincoln logo.
6-91-49 MARINE LIFE RESCUE 1991
White body, blue . . .
6-91-50 MENINGITIS TRUST 1991
Yellow body, blue chassis and roof, the Meningitis Trust logo.
6-91-51 MILTON KEYNES CITY CHURCH 1991
Blue body, black chassis and roof, Milton Keynes City Church logo.
6-91-52 MONK BAR MODEL SHOP 1991
Cream body, red chassis and roof, Monk Bar Model Shop logo.
6-91-53 MULLION MODEL MUSEUM 1991
Blue body, white . . , red . .
6-91-54 NEWARK ADVERTISER 1991
Blue body, black . . .
6-91-55 NORTHAMPTON & COUNTY POLICE 1991
Black body, chassis and roof . . .
6-91-56 NORTHAMPTON VISITOR CENTRE 1991
Maroon body, cream . . .
6-91-57 NORWICH CITY F. C. 1991
Yellow body, green . . .
6-91-58 NOTTS ELECTRICAL CLUB 1991
Maroon body, black . . .
6-91-59 OVER TO YOU, JOHN 1991
White body, black . . .
6-91-60 PENISTONE UNITED PATTERNS 1991
Light yellow body, blue chassis and roof, Penistone Patterns Ltd. and P U P emblem logo.
6-91-61 PILGRIM CHILDREN'S WARD 1991
Yellow body, brown . . .
6-91-62 PIONIER AUTOMOBILIEN CLUB 1991
Blue body, red . . ., black . . .
6-91-63 POPLAR FARM RESTAURANT 1991
White body, green . . .
6-91-64 PORTSMOUTH CARPETS 1991
Red body, black . . .
6-91-65 PORTSMOUTH EVENING NEWS 1991
Black body, chassis and roof, Evening News logo.
6-91-66 PRESTON GUILD 1991
White body, light blue . . .
6-91-67 RACKHAMS 1991
White body, dark green . . .
6-91-68 RADIO SOCIETY OF GREAT BRITAIN 1991
Light blue body, white . . .
6-91-69 RINGTONS TEA 1991
Black body, yellow chassis and roof, Ringtons Tea logo.
6-91-70 ROSPA ADVANCED DRIVERS 1991
Green body, black chassis and roof, RoSPA Advanced Drivers Association logo.

6-91-71 ROYAL MAIL--BYPOST 1991
Red body, black chassis and roof, Royal Mail and #251 logo, special Bypost box.
6-91-72 SCHNEIDER AIR RACE 1991
Black body, white . . .
6-91-73 SHIPSTONES BITTER 1991
Red body, chassis and roof, Shipstones local bitter logo.
6-91-74 SIRDAR 1991
White body, red . . .
6-91-75 SMARTIES 1991
Dark green body, black chassis, Smarties logo.
6-91-76 SMITHS CHEMISTS 1991
Red body, white . . .
6-91-77 SOMERSET SCOUTS 1991
White body, blue chassis, red roof, Somerset Cub Scouts 75 logo.
6-91-78 SOUTHPORT FLOWER SHOW 1991
Light blue body, crewam chassis and roof, Southport Flower Show logo.
6-91-79 SOUTHPORT STAR 1991
White body, blue . . .
6-91-80 SOUTH STAFFS WATER 1991
Green body and roof . . .
6-91-81 SOUTH WALES CONSTABULARY 1991
White body, black chassis and roof, South Wales Constabulary emblem logo.
6-91-82 THE SPORTING LIFE 1991
Green body, black chassis, white roof, The Sporting Life logo.
6-91-83 STONELEIGH TOY FAIR 1991
Green body, black . . .
6-91-84 SYLVAC COMPANION 1991
Light gray body and roof . . .
6-91-85 SYLVAC STORY 1991
Gray body, black . . .
6-91-86 TEMPLE GROVE SCHOOL 1991
White body, green . . .
6-91-87 TRADER NEWSPAPER SERIES 1991
Maroon body, black chassis and roof, Trader Newspaper Series 21st Anniversary logo.
6-91-88 TRANSPLANT GAMES 1991
Yellow body, black . . .
6-91-89 TREBOR BASSETT 1991
White body, blue . . .
6-91-90 WALLS ICE CREAM 1991
Black body, cream . . .
6-91-91 WARBURTON'S 1991
Orange body, brown chassis and roof, Warburton's Family Bakers Since 1876 logo.
6-91-92 WARWICKSHIRE CONSTABULARY 1991
Navy blue body, black . . .
6-91-93 WEST MIDLANDS POLICE 1991
Navy blue body, black . . .

163

6-91-94 WIGAN PIER 1991
Red body, black . . .
6-91-95 YORK CASTLE 1991
Maroon body, cream chassis and roof . . .
6-92-1 ABACUS FROZEN FOODS 1992
White body, red . . .
6-92-2 ABBEY HOUSE MUSEUM 1992
Green body, black chassis and roof, Abbey House Museum logo.
6-92-3 ADAMS CHILDREN'S WEAR 1992
Cream body, green . . .
6-92-5 ALDERMASTON MANOR 1992
Maroon body . . .
6-92-6 ALTON BOX 1992
White body, chassis and roof, Alton Box Ltd. logo.
6-92-7 ALTON TOWERS 1992
Yellow body, gray . . .
6-92-8 ANGLO AMERICAN 1992
Blue body, white . . .
6-92-9 ANTHONY NOLAN TRUST 1992
White body, black . . .
6-92-10 ASTON VILLA 1992
Maroon body, yellow . . .
6-92-11 AYRSHIRE SECURITY ALARMS 1992
White body, blue . . ., red . . .
6-92-13 AYRSHIRE SOUVENIR AUTOS 1992
White body, red . . ., blue . . .
6-92-14 BAIN CLARKSON 1992
Red body, black . . .
6-92-15 BAPTIST UNION 1992
Black body, bronze . . .
6-92-16 BAXTER WOODHOUSE & TAYLOR 1992
White body, red chassis and roof, Baxter Woodhouse & Taylor logo.
6-92-17 BEAULIEU 1992 1992
Maroon body . . .
6-92-18 BEES ELECTRICAL 1992
Blue body, white . . .
6-92-19 BERKS & READING FIRE 1992
Red body . . .
6-92-20 BINNS ROAD CO. 1992
Blue body, white . . .
6-92-21 BRANSTON PICKLE 1992
Dark blue body, black chassis, cream roof, Crosse & Blackwell's Branston Pickle logo.
6-92-22 BROADWAY PRESS 1992
Yellow body, black . . .
6-92-23 CADBURYS HOT CHOCOLATE 1992
Purple body, tan . . .
6-92-24 CAITHNESS NATURAL WORLD 1992
White body, green . . .
6-92-25 CHARLES BAKER 1992
Navy blue body . . .

6-92-26 CHELTENHAM F. C. 1992
Red body, white . . .
6-92-27 CHESTER ZOO 1992
Tan body, green . . .
6-92-28 CHILDREN'S WORLD 1992
White body, red . . .
6-92-29 CLASSIC CAR 1992
White body, maroon . . .
6-92-30 THE CORNISHMAN 1992
Blue body . . .
6-92-31 T. A. COWAP 1992
Red body, black . . .
6-92-32 D. & R. LTD. 1992
White body . . .
6-92-33 DAVID SUMNER 1992
Blue body and roof, black chassis, David Sumner, Garden Maintenance logo.
6-92-34 DEL MONTE 1992
Green body . . .
6-92-35 DENTONS CATERING 1992
Light blue body and roof, black chassis, Dentons Catering Equipment Inc. logo.
6-92-36 DERBY COUNTY F. C. 1992
White body, dark blue chassis and roof, Derby County F. C. logo with ram figure.
6-92-37 DERBYSHIRE CONSTABULARY (Pear Tree) 1992
White body, black chassis and roof, Derbyshire Constabulary emblem and Pear Tree Police Station logo.
6-92-38 DIGITAL LOGISTICS CHALLENGE 1992
Yellow-orange body, light blue chassis and roof, Digital Logistics Challenge logo, Avenue School header.
6-92-39 DUERRS (2nd) 1992
Green body . . .
6-92-40 EDWARDIAN CIGARETTE CARD CO. 1992
Red body, black . . .
6-92-41 EUROPEAN IND. SERVICES 1992
White body, black . . .
6-92-42 EVENING ADVERTISER 1992
White body, blue chassis and roof, Evening Advertiser logo.
6-92-43 FARRANTS 1992
White body, black . . .
6-92-44 FERODO 1992
Green body, black . . .
6-92-45 FURNELL TRANSPORT 1992
Blue body, white . . .
6-92-46 GRIMSBY TOWN F. C. 1992
White body, black chassis and roof, Grimsby Town FC logo.
6-92-47 GUIDE DOGS (2nd issue) 1992
Tan body . . .
6-92-48 GUIDE DOGS--60 YEARS (1st issue) 1992
Green body, blue . . .

6-92-49 HADRIAN CRYSTAL 1992
Silver body, black . . .
6-92-50 HASSENFELD BROTHERS 1992
Light blue body, black . . .
6-92-51 HAWTHORNS 1992
Dark blue body, red . . .
6-92-52 HEINZ OVEN BAKED BEANS 1992
White body, chassis and roof, Heinz Oven Baked Beans logo.
6-92-53 HESLEY WOOD 1992
White body, dark green . . .
6-92-54 HOME AMBULANCE SERVICE 1992
Green body, black chassis and roof, Order of St. John's & British Red Cross Home Ambulance Service logo, +/- lower panel lettering re Lledo International Model Show in Wroughton, Guy's Evelina Children's Hospital box.
　　1. With Lledo Model Show lettering.
　　2. Without Lledo Model Show lettering.
6-92-55 HORNBY RAILWAYS 1992
Red body, yellow . . .
6-92-56 INTERLINK EXPRESS 1992
White body . . .
6-92-57 INTERNATIONAL POLICE TATTOO 1992
Black body . . .
6-92-58 JOHN WEST'S SALMON 1992
Green body and chassis, black roof, John West's "Middle-Cut" Salmon logo.
6-92-59 JONES UPHOLSTERY 1992
Dark green body, chassis and roof, Jones Upholstery Services logo.
6-92-60 KP KACTORS 1992
Green body, black . . .
6-92-61 KENT MESSENGER 1992
Yellow body, black . . .
6-92-62 KING'S APPEAL 1992
White body, blue . . .
6-92-63 KLEENEX TRAVEL TISSUES 1992
White body and roof, red chassis, Kleenex Travel Tissues logo.
6-92-64 KNOWSLEY SAFARI PARK 1992
White body, black . . .
6-92-65 LAKELAND PENNINE 1992
White body, blue . . .
6-92-66 LANCASHIRE CC 1992
White body, red . . ., green . . .
6-92-67 LANCASHIRE CONSTABULARY 1992
Black body, white . . .
6-92-68 LANCASHIRE EVENING TELEGRAPH 1992
Red body, black chassis and roof, Lancashire Evening Telegraph logo.
6-92-69 LEEDS UNITED 1992
White body, yellow . . .
6-92-70 LEEDS WEEKLY NEWS 1992
White body, black . . .

6-92-71 LEWIS DMR 1992
White body, yellow . . .
6-92-72 LILLIPUT LANE 1992
Maroon body, gray . . .
6-92-73 LINCOLN CITY F. C. 1992
Red body, white . . .
6-92-74 LINCOLNSHIRE STANDARD 1992
White body, red . . .
6-92-75 LIVERPOOL F. C. 1992
White body, red . . .
6-92-76 LIVERPOOL OVERHEAD RAILWAY 1992
Black body . . .
6-92-77 LLOYDS BANK--ST. JULIAN'S 1992
White body, green . . .
6-92-78 LOVE ROMANIA 2 1992
White body, blue . . .
6-92-79 MAGIC MILLION 1992
White body, orange . . .
6-92-80 MANCHESTER UNITED 1992
Red body, black . . .
6-92-81 MECCANO 1992
Black body, red . . ., white . . .
6-92-82 MITA (UK) LTD. 1992
Green body, black . . .
6-92-83 NEWCASTLE UNITED F. C. 1992
White body, black . . .
6-92-84 NORFOLK CONSTABULARY 1992
Black body . . .
6-92-85 H. NORMANSELL 1992
Brown body . . .
6-92-86 ORCHARD SCHOOL 1992
Red body, black chassis, white roof, Orchard School logo.
6-92-87 OXFAM FIFTY YEARS 1992
Green body, chassis and roof, Fifty Years Oxfam Working for a Fairer
World logo. (Letter O is a globe.)
6-92-88 E. D. PALMER 1992
Light blue body, white . . .
6-92-89 PARSONAGE COLLIERY 1992
Black body, red . . .
6-92-90 PEARSON CANDY 1992
Red body . . .
6-92-91 PILGRIM FETAL HEART MONITOR 1992
White body, silver . . .
6-92-92 PLEASURE ISLAND 1992
White body, light blue . . .
6-92-93 PORTHYWEN SILVER BAND 1992
Maroon body, cream . . .
6-92-94 POWERVACS 1992
Light blue body and chassis, blue roof, Powervacs Vacuum Cleaner
Specialists logo.

6-92-95 PRESTON GUILD 92 1992
White body, light blue . . .
6-92-96 PROVOST PARADE 1992
Black body . . .
6-92-97 R.A.F. GATEWAY 1992
Black body . . .
6-92-98 R.A.F. POLICE 1992
Black body . . .
6-92-99 R.A.O.B. 1992
Green body, white . . .
6-92-100 C. B. RANSOM 1992
Light blue body . . .
6-92-101 READING POLICE 1992
Black body . . .
6-92-102 ROSPA 75TH ANNIVERSARY 1992
Red body, chassis and roof, Rospa Anniversary logo.
6-92-103 ROTHERHAM UNITED F. C. 1992
White body, red . . .
6-92-104 ROYAL MAIL, EASTWOOD 1992
Red body and roof, black chassis, Royal Mail Post Office, Eastwood
1991 logo.
6-92-105 ROYAL MILITARY POLICE 1992
Olive body . . .
6-92-106 RUFFORD COLTS F. C. 1992
Yellow body, black . . .
6-92-107 ST. GEORGE'S HOSPITAL 1992
White body . . .
6-92-108 SAKEJI SCHOOL, ZAMBIA 1992
White body, red . . ., green . . .
6-92-109 SF ELECTRIC 1992
White body . . .
6-92-110 W. H. SMITH & SON 1992
Red body, black chassis, white roof,f W. H. Smith & Son logo.
6-92-111 SOUTHPORT 200 1992
White body, red . . .
6-92-112 SOUTH WALES ARGUS 1992
Dark green body, black . . .
6-92-113 SPARTAN 1992
Red body, black chassis, white roof, Spartan logo.
6-92-114 STANLEY GIBBONS 1992
Blue body . . .
6-92-115 SWAN OF WITNEY 1992
White body . . .
6-92-116 TELETHON '92 1992
Tan body . . .
6-92-117 TORQ 1992
Black body, silver . . .
6-92-118 TOWN & COUNTRY FESTIVAL 1992
Light blue body, black . . .
6-92-119 TOYTOWN MODELS 1992
Yellow body, red . . .

6-92-120 TRADER NEWS 1000TH EDITION 1992
Black body, chassis and roof, Trader News, April 10th, 1992, 1000th
Edition logo.
6-92-121 TRENT COMMERCIAL 1992
Gold body, black . . .
6-92-122 UNCLE JOE'S MINTBALLS 1992
Blue body, orange . . .
6-92-123 UNIPLEX UK LTD. 1992
White body, red . . ., gray . . .
6-92-124 THE UNIVERSE 1992
Green body . . .
6-92-125 VALOR HEATING 1992
Red body, white . . .
6-92-126 WAWA DAIRY FARMS 1992
Black body . . .
6-92-127 THE WEST BRITON 1992
Green body, white . . .
6-92-128 WESTBROOK GUIDES--ALTON SCOUTS 1992
Blue body, green . . .
6-92-129 WIGAN OBSERVER 1992
White body, maroon . . .
6-92-130 WILLOWDALE MILL 1992
Cream body, brown . . .
6-92-131 WILSDON 100 YEARS 1992
Cream body, black . . .
6-92-132 WILTSHIRE CONSTABULARY 1992
Black body, chassis and roof, Wiltshire Constabulary logo.
6-92-133 WORLD SCOUT JAMBOREE 1992
White body, green chassis, maroon roof, World Jamboree logo.
6-92-134 WORTHING LIONS 1992
Blue body . . .
6-92-135 YEOMANS ARMY STORES 1992
Yellow body, red . . .
6-93-1 ABBEY LIGHT RAIL 1993
Green body, black . . .
6-93-2 ANTHONY NOLAN TRUST (no. 2) 1993
White body . . .
6-93-3 ARKWRIGHT COLLIERY 1993
Navy blue body . . .
6-93-4 ASPALL CYDER 1993
Blue body . . .
6-93-5 ASPRO 1993
Pink body, black chassis and roof, Aspro since 1912 logo.
6-93-6 BATTERSEA DOGS' HOME 1993
Red body, cream . . .
6-93-7 BENTLEY COLLIERY 1993
No data.
6-93-8 BIRMINGHAM CHILDREN'S HOME 1993
White body, black . . .
    1. Incorrect "Birmiingham" spelling.
    2. Correct "Birmingham" spelling.

6-93-9 BOOTLE COUNTY POLICE 1993
Black body, white . . .
6-93-10 BRECONSHIRE CONSTABULARY 1993
Black body and chassis, ? roof, Breconshire Constabulary logo.
6-93-11 BRITISH RED CROSS 1993
Khaki body . . .
6-93-12 CADBURYS ECLAIRS 1993
Purple body, red . . .
6-93-13 CALKIT CLEANING 1993
White body, blue chassis and roof, Calkit Cleaning Equipment logo.
6-93-14 CAMA REAL ALE 1993
Silver body, red . . ., black . . .
6-93-15 CARBURETTOR HOSPITAL 1993
White body, black . . .
6-93-16 CHESTERFIELD & DISTRICT CO-OP 1993
Red body, black . . .
6-93-17 S. CLAUS 1993
Red body, green chassis, white roof, S. Claus Gofts & Presents logo,
S. Claus on header.
6-93-18 CLUEDO 93 1993
Tan body, black . . .
6-93-19 CORNWALL AMBULANCE SERVICE 1993
Cream body, black . . .
6-93-20 COULTERS GARAGE 1993
Blue body, white chassis and roof, Coulters Garage Ford 9Evesham)
Limited logo.
6-93-21 DAILY MIRROR 1993
Navy blue body . . .
6-93-22 DERBYSHIRE CRICKET CLUB 1993
Blue body, gold . . .
6-93-23 L. J. DIFFORD 1993
Red body, black . . .
6-93-24 DINNINGTON & MALTBY TRADER NEWS 1993
Brown body, chassis and roof, Dinnington & Maltby Trader News
21st Anniversary logo.
6-93-25 DONCASTER STAR 1993
White body, red . . ., black . . .
6-93-26 DOUWE EGBERTS 1993
Blue body, cream . . .
6-93-27 DUDLEY ROAD HOSPITAL 1993
White body, red . . ., black . . .
6-93-28 EASON & SON, BELFAST 1993
Red body . . .
6-93-29 EAST MIDLANDS ORCHID SOCIETY 1993
Yellow body, chassis and roof, East Midlands Orchid Society emblem
logo.
6-93-30 EPSOM STAMP COMPANY 1993
Light blue body, blue . . .
6-93-31 ESSEX RADIO 1993
White body, red . . .

6-93-32 EXCHANGE & MART 125TH 1993
Black body, red chassis and roof, Exchange & Mart 125th Year logo.
6-93-33 FELL END CARAVAN PARK 1993
White body, green . . .
6-93-34 FINCHES 1993
White body, yellow chassis, orange roof, Finches Sparkling Orange
logo.
6-93-35 FLEDGLINGS TRUST 1993
Light blue body . . .
6-93-36 FOREST FOR THE COMMUNITY 1993
Tan body, green . . ., red . . .
6-93-37 FREEWAY MARKETING 1993
White body, orange . . .
6-93-38 GOSNALL PLAYERS 1993
Red body, cream . . .
6-93-39 GRIMETHORPE COLLIERY 1993
Navy blue body . . .
6-93-40 HAPPY PET 1993
Yellow body, blue . . .
6-93-41 HENRY ADLAM 1993
Cream body, black . . .
6-93-42 HOLDENS BREWERY 1993
Green body, red . . ., black . . .
6-93-43 IMPERIAL CANCER RESEARCH FUND 1993
Yellow body, blue chassis and roof, in aid of the Imperial Cancer
Research Fund logo.
6-93-44 JENNY LIND 1993
Yellow body, pink . . ., blue . . .
6-93-45 JOHN HARVEY 1993
Maroon body . . .
6-93-46 KELLINGLEY COLLIERY 1993
Navy blue body . . .
6-93-47 KEN ASH 1993
White body, green . . .
6-93-48 KENT COUNTY CONSTABULARY 1993
Black body, chassis and roof, Kent County Constabulary logo.
6-93-49 KENT MESSENGER 1993
Yellow body, black . . .
6-93-50 KIVETON PARK COLLIERY 1993
Black body . . .
6-93-51 LANCASTER 800 1993
Tan body, maroon . . .
6-93-52 L L CLUB 1993
White body, green . . .
6-93-53 M & B 1993
Red body, black . . .
6-93-54 MARKHAM COLLIERY 1993
Black body . . .
6-93-55 MASTER BAKER 1993
Green body, black . . .

6-93-56 MERSEYSIDE POLICE 1993
White body . . .
6-93-57 MIDLAND BUSINESS EQUIPMENT 1993
Black body, chassis and roof, Midland Business Equipment &
Stationery Ltd. logo.
6-93-58 MOORFIELD EYE HOSPITAL 1993
Cream body, blue . . .
6-93-59 THE MUSIC MUSEUM 1993
Tan body . . .
6-93-60 NEAL'S TOYS AND PRAMS 1993
White body, black . . .
6-93-61 NORTHERN DAIRIES 1993
Cream body and roof, green chassis, Northern Dairies logo.
6-93-62 N. U. M. DERBYSHIRE 1993
Green body, black . . .
6-93-63 OLIVE OYL 1993
White body, black chassis and roof, Olive Oyl & Swee'pea logo,
Popeye header.
6-93-64 ONE STOP SHOP 1993
White body, blue . . .
6-93-65 OSHKOSH NORTHWESTERN 1993
Dark blue body, black . . .
6-93-66 THE OVERHEAD DOOR 1993
Black body, red . . .
6-93-67 J. C. PENNEY 1993
Black body, chassis and roof, J. C. Penney Co. logo (also on header),
Est. 1902 on doors.
6-93-68 PRETTIGE FEESTDAGEN (dark blue) 1993
Dark blue body, black . . .
6-93-69 PRETTIGE FEESTDAGEN (light blue) 1993
Light blue body, white . . .
6-93-70 PUNJANA TEA 1993
Red body, cream . . .
6-93-71 RADLEY CONSERVATORIES 1993
White body, orange . . .
6-93-72 RICHARD SCOLLINS FUND 1993
Black body and roof, white chassis, The Richard Scollins Fund logo
with "Ey up mi duck!".
6-93-73 ROYAL NATIONAL LIFEBOAT INSTITUTION 1993
Navy blue body, white . . .
6-93-74 ROSE RESTAURANT 1993
White body, maroon . . ., gray . . .
6-93-75 SAIT RADIO HOLLAND 1993
White body, navy blue . . .
6-93-76 SHERIFF'S HONEY 1993
White body, maroon . . .
6-93-77 SHIREBROOK COLLIERY 1993
Dark blue body, black . . .
6-93-78 SLIME 1993
Black body . . .

6-93-79 SOUTHPORT POLICE 1993
Navy blue body, black . . .
6-93-80 SPORS SURFACE INSTAL 1993
White body, green . . .
6-93-81 A. T. SPRACK 1993
Black body, red . . .
6-93-82 STANDARD FIREWORKS 1993
Dark blue body, blue . . .
6-93-83 STANLEY GIBBONS 1993
Maroon body, black . . .
6-93-84 SUN LIFE OF CANADA 1993
White body, black . . .
6-93-85 SWINDON TOWN F. C. 1993
White body, green . . ., red . . .
6-93-86 TITANIC ANTIQUES 1993
Tellow body, black . . .
6-93-86 TRICKY DICKY SURFWEAR 1993
Black body . . .
6-93-87 VENTNOR RACING PIGEON CLUB 1993
Navy blue body, gray . . .
6-93-88 WESSEX EVENING CHRONICLE 1993
Light blue body, gray . . .
6-93-89 WOLVERHAMPTON BOYS BRIGADE 1993
Navy blue body . . .
6-94-1 1ST COOMBS WOOD SCOUTS 1994
Blue body, black chassis, white roof . . .
6-94-2 ADAMS--SAVE THE CHILDREN 1994
Red body, green . . ., yellow . . .
6-94-3 ALDERSHOT NEWS 1994
No data.
6-94-4 ANADIN 1994
Yellow body, green . . .
6-94-5 ARJO WIGGINS 1994
White body, blue chassis, red roof, Arjo Wiggins logo.
6-94-6 ARSENAL FOOTBALL CLUB 1994
White body, red . . .
6 94 7 ASHFORDBY COLLIERY 1994
Navy blue body, black . . .
6-94-8 AUTO TRADER 1994
Red body, black . . .
6-94-9 BARCLAYS FINANCIAL SERVICES 1994
Blue body, white . . .
6-94-10 BASSETTS ALLSORTS 1994
Black body, chassis and roof . . .
6-94-11 BAYTREE NURSERIES 1994
Green body, black . . .
6-94-12 BEAULIEU 1994
Green body, black . . .
6-94-13 BILSTHORPE COLLIERY 1994
Blue-black body, chassis and roof, Bilsthorpe Colliery, at the heart of safety emblem, gold lettering, British Coal on header.

6-94-14 BLOBBY CHRISTMAS 1994
Blue body and chassis, yellow roof, Blobby Christmas logo with Santa-and-chimney scene, Mr. Blobby on header, Mr. Blobby box.
6-94-15 BOBBIES ON BIKES 1994
White body, black . . .
6-94-16 BOLSOVER COLLIERY 1994
Navy blue body, black . . .
6-94-17 BRITISH COAL, MIDLANDS 1994
Navy blue body, black . . .
6-94-18 BRITISH TRANSPORT POLICE 1994
White body, black chassis and roof, British Transport Police logo.
6-94-19 CANDEREL 1994
White body, red . . .
6-94-20 CAROUSEL ENCHANTMENT 1994
White body, blue . . ., red . . .
6-94-21 CENTER PARCS 1994
Green body, black . . .
6-94-22 CONCORD FOODS 1994
Maroon body, black . . .
6-94-23 COOKIE COACH 1994
Red body . . .
6-94-24 CRAWLEY TOWN F.C. 1994
White body, red chassis and roof, Crawley Town F.C. emblem and Crawley Town Supporters Club logo, Follow the Reds on header.
6-94-25 DANNIMAC 75TH 1994
Dark green body, black . . .
6-94-26 DAVO MOUNTS 1994
Navy blue body . . .
6-94-27 DAW MILL COLLIERY 1994
Navy blue body, black . . .
6-94-28 DORSET EVENING ECHO 1994
White body, green . . .
6-94-29 DULUX WOODSTAIN 1994
Black body, white . . .
6-94-30 EASTWOOD AND KIMBERLEY ADVERTISER 1994
White body, black chassis and roof, Eastwood and Kimberley Advertiser 100 Years logo, Advertiser on header.
6-94-31 ELIZABETH SHAW 1994
Cream body, blue . . .
6-94-32 ELLINGTON COLLIERY 1994
Navy blue body, black . . .
6-94-33 ESSEX CHRONICLE 1994
Light blue body, black . . .
6-94-34 ESSEX COUNTY CRICKET CLUB 1994
White body, red . . .
6-94-35 EXPRESS CHRONICLE 1994
Blue body, black . . .
6-94-36 M. FIRKIN 1994
Dark green body . . .

6-94-37 FRED DIBNAH (1st) 1994
No data.
6-94-38 FRED DIBNAH (2nd) 1994
Navy blue body . . .
6-94-39 GLASGOW RANGERS F. C. 1994
Blue body, red . . ., white . . .
6-94-40 GUINNESS EXTRA STOUT 1994
Black body and chassis, cream roof, Guinness Extra Stout logo.
6-94-41 HAMMERITE--SOLVOL 1994
White body, black . . .
6-94-42 HELP INTERNATIONAL 1994
White body, green . . .
6-94-43 HENRY WALKER 1994
White body, maroon . . .
6-94-44 HOUSE OF ELIOTT 1994
Cream body, maroon chassis and roof, The house of Eliott logo.
6-94-45 ILKESTON CO-OP 1994
Blue body, black . . .
6-94-46 LEEDS INTERNATIONAL 1994
White body, black . . .
6-94-47 LEICESTER CHRONICLE 1994
Yellow body and roof, black chassis, Illustrated Leicester Chronicle, Your Pictorial Weekly logo, Illustrated Chronicle on blade.
6-94-48 LEYTON ORIENT FOOTBALL CLUB 1994
Red body, white . . .
6-94-49 LINCOLN UNITED FOOTBALL CLUB 1994
White body, black chassis and roof, Lincoln United F.C. logo.
6-94-50 LINCOLNSHIRE POLICE 1994
White body, black . . .
6-94-51 MANCHESTER CITY FOOTBALL CLUB 1994
Black body, red . . .
6-94-52 MANCHESTER DOCK POLICE 1994
Black body, chassis and roof . . .
6-94-53 MANTON COLLIERY 1994
Navy blue body, black . . .
6-94-54 MIDLAND BANK 1994
Navy blue body . . .
6-94-55 MILLWALL FOOTBALL CLUB 1994
Blue body, white . . .
6-94-56 MOTIVATION 1994
Tan body, green . . ., maroon . . .
6-94-57 NEPTUNE'S CAVE 1994
Red body, chassis and roof, Neptune's Cave, Ilfracombe logo.
6-94-58 OLLERTON COLLIERY 1994
Navy blue body, black . . .
6-94-59 OXFORD CITY POLICE 1994
Black body, gray . . .
6-94-60 PAYNES POPPETS 1994
Blue body and roof, black chassis, Geo. Paynes Poppets logo.
6-94-61 PLYMOUTH ARGYLE F. C. 1994
White body, black . . .

167

6-94-62 POINT OF AYRE COLLIERY 1994
Navy blue body, black . . .
6-94-63 PRINCE OF WALES COLLIERY 1994
Navy blue body, black . . .
6-94-64 QUEEN CONCERT 1994
Black body . . .
6-94-65 R T M D C 1994
White body, green . . .
6-94-66 THE REPOSITORY 1994
White body, blue . . .
6-94-67 RETFORD TRADER 1994
Green body . . .
6-94-68 ROCHDALE EQUITABLE PIONEERS 1994
Maroon body, brown chassis, white roof, Rochdale Equitable
Pioneers logo, Est. 1844 on header.
6-94-69 ROY CASTLE APPEAL 1994
White body, blue . . ., yellow . . .
6-94-70 ROYAL NATIONAL LIFE-BOAT INST. 1994
Navy blue body, blue . . .
6-94-71 RUPERT BEAR 1994
Red body, white chassis and roof, Little Lost Bear scene logo.
6-94-72 ST. IVEL CHEESE 1994
Dark blue body, black chassis, cream roof, St. Ivel 'Lactic' Cheese
logo, St. Ivel on header.
6-94-73 SANDWELL VEHICLE WATCH 1994
White body, black . . .
6-94-74 SHEFFIELD UNITED F. C. 1994
White body, red . . .
6-94-75 SHEFFIELD WEDNESDAY F. C. 1994
White body, blue . . .
6-94-76 SHEFFIELD WEDNESDAY SUP. CLUB 1994
Navy blue body, white . . .
6-94-77 SNODLAND MOTOR REPAIRS 1994
White body, blue-black chassis, red roof, Snodland Motor Repairs
Ltd. logo, S.M.R.L. on header.
6-94-78 SOUTHAMPTON FOOTBALL CLUB 1994
White body, red . . .
6-94-79 SPIRE PROMOTIONS 1994
Navy blue body, black . . .
6-94-80 STEVELYN 500TH 1994
Gold body, navy blue chassis and roof, To Celebrate the 500th logo.
6-94-81 SUBBUTEO 1994
Green body, black . . .
6-94-82 SUBBUTEO--WORLD CUP 1994
White body, blue . . ., red . . .
6-94-83 TIMBERCRAFT 1994
Gray body, green . . .
    1. Main logo on left side.
    2. Ben logo on left side.
6-94-84 TRANSPORT TOYS & MODELS 1994
Yellow body, dark green . . .

6-94-85 UNIFIX 1994
No data.
6-94-86 URCH HARRIS 1994
No data.
6-94-87 WELBECK HOTEL 1994
Cream body, dark brown . . .
6-94-88 WEST HAM FOOTBALL CLUB 1994
Maroon body, blue . . .
6-94-89 WHITE CROSS TO ROMANIA 1994
White body, blue . . ., red . . .
6-94-90 WIGAN PIER 1994
Black body, chassis and roof . . .
6-94-91 WIMBLEDON FOOTBALL CLUB 1994
Black body, yellow . . .
6-94-92 WINTERWARM 1994
Blue body, black . . .
6-94-93 YORK CASTLE MUSEUM 1994
Blue body, cream chassis and roof, York Castle Museum logo.
7 FORD WOODY WAGON 1984
7-86-1 FERGUSON'S FORD 1986
White body, blue chassis.
7-87-1 KLM 1987
Light blue body, blue chassis, "KLM" on blade, "all animal
transport" logo. In boxed set of three models.
7-88-1 GINGER CONSERVE 1988
Cream and green body, green chassis, "Ginger Conserve" logo.
7-89-1 3M AUTOMOTIVE TRADES 1989
Light tan body, brown chassis, "3M Brand Coated Abrasives" logo.
7-89-2 BOOTS 1989
Blue and white . . .
7-90-1 HAPPY EATER 1990
Yellow body, red chassis and blade, Happy Eater logo and symbol.
7-93-1 MAYNARDS WINE GUMS 1993
Green body, maroon chassis . . .
8 MODEL T FORD TANKER 1984
8-85-1 BRITISH PETROLEUM 1985
Dark green body, red tank, black chassis, white roof, "British
Petroleum" and "BP" logo.
8-86-1 BONDY OIL 1986
Light blue body and chassis, silver tank, white roof, "Bondy Oil Inc."
logo.
8-86-2 MARSHALL'S TRUCKING 1986
Green body, silver tank, white roof and chassis, "Marshall Trucking
Inc." logo.
8-86-3 MIDWEST MINIATURE BOTTLE CLUB 1986
Black body and tank, red chassis and roof, "Midwest Miniature
Bottle Collector's Club" logo.
8-86-4 SHELL-MEX 1986
Red body and tank, black chassis, white roof, "Shell-Mex Ltd. Fuel
Oil" logo. Like DG 8011 but with LP base.

8-86-5 SMALL WHEELS 1986
Black body, roof, tank and chassis, "Small Wheels" logo.
8-87-1 B P CHEMICALS 1987
White body and tank, blue chassis and roof, "BP Chemicals" logo.
8-87-2 CASTROL 1987
Green body and tank, black chassis, white roof, "Castrol" and
"Wakefield Motor Oil" logo.
8-87-3 CLIFFORD AND SON 1987
Red body, black chassis . . .
8-87-4 COLE'S 1987
Red body, green chassis, tank and roof, "Cole's Factors Motor Spirit--
Paraffin" logo.
8-87-5 MILK 1987
Blue body and chassis, white tank and roof, "Milk fresh from the
farm: logo.
8-88-1 AMPOL 1988
Light blue body, blue chassis and roof, white tank, "Ampol" logo,
mounted on plinth.
8-88-2 KLM FUEL 1988
Light blue body and tank, blue chassis, white roof, "KLM" logo.
8-88-3 LAPORTE CHEMICALS 1988
Green body, cream . . .
8-88-4 NICHOLAS SMITH TRAINS 1988
Orange body, blue chassis, tank and roof, "Nicholas Smith" logo.
8-88-5 SHELL FUEL SUPPLIES 1988
Yellow body, gray . . .
8-89-1 BOEHMERS 1989
Yellow body and tank, green chassis and roof, "Boehmers, always
glad to help" logo.
8-89-2 SOUTH BUCKS EFFLUENT CO. 1989
Yellow body . . .
8-89-3 UNIGATE 1989
Red body, white tank, black chassis and roof, Unigate Fresh Milk
logo.
8-90-1 3M BODYGARD 1990
Red body and chassis, black tank and roof, 3M emblem, Bodygard
Stonechip Coating logo.
8-90-2 DAIRY FARM 1990
Cream body, blue chassis, roof and tank, Dairy Farm Direct Farm
Supply logo.
8-90-3 STAUFFER CHEMICALS 1990
Red and black . . .
8-90-4 WYNNS 1990
Light blue and white . . .
8-91-1 CADBURYS 1991
Purple . . .
8-91-2 EXPRESS DAIRIES 1991
Black and white . . .
8-91-3 KODAK 1991
Red and yellow . . .

8-91-4 RED CROWN 1991
Black and white . . .
8-91-5 SHELL ROAD TRANSPORT 1991
Red, white and black . . .
8-91-6 WALKERS CRISPS 1991
Red body and tank, blue chassis, white roof, Walkers Potato Crisps logo.
8-91-7 WEOLEY SERVICE STATION 1991
Blue and white . . .
8-92-1 ANADIN 1992
Yellow and red . . .
8-92-2 BRIGGS OIL 1992
Dark green and red . . .
8-92-3 SOUTH STAFFS WATER 1992
Dark green . . .
8-92-4 TEXACO 1992
Red and black . . .
8-92-5 UNITED MOLASSES 1992
Blue and gray . . .
8-93-1 CARLTON FUELS 1993
No data.
8-93-2 GOLDEN FIELDS 1993
Green body, yellow . . .
8-93-3 GUNGE TANKER 1993
Dark green body, cream . . .
8-93-4 NESTON TANK 1993
Purple body, blue . . .
8-93-5 NORTHERN DAIRIES 1993
Cream body, tank and roof, black chassis, Northern Dairies logo.
8-93-6 R A F CHIVENOR/AVIATION SPIRIT 1993
Yellow body, chassis, roof and tank, Aviation Sprit and roundel logo, RAF Chivenor on header.
8-93-7 RED CROWN--AMOCO 1993
Red body, white . . ., black . . .
8-93-8 SOUTHPORT FLOWER SHOW 1993
Blue body, cream . . .
8-94-1 ENGEN 1994
Blue body, white . . .
8-94-2 PETERBOROUGH CO-OP MILK 1994
Maroon body, cream . . .
9 MODEL T FORD TOURING CAR 1984
9-86-1 CAVE PHOTOGRAPHIC 1986
Silver body, Cave Photographic Picture Framing logo.
10 ALBION SINGLE DECKER COACH 1984
10-85-1 CENTRAAL NEDERLAND 1985
Yellow body and roof, gray chassis, "Centraal Nederland" logo.
10-85-2 L. N. E. R. 1985
Green body and chassis, cream roof, "L N E R" logo.
10-85-3 TANDHAUS 1985
Cream body and roof, blue chassis, "Tandhaus Miniature Cars" logo.

10-85-4 THORPE HALL SCHOOL 1985
Green body, black chassis, light orange roof, "Thorpe Hall School" logo.
10-86-1 AMSTERDAM OLYMPICS 1986
Yellow body, gray chassis, cream roof, silver or gold grille, "Amsterdam 1992" on roof, side logo in 2 of 4 languages.
  1. English and Dutch logo.
  2. French and Spanish logo.
10-86-2 HAPPY DAYS 1986
Red body, cream chassis and roof, "Happy Days" logo.
10-86-3 IRONBRIDGE MUSEUM 1986
Blue-black body, cream chassis and roof, "Visit the museums at Ironbridge" logo.
10-87-1 DUNDEE CORPORATION 1987
Dark blue body and chassis, light blue roof, "Corporation Transport" logo, "Dundee" front board.
10-87-2 GLASGOW CORPORATION 1987
Orange body, black chassis, green roof, "Glasgow Corporation" logo.
10-87-3 G. W. R. MUSEUM 1987
Brown body and chassis, cream roof, "G. W. R. Museum, Swindon" logo.
10-87-4 K L M PASSENGER TRANSPORT 1987
Light blue body, blue chassis, white roof, "KLM Passenger Transport" logo.
10-87-5 LAKESIDE TOURS 1987
Red body, dark red chassis, cream roof, "Lakeside Tours: logo.
10-87-6 LOTHIAN 1987
Maroon body, black chassis, white roof, "Lothian" logo.
10-87-7 MAIDSTONE & DISTRICT 1987
Dark green body and chassis, cream roof, "Maidstone & District" logo.
10-87-8 OXFORD 1987
Red body, black chassis, red-brown roof, "Oxford" logo.
10-88-1 BARCLAYS 1988
Dark blue body and chassis, light blue roof, "Connect with Barclays" logo.
10-88-2 BOURNEMOUTH CORPORATION 1988
Yellow body, cream roof.
10-88-3 CITY OF COVENTRY 1988
Maroon body, cream roof.
10-88-4 DEVON AND DORSET SERVICE 1988
Gold body, dark green chassis and roof, "Devon & Dorset Service" logo.
10-88-5 HARRY MARGHAM AND SONS 1988
Magenta body, black chassis, cream roof, "Harry Margham & Sons Centenary" logo.
10-88-6 THE MANOR HOUSE 1988
Light brown body and chassis, cream roof, "The Manor House at Castle Combe" logo.
10-88-7 NORTHANTS CORPORATION 1988
Red body, cream . . .

10-88-8 STAPELEY WATER GARDENS 1988
Yellow body, black chassis and roof, "Stapeley Water Gardens" logo.
10-88-9 STEVENSONS 1988
Yellow body and chassis, black roof, "Stevensons Bus Services" logo.
10-89-1 EASTER SEALS CAMP 1989
White body, gray chassis and roof, "Camping Fun for Easter Seal Kids" logo.
10-89-2 KODAK EKTACHROME 1989
Yellow body, blue . . .
10-90-1 HARRY RAMSDEN 1990
Yellow body, white roof, "Harry Ramsden's world famous fish & chips" logo.
10-90-2 SOUTH HAYES NURSING HOME 1990
White body . . .
10-90-3 VECTIS MODELS 1990
Blue body, red roof, Vectis on sides, Southern Vectis on rear.
10-90-4 WALSALL CORPORATION 1990
Navy blue body, light blue roof, "Walsall Corporation" logo.
10-90-5 WEST BROMWICH CORPORATION 1990
Navy blue body, light blue roof, "West Bromwich Corporation" logo.
10-91-1 ST. ANDREWS POLICE CONVALESCENT HOME 1991
Navy boue body, cream roof . . .
11 HORSE DRAWN VAN 1984
11-85-1 CITY OF LONDON POLICE/PRISONS 1985
Different colors, "City of London Police" adhesive labels.
  1. Blue-black body, black chassis and roof (police van).
  2. Mustard body and chassis, dark brown roof (prison van).
11-86-1 EXCHANGE AND MART 1986
Tan body, light green chassis, green roof, "Exchange and Mart" logo.
11-86-2 TEXAS SESQUICENTENNIAL 1986
White body, blue chassis, red roof, "Texas Sesquicentennial" logo.
11-87-1 BRANTH-CHEMIE 1987
Yellow body, red chassis, blue roof, "Branth-Chemie" logo.
11-88-1 ST. JOHN AMBULANCE 1988
Black body and chassis, white roof, "St. John Ambulance" logo.
11-89-1 MAY & BAKER 1989
Dark green body, black chassis . . .
11-89-2 ROYAL MAIL 1989
Red body, black chassis, white roof, "Royal Mail" logo.
11-90-1 ESSEX CONSTABULARY 1990
Dark blue body, black chassis and roof, "Essex Constabulary" logo.
11-90-2 STAUFFER CHEMICALS 1990
White body, red . . .
11-91-1 BIRMINGHAM CITY POLICE 1991
Green body, white . . .
11-91-2 ENGLISH AMBULANCE 1991
Tan body, black chassis, dark brown roof, Services of the English Ambulance logo, British Red Cross box.

11-92-1 LONDON CITY POLICE 1992
Dark blue body, black chassis, City of London Police, A Division, Moor Lane logo.
11-93-1 MAY & BAKER 1993
Dark green body, black . . .
11-93-2 THOMAS RING & SON 1993
Cream body and roof, black chassis, Thos. Ring & Son logo.
12 ALBION FIRE ENGINE 1985
12-85-1 G.W.R. FIRE BRIGADE 1985
Brown body, cream chassis, fixed ladder, "G.W.R. Fire Brigade" logo.
12-85-2 SURREY FIRE BRIGADE 1985
Red body, black chassis, "Surrey Fire Brigade" logo.
 1. Fixed ladder.
 2. Removable wheeled ladder.
12-86-1 BOROUGH GREEN 1986
Red body, white chassis, fixed ladder, "Borough Green & District" logo.
12-86-2 CHELMSFORD TOWN 1986
Red body and chassis, wheeled ladder, "Chelmsford Town Fire Brigade" logo.
12-86-3 GUILDFORD 1986
Dark green body and chassis, fixed ladder, "Guildford Fire Brigade" logo.
12-86-4 JAMES WALKER & CO. 1986
Plum body, black chassis, fixed ladder, "James Walker & Co." logo.
12-86-5 LONDON C. C. 1986
Red body, black chassis, wheeled ladder, "L.C.C. London Fire Brigade" logo.
12-86-6 MILTON--BRISBANE 1986
Red body, white chassis, fixed ladder, "Milton Volunteer Brigade, Brisbane" logo.
12-86-7 NATIONAL FIRE SERVICE 1986
Light gray body, white chassis, fixed ladder, "National Fire Service" logo.
12-87-1 WARRINGTON 1987
Red body and chassis, wheeled ladder, "Warrington Fire Brigade" logo.
12-88-1 CHIVERS & SONS 1988
Red body and chassis, wheeled ladder, "Chivers & Sons Ltd." logo.
12-88-2 HERTFORDSHIRE 1988
Red body, black chassis.
12 88 3 INVERCARGILL 1988
Red body and chassis, wheeled ladder, "Invercargill Fire Board N.Z." logo.
12-88-4 NEW SOUTH WALES 1988
Red body and chassis, fixed ladder, "N.S.W. Fire Brigade" logo.
12-88-5 WAKEFIELD 1988
Red body, white chassis.

12-89-1 DERBYSHIRE FIRE SERVICE 1989
Red body, black chassis, wheeled ladder, "Derbyshire Fire Service" logo.
12-89-2 K L M 1989
Light blue body, blue chassis, fixed ladder, "KLM" logo.
12-89-3 SANDRINGHAM FIRE BRIGADE 1989
Red body, white chassis, wheeled ladder, "Sandringham Fire Brigade" logo.
12-89-4 UTRECHTSE BRANDWEER 1989
Red body . . .
12-90-1 CITY OF COVENTRY 1990
Red body . . .
12-90-2 MANCHESTER SQUARE, LONDON 1990
Red body, black chassis, wheeled ladder, "Manchester Square Fire Station, London Fire Brigade" logo.
12-90-3 NORFOLK FIRE SERVICE 1990
Red body and chassis, fixed ladder, "Norfolk Fire Service" logo.
12-91-1 DEVON COUNTY FIRE SERVICE 1991
Red body, black chassis . . .
12-91-2 ENFIELD AND DISTRICT 1991
Red body, black chassis . . .
12-91-3 I. F. P. A. 1991
Red body . . .
12-91-4 NATIONAL FIRE SERVICE 1991
Light gray body and chassis, wheeled ladder, NFS emblem.
12-91-5 REFINERY FIRE DEPARTMENT 1991
Red body, black . . .
12-91-6 WANGANUI FIRE BRIGADE 1991
Red body, black . . .
12-92-1 CROWBOROUGH (red) 1991-92
Red body . . .
12-92-2 CROWBOROUGH (green) 1992
Green body . . .
12-92-3 LEICESTER FIRE SERVICE 1992
Red body and chassis, wheeled ladder, Leicester City logo.
12-93-1 ALTON FIRE BRIGADE 1993
Red body...
12-93-2 CLEETHORPES FIRE SERVICE 1993
Red body, black chassis, fixed ladder, Cleethorpes Fire Service logo.
12-93-3 ESSEX COUNTY FIRE BRIGADE 1993
Red body, white chassis, Essex County Fire Brigade logo.
12-93-4 JOHNSONVILLE VOLUNTEER F. B. 1993
Red body and chassis, Johnsonville Volunteer Fire Brigade logo.
12-93-5 SURREY FIRE BRIGADE 1993
Red body, black chassis, fixed ladder, Surrey Fire Brigade logo.
12-93-6 UK FIRE BRIGADE CHALLENGE 1993
Gold body; mounted on plinth.
12-94-1 BEAULIEU 1994
Red body . . .

12-94-2 BOROUGH OF MANSFIELD 1994
Gray body . . .
12-94-3 CITY OF NOTTINGHAM 1994
Red body, black chassis, wheeled ladder, City of Nottingham logo.
12-94-4 CITY OF OXFORD 1994
Red body . . .
12-94-5 LONDON FIRE BRIGADE 1994
Red body, black chassis and floor, brown ladder, London Fire Brigade, Blackwall Division logo, London's Burning box.
12-94-6 OHIO OIL COMPANY 1994
Red body . . .
13-85-1 A.I.M./HAROLD'S PLACE 1985
Dark red body, black chassis, tan roof and blade, AIM emblem, 1970-1985 logo, Harold's Place, Inc. on blade.
13-85-2 BLACKPOOL EVENING GAZETTE 1985
Yellow body, black chassis and roof, Evening Gazette, Victoria St. Blackpool logo.
13-85-3 BUCKTROUT & CO. 1985
Dark blue body, black chassis and roof, Bucktrout & Company Limited logo.
13-85-4 EL PASO--SUN BOWL 1985
Light blue body, black chassis and roof, El Paso, Texas and Sun Bowl logo.
13-85-5 FINDLATER MACKIE TODD 1985
Dark green body, chassis and roof, Findlater Mackie Todd & Co. Ltd. logo.
13-85-6 FOTORAMA 1985
White body, red chassis and roof, Fotorama, A World of Colour logo.
13-85-7 HAROLD'S PLACE/MERRY CHRISTMAS 1985
Green body, red chassis, roof and blade, Harold's Place, Inc. logo, Merry Christmas on blade.
13-85-8 HARROW 18 PLUS 1985
Cream body, green chassis, roof and blade, Harrow 18 Plus logo.
13-85-9 ILLINOIS TOY SHOW 1985
Black body, chassis and roof, 5th Illinois Plastic Kit & Toy Show Sept. 22, 1985 logo.
13-85-10 ISLE OF WIGHT WEEKLY POST MOTOR SHOW 1985
Yellow body, black chassis, red roof and blade, '85 Motor Show, St. Clare Holiday Centre logo, Isle of Wight Weekly Post on blade.
13-85-11 KITCHENER COIN MACHINE 1985
Blue body, red chassis, roof and blade, Kitchener coin machine co. ltd. logo, Service and phone number on blade.
13-85-12 LEICESTER MERCURY 1985
Dark blue body, black chassis, white roof, Leicester Mercury Largest Circulation logo.
13-85-13 LINCOLNSHIRE ECHO 1985
Red body . . .
13-85-14 MANCHESTER EVENING NEWS 1985
Yellow body, chassis, roof and blade, Manchester Evening News, a friend dropping in! logo.

13-85-15 NEWEY & EYRE 1985
Blue body, chassis and roof, Newey & Eyre Ltd. logo.
13-85-16 NEDERLANDSE LLEDO 1985
Cream body, blue chassis, red roof and blade, Nederlandse Lledo
Verzamelaars Vereniging logo, same on blade.
13-85-17 O'HARA BAR COFFEE SHOP 1985
Dark blue body, gray chassis, roof and blade, O'Hara Bar Bodega
Coffee Shop, Thai and Dutch Food logo, De Koffie is Klaar on blade.
13-85-18 POLK'S HOBBIES 1985
Cream body, black chassis, roof and blade, Polk's Model Craft
Hobbies Inc. logo, 50 Years of Service on blade.
13-85-19 SWAN PENS 1985
Black body, chassis and roof, Swan Pens logo.
13-85-20 VIMTO 1985
Plum body, black chassis, black or white roof and blade, Drink Vimto
and Keep Fit logo, J. N. Nichols & Co. Ltd. on blade.
    1. White roof and blade with red lettering.
    2. Black roof and blade with yellow lettering.
13-85-21 WEST POINT TOY SHOW 1985
Cream body, green chassis, roof and blade, West Point Toy show,
June 23 1985 logo, blade may have lettering.
    1. Hotel Thayer lettering on blade.
    2. No lettering on blade.
13-85-22 YOUNGS OF HAYES 1985
Blue body, chassis, roof and blade, Youngs Hayes logo, First with the
News on blade.
13-86-1 BAGEL WORLD 1986
Salmon body, brown chassis and roof, Bagel World logo.
13-86-2 BBC FIFTY YEARS/RADIO TIMES 1986
Dark green body, black chassis, roof and blade, BBC 1936-1986,
Fifty Years of Television logo, Radio Times 2d Every Friday on
blade.
13-86-3 BEAVER LUMBER 1986
Yellow body, chassis, roof and blade, Beaver Lumber logo, Your
Lumber One Store on blade.
13-86-4 BILL GEAR 1986
Cream body, black chassis and roof, Bill, shield and and You Cannot
Buy Better Gear logo.
13-86-5 CADBURY'S CHOCOLATE--BOURNVILLE 1986
Purple body and roof, brown chassis, Cadbury's Chocolate and
Bournville logo.
13-86-6 CARR'S PET STORES 1986
Cream body, green chassis and roof, Carr's Pet Stores logo.
13-86-7 CHARCOAL STEAK HOUSE 1986
Cream body, brown chassis and roof, Charcoal Steak House logo.
13-86-8 CHERRY CIGARETTES 1986
Cream body, black chassis, red roof, Cherry Cigarettes logo.
13-86-9 CHUBB LIFE AMERICA 1986
White body, blue chassis, roof and blade, Chubb Life America logo,
Group Insurance on blade.

13-86-10 CLOWNS CONVENTION 1986
Tan body, black chassis, roof and blade, Clowns Convention logo,
2nd International Clowns Convention on blade.
13-86-11 ERNIE WHITT CLASSIC 1986
White body, black chassis and roof, Ernie White Charity Classic
August 18th 1986 logo.
13-86-12 EVENING SENTINEL 1986
Navy blue body, black chassis, roof and blade, Evening Sentinel logo,
Festival Year on blade.
13-86-13 EXCHANGE & MART 1986
White body, black chassis, roof and blade, The Exchange & Mart
logo, 4d Every Thursday on blade.
13-86-14 EXPRESS AND STAR 1986
Red body, black chassis, white roof, Express & Star logo.
13-86-15 FARNHAM MALTINGS 1986
Dark green body, red chassis, yellow roof and blade, Farnham
Maltings Swapmeet logo, The Best In The south on blade.
13-86-16 HORNBY'S DAIRIES 1986
Red body, black chassis, white roof, Hornby's Dairies, Bristol's
Safest Milk logo.
13-86-17 ISLE OF MAN TT 1986
Light blue body, black chassis, gray roof, Isle of Man TT 86 logo.
13-86-18 JAMES NEALE & SONS 1986
Yellow body, blue chassisn white roof, James Neale & Sons Limited
logo.
13-86-19 JELLY BEANS TV SHOW 1986
White body, red chassis and roof, Jelly Beans TV Show with your
host Danny Coughlan logo.
13-86-20 KALAMAZOO 1986
Black body, chassis and roof, Kalamazoo Loose Leaf Books logo.
13-86-21 KUNTZ ELECTROPLATING 1986
Dark blue body, black chassis and roof, Kuntz Electroplating Inc.
logo.
13-86-22 LIONEL LINES 1986
Orange body, blue chassis, roof and blade, Lionel Lines Service
Truck logo, Nicholas Smith est. 1909 on blade.
13-86-23 MERCANTILE CREDIT 1986
Dark blue body, chassis and roof
13-86-24 MICHAEL GERSON 25 YEARS 1986
Silver body, green or black chassis and roof, Michael Gerson 25
Years logo.
    1. Green chassis, roof, wheels and logo.
    2. Black chassis, roof, wheels and logo.
13-86-25 MITRE 10 1986
Light brown body, black chassis and roof, Mitre 10 logo.
13-86-26 NEWS PLUS 1986
White body, blue chassis, roof and blade, News Plus Newsagent logo,
We're more than just newsagents on blade.
13-86-27 NIAGARA FALLS 1986
Red or light blue body, black chassis and roof, Niagara Falls Canada
logo.

    1. Red body and wheels, black tires.
    2. Light blue body, black wheels, white tires.
13-86-28 NORFRAN PRODUCTS 1986
Blue body, chassis and roof, Norfran Products Ltd. logo.
13-86-29 OLD TOYLAND SHOWS 1986
Dark orange body, black chassis, dark brown roof and blade, logo
with fire truck, show locations and U.S.A. 1986, Old Toyland Shows
on blade.
13-86-30 ONTARIO BEAVER PELTS 1986
Cream body, brown chassis and roof, Ontario Beaver Pelts logo.
13-86-31 PETERBOROUGH PARACHUTE CENTRE 1986
Maroon body, cream chassis, roof and blade, Peterborough Parachute
Centre logo, Learn to Skydive on blade.
13-86-32 SWISS CENTRE 1986
Maroon body, black chassis, white roof, Swiss Centre Restaurants &
Shops logo.
13-86-33 TELEGRAPH CENTENARY 1986
Red body, black chassis and roof, Telegraph 1886 Centenary 1986
logo.
13-86-34 THE TIMES 1986
Yellow body, chassis, roof and blade, First with the News logo, The
Times on blade.
13-86-35 TIMEX CPGA CHAMPIONSHIP 1986
White body, blue chassis and roof, Timex CPGA Championship logo.
13-86-36 TURANO BREAD 1986
Cream body, brown or black chassis and roof, Turano Old Fashioned
French & Italian Bread .ogo.
    1. Brown chassis and roof.
    2. Black chassis and roof (1987).
13-86-37 VECTIS MODELS 1986
Dark green body, red chassis, yellow roof and blade, The Island's
Premier Diecast Centre V M logo, Vectis Models on blade.
13-86-38 ZEALLEY 1986
Blue body, black chassis and roof, Zealley, Newton 67676, Est. 1836
logo.
13-87-1 ALFRED QUAIFE 1987
Black body, chassis and roof . . .
13-87-2 BRISTOL EVENING POST 1987
Yellow body, black chassis, roof and blade, Bristol Evening Post
logo, Latest News on blade.
13-87-3 CHICHESTER OBSERVER CENTENARY 1987
Light blue body, chassis, roof and blade, Chichester Observer
Centenary logo, 1887-1987 on blade.
13-87-4 COCA-COLA 1987
Red body, black chassis and roof, Drink Coca-Cola registered trade
mark logo.
13-87-5 ETS. COMM. HOLL. MAROCAIN 1987
Cream body, blue chassis, yellow roof, Ets. Comm. Holl. Marocain
logo on left side, Moroccan flag and Arabic logo on right.

13-87-6　EVENING ARGUS　1987
Green body, black chassis, roof and blade, Evening Argus logo, Incorporating Sussex Daily News on blade.

13-87-7　EVENING TELEGRAPH　1987
Red body, black chassis and roof, Evening Telegraph logo.

13-87-8　FARNHAM MALTINGS　1987
Red body, black chassis and roof . . .

13-87-9　FOTORAMA　1987
Silver body, red chassis, roof and blade, Fotorama, A World of Colour logo, Colour Print Film on blade.

13-87-10　H. & G. RESTAURANTS　1987
Black body, chassis, roof and blade, H & G Restaurant logo, 40th Anniversary on blade.

13-87-11　HARRY RAMSDEN'S FISH & CHIPS　1987
Cream or yellow body, blue chassis and roof, Harry Ramsden's, the most famous Fish & Chip Store in the world logo.
　1. Cream body.
　2. Yellow body (1989).

13-87-11　HEWITT FORD OF CHIPPENHAM　1987
White body, blue chassis and roof . . .

13-87-12　HEWITT FORD OF WEYMOUTH　1987
White body, blue chassis and roof . . .

13-87-13　HOLME VALLEY EXPRESS　1987
Blue body, black chassis, yellow roof and blade, Holme Valley Express logo, The Voice of the Valley on blade.

13-87-14　KELLOGG CORN FLAKES　1987
White body, red chassis and roof, Kellogg Toasted Corn Flake Co. logo with cereal box design.

13-87-15　THE KENTISH MERCURY　1987
Yellow body, black chassis, roof and blade, The Kentish Mercury logo, The Best Local Paper on blade.

13-87-16　K L M PARTY AND CATERING　1987
Light blue body, blue chassis, white roof, Party and Catering Service logo.

13-87-17　LE CRUNCH BUNCH　1987
Cream body, black chassis, green roof, le crunch bunch, Delicious Apples from France logo.

13-87-18　LINCOLNSHIRE STANDARD　1987
White body, red chassis . . .

13-87-19　NORTH LONDON ADVERTISER　1987
White body, light green chassis, roof and blade, North London Group Advertiser logo, Delhome Distribution on blade.

13 87-20　ROBERTS BAKERY　1987
Green body, black chassis, roof and blade, Roberts Bakery Centenary logo, Roberts Bakery on blade.

13-87-21　SOUTH ESSEX TOY FAIR　1987
Black body, black chassis, roof and blade, South Essex Diecast Model Club, Toy Fair '87 logo, Tinplate-Diecasts-Model Railways on blade.

13-87-22　TAYLORS OF WOODFORD　1987
White body, black chassis, blue roof, Taylors of Woodford Ltd. Retail Dealer logo, Ford emblem.

13-87-23　TOWN CRIER　1987
Orange-yellow body, roof and blade, black chassis, Cambridgeshire's Free Newspaper logo, Town Crier on blade.

13-87-24　TWININGS TEA　1987
Black body, chassis and roof, two different logo designs.

13-87-25　VICTORIA WINE　1987
Dark green body, black chassis and roof, The Victoria Wine Company logo.

13-88-1　ABERDEEN EVENING EXPRESS　1988
Red body . . .

13-88-2　ANCHOR BUTTER AND CHEESE　1988
Yellow body, black chassis and roof . . .

13-88-3　AUTOBAR　1988
Tan body, brown . . .

13-88-4　BARCLAYS BANK　1988
Light gray body, black chassis, blue roof and blade, You're better off talking to Barclays logo, Barclays on blade.

13-88-5　BEAMISH MUSEUM　1988
Red-brown body, cream chassis and roof, Beamish, the North of England Open Air Museum logo.

13-88-6　BOWERS MOTORCYCLES　1988
Red body, black chassis and roof, Bowers Motorcycles, 60 Years 1928-1988 logo.

13-88-7　BRADFORD INDUSTRIAL MUSEUM　1988
Dark green body, black chassis and roof, Bradford Industrial Museum logo.

13-88-8　BROKEN HILL PROPRIETARY CO.　1988
Gray body, dark blue chassis and roof, BHP, The Broken Hill Proprietary Co. Ltd. logo, on plinth.

13-88-9　CHIVERS MARMALADE　1988
Light blue body, blue chassis, roof and blade, Chivers Breakfast Marmalade logo, Preserves Chivers Marmalades on blade.

13-88-10　COVENT GARDEN GENERAL STORE　1988
Dark green body, black chassis, roof and blade, The Covent Garden General Store logo, More fun than just shopping on blade.

13-88-11　COVENTRY DIECAST MODEL CLUB　1988
Cream body, magenta chassis, plum roof and blade, Coventry Diecast Model Club logo, News from Wheelspin on blade.

13-88-12　DERBY DAILY TELEGRAPH　1988
Red body . . .

13-88-13　DERBYSHIRE CONSTABULARY　1988
Dark blue body, black chassis and roof, Derbyshire Constabulary logo.

13-88-14　DORSET DAILY ECHO　1988
Green body, black chassis, roof and blade, Dorset Daily Echo logo, Dorset's own Paper on blade.

13-88-15　GLASGOW GARDEN FESTIVAL　1988
Cream body, red chassis and roof, Glasgow Garden Festival '88 logo.

13-88-16　GLOUCESTERSHIRE ECHO　1988
Red body and roof, black chassis, Gloucestershire Echo logo.

13-88-17　HULL DAILY MAIL　1988
Red body, black chassis, roof and blade, Hull Daily Mail logo, All you need to read on blade.

13-88-18　JERSEY LAVENDER　1988
Lilac body, black chassis, roof and blade, Jersey Lavender logo, A Fragrant Experience on blade.

13-88-19　JIM BEAM　1988
Yellow body, black . . .

13-88-20　NEWCASTLE JOURNAL　1988
Blue body, roof and blade, black chassis, Newcastle Journal and North Mail logo, Quality Voice of the North on blade.

13-88-21　ODD FELLOWS　1988
Blue body, cream chassis, yellow roof and blade . . .

13-88-22　OLDHAM CHRONICLE　1988
Yellow body, black chassis and roof, Oldham Chronicle logo.

13-88-23　OPTREX　1988
Blue body and chassis, white roof and blade, Optrex and Crookes Healthcare emblem logo, Sight for Sore Eyes on blade.

13-88-24　K. G. ORREY & SON　1988
Light blue body, blue chassis and roof, K. G. Orrey & Son Plumbing & Heating logo.

13-88-25　OUTSPAN　1988
Blue body, chassis, roof and blade, Small ones are more juicy, Outspan on blade.

13-88-26　THE PALMS　1988
Yellow body, black chassis, white roof and blade, The Palms Tropical Oasis logo, The Palms on blade.

13-88-27　PORT PLUMBING　1988
Light blue body, blue chassis and roof, Port Plumbing, Iain Barr logo.

13-88-28　POTTERS 100　1988
White body, blue chassis and roof, Potters 100 Road Trials logo.

13-88-29　SHELL FUEL SUPPLIES　1988
Yellow body, gray chassis, white roof, Shell Maintenance Service, Fuel Supplies (C.I.) Ltd. logo.

13-88-30　SHOWGARD MOUNTS　1988
Red body, black chassis and roof, Showgard Mounts logo.

13-88-31　STANLEY GIBBONS　1988
Red body . . .

13-88-32　TER MEULEN POST　1988
Orange body, black chassis, white roof and blade . . .

13-88-33　THORNTONS TOFFEE　1988
Cream body, tan chassis and roof, Thornton's Special Toffee delivered fresh each week logo.

13-88-34　UNIVERSITY OF HULL　1988
White body, blue chassis and roof . . .

13-88-35　WM. YOUNGER ALES　1988
Black body, chassis and roof, Wm. Younger's famous traditional Ales logo.

13-89-1　BOOTS QUALITY PRODUCTS　1989
Blue body and chassis, white roof, Boots Quality Products logo.

13-89-2 CHRONICLE & ECHO 1989
White body and roof, red chassis, Chronicle & Echo, Mercury & Herald logo.
13-89-3 CUMBRIA CLASSIC/WIGTON 1989
White body and roof, black chassis, "Cumbria Classic and Cumbria News logo, Wigton Motor Club Ltd. on blade.
13-89-4 DAILY EXPRESS (war) 1989
White body, black chassis, roof and blade, Daily Express logo, War declared on blade.
13-89-5 DAILY EXPRESS (V-E) 1989
White body, black chassis, roof and blade, Daily Express logo, V. E. Day--The King Speaks on blade.
13-89-6 EASTERN EVENING NEWS 1989
White body, black . . .
13-89-7 EDWARDS THE TRADEMASTERS 1989
Blue body, black chassis, roof and blade, Edwards The Trademasters logo, War Declared on blade.
13-89-8 EMULSIDERM BATHTIME FAVORITE 1989
Blue body and chassis, white roof and blade, Bathtime Favourite logo, Emulsiderm on blade.
13-89-9 EVENING ECHO 1989
White body, blue chassis and roof, Evening Echo logo.
13-89-10 EVENING GAZETTE 60 YEARS 1989
Yellow body, black chassis, roof and blade, Evening Gazette 60 Years Young, Diamond Jubilee 1929-1989 on blade.
13-89-11 FULLERS BEER 1989
Green body, red . . .
13-89-12 GUILDFORD DIVISION 1989
Gray body, black roof and chassis, Guildford Division logo, red crosses.
13-89-13 HAYES GARDEN WORLD 1989
White body, green chassis and roof, Hayes Garden World logo.
13-89-14 WM. JACKSON & SON 1989
Maroon body, black chassis and roof, Wm. Jackson & Son Ltd. logo.
13-89-15 MOTHERS PRIDE BUTTER 1989
Dark cream body and chassis, brown roof, Mothers Pride on right, Pure Butter--Naturally logo on both sides.
13-89-16 NORTHERN ECHO 1989
Red body and roof, black chassis, Northern Echo logo.
13-89-17 PROTIM 1989
Blue body, roof and chassis, Protim logo with emblem.
13-89-18 ROAD HAULAGE ASSOCIATION 1989
Blue body, white . . .
13-89-19 ROYAL MAIL 1989
Red body, black chassis, roof and blade, Royal Mail logo, Help the post get through on blade.
13-89-20 ST. JOHN AMBULANCE, DOWLAIS 1989
Black body and chassis, white roof, Dowlais Division Glamorganshire, St. John Ambulance Brigade on blade.

13-89-21 TETLEY'S TEAS 1989
Dark blue body, white roof, black chassis, Tetley's Teas Est. 1837 logo.
13-89-22 UNIGATE 1989
Red body, black chassis and roof, Unigate emblem logo.
13-89-23 UNWINS WINE MERCHANTS 1989
Dark green body and roof, black chassis, Unwins Wine Merchants logo.
13-90-1 AIR CANADA 1990
White body, red . . .
13-90-2 ALDERSHOT & DISTRICT 1990
Dark green body, chassis and roof, Aldershot & District Traction Co. Ltd. Route Servicing logo.
13-90-3 BASSETTS ALLSORTS 1990
Black body, chassis and roof, Bassetts Liquorice Allsorts logo.
13-90-4 CADBURYS 1990
Purple body . . .
13-90-5 CADBURYS DAIRY MILK 1990
Purple body, white . . .
13-90-6 CASTROL 1990
Green body, black . . .
13-90-7 COVENTRY EVENING TELEGRAPH 1990
Black body, chassis and roof, Coventry Evening Telegraph logo.
13-90-8 DAILY/SUNDAY EXPRESS (Dunkirk) 1990
White body, black chassis, roof and blade, Daily Express logo on left, Sunday Express on right, Four-fifths of B.E.F. home and Dunkirk-The last thin line on blade.
13-90-9 DAILY MIRROR 1990
Black body, chassis, roof and blade, Daily Mirror Est. 1903 logo, On sale daily-Price 1d on blade.
   1. First day of war headline in red.
   2. First day of war headline in black.
13-90-10 DAIRY FARM 1990
Dark blue body, red chassis, white roof and blade, Dairy Farm Rich Clean Milk logo, Fresh milk, cream and eggs on blade.
13-90-11 DAN-AIR 1990
Blue body, and roof, white chassis, Dan-Air logo.
13-90-12 FORD LEAMINGTON PLANT 1990
Dark blue body, chassis and roof, Ford Leamington Plant 1940-1990 logo.
13-90-13 ISLE OF THANET GAZETTE 1990
Blue body, black chassis, white roof and blade, Isle of Thanet Gazette logo, your news your views your paper on blade.
13-90-14 KEILLER BUTTERSCOTCH 1990
Cream body, maroon . . .
13-90-15 KLLEENEX 1990
White body, blue chassis, roof and blade, Kleenex Tissues, Softness is our strength logo, same on blade. [check]
13-90-16 LE GRAND HOTEL, PARIS 1990
Cream body, dark green chassis and roof, Le Grand Hotel Paris logo.

13-90-17 LMS AMBULANCE 1990
Black body and chassis, white roof, LMS logo with Maltese cross.
13-90-18 R. S. MALCOLM BANBURY CAKES 1990
Cream body, brown chassis, roof and blade, R. S. Malcolm Family Baker & Confectioner logo, Banbury Cakes on blade.
13-90-19 NOTTINGHAM FIRE SERVICE 1990
Red body, black chassis and roof, Nottingham Fire and Rescue Service logo.
13-90-20 ROY SCOT DRIVE 1990
White body, blue chassis and roof, Roy Scot Drive logo with emblem, phone number on blade.
13-90-21 ST. JOHN AMBULANCE SIDMOUTH 1990
Black body and chassis, white roof, St. John Ambulance, Sidmouth logo.
13-90-22 SCHNEIDERS 1990
Orange body, blue . . .
13-90-23 SEVENOAKS CHRONICLE 1990
Blue body, black chassis, roof and blade, Sevenoaks Chronicle logo, All your local news on blade.
13-90-24 SMARTIES 1990
Brown body and chassis, cream roof and blade, Smarties logo with Rowntrees emblem, Smarties on blade.
13-90-25 SOUTHERN DELIVERY 1990
White body, black . . .
13-90-26 SUNDAY/DAILY EXPRESS (Victory) 1990
Black body, chassis, roof and blade, Sunday Express logo on left side, Daily Express on right, Third Great Victory on blade.
13-90-27 SWAN VESTAS 1990
Yellow body, green chassis and roof, Swan Vestas, Bryant & May logo.
13-90-28 TIVERTON GAZETTE 1990
Blue body, black . . .
13-90-29 VICTORIA WINE 1990
Green body, black . . .
13-90-30 WALKERS CRISPS 1990
Maroon body, black chassis, roof and blade, Walkers Crisps logo, Walkers the Perfect Crisp on blade.
13-90-31 YORKSHIRE EVENING POST 1990
Tan body, black chassis and roof, Yorkshire Evening Post logo.
13-91-1 DAILY EXPRESS (Germany) 1991
Black body, chassis, roof and blade, Daily Express logo, Germany invades Russia and RAF attack Nazi lines on blade.
13-91-2 DAIRY FARM BAKERY 1991
Cream body, tan chassis, roof and blade, Dairy Farm Bakery logo, Fresh bread delivered to your door on blade.
13-91-3 A. J. EVANS 1991
Light blue body, white . . .
13-91-4 FORD VAN WEEK 1991
Yellow body, green . . .

13-91-5 HORNIMANS TEA 1991
Red body, black . . .
13-91-6 J. O. 1991
Brown body, white . . .
13-91-7 KODAK 1991
White body, red . . ., blue . . .
13-91-8 LEWIS DMR 1991
White body, yellow . . .
13-91-9 MAIDSTONE CO-OP SOCIETY 1991
Dark green body, black chassis and roof, Maidstone Co-operative
Societyy Ltd, The Kentish Milk logo.
13-90-10 PAMS 1991
White body, red . . .
13-91-11 PAXO 1991
Dark blue body, black chassis and roof, Paxo logo.
13-91-12 THE PEOPLE 1991
Blue body, chassis and roof, The People logo.
**13-91-13 RETFORD GAINSBOROUGH & WORKSOP TIMES
  1991**
Yellow body, blue chassis, black roof and blade, Retford,
Gainsborough & Worksop Times logo, The county Newspaper for
North Notts on blade.
13-91-14 ROYAL MAIL--BYPOST 1991
Red body, black chassis and roof, Royal Mail logo, Bypost box.
13-91-15 ST. JOHN AMBULANCE 1991
Gold body . . .
13-91-16 THE SPORTING LIFE 1991
Green body, black chassis, white roof and blade, The Sporting Life
logo, On sale daily on blade.
13-91-17 YORKSHIRE EVENING PRESS 1991
Red body and roof, black chassis, The Yorkshire Evening Press logo.
13-92-1 BROADWAY PRESS 1992
Yellow body, black . . .
13-92-2 CADBURY DAIRY MILK CHOCOLATE 1992
Purple body, white . . ., logo with border.
13-92-3 CADBURYS IRELAND 1992
Purple body, white . . .
13-92-4 CASTROL 1992
Red body, black . . .
13-92-5 DAILY EXPRESS (Singapore) 1992
Black body, chassis and roof, Singapore mentioned . . .
13-92-6 DAILY MIRROR (Andy Capp) 1992
Yellow body, white . . .
  1. Figure of Andy.
  2. Figure of Flo.
13-92-7 DAIRY FARM BUTCHERS 1992
Blue body, cream . . .
13-92-8 EUROPA SERVICE 1992
Dark blue body, black chassis, yellow roof and blade, E S Europa
Service logo, same on blade.

13-92-9 J & B RARE 1992
Light orange body and chassis, black roof, J & B Rare Scotch Whisky
logo.
13-92-10 KENT RED CROSS 1992
Navy blue body, cream . . .
13-92-11 KLEENEX VELVET TISSUES 1992
White body and roof, blue chassis, Kleenex Velvet Toilet Tissue logo.
13-92-12 LAGADU'S 1992
Blue body . . .
13-92-13 LEEDS CITY MUSEUM 1992
Yellow body, black chassis, white roof, Leeds City Museum
Collecting Since 1819 logo.
13-92-14 METROPOLITAN POLICE 1992
Dark blue body, gray . . .
13-92-15 MORRIS & CO., SHREWSBURY 1992
Green body, black . . .
13-92-16 ROUND TABLE 1992
Black body, red . . .
13-93-1 AA ROAD SERVICES 1993
Yellow body, black . . .
13-93-2 BRIDGEWATER MERCURY 1993
Red body, black . . .
13-93-3 DAILY MIRROR 1993
Navy blue body . . .
13-93-4 DAILY MIRROR/ANDY CAPP 1993
White body, red chassis and roof, Andy Capp everyday in the Daily
Mirror logo.
  1. Figure of Andy.
  2. Figure of Flo.
13-93-5 DAYS GONE 1993
Green body, black chassis and roof, Days Gone, the Ultimate
Promotion Vehicle logo.
13-93-6 ENFIELD PAGEANT 1993
Dark blue body, black . . .
13-93-7 GOD SAVE THE QUEEN 1993
Red body, black chassis, cream roof, Admiralty Arch and Coronation
Souvenir logo.
13-93-8 HARROGATE ADVERTISER 1993
Dark green body, black . . .
13-93-9 HINDLEYS 1993
Maroon body, white . . .
13-93-10 JENNINGS ALES 1993
Dark blue body and chassis, black roof, Jennings Great Cumberland
Ales logo.
13-93-11 LEIGHTONS OF HULL 1993
Navy blue body, black chassis, roof and blade, Leightons of Hull
logo, Carpets & Curtains on blade.
13-93-12 LILLIPUT LANE 1993
Cream body, green . . .
13-93-13 MILKY WAY 1993
Blue body, red . . .

13-93-14 N D B I 1993
Blue body, maroon . . ., white . . .
13-93-15 NEWS OF THE WORLD 1993
Green body, black chassis, roof and blade, News of the World logo,
Best Sunday Paper on blade.
13-93-16 J. C. PENNEY 1993
Red body, black chassis and roof, J. C. Penney Co., 297 Stores logo,
Est. 1902 on doors.
13-93-17 PRIORY OF WALES 1993
Black body, white . . .
13-93-18 ROYAL MAIL, JERSEY 1993
Red body, white . . .
13-93-19 ST. JOHN'S AMBULANCE--BEESTON 1993
Black body, chassis and roof, Order of St. John . . . Beeston Notts
Branch logo.
13-93-20 ST. JOHN'S AMBULANCE--ENFIELD 1993
White body, black . . .
13-93-21 SCHWEPPES 1993
Blue body, roof and blade, red chassis, Schweppes logo with emblem,
Schweppes on blade.
13-93-22 SOUTH STAFFORDSHIRE WATER 1993
Dark green body, roof and blade, black? chassis, The South
Staffordshire Water Company Local Water logo, Water on blade.
13-93-23 TOMS ROASTED PEANUTS 1993
Silver body, black . . .
13-93-24 THE TOY SHOP 1993
White body, blue . . .
13-93-25 T S I 1993
Green body, black . . .
13-94-1 3M 1994
Green body, black chassis . . .
13-94-2 APEX 1994
No data.
13-94-3 AUTOMOBILE ASSOCIATION 1994
Yellow body, black chassis, roof and blade, AA emblems and Road
Service logo, same on blade.
13-94-4 BLACK & DECKER 1994
Black body, roof and chassis . . .
13-94-5 DAMART 1994
Cream body, red roof, black chassis . . .
13-94-6 DULUX NATURAL WOOD 1994
Green body
13-94-7 EXPRESS AND ECHO 1994
Red body, white . . .
13-94-8 G K PRINTING 1994
Cream body, blue chassis . . .
13-94-9 HAMMERITE--WAXOYL 1994
Yellow body, black chassis . . .
13-94-10 HENRY DENNY 1994
Navy blue body, white . . .

13-94-11 JERSEY FLOWER CENTRE 1994
Pale green body, apple green chassis and roof, Retreat Farm, Jersey Flower Centre, The Home of Flying Flowers logo, A Floral Paradise on blade.

13-94-12 LILLIPUT LANE 1994
Black body, roof and chassis, Lilliput Lane, Fine Gifts and Collectables logo.

13-94-13 MICHELIN 1994
Yellow body, blue chassis . . .

13-94-14 MORTGAGE COMPANY 1994
Green body, black chassis . . .

13-94-15 PETERBOROUGH CO-OP BAKERY 1994
Maroon body, cream . . .

13-94-16 RADIO TIMES/CRINKLEY BOTTOM 1994
Black body, chassis, roof and blade, Radio Times best programme guide logo, Crinkley Bottom Newsagent on blade.

13-94-17 RUPERT BEAR 1994
Blue body, red chassis, dark blue roof and blade, Rupert and Express design logo, Daily Express/Sunday Express on blade.

13-94-18 ST. JOHN AMBULANCE GPO BRIGADE 1994
Black body, chassis, roof and transverse blade, St. John Ambulance GPO Brigade logo, Ambulance on blade.

13-94-19 TELEGRAPH & ARGUS 1994
Yellow body, black . . .

14 MODEL A FORD TOURING CAR 1985
14-86-1 METROPOLITAN POLICE 1986
Black body, chassis, top and interior, Metropolitan Police logo.

14-86-2 STATE FARM INSURANCE 1986
White body, red chassis, cream or black top and interior, Harold L. Bennett Insurance Agency Ltd. and State Farm Insurance logo.
    1. Black top and interior.
    2. Cream top and interior.

14-86-3 TAXI (black) 1986
Black body, chassis, top and interior, TAXI logo.

14-87-1 K L M 1987
Light blue body, blue chassis, white top and interior, KLM and Travel Agencies logo.

14-87-2 WESTERN STUDIOS 1987
Cream body, red chassis, white top and interior, Western Studios film crew logo.

14-88-1 HAPPY EATER 1988
Yellow body and chassis, red roof and interior, Happy Eater Restaurants logo.

14-88-2 OTTAWA CITIZEN 1988
Yellow body, black chassis, roof and interior, The Ottawa Citizen, since 1843 logo.

15 AEC DOUBLE DECK BUS 1985
The upper and lower logo of most models are separated by the word "and".

15-85-1 ADMIRAL'S CUP 1985
Green body, cream . . ., Southern Vectis and Admirals' Cup '85 logo.

15-85-2 BARCLAYS IN MILTON KEYNES 1985
Dark lbue body and chassis, yellow roof and windows, Barclays in Milton Keynes and Ask Barclays First! logo.

15-85-3 B.I.S.--SPLIT 1985
Dark green body and chassis, brown roof, cream windows, 85 B.I.SD.--Split and London Transport logo.

15-85-4 BROOKLANDS 1985
Red body, black chassis, silver roof, cream windows, Visit Brooklands Motorcourse and General logo.

15-85-5 CHASEWATER LIGHT RAILWAY 1985
Navy blue body, black chassis, cream roof and windows, Chasewater Light Railway Transport Rally 1985 logo.

15-85-6 CITY OF COVENTRY 1985
Magenta body and chassis, cream roof and windows, 100 Years of Public Transport in Coventry and City of Coventry logo.

15-85-7 FARNHAM MALTINGS 1985
Red body, chassis and roof, tan windows, Farnham Maltings and Alder Valley logo.

15-85-8 FOTORAMA A WORLD OF COLOR 1985
Red body and roof, black chassis, cream windows, Fotorama a World of Color and London Transport logo.

15-85-9 FOTORAMA FILM 1985
Red body and roof, black chassis, cream windows, Fotorama Film and London Transport logo.

15-85-10 GEMINI DIECAST 1985
Pink body and roof, black chassis, cream windows, Gemini Diecast and Shropshire logo.

15-85-11 HALL'S WINE/HASTINGS 1985
Maroon body and chassis, silver roof, cream windows, Take Hall's Wine and defy Influenze and Hastings & District logo.

15-85-12 ISLE OF WIGHT STEAM RALLY 1985
Green body and chassis, cream roof and windows, Isle of Wight Steam Rally August 1985 and Westridge logo.

15-85-13 ISLE OF WIGHT WEEKLY POST 1985
Green body and chassis, cream roof and windows, Isle of Wight Weekly Post 1975-1985 and Southern Vectis logo.

15-85-14 SHOWGARD MOUNTS 1985
Red body, black chassis, cream roof and windows, Showgard Mounts for stamps of all nations and General logo.

15-85-15 STOCKTON CORPORATION 1985
Dark green body, chassis and roof, cream windows, Stockton Corporation logo.

15-85-16 STRETTON MODELS 1985
Dark blue body and roof, black chassis, cream windows, Stretton Models and Shropshire logo.

15-86-1 AVON DIECAST 1986
Dark green body and roof, black chassis, cream windows, 1st Avod Diecast Club Swapmeet 27/2/86 and Bristol logo.

15-86-2 BARCLAYS--ST. JOHN'S WOOD 1986
Dusty blue body and roof, cream chassis and windows, Barclays Founded 1896 and Wellington Road, St. John's Wood, London logo. Eagle on upper logo may face left or right.

15-86-3 BOURNEMOUTH TRANSPORT MUSEUM 1986
Yellow body, black chassis, brown or cream roof, yellow or cream windows, Visit Bournemouth Transport Museum and Corporation Transport logo.
    1. Cream roof and windows, red upper logo background.
    2. Brown roof, yellow windows, green upper logo background.

15-86-4 CANADIAN/GENERAL (blue) 1986
Light blue body and roof, black chassis, cream windows, varying upper (as below) and General lower logo.
    1. City of Edmonton.   6. City of Toronto.
    2. Guelph, the Royal City. 7. Toronto Harbour Front.
    3. City of Kitchener.   8. City of Vancouver.
    4. Ville de Montreal.   9. City of Waterloo.
    5. Quebec City.   10. Waterloo and District.

15-86-5 CANADIAN/GENERAL (red) 1986
Red body, black chassis, cream roof and windows, varying upper (as below) and General lower logo.
    1. Guelph, the Royal City.
    2. City of Kitchener.
    3. Toronto Harbour Front.
    4. City of Waterloo.
    5. Yorkville & District.

15-86-6 CANADIAN/GENERAL (red/silver) 1986
Red body, black chassis, silver roof, cream windows, varying upper (as below) and General lower logo.
    1. Banvil Milton.   7. City of Toronto.
    2. City of Edmonton.   8. Toronto Harbour Front.
    3. Guelph, the Royal City. 9. City of Vancouver.
    4. City of Kitchener.   10. City of Waterloo.
    5. Ville de Montreal.   11. Yorkville and District.
    6. Quebec City.

15-86-7 CANADIAN/GENERAL (yellow) 1986
Yellow body, black chassis, cream roof and windows, varying upper (as below) and General lower logo.
    1. Guelph, the Royal City
    2. City of Kitchener.
    3. Toronto Harbour Front.
    4. City of Waterloo.
    5. Yorkville and District.

15-86-8 CHORLEY GUARDIAN 1986
Red body, black chassis and roof, cream windows, Chorley Guardian and Ribble logo.

15-86-9 EXPRESS AND STAR 1986
Green body and roof, black chassis, yellow windows, First With the News, Express & Star Est. 1874 and Wolverhampton Corporation Transport logo.

175

15-86-10 FLEETWOOD 150 1986
Cream body, brown chassis, roof and windows, Fleetwood 150 Celebrations 1836-1986 and Fleetwood logo.
15-86-11 GREAT WESTERN SOCIETY 1986
Brown body, black chassis, cream roof and windows, GWS 25th Anniversary 1961-1986 and Great Western Society logo.
15-86-12 HANNINGTONS 1986
Red body, chassis and roof, cream windows, Hanningtons Dept. Store and Brighton Corporation Transport logo.
15-86-13 HAPPY EATER 1986
Red body, black chassis, silver roof, cream windows, Happy Eater Family Restaurants and Look Out For Our Signs logo.
15-86-14 LINCOLNSHIRE ECHO 1986
Olive or green body, chassis and roof, cream windows, Lincolnshire Echo and City of Lincoln Transport logo.
  1. Olive body, maroon logo.
  2. Olive body, red logo.
  3. Green body, red logo.
15-86-15 LITTLE JOE'S--VIENNA BEEF 1986
Yellow body, blue chassis and windows, yellow or blue roof, Vienna Beef and Little Joe's, Countryside IL logo.
  1. Yellow roof.
  2. Blue roof.
15-86-16 LONDON MODEL CLUB 1986 1986
Yellow body and windows, black chassis and roof, London Model Club--1986 logo.
15-86-17 MAIDSTONE & DISTRICT 1986
Dark green body, chassis and roof, cream windows, See the Countryside by M & D Bus and Maidstone & District Motor Services Co. logo, 75 years behind us on rear.
15-86-18 MANCHESTER EVENING NEWS 1986
Maroon body, chassis and roof, cream windows, Manchester Evening News and Manchester Corporation logo.
15-86-19 MSMC WINDSOR SWAPMEET 1986
Dark blue body, black chassis, silver roof, cream windows, Windsor Swapmeet and MSMC logo.
15-86-20 NATIONAL AND PROVINCIAL 1986
Red body, chassis, roof and windows . . .
15-86-21 NATIONAL GARDEN FESTIVAL 1986
Red body and roof, green chassis, cream windows, National Garden Festival 1986 and Stoke-on-Trent logo.
15-86-22 NEWS OF THE WORLD 1986
Red body, chassis and roof, cream windows, Best Sunday Paper, News of the World, World's Record Sale and London Transport logo.
15-86-23 NIAGARA FALLS 1986
Red body and roof, black chassis, cream windows, Niagara Falls--Canada and General logo.
15-86-24 NORFOLK SWAPMEET 1986
Black body, chassis, roof and windows, Sunday 30th November 1986, 6th Norfolk Swapmeet and The East Anglian Diecast Model Club logo.

15-86-25 NOTTINGHAM GUARDIAN-POST/EVENING POST 1986
Dark green body, chassis and roof, cream windows, newspaper name and Nottingham Corporation Passenger Transport Department logo.
  1. Guardian-Post Morning-Evening logo.
  2. Nottingham Evening Post logo.
15-86-26 OXFORD MAIL 1986
Red body, black chassis, maroon roof and windows, Read the Oxford Mail Daily and Oxford logo, Visit the Oxford Bus Museum on rear.
  1. Light gray-green stripes.
  2. Blue stripes.
15-86-27 RADIO TIMES 1986
Red body, chassis and roof, cream windows, Radio Times Every Friday 2d and London Transport logo.
15-86-28 RED FUNNEL GROUP 1986
Black body, light blue chassis, white roof, red windows, 1986 Southampton Isle of Wight and South of England, Royal Mail Steam Packet Company Limited 1861 and Red Funnel Group 125th Anniversary logo. One date on each side.
15-86-29 REDBRIDGE VICTIMS SUPPORT 1986
Red body and roof, black chassis, cream windows, Redbridge Victims Support Scheme and London Transport logo.
15-86-30 RYDE HARRIERS 1986
Red body, white chassis, roof and windows, 30th Isle of Wight Marathon Ryde Harriers and Southern Vectis logo.
15-86-31 RYDE RAIL FESTIVAL 1986
Dark blue body, light gray chassis and roof, cream windows, Ryde Rail Festival and Ryde Rail 1986 logo.
15-86-32 SPRING GARDEN SHOW 1986
Cream body and windows, light blue chassis and roof, The Spring Garden Show 1986 and County Showground logo.
15-86-33 STAFFORDSHIRE COUNTY SHOW 1986
Cream body and windows, green chassis and roof, Staffordshire County Show May 28-29 1986 and Staffordshire Agricultural Society logo.
15-86-34 TOYFAIR AT THE CENTRE HALLS 1986
Tan body and chassis, silver roof, brown windows, The Toyfair at the Centre Halls and Surrey logo.
15-86-35 VIGIL RESCUE 1986
Dark green body, chassis and roof, silver roof, cream windows, Vigil Rescue and London Transport logo.
15-86-36 VIMTO 1986
Red body, black chassis, cream roof, brown windows, Vimto Keeps You Fit and General logo.
15-87-1 ADMIRALS' CUP 1987
Green body, chassis and roof, white windows, 1987 Admirals' Cup and Southern Vectis logo.
15-87-2 ALTON TOWERS 1987
Magenta body, cream chassis and windows, silver roof, Alton Towers, Europe's Premier Leisure Park and gold emblem logo.

15-87-3 AUSTRALIAN BICENTENARY 1987
Green body, black chassis, cream roof and windows, Australian Bicentenary Celebrations and Southern Vectis logo.
15-87-4 AUTOCAR 1987
Purple body and chassis, cream roof and windows, Autocar logo, destination Uckfield.
15-87-5 BANBURY STEAM SOCIETY 1987
Dark green body and windows, black chassis and roof, 12st Anniversary Rally 1987, Bloxham and Banbury Steam Society logo.
15-87-6 BARCLAYS EALING 1987
Red body and roof, cream chassis and windows, Barclays Ealing and London Transport logo.
15-87-7 BARCLAYS SUPER SAVERS 1987
Dusty blue body and roof, cream chassis and windows, Barclays Founded 1896 and Super Savers Club logo.
15-87-8 BEAMISH 1987
Red body, black chassis, light cream roof, dark cream windows, Beamish and Northern logo.
15-87-9 BIRD'S 1987
Red body and roof, black chassis, cream windows, Bird's and London Transport logo.
15-87-10 BRIGADE AID 1987
Light blue body and roof, blue chassis, orange windows, Brigade Aid and Water Means Life logo.
15-87-11 BOURNEMOUTH TRANSPORT MUSEUM/HANTS & DORSET 1987
Dark green body, black chassis, cream roof and windows?, Visit the Transport Museum in Bournemouth and Hants & Dorset logo.
15-87-12 BOURNEMOUTH TRANSPORT MUSEUM/ VERWOOD 1987
Dark blue body and roof, black chassis, light blue windows, Visit Bournemouth Transport Museum and Verwood Transport logo.
  1. Destination Poole.
  2. Destination Verwood.
15-87-13 BUCKINGHAM AND STANLEY 1987
Light blue body . . .
15-87-14 CANADIAN/GENERAL (gray) 1987
Gray body, yellow . . ., varying upper (as below) and General lower logo.
  1. City of Edmonton.   6. City of Toronto.
  2. Guelph, the Royal City. 7. Toronto Harbour Front.
  3. City of Kitchener.   8. City of Vancouver.
  4. Ville de Montreal.   9. City of Waterloo.
  5. Quebec City.   10. Yorkville and District.
15-87-15 CASTROL 1987
Red body and roof, black chassis, cream windows, Castrol, The Masterpiece in Oils and London Transport logo.
15-87-16 CATHERINE COOKSON/SOUTH SHIELDS 1987
Dark blue body and chassis, cream roof and windows, Catherine Cookson Country and South Shields Corporation logo.

15-87-17 COUNTRY LIFE BUTTER 1987
Red body, black chassis, cream roof and windows, Country Life English Butter and You'll never put a better bit of butter on your knife logo.

15-87-18 COWES TOY AND MODEL MUSEUM (green) 1987
Green body, black chassis, cream roof and windows, Cowes Toy and Model Museum and Southern Vectis logo.

15-87-19 COWES TOY AND MODEL MUSEUM (brown) 1987
Dark brown body, tan chassis and roof, white windows, Cowes Toy and Model Museum and High Street, West Cowes logo.

15-87-20 THE DELAINE 1987
Dull blue body, black chassis and roof, cream windows, The Delaine logo, destination Bourne.

15-87-21 DONINGTON AUTOJUMBLE 1987
Blue body and roof, cream chassis and windows, Donington International 1st Autojumble 87 and Donington logo.

15-87-22 ESSEX TOY FAIR 1987
White body, black chassis, green roof, dark green windows, Essex Toy Fair and For Collectors Of Tinplate, Die Cast & Model Railways logo.
1. Red logo.
2. Black logo.

15-87-23 EXCHANGE AND MART 1987
Red body, black chassis, silver roof, cream windows, Exchange & Mart Every Thursday, Just the Ticket and General logo.

15-87-24 EXPRESS AND ECHO 1987
Red body and roof, black chassis, cream windows, Express & Echo, Your Local Evening Newspaper and Exeter Corporation logo.

15-87-25 EVENING ARGUS 1987
Lime green body, dark green chassis and roof, cream windows, Read the Evening Argus, your local paper and Southdown logo.

15-87-26 EVENING TELEGRAPH 1987
Dark green body and roof, black chassis, cream windows, Evening Telegraph and Lincolnshire Road Car Co. Ltd. logo.

15-87-27 ISLE OF WIGHT STEAM RAILWAY 1987
Green body, black chassis, cream roof and windows, Isle of Wight Steam Railway and Southern Vectis logo.

15-87-28 K L M 1987
Light blue body, blue chassis, cream roof and windows, Fly With KLM The No. 1 and The Reliable Airline KLM logo.

15-87-29 LAMBETH BUILDING SOCIETY 1987
Red body and roof, black chassis, white windows, Lambeth Building Society, A safe home for investors since 1852 and London Transport logo.

15-87-30 M G (MICHAEL GERSON) 1987
Red or white body and roof, black or green chassis, cream or green windows, MG emblem plus Japanese lettering and Japanese lettering plus phone number logo.
1. Red body, roof and wheels, black chassis, cream windows.

2. White body and roof, green chassis, windows and wheels.

15-87-31 MODEL MOTORING/DUNDEE 1987
Dark blue body and chassis, light blue roof and windows, Model Motoring and Corporation Transport No. 15 logo.

15-87-32 MODEL MOTORING/GLASGOW 1987
Orange body and chassis, green roof and windows, Model motoring and Glasgow Corporation logo.
1. Medium green roof and windows.
2. Dark green roof and windows.

15-87-33 MODEL MOTORING/LOTHIAN 1987
Maroon body, black chassis, white roof and windows, Model Motoring and Lothian logo.

15-87-34 NORTHERN DAILY MAIL 1987
Maroon body, black chassis, light gray roof, cream windows, Don't Miss The Northern Daily Mail and emblem logo.

15-87-35 PERSIL 1987
Red body and roof, black chassis, white windows, Persil washes whiter and London Transport logo.

15-87-36 PLYMOUTH ARGYLE FOOTBALL CLUB 1987
Green body, roof and windows, black chassis, Plymouth Argyle Football Club and Western National logo.

15-87-37 S. R. A./LONDON TRANSPORT 1987
Red body . . ., London Transport lower logo.
1. SRA upper logo.
2. SRA Global upper logo.

15-87-38 STEVENSON'S BUS SERVICES 1987
Yellow-orange body and windows, black chassis and roof, Stevenson's Bus Services and Stevensons logo.

15-87-39 TOWN CRIER 1987
Red body and roof, black chassis, white windows, Town Crier and Ortona, Cambridge logo.

15-87-40 UNITED 75 YEARS 1987
Red body and roof, black chassis, cream windows, Serving the North East for 75 Years and United 75 logo.
1. As above.
2. Plus The Model Bus Federation logo on rear.

15-87-41 VISIT OF H. M. THE QUEEN 1987
Green body, black chassis, cream roof and windows, Visit of H. M the Queen and Southern Vectis logo.

15-88-1 BASSETTS ALLSORTS 1988
Black body, chassis, roof and windows, Bassetts Allsorts Liquorice and candy design logo, The Original Allsorts rear logo.

15-88-2 BELL VUE/PEMBROKE 1988
Light blue body, navy blue chassis and roof, cream windows, Bell Vue Promotions Aug. 1988 and gold bell symbol logo.
1. Destination Canada.
2. Destination Pembroke Dock.

15-88-3 BRADFORD INDUSTRIAL MUSEUM 1988
Blue body and roof, black chassis, cream windows, Bradford Industrial Museum and Bradford's world of industry logo.

15-88-4 CANADIAN/GENERAL (red) 1988
Red body and roof, black chassis, cream windows, varying upper (as below) and General lower logo.
1. Banvil Milton.	5. City of Toronto.
2. City of Edmonton.	6. Toronto Toy Fair.
3. Ville de Montreal.	7. City of Vancouver.
4. Quebec City.	

15-88-5 CANADIAN/GENERAL (yellow/silver) 1988
Yellow body, black chassis, silver roof, cream windows, varying upper (as below) and General lower logo.
1. City of Edmonton.	9. Quebec City.
2. Guelph, the Royal City.	10. City of Toronto.
3. Just Wheels.	11. Toronto Harbour Front.
4. City of Kitchener.	12. City of Vancouver.
5. Ville de Montreal.	13. Victoria, B. C.
6. Niagara Falls.	14. City of Waterloo.
7. Niagara-on-the-Lake.	15. Yorkville and District.
8. Northwest Territories.	16. Yukon Territory.

15-88-6 CHATHAM OBSERVER 1988
Green body . . ., Chatham Observer and Maidstone & District logo.
1. Destination Chatham.
2. Destination Hoo.

15-88-7 DEVON GENERAL 1988
Maroon body, cream . . ., Devon General logo.
1. Destination Paignton.
2. Destination Torquay.

15-88-8 EVENING SENTINEL 1988
Dark blue body and roof, black chassis, cream windows, Evening Sentinel and A Friend of the Family logo.

15-88-9 EVENING TELEGRAPH 1988
White body, windows and roof, black chassis, Evening Telegraph logo.

15-88-10 EXPRESS AND STAR (blue) 1988
Blue body, chassis and roof, pale blue windows, First with the News/ Express & Star Est. 1874 amd Walsall Corporation logo.

15-88-11 FISHERMAN'S FRIEND 1988
Red body . . ., Fisherman's Friend and London Transport logo.

15-88-12 GLAMORGAN GAZETTE 1988
Plum body, chassis and roof, cream windows, The glamorgan Gazette and Porthcawl Omnibus Co. Ltd. logo.
1. Destination Bridgend.
2. Destination Nottage.

15-88-13 HORNBY DUBLO 1988
Dark green body, chassis, roof and windows, 50th Anniversary Hornby Dublo 1938-1988 and Southern Vectis logo.

15-88-14 LEICESTER MERCURY 1988
Purple body and chassis, cream roof and windows, Leicester Mercury and Leicester Tramways logo.

15-88-15 NATIONAL EISTEDDVOD 1988
Green body, yellow . . .

15-88-16 ORANGE SHRED 1988
Red body, roof and windows, green chassis, Tangy Orange Shred and Chivers logo.
15-88-17 RdP COLLECTORS GUIDE 1988
Cream body and roof, red chassis and windows, RdP Lledo Information Service 1988 and RdP Publications logo.
15-88-18 SKODA FORTUNE AUTO SALES 1988
Dark blue body, black chassis, cream roof and windows?, Harris Buses lower logo.
15-88-19 STAPELEY WATER GARDENS 1988
Yellow body, black chassis, roof and windows, Stapeley Water Gardens and The Palms, Tropical Oasis logo.
15-88-20 SWEETEX 1988
Green body and chassis, white roof and windows, Sweetex and Nottingham Transport logo.
15-88-21 THANET GAZETTE 1988
Maroon body and chassis, cream roof and windows, Thanet Gazette every Friday, price 3d and East Kent logo.
    1. Destination Margate.
    2. Destination Ramsgate.
15-88-22 THANET TIMES 1988
Maroon body and chassis, white roof and windows, Thanet Times every Tuesday, price 2d and East Kent logo.
    1. Destination St. Peter.
    2. Destination Westgate.
15-88-23 WATFORD SWAPMEET 1988
Green body, cream . . ., London Transport lower logo.
15-89-1 AB MOTOR CO. 1989
Dark blue body . . .
15-89-2 ADMIRALS' CUP 1989 1989
Cream body, green . . ., Admirals' Cup 1989 and Southern Vectis logo.
15-89-3 FISHERMAN'S FRIEND 1989
Red body . . ., Extra strong lozenges logo.
15-89-4 W. GASH & SONS 1989
Dark blue body . . ., cream . . . .
    1. Destination Elston.
    2. Destination Newark.
15-89-5 HACKNEY GAZETTE 1989
Red body . . ., London Transport lower logo.
15-89-6 MOSELEY POTTERY 1989
Green body, cream . . ., Green Bus Service lower logo.
    1. Destination Cannock.
    2. Destination Walsall.
15-89-7 ODD FELLOWS/MANCHESTER 1989
Maroon body, chassis and roof, cream windows, Manchester Corporation lower logo.
    1. Destination Eccles.
    2. Destination Salford.

15-89-8 THE OLD BANK, LEWES 1989
Light blue body and roof, black chassis, cream windows, The Old Bank Lewes and 1789 Bicentenary 1989 logo.
15-89-9 PEAT MARWICK 1989
Red body . . ., London Transport lower logo.
    1. Destination Blackfriars.
    2. Destination Fleet St.
15-89-10 POST EARLY FOR CHRISTMAS 1989
Red body, roof and windows, black chassis, Post Early For Christmas and London Transport logo.
15-89-11 POTTERTON GAS HEATING 1989
White body and roof, black chassis and windows, Potterton the best in gas central heating and address logo.
15-89-12 ROBIN HOOD MARATHON 1989
Green body and roof, black chassis, cream windows, Pork Farms Robin Hood Marathon and Nottingham City Transport logo.
15-89-13 RPP BUILDING SERVICES 1989
Brown body and chassis, cream roof and windows, Enterprise & Silver Dawn lower logo.
    1. Destination Brigg.
    2. Destination Lincoln.
15-89-14 SGT. PEPPERS CONCERT PARTY 1989
Red body and roof, black chassis, cream windows, Sgt. Peppers Concert Party and Berkhamsted logo.
15-89-15 WAKEFIELD CASTROL MOTOR OIL 1989
Red body and roof, black chassis, cream windows, Wakefield Castrol Motor Oil, The Masterpiece in Oils and General logo.
15-89-16 WALSALL ILLUMINATIONS 1989
Dark green body, red chassis, windows and roof, The 1989 Illuminations and Walsall MBC logo.
15-89-17 W.C.D.N.T./CASTROL 1989
Orange-red body and roof, black chassis, cream windows, 12th W.C.D.N.T. Amsterdam 1989 and Castrol logo.
15-90-1 AB MOTOR CO. 70TH ANNIVERSARY 1990
No data except:
    1. Red body . . .
    2. Green body, dark green . . .
15-90-2 THE ADVERTISER 1990
Red body, black chassis and windows, cream roof, Advertiser 1975-1990 and Potteries logo.
15-90-3 AIR CANADA 1990
Red body, white . . .
15-90-4 BOWLERS/MANCHESTER TOY FAIR 1990
Plum body, chassis and roof, cream windows, Bowlers and Manchester Toy Fair Oct 1990 logo.
    1. Destination Salford.
    2. Destination Trafford Park.
15-90-5 BROBAT 1990
Blue body . . ., Middlesborough Corporation lower logo.
    1. Destination Redcar.
    2. Destination Southbank.

15-90-6 THE CHILDREN'S SOCIETY 1990
White body and windows, yellow chassis, red roof, The Children's Society and figures logo.
    1. Destination Shirburn.
    2. Destination The Starting Point.
15-90-7 CITIZEN MOTOR SHOW 1990
Maroon body, cream . . ., Ribble lower logo.
15-90-8 CLARENDON COLLEGE 1990
Green body and roof, black chassis, white windows, Clarendon plus emblems and Nottingham County Council Education logo.
    1. Destination Mansfield.
    2. Destination Pelham Ave.
15-90-9 DAN-AIR 1990
Red body and roof, black chassis, cream windows, Dan-Air and London Transport logo.
15-90-10 DONINGTON 1990
Navy blue body, white . . .
    1. Destination Airport.
    2. Destination 1990.
15-90-11 DRIVING THE DREAM 1990
White body . . ., Manchester lower logo.
15-90-12 ENGINEERING & FASTENERS 1990
Silver body and roof, black chassis, gray windows, Engineering & Fasteners Trade Union and address logo.
    1. Destination Bearwood.
    2. Destination Oldbury.
15-90-13 FARNHAM MALTINGS 1990
Dark green body, green . . ., Aldershot & District lower logo.
    1. Destination Camberley.
    2. Destination Farnham.
15-90-14 FORCE FLAKES 1990
Red body . . ., London Transport lower logo.
15-90-15 GILBEYS GIN/GREEN LINE 1990
Green body . . ., Green Line lower logo.
    1. Destination Ilford.
    2. Destination Stratford.
15-90-16 THE GROCER 1990
Red body, black chassis and roof, white windows, The Grocer Est. 1861 and General logo.
15-90-17 KLEENEX BOUTIQUE 1990
Red body and roof, black chassis, cream windows, Kleenex Boutique Tissues and London Transport logo.
15-90-18 LINCOLNSHIRE TOY & TRAIN 1990
Yellow body, blue chassis, roof and windows, The lincolnshire toy & Train Collectors Extravaganza and Promoted by Julie & John Webb logo.
15-90-19 LITTLEWOODS 1990
Red body, roof and windows, black chassis, Littlewoods and Rhondda logo.
    1. Destination Merthyr.
    2. Destination Porth.

15-90-20 LYTHAM ST. ANNE'S PHILATELIC SOCIETY 1990
Light blue body and roof, black chassis, cream windows, Kytham St. Anne's Philatelic Society Annual Fair and 150th Anniversary Penny Black Postage Stamp logo.

15-90-21 MEW LANGTONS ALES 1990
Light green body, cream . . ., Southern Vectis lower logo.

15-90-22 MORNFLAKE OATS 1990
Red body, chassis and roof, cream windows, Take good care of yourself with Mornflake oats logo.

15-90-23 NATIONAL GARDEN FESTIVAL 1990
Cream body and windows, black chassis, blue roof, National Garden Festival and Gateshead 1990 logo.

15-90-24 ROMANDO BAND 1990
Red body . . .
  1. Destination Eastbourne.
  2. Destination Southport.

15-90-25 ST. DAVID'S FOUNDATION 1990
Brown body, cream . . .

15-90-26 ST. JULIAN'S BAPTIST 1990
Navy blue body, red . . .

15-90-27 SANDOWN TOY EXTRAVAGANZA 1990
Maroon body and roof, black chassis, dark maroon windows, Sandown Toy Extravaganza and Barry Potter Fairs logo.
  1. Destination Esher.
  2. Destination Sandown.

15-90-28 THE STANDARD 1990
White body and windows, light green chassis and roof, The Standard and part of life in Lincolnshire logo.

15-90-29 THE STAR 1990
Dark blue body, black chassis, cream roof and windows, The Star Est. 1887 and Sheffield Corporation Motors logo.
  1. Destination Dore.
  2. Destination Middlewood.

15-90-30 SUTTON SCHOOL OF GYMNASTICS 1990
Cream body and windows, maroon chassis and roof, Sutton's new Gymnastics Centre and Sutton School of Gymnastics logo.

15-90-31 TRANSPORT 90 1990
Red body, chassis and windows, white roof, Transport '90 and Eastern Counties logo.

15-90-32 VEN (Dieman/Alkmaar) 1990
White body . . ., blue . . .
  1. Destination Alkmaar.
  2. Destination Dieman.

15-90-33 VEN (Haarlem/Marktweg) 1990
White body and windows, jade green chassis and roof, Ven, ver vooruit in food en non-food en VEN logo.
  1. Destination Haarlem.
  2. Destination Marktweg.

15-90-34 WESTERN 1990
White body, black chassis, windows and roof, Western logo.
  1. Destination Paisley.
  2. Destination Queen Street.

15-91-1 ADMIRALS' CUP 1991 1991
Green body, cream . . ., Southern Vectis lower logo. Apparently two variations.

15-91-2 BIG BEN'S OF LONDON 1991
Red body, roof and windows, black chassis, Columbus 70 West, Big Ben's of London and Big Ben Fudge Shop logo.

15-91-3 BLUE BUS SERVICE 1991
Blue body, chassis and roof, tan windows, Blue Bus Service logo.
  1. Destination Burton.
  2. Destination Derby.

15-91-4 CLIFFORD'S DAIRIES 1991
Red body, cream chassis, roof and windows, Clifford's Dairies and coat of arms logo.

15-91-5 EAST ANGLIA
Maroon body, cream . . ., East Anglia TM and Lowestoft Corporation logo.
  1. Destination Corton.
  2. Destination Sparrows N.

15-91-6 FOX'S BISCUITS 1991
Red body . . .

15-91-7 GUIDE DOGS 1991
White body and windows, blue chassis, light green roof, Guide Dogs for the Blind Association Diamond Jubilee Year 1991 and 1991 with figure logo.
  1. Destination Exeter.
  2. Destination Torquay.

15-91-8 LLEDO SHOW 1991
Red body, silver . . ., 2nd Lledo Show and Midland Red logo.

15-91-9 N E C TOYFAIR 1991
Dark blue body, cream . . ., Birmingham Corporation lower logo. Apparently two variations.

15-91-10 NOTTINGHAMSHIRE TOY & TRAIN 1991
Pinkish cream body, dark green chassis, roof and windows, Nottinghamshire Toy & Train Collectors Extravaganza and Kime's Coaches logo.
  1. Destination Folkingham.
  2. Destination Newark Showground.

15-91-11 PORTSMOUTH CORPORATION 1991
Red body . . .
  1. Destination Dockyard.
  2. Destination Red Lion.

15-91-12 ST. DAVID'S FOUNDATION 1991
Green body and chassis, red roof, cream windows, Eissedvod Genedlaethol Frenhinol Cymru and St. David's Foundation, Newport Gwent 1991 logo.

15-91-13 SALVATION ARMY 1991
Green body, cream . . ., Chatham & District lower logo.
  1. Destination Luton.
  2. Destination Strand.

15-91-14 SOUTHPORT FLOWER 1991
Light blue body, cream . . .
  1. Destination Botanical Gardens.
  2. Destination Southport.

15-91-15 STEVENSONS 1991
Yellow body, black . . ., Stevensons logo.
  1. Destination Burton.
  2. Destination Uttoxeter.

15-91-16 VICTOR ARTS 1991
Blue body . . .

15-91-17 WHITTAKER COACHES 1991
Light green body, red . . ., W. Whittaker and Whittaker Coaches logo.
  1. Destination Halesowen.
  2. Destination Hill Top.

15-91-18 WIGAN PIER 1991
Maroon body, black . . ., Wigan Pier and Wigan Lancs logo.

15-92-1 BARCLAY PLUS 1992
Light blue body . . .

15-92-2 COVENTRY TRANSPORT 1992
Cream body . . .
  1. Destination Coundon.
  2. Destination Holbrooks.

15-94-3 FAIRVIEW INN 1992
Red body . . ., Midland ML lower logo.

15-92-4 JUBILEE STOUT 1992
Dark red body, chassis and roof, maroon windows, Jubilee Stout and Hebble logo.

15-92-5 LINCOLNSHIRE STANDARD 1992
Red body . . .

15-92 6 LYONS TEA 1992
Red body and roof, black chassis, cream windows, Lyons Tea and coat of arms logo.

15-92-7 MAKE & MOVE 1992
Blue body, white . . ., JBS lower logo.

15-92-8 OXFORD MAIL 1992
Red body . . ., Oxford lower logo.

15-92-9 ST. IVEL CHEESE 1992
Blue body, chassis and hubs, cream roof and windows, St. Ivel Cheese, The Pride of the West Countrie and Thamesdown logo.

15-92-10 SILVER QUEEN 1992
Silver body, white . . .
  1. Destination Brace Brd.
  2. Destination Lincoln.

15-92-11 SOUTH WALES ARGUS 1992
Green body and windows, black chassis and roof, 1892 South Wales Argus 1992 and Gwent's Evening Newspaper logo.

15-92-12 SUBBUTEO 1992
Green body . . .
15-92-13 TRANSTAR 1992
Dark blue body . . ., West Bromwich lower logo.
15-92-14 VB MODELS 1992
White body, blue . . .
    1. Destination Cape.
    2. Destination Hawthorns.
15-92-15 WOODWARD'S 1992
Red body, roof and hubs, cream windows, Woodward's British
Promotion and London Transport logo.
15-93-1 ADMIRALS' CUP 1993
Cream body . . .
    1. Destination Cowes.
    2. Destination East Cowes.
15-93-2 CHAMPION SPARK PLUGS 1993
Red body . . .
15-93-3 EAST LANCASHIRE RAIL 1993
Green body, white . . .
15-93-4 HARRY RAMSDEN 1993
Green body, white . . .
15-93-5 HOVE SCOUTS/BRIGHTON 1993
Blue body . . ., 6th Hove Scouts and Brighton logo.
    1. Destination Hurst Crescent.
    2. Destination P Charles.
15-93-6 LANGS SCOTCH WHISKY 1993
Red body, chassis and roof, cream windows, Langs Supreme Scotch
Whisky and London Transport logo.
15-93-7 ST. DAVIDS 1993
Light blue body, cream . . .
15-93-8 ST. JULIANS 1993
Green body, brown . . .
15-93-9 TINTAGEL TOY 1993
Dark green body, Western National lower logo.
    1. Destination Bude.
    2. Destination Plymouth.
15-94-1 ALLIANCE & LEICESTER/GENERAL 1994
Dark gray body . . .
15-94- CHURCHILLS 1994
Red body . . ., London Transport lower logo, destination London
Bridge Station.
15-94- DOUBLE DECCA 1994
Red body . . ., London Transport lower logo.
15-94- HERMETITE/NEWCASTLE 1994
Yellow body, cream . . .
15-94- WIGAN PIER 1994
Black body . . ., Wigan Lancs lower logo.
16 DENNIS PARCELS VAN
Here again, the stated chassis color of models I have not seen may
actually be the roof color. The "front" occasionally noted is the front
of the rear box, above the cab.

16-85-1 AVON DIECAST SOCIETY 1985
Black body, chassis and roof, Avon Diecast And Model Collectors
Society logo, plus 1985 on front.
16-85-2 J. J. BRODSKY AND SONS 1985
Cream body, blue chassis and roof, J. J. Brodsky & Sons, Inc.
Wholesale Distributors logo.
16-85-3 FERGUSON'S CARRIERS 1985
Light blue body and chassis, cream roof, Ferguson's Carriers
Removers, Bath Lane, Blyth logo.
16-85-4 MICHAEL GERSON 1985
Dark grren body, black chassis and roof, Overseas Removals,
Michael Gerson logo.
16-85-5 NMCC MINIATURE CAR YEAR 1985
Dark yellow body, black chassis and roof . . .
16-85-6 OLD TOYLAND SHOWS 1985
Light gray body, red chassis and roof, On The Move With Old
Toyland Shows logo.
16-85-7 OVER'S OF CAMBERLEY 1985
Red body, black chassis, white roof, Internationale Mobelspedition
Removals Storage Packing Shipping and Over's of Camberley logo.
16-85-8 SCALE AUTO ENTHUSIAST 1985
Light gray body, black chassis and roof, Scale Auto enthusiast,
world's leading automotive modeling magazine logo.
16-85-9 SURREY DIECAST MODEL CLUB 1985
Tan body, black chassis, brown roof, Surrey Diecast Model Club
logo, plus September 1985 on front.
16-85-10 THRESHOLD RECORDS & TAPES 1985
White body, black chassis, blue roof, Threshold Records & Tapes
logo.
16-86-1 ALAN GREENWOOD 1986
Red body, black chassis, white roof, Alan Greenwood International
Removal Specialists logo.
16-86-2 ALFRED QUAIFE 1986
Black body, chassis and roof. Sometimes on plinth?
16-86-3 ALLIED VAN LINES 1986
Dull orange body and chassis, white roof, Allied, The Careful Movers
logo with maple leaf.
16-86-4 APURA 1986
White body and roof, black chassis, Apura, efficient en betrouwbar--
ook in service logo.
    1. One A emblem on rear doors.
    2. Two A emblems on rear doors.
16-86-5 ASSOCIATION OF MODEL RAILWAY CLUBS 1986
Light yellow body, blue chassis and roof, Association of Model
Railway Clubs Wales & West of England Ltd. logo.
16-86-6 BRATT VEHICLE HIRE 1986
Orange body, black chassis and roof, Bratt vehicle hire specialists
logo.
16-86-7 CAVALIER REMOULDS 1986
Black body, chassis and roof, Cavalier H.G.V. Remoulds logo with
cavalier figure.

16-86-8 P. H. CHANDLER 1986
Cream body, brown chassis and roof, P. H. Chandler logo.
16-86-9 COLD CHOICE--PELHAM MEATS 1986
Cream body, black chassis and roof, Cold Choice, Pelham Meats Ltd.
logo.
16-86-10 DUNLOP 1986
Red body, black chassis, white roof, Dunlop, The World's Master
Tyre logo.
16-86-11 ENFIELD PAGEANT OF MOTORING 1986
Black body, chassis and roof . . .
16-86-12 EXCHANGE AND MART 1986
Black body, red chassis, white roof, Exchange & Mart packed full of
bargains Every Week! logo.
16-86-13 GREAT WESTERN SOCIETY 1986
Brown body, black chassis, cream roof . . .
16-86-14 GRIMLEY AND SON 1986
Red body, black chassis, white roof . . .
16-86-15 HAROLD'S PLACE/CHRISTMAS 1986
Green body and chassis, dark green roof, Merry Christmas 1986 to
our Customers, Harold's Place, Inc. logo.
16-86-16 HISTORIC COMMERCIAL VEHICLE RUN 1986
Dark green body, black chassis, cream roof, The Historic Commercial
Vehicle Run London-Brighton logo on left, Wheels of Yesterday
Rally on right.
16-86-17 L M S EXPRESS PARCELS 1986
Magenta body, black chassis and roof, L M S Express Parcels Service
logo.
16-86-18 LUCKING FURNITURE 1986
Blue body, white . . .
16-86-19 MANNERS AND HARRISON 1986
Cream or white body, black or blue chassis and roof, Manners &
Harrison Auction Department, Chartered Surveyors logo.
    1. Cream body, black chassis and roof.
    2. White body, blue chassis and roof, reversed logo colors.
16-86-20 NATIONAL FIRE SERVICE 1986
Red body, black chassis. white roof, NFS emblem logo with doors,
windows and checkered stripes.
16-86-21 NATIONAL SYSTEMS 1986
Yellow-orange body, green chassis and roof, National Systems Co.
P.O. Box 157, Waterloo, Ontario logo.
16-86-22 NORTHLAND LUMBER 1986
Yellow-orange body, dark green chassis and roof, Northland Lumber
logo, Canada on front.
16-86-23 NOTTINGHAM IDEAL HOME EXHIBITION 1986
Cream body, red chassis and roof, The Nottingham Ideal Home
Exhibition logo.
16-86-24 J. & B. PEARCE 1986
Light blue body, dark blue chassis, white roof, J & B Pearce & Co
Agricultural Supplics logo.
16-86-25 RELIANCE WHOLESALE ELECTRICAL 1986
Cream body, brown . . .

16-86-26 SLUMBERLAND BEDS 1986
Red body and roof, black chassis, Slumberland Beds, over 20 years of Posture Springing logo.
16-86-27 SOUTH ESSEX TOY FAIR 1986
White body, black chassis, brown roof, South Essex Diecast Model Club Toy Fair '86, Basildon, Essex logo.
16-86-28 VAKUUM VULK 1986
Black body, chassis and roof, Vakuum Vulk, The Long Distance Retread logo.
16-86-29 VAN MAGAZINE 1986
White body, red chassis and roof, V A N Magazine at your Newsagent Now! logo.
16-86-30 VEN GROOTHANDELCENTRUM 1986
White body, green chassis and roof, VEN Groothandelcentrum logo.
16-86-31 VEN VERS MARKT 1986
White body, green chassis and roof, VEV Internationale Vers Markt logo. Sometimes on plinth.
16-86-32 WESTWARD TOOLS 1986
White body, blue chassis and roof, Westward Tools and Equipment Fully Guaranteed Across Canada logo.
16-87-1 ALTON TOWERS 1987
Cream body, black chassis, brown roof, Alton Towers, Europe's Premier Leisure Park logo.
16-87-2 ANCHOR BUTTER 1987
Light yellow body, green chassis and roof, Anchor Butter and Cheese logo.
16-87-3 BRIGHTON EQUITABLE SOCIETY 1987
Red body, cream chassis and roof, Brighton Equitable Society Ltd. Cooperative logo.
16-87-4 BRITISH POLICE QUEST 1987
Navy blue body, black chassis and roof, British Police Sponsored Quest, England 1987 Turkey logo.
16-87-5 CO-OP ENGLISH BUTTER 1987
Dark green body, chassis and roof, Co-Op English Butter logo with farm scene.
16-87-6 ENFIELD PAGEANT OF MOTORING 1987
Silver body, red chassis . . .
16-87-7 JONES AND SON 1987
Light brown body, cream chassis and roof, Jones & Son Horse & Pony Transport Services logo.
16-87-8 THE KLEEN-E-ZE MAN 1987
Blue body, blue chassis, white roof, The Kleen-e-ze Man stands for satisfaction, See him when he calls logo.
    1. Pale blue body, light blue chassis and wheels.
    2. Rich blue body, chassis and wheels.
16-87-9 K L M CARGO 1987
Light blue body, blue chassis, white roof, KLM Doorspeed Cargo logo, Amsterdam on front.
16-87-10 MINSTER TOY & TRAIN FAIR 1987
Maroon body, black chassis, tan roof, The 1st Minster 1987 Toy & Train Fair logo.

16-87-11 NATIONAL FIRE SERVICE 1987
Light gray body, white chassis, gray roof, NFS emblem logo with doors, windows and checkered stripes.
16-87-12 READING MLO, ROYAL MAIL 1987
Red body, black chassis and roof, Reading M.L.O., Royal Mail, Operational 1987 logo.
16-87-13 SHELTONS 1987
White body, black chassis, brown roof, Sheltons, East Anglia's Largest Independent Furniture Center logo.
16-87-14 STONEY CREEK FURNITURE 1987
Cream body, brown chassis and roof, Stoney Creek Furniture, Real Furniture at Realistic Prices logo.
16-87-15 VERNONS PLAICE 1987
Dark naroon body, black chassis, tan roof, Vernon's Plaice logo with fish design.
16-88-1 AUTOBAHN 88 1988
White body, black chassis and roof, Autobahn 88 logo.
16-88-2 AUXILIARY FIRE SERVICE 1988
Olive body, black chassis . . .
16-88-3 BARCLAYS 'ON THE MOVE' 1988
Gray body, nlack chassis . . .
16-88-4 BARCLAYS BANK, SUDBURY HILL 1988
Red body, gray chassis, cream roof, Barclays Bank, Sudbury Hill, Spread Eagle House logo.
16-88-5 BARTON ENGINEERING 1988
White body, red chassis . . .
16-88-6 BE-RO FLOUR 1988
Green body and roof, black chassis, Be-Ro Self-raising Flour logo.
16-88-7 BRITISH COMMERCIAL VEHICLE MUSEUM 1988
Dark green body, black chassis and roof, British Commercial Vehicle Museum logo.
16-88-8 DEMON TWEEKS 1988
White body and roof, black chassis, Demon Tweeks logo.
16-88-9 ENFIELD PAGEANT OF MOTORING 1988 1988
Cream body, dark green . . .
16-88-10 EXCHANGE AND MART 1988
White body, red chassis . . .
16-88-11 FARLEYS RUSKS 1988
Pink body, white chassis and roof, Farley's Rusks and Crookes Healthcare logo.
16-88-12 G.W.R. MUSEUM, SWINDON 1988
Dark green museum, black chassis and roof, G.W.R. Museum, Swindon logo.
16-88-13 HADLEY AND OTTAWAY 1988
Dark blue body and roof, black chassis, Removals, Storage, Hadley & Ottaway Ltd., Norwich logo.
16-88-14 HOUSE OF FRASER 1988
White body, green chassis . . .
16-88-15 OVEN FRESH HOME BAKERS 1988
Cream body, brown chassis and roof, Oven Fresh Home Bakers logo.

16-88-16 ROBERT BROTHERS CIRCUS 1988
White body, red chassis and roof, Robert Brothers famous Circus logo.
16-88-17 ROMNEY, HYTHE AND DYMCHURCH RAILWAY 1988
Brown body, black chassis and roof . . .
16-88-18 SAYERS BROTHERS 1988
White body, green chassis and roof, Sayers Brothers logo with house design.
16-88-19 STANLEY GIBBONS 1988
Blue body, black chassis and roof, Stanley Gibbons Publications Limited logo with SG design.
16-88-20 WESTWARD TOOLS 25TH ANNIVERSARY 1988
Blue body, chassis and roof, Westward Tools & Equipment 25th Anniversary 1963-1988 logo.
16-88-21 WESTWOODS CARPETS 1988
Cream body, brown chassis and roof, Westwoods Carpets Ltd. logo.
16-88-22 WILTSHIRE-BRINTON ASSOCIATES 1988
Light gray body, black chassis, white roof, Building a better business with WBA logo, Wiltshire-Brinton Associates on front.
16-89-1 CLAN DEW 1989
Tan body, red-brown chassis, brown roof, The Original Clan Dew logo.
16-89-2 CLIFFORD'S DAIRIES CATERING SERVICE 1989
White body and roof, black chassis, Clifford's Dairies Catering Service logo.
16-89-3 COOK'S MATCHES 1989
Tan body, black chassis and roof, The original Cook's Matches emblem logo.
16-89-4 DEILCRAFT 1989
Dark gray body, maroon . . .
16-89-5 DERBYSHIRE AMBULANCE SERVICE 1989
Cream body and roof, black chassis, Derbyshire Ambulance Service logo with emblem.
16-89-6 ENFIELD PAGEANT OF MOTORING 1989 1989
Yellow body, white . . .
16-89-7 EXELBEE 1989
Black body, chassis and roof . . .
16-89-8 MODEL OF THE MONTH CLUB 1989
Dark green body, black chassis and roof, Model of the Month Club Autumn 1989 logo.
16-89-9 NOTTINGHAMSHIRE AMBULANCE SERVICE 1989
Cream body and roof, black chassis, Nottinghamshire Ambulance Service logo with emblem.
16-89-10 NOTTINGHAMSHIRE COUNTY LIBRARY 1989
Green body, cream chassis, ivory roof, Nottinghamshire County Library, 1889-1989 on front.
16-89-11 NUSS REMOVALS 1989
Tan body, white . . .

16-89-12 OUTSPAN 1989
White body, orange chassis and roof, Outspan, small ones are more juicy logo.

16-89-13 ROYAL MAIL 1989
Red body, black chassis and roof, Royal Mail Parcels, Mount Pleasant Sorting Office logo.

16-90-1 BASSETTS JELLY BABIES 1990
Yellow body and chassis, red roof, Bassetts Jelly Babies logo.

16-90-2 CHIVERS OLD ENGLISH MARMALADE 1990
Black body and chassis, yellow roof, Chivers Old English Marmalade logo, The Morning Tonic on rear.

16-90-3 ENFIELD PAGEANT OF MOTORING 1990 1990
Blue body, white . . .

16-90-4 ESSEX CONSTABULARY 1990
Dark blue body, black chassis and roof, Essex Constabulary Control Unit logo.

16-90-5 FOLGATE INSURANCE 1990
White body . . .

16-90-6 WALKERS CRISPS 1990
Blue body, and roof, black chassis, Walkers Crisps, The Perfect Crisp logo.

16-90-7 WIGTON MOTOR CLUB CUMBRIA CLASSIC 1990
Dark blue body and roof, black chassis, Wigton Motor Club Cumbria Classic logo, Cumberland News on front.

16-90-8 WILLIAMS GRIFFIN 1990
Green body, tan . . .

16-91-1 AIR CANADA 1991
Red body, white . . .

16-91-2 BINNS 1991
Green body and roof . . .

16-91-3 BIRMINGHAM POLICE HORSES 1991
Brown body, black? chassis, white roof, Horses logo with police emblem, Police on front.

16-91-4 CEREBOS TABLE SALT 1991
Dark blue body and chassis, yellow roof, Cerebos Extra Fine Table Salt logo.

16-91-5 DAILY EXPRESS (Bismarck sunk) 1991
Black body, chassis and roof, Daily Express logo with Bismarck Sunk panel.

16-91-6 DAILY EXPRESS (Japs declare) 1991
Black body, chassis and roof, Daily Express logo with Japs declare war . . .

16-91-7 HAMMONDS 1991
White body, green chassis and roof, Hammonds and Frasercard logo.

16-91-8 KENDAL MILNE & CO. 1991
Dark green body, cream . . .

16-91-9 LEWIS DMR 1991
White body, yellow . . .

16-91-10 RANDALL'S STORES 1991
Tan body, brown chassis and roof, Randall's Stores logo.

16-91-11 SALVATION ARMY MOBILE CANTEEN 1991
Dark blue body, black chassis. light gray roof, Mobile Canteen logo with The Salvation Army shield.

16-91-12 STOKES QUALITY SHOPFITTERS 1991
Blue body, chassis and roof, Stokes Quality Shopfitters logo.

16-91-13 VALOR BLACK BEAUTY 1991
Black body and chassis, white roof, Valor Black Beauty logo.

16-92-1 BIRMINGHAM POLICE 1992
Navy blue body, roof . . .

16-92-2 BROADWAY PRESS 1992
Yellow body, black chassis and roof, For a complete printing service, Broadway Press logo.

16-92-3 CHILDRENS WORLD 1992
White body, black . . .

16-92-4 CITY OF GLOUCESTER TRAMWAYS 1992
Cream body, maroon chassis and roof, City of Gloucester Tramways Parcel Delivery Service logo.

16-92-5 CITY OF LONDON POLICE 1992
Dark blue body, black chassis and roof, City of London Police logo with coat of arms.

16-92-6 DAIRY FARM BAKERY 1992
Tan body and chassis, cream roof, Dairy Farm Bakery logo, Fresh Bread delivered daily on rear.

16-92-7 DAS MODELL LADCHEN 1992
Tan body, brown . . .

16-92-8 EXPRESS DAIRY 1992
Blue-black body and chassis, white roof, Express Dairy Milk logo.

16-92-9 LEICESTERSHIRE FIRE AND RESCUE 1992
Red body, black chassis and roof, Leicestershire Fire and Rescue Service Mobile Control Unit logo.

16-92-10 MAYNARDS WINE GUMS 1992
Plum body and chassis, green roof, Maynords Original Wine Gums logo.

16-92-11 MUSIC SALES 1992
White body, red . . .

16-92-12 WALL'S 1992
Brown body, black chassis, cream roof, Eat well--eat Wall's logo.

16-92-13 WEETAFLAKES 1992
Blue body, yellow chassis and roof, Weetabix crunchy whole wheat flakes logo.

16-93-1 3M BODY GUARD 1993
Blue body, black . . .

16-93-2 BEBE JUMEAU 1993
Maroon body and roof . . .

16-93-3 GRACE BROS. DEPARTMENT STORE 1993
Red body, black chassis, white roof, Grace Bros. Department Store logo.

16-93-4 HALFORD CYCLE CO. 1993
Brown body, black chassis and roof, The Halford Cycle Co. Ltd. logo.

16-93-5 LINCOLN YMCA TEA CAR 1993
Olive body, chassis and roof, logo presumably names Lincoln.

16-93-6 NEALS TOYS 1993
No data.

16-93-7 ROYAL NATIONAL LIFE-BOAT INSTITUTION 1993
Blue body, black chassis and roof, Our Life-Boat Men and Royal National Life-Boat Institution logo.

16-93-8 ST. MARYS THEATRE CLUB 1993
Black body, chassis and roof . . .

16-93-9 YMCA TEA CAR 1993
Olive body, chassis and roof, Y M C A Tea Car logo.

16-94-1 CARDIFF CITY POLICE 1994
Blue body, black chassis, gray roof, Cardiff City Police, Law Courts Cardiff logo.

16-94-2 EDRADOUR DISTILLERY 1994
1. Cream body, red . . .
2. Black body, red . . .

16-94-3 HAMMERITE UNDERBODY SEAL 1994
Black body, red . . .

16-94-4 WILTS UNITED DAIRIES 1994
Tan body, dark green chassis and roof, Wilts United Dairies Ltd., The "Moonraker" Brand logo, Wilts United Dairies Ltd. on front.

17 AEC REGAL SINGLE DECK BUS

17-85-1 EAST KENT 1985
Maroon body and chassis, cream roof and windows, East Kent logo.
1. Destination Ashford, lighter maroon body and chassis.
2. Destination Dover, darker maroon body and chassis.

17-85-2 HEDINGHAM AND DISTRICT 1985
Dark blue body, black chassis, cream roof and windows, Hedingham & District logo, destination Gosfield-Hedingham.

17-85-3 LONDON TRANSPORT (red) 1985
Red body, roof and windows, black chassis, London Transport logo, destination 213A.

17-85-4 MAIDSTONE AND DISTRICT 1985
Dark green body and chassis, cream roof and windows, Maidstone & District Motor Services Ltd. logo.
1. Destination Maidstone.
2. Destination Rye.

17 85 5 SOUTHDOWN 1985
Light green body and roof, dark green chassis, cream windows, Southdown logo.
1. Destination Brighton.
2. Destination Worthing.

17-85-6 SUTTON SCHOOL OF GYMNASTICS 1985
Cream body, roof asnd windows, black chassis, Sutton School of Gymnastics logo.

17-86-1 ALDERSHOT & DISTRICT 1986
Lime green body, black chassis, dark green roof and windows, Aldershot & District logo.
1. Destination Alton.
2. Destination Guildford.

17-86-2 EASTBOURNE CORPORATION 1986
Navy blue body and chassis, cream roof and windows, Eastbourne
Corporation logo, sometimes with gold stripe.
  1. Destination Brighton, without stripe.
  2. Destination Old Town, with or without stripe.
17-86-3 HAPPY DAYS 1986
Red body, cream chassis, roof and windows, Happy Days and
Austin's logo.
17-86-4 ISLE OF MAN TT 1986
Light blue body, yellow chassis, light gray roof, cream windows, Isle
of Man TT86 26 May-6 June logo.
17-86-5 LONDON TRANSPORT (green) 1986
Dark green body, chassis, roof and windows, London Transport logo,
destination Cobham.
17-86-6 MIDDLESBOROUGH CORPORATION 1986
Blue body, roof and windows, black chassis, Middlesborough
Corporation logo.
17-86-7 POTTERIES 1986
Red body and windows, black chassis, cream roof, Potteries logo.
17-86-8 RDP LLEDO COLLECTORS GUIDE 1986
Cream body and roof, red chassis and windows, RDP Lledo
Collectors Guide 1986 logo. Destination Halesowen.
17-86-9 RIBBLE 1986
Red body, black chassis, cream roof and windows, Ribble logo,
destination Preston.
17-86-10 STEVENSON'S BUS SERVICES 1986
Dark yellow body and roof, black chassis and windows, Stevenson's
Bus Services logo.
17-87-1 ALTON TOWERS 1987
Red body, black chassis, cream roof and windows, Alton Towers,
Europe's Premier Leisure Park logo, destination Alton.
17-87-2 BLACKBURN TRANSPORT 1987
Green body and chassis, dark green roof, cream windows, Blackburn
Transport logo.
17-87-3 BOURNEMOUTH CORPORATION 1987
Yellow body and windows, black chassis, cream roof, Bournemouth
Corporation Motors logo, destination Moordown.
17-87-4 BRISTOL 1987
Cream body, roof and windows, black chassis, Bristol logo,
destination Yate 87.
  1. As above.
  2. Avon Diecast Club 3rd Swapmeet label on rear.
17-87-5 THE DELAINE 1987
Dark blue body, black chassis and roof, cream windows, The Delaine
logo, destination Bourne.
17-87-6 DEVON GENERAL 1987
Red body and roof, black chassis, dark red windows, Devon General
logo, destination Torquay.
17-87-7 DUNDEE CORPORATION 1987
Dark blue body and chassis, light blue roof and windows,
Corporation Transport logo with emblem, destination Dundee.

17-87-8 EXCHANGE AND MART 1987
Red body and roof, black chassis, white windows, Exchange & Mart
Every Thursday 3d and London Transport logo.
17-87-9 G & B MOTOR SERVICES 1987
Light brown body, black chassis, roof and windows, G & B Motor
Services logo, destination Durham.
17-87-10 GLASGOW CORPORATION 1987
Orange body, black chassis, green roof and windows, Glasgow
Corporation logol, destination Johnstone.
  1. Jade green roof and windows.
  2. Dark green roof and windows.
17-87-11 HEDINGHAM & DISTRICT (cream) 1987
Cream body and windows, black chassis, blue roof, Hedingham &
District logo, destination Sudbury.
17-87-12 LOTHIAN 1987
Maroon body, black chassis, white roof and windows, Lothian logo,
destination Broughton St.
17-87-13 MAIDSTONE & DISTRICT 1987
Cream body, dark green chassis, roof and windows, Maidstone &
District Motor Services Ltd. logo, destination Leysdown.
17-87-14 OXFORD (cream) 1987
Cream body and windows, broan chassis and roof, Oxford logo,
destination Didcot.
17-87-15 SOUTHERN VECTIS (black chassis) 1987
Green body, black chassis, cream roof and windows, Southern Vectis,
Nelson Road, Newport logo.
  1. Destination Cowes.
  2. Destination Newport.
17-87-16 SOUTHERN VECTIS (green chassis) 1987
Cream body, windows and roof, green chassis, Southern Vectis logo,
destination Newport.
17-87-17 SOUTHERN VECTIS (green roof) 1987
Cream body and windows, green chassis and roof, Southern Vectis
logo, destination Newport.
17-87-18 ULSTER TRANSPORT 1987
Dark green body and chassis, cream roof and windows, Ulster
Transport emblem logo.
  1. As above.
  2. Greenish cream stripe.
  3. Destination Belfast, greenish cream stripe.
17-87-19 WEST BROMWICH CORPORATION 1987
Navy blue body, black chassis, dark greenish-blue roof, light blue
windows, West Bromwich Corporation logo with coat of arms,
destination Oldbury.
17-87-20 YORK CASTLE MUSEUM 1987
Blue body and roof, cream chassis and windows, York Castle
Museum logo.
17-88-1 ALDERSHOT & DISTRICT/L.S.W.R. 1988
Lime green body, black chassis, dark green roof and windows,
Aldershot & District logo, The Mid-Hants Celebrates L.S.W.R. 150
on boards, destination Ropley 215.

17-88-2 CLAYTON HIGH SCHOOL 1988
Maroon body, gray chassis and roof, cream windows, P.S.A. Bus
Fund logo, Clayton High School on boards.
**17-88-3 EXCHANGE AND MART/HANTS AND DORSET
1988**
Green body, black chassis, white roof, cream windows, Hants &
Dorset logo, Exchange & Mart Every Thursday on boards,
destination Poope Dorset.
17-88-4 LEICESTER MERCURY 1988
Plum body and roof, black chassis, cream windows, Leicester City
Transport logo, Leicester Mercury largest circulation on boards,
destination Town Centre 27.
17-88-5 LINCOLNSHIRE ECHO 1988
Dark green body and roof, black chassis, cream windows . . .,
destination 60 Years.
17-88-6 MacBRAYNES/SCOTSMAN 1988
Red body, black chassis, lime roof, cream windows, Macbraynes
logo, The Scotsman, your Scottish Daily on boards, destination Fort
William. Plain or fancy logo?
17-88-7 MERLEY HOUSE & MODEL MUSEUM 1988
White body, roof and windows, gray chassis, Merley House & Model
Museum logo, destination Wimborne.
17-88-8 MIDLAND 1988
Dull blue body and roof, black chassis and windows, Midland logo,
destination Airdrie.
17-88-9 MIDLAND RAILWAY CENTRE 1988
Maroon body . . ., destination Butterley.
17-88-10 NORFOLK SWAPMEET/ROBERTSON 1988
Light gray body and chassis, cream roof and windows, Norwich-
Sprowston-Wroxham-Hoveton-Stalham, Robertson and 8th Norfolk
Swapmeet logo, Robertson of Stalham on rear, destination Norwich.
17-88-11 NORTHERN 75 YEARS 1988
Maroon body, black chassis, cream roof and windows, Northern 75
Years of local bus services logo, destination Chester-le-Street.
  1. Light maroon body.
  2. Dark maroon body.
17-88-12 OXFORD (red) 1988
Red body, brown chassis, roof and windows, Oxford logo, destination
Thame.
17-88-13 ROYAL NAVY 1988
Navy blue body, black chassis and windows, white roof, Royal Navy
logo, destination HMS Vernon.
17-88-14 SOUTH ESSEX DIECAST CLUB TOY FAIR 1988
Black body, white chassis, roof and windows, destination S.E.D.M.C.
17-88-15 THAMES VALLEY 1988
Red body and roof, black chassis, red or cream windows, Thames
Valley logo, destination Henley 8.
  1. Red windows.
  2. Cream windows.
17-88-16 THANET GAZETTE/EAST KENT 1988
Maroon body . . ., destination Margate.

17-88-17 TIME MACHINE 1988
Dark blue body, pale blue chassis and roof, white windows, Time Machine 1983 non-stop service 1988 logo, destination Earlsdon.

17-88-18 WEALD OF KENT 1988
Yellow body, blue chassis, ivory roof and windows, Weald of Kent Transport Co. logo, destination Headcorn.

17-89-1 ADVERTISER WISE/POTTERIES 1989
Red body and windows, black chassis, white roof, Potteries logo, be Advertiser wise on boards.

17-89-2 ALDERSHOT AND DISTRICT 1989
Dark green body, chassis, windows and roof, Aldershot & District Traction Co. Ltd. logo.

17-89-3 BELFAST CORPORATION/GREEN ISLAND 1989
Red body and chassis, cream roof and windows, Belfast Corporation, Green Island Newsagency on boards.
1. Destination City Hall.
2. Destination Stormont.

17-89-4 BOULTONS OF SHROPSHIRE 1989
Tan body and roof, red chassis, white windows, Boultosn of Shropshire logo, destination Clive.

17-89-5 BUCKLAND BUS SERVICES 1989
Red body and windows, black chassis, cream roof, Buckland Bus Services logo, Vintage Omnibus Hire on boards.

17-89-6 BURNLEY COLNE AND NELSON 1989
Maroon body, black chassis, cream roof and windows, Burnley Colne & Nelson Joint Transport logo, destination 504 Burnley.

17-89-7 COPELAND'S TOURS (CT) 1989
Blue body, roof and windows, dark blue chassis, CT monogram logo, Copeland's Tours on rear.

17-89-8 COVENTRY TRANSPORT 1989
Plum body and roof, black chassis, maroon windows, Coventry Transport logo, destination Berkswell 15.

17-89-9 DAILY INDEPENDENT/SHEFFIELD CORPORA- TION 1989
Blue-black body, black chassis, light gray roof, cream windows, Sheffield Corporation Motors logo, 1d Daily Independent on boards.
1. Destination Barnsley.
2. Destination Chesterfield.

17-89-10 E & F TRADE UNION 1989
Silver body . . .
1. Destination Smethwick.
2. Destination Warley.

17 89 11 EMERGENCY MEDICAL SERVICES 1989
Gray body . . ., destination Ambulance.

17-89-12 EXPRESS AND STAR/WOLVERHAMPTON 1989
Green body and chassis, yellow roof and windows, Wolverhampton Corporation Transport logo, Express & Star, First with the News on boards, destination Sedgley 28.

17-89-13 FIRST BUDE SCOUTS 1989
Red body, cream . . ., destination 1st Bude Scouts.

17-89-14 GREAT WESTERN RAILWAY 1989
Dark brown body, black chassis, cream roof and windows, Great Western logo with coat of arms, destination Swindon.

17-89-15 G. W. R. PADDINGTON 1989
Dark brown body, black chassis, pale yellow roof, cream windows, G. W. R. Paddington logo.
1. Destination Paddington.
2. Destination Swindon.

17-89-16 GREEN BUS SERVICES 1989
Dark green body, cream . . .
1. Destination Bloxwich.
2. Destination Great Wyrley.

17-89-17 GUIDE DOGS/TORBAY 1989
White body, brown chassis, orange roof . . .
1. Destination Goodrington.
2. Destination Paignton.

17-89-18 KINGSTON UPON HULL 1989
Blue body . . ., destination Hull Station.

17-89-19 LINCOLNSHIRE EVENING TELEGRAPH 1989
Dark green body and roof, black chassis, cream windows, Lincolnshire Evening Telegraph your local paper logo.
1. Destination Grimsby.
2. Destination Scunthorpe.

17-89-20 L M S RAILWAY 1989
Maroon body, black chassis, white roof, LMS 55F logo, London Midland and Scottish Railway on boards.
1. Destination Manchester.
2. Destination Sheffield.
3. Destination Station.

17-89-21 L N E R 1989
Green body, black chassis, cream roof and windows, London & North eastern Railway with coat of arms, destination Durham.

17-89-22 SHEFFIELD CORPORATION 1989
Dark blue body, cream . . .
1. Destination Lodge Moor.
2. Destination Moorhead.
3. Destination Woodhouse.

17-89-23 STEVENSON'S BUS SERVICES 1989
Yellow body and windows, black chassis and roof, Stevenson's Bus Services logo, Stevenson's on boards.

17-89-24 TWICKENHAM RUGBY 1989
Red body and roof, black chassis, London Transport logo, Twickenham--The Home of English Rugby on boards, destination Twickenham.

17-89-25 WOLVERHAMPTON WANDERERS 1989
Light orange body and roof, black chassis and windows, One Hundred Years of Molineux 1889-1989 logo, Wolverhampton Wanderers F. C, on boards, destination Wolves.

17-90-1 ALDERSHOT AND DISTRICT 1990 (early)
Light green body, black chassis, dark green windows and roof, Aldershot & District Traction Co. Ltd. logo.
1. Destination Aldershot.
2. Destination London.

17-90-2 ALDERSHOT AND DISTRICT 1990 (late)
Lime green body, black chassis, dark green roof and windows, Aldershot & District Traction Co. Ltd. logo with stripe.
1. Destination Camberley.
2. Destination Guildford.

17-90-3 AMERSHAM & DISTRICT 1990
Green body and chassis, cream roof and windows, Amersham & District logo with emblem, Tring via Chesham on boards.
1. Destination Tring.
2. Destination Watford.

17-90-4 ASH GREEN SCHOOL 1990
Lime green body, black chassis, pale gray roof, white windows, white emblem logo, Ash Green School--Trentham on boards.

17-90-5 BEDWORTH ALMSHOUSES/MIDLAND 1990
Red body and windows, black chassis, silver roof, Midland logo, Bedworth Almshouses 1840-1990 on boards.
1. Destination Bedworth.
2. Destination Coventry.

17-90-6 BRITISH COAL/COTGRAVE COLLIERY 1990
Blue-black body, roof and windows, black chassis, British Coal logo, Cotgrave Colliery, Nottinghamshire on boards.
1. Destination Cotgrave.
2. Destination Nottingham.

17-90-7 BUDE SCOUTS 1990
Red body, white . . ., green . . ., destination Scorze.

17-90-8 BURTON COACHES 1990
Dark green body and windows, light gray chassis and roof, Burton Coaches logo.
1. Destination Brixham.
2. Destination Kingswear.

17-90-9 COVENTRY CORPORATION 1990
Cream body and roof, maroon chassis and windows, coat of arms logo with maroon stripe, destination Bagington.

17-90-10 DAN-AIR 1990
Blue body and roof, white chassis and windows, Dan-Air Scheduled Services logo, destinations on boards as below.
1. London-Aberdeen.
2. London-Inverness.
3. London-Manchester.
4. London-Newcastle.

17-90-11 FRIENDS OF ROSE MEADOW/SAFEWAY 1990
Red body and windows, maroon chassis and roof, Safeway Services emblem logo, Friends of Rose Meadow on boards.
1. Destination Taunton.
2. Destination Yeovil.

184

17-90-12 GREEN LINE 1990
Mint green body, chassis and roof, jade green windows, Green Line
London Transport logo.
1. Destination Barnet.
2. Destination Windsor.
17-90-13 GREENLINE DIAMOND JUBILEE 1990
Green body, black chassis, silver roof, light green windows,
Greenline and London Transport logo, 1930 1990 Greenline
Diamond Jubilee on boards, destination Reigate.
17-90-14 HULLEY'S OF BASLOW 1990
Orange-red body and chassis, cream roof and windows, Hulley's of
Baslow, Baslow Carnival logo.
17-90-15 L N E R 1990
Green body, black chassis, cream roof and windows, London and
Northeastern Railway L.N.E.R. logo.
1. Destination Special.
2. Destination Station.
17-90-16 METROPOLITAN RAILWAY 1990
Brown body and chassis, white roof and windows, Metropolitan
Railway logo with coat of arms.
1. Destination Aldgate.
2. Destination Watford.
17-90-17 MIDLAND GENERAL 1990
Dark blue body and roof, black chassis, cream windows, Midland
General logo, Midland General for private hire on boards.
1. Destination Ripley.
2. Destination Swingate.
17-90-18 MIDLAND (red) 1990
Red body, chassis and windows, silver roof, Midland logo,
destination Dudley.
17-90-19 NORTHERN--BEAMISH 1990
Maroon body, cream . . ., destination Chester Le Street.
1. Correct logo.
2. Incorrect logo (only Beamish).
17-90-20 P G TAGS 1990
Green body, cream . . .
17-90-21 RHONDDA 1990
Red body . . .
1. Destination Caerphilly.
2. Destination Pontypridd.
17-90-22 SOUTHERN RAILWAY 1990
Green body, black chassis, cream roof and windows, Southern
Railway Bideflrd Clovelly logo.
1. Destination Bideford.
2. Destination Clovelly.
17-90-23 SOUTHERN VECTIS 1990
Light green body . . ., destination Cowes.
17-90-24 TAUNTON SCOUTS 1990
Tan body, green chassis, roof and windows, Taunton Scouts 80 Years
logo, Taunton 1990 and emblem on rear, destination Taunton.

17-90-25 THAMES VALLEY 1990
Red body and roof, black chassis, cream windows, Thames Valley
logo.
1. Destination Newbury.
2. Destination Oxford.
3. Destination Reading.
17-90-26 TRENT FM CHARITY APPEAL 1990
White body, roof and windows, dark blue chassis, Trent FM 1990
Charity Appeal logo, --today's FM station-- on boards.
1. Destination Burton.
2. Destination Derby.
17-90-27 VEN 40TH 1990
White body, red . . .
1. Destination Rotterdam.
2. Destination Zichtenbur.
17-90-28 WALSALL ILLUMINATIONS 1990
Dark green body, red chassis, roof and windows, Walsall Leisure for
all logo, also on rear, 1990 Walsall Illuminations at the Arboretum on
boards, destination Brownhills.
**17-90-29 WESTERN MORNING NEWS/WESTERN
       NATIONAL 1990**
Green bnody, black chassis, cream roof and windows, Western
National logo, The Western Morning News on boards, destination
Tavistock.
17-90-30 WESTERN (SCOTTISH) 1990
White body, black . . .
1. Destination Glasgow.
2. Destination London.
17-90-31 WORTH VALLEY 1990
Maroon body and roof, black chassis, cream windows, Worth Valley
emblem logo, destinations on boards.
17-91-1 ALTONIAN COACHES 1991
Orange body, chassis and roof, orange-red windows, black emblem
on cream side panel, Altonian on cream rear panel.
1. Destination Excursion.
2. Destination Tour.
17-91-2 BELLE COACHES/NORFOLK TOY & TRAIN 1991
Tan body, blue chassis, roof and windows, Belle Coaches Lowestoft
4669 logo, The Norfolk Toy & Train Extravaganza on boards.
1. Destination Lowestoft Terminus.
2. Destination Norfolk.
17-91-3 BIRMINGHAM CITY TRANSIT 1991
Dark blue body, cream . . ., destination Dudley.
17-91-4 BLUE BUS SERVICE 1991
Cream body, blue . . .
1. Destination Derby.
2. Destination Willington.
17-91-5 BRITISH RAILWAYS 1991
Dark red body, cream . . .
1. Destination Relief.
2. Destination Station.

17-91-6 BUDE SCOUTS 1991
Yellow body, blue . . ., destination Jacobstow.
**17-91-7 CHELTENHAM & DISTRICT/GLOUCESTERSHIRE
       ECHO 1991**
Red body, black chassis, cream roof and windows, Cheltenham &
District logo, Gloucestershire Echo on boards, destination
Leckhampton.
17-91-8 DEVON SERVICES 1991
Dark blue body, black chassis and roof, white windows, Devon
Services logo, Friends of Steps Cross on boards.
1. Destination Totnes.
2. Destination Watcombe.
17-91-9 EAST KENT 75 YEARS 1991
Maroon body, cream . . ., destination Canterbury.
17-91-10 G W R MUSEUM 1991
Blue body . . ., destination Swindon.
17-91-11 HAPPY EATER 1991
Green body, black chassis, light orange roof and windows, Look Out
For Our Signs logo, Happy Eater Family Restaurants on boards.
17-91-12 HEDINGHAM AND DISTRICT 1991
Red body, cream . . ., destination Braintree.
17-91-13 LAMCOTE INTERNATIONAL 1991
Green body and roof, black chassis, cream windows, Lamcote
International logo, British & Continental Tours on boards.
1. Destination Nottingham.
2. Destination Radcliffe.
17-91-14 LIVERPOOL FOOTBALL CLUB 1991
Red body, white . . ., destination Wembley.
17-91-15 MAIDSTONE & DISTRICT 1991
Cream body . . ., dark green . . ., Maidstone & District logo,
destination London E1.
17-91-16 MAJESTIC 1991
White body, black chassis, roof and windows, Majestic logo with
emblem, Glasgow-Edinburgh-Newcastle-London on boards.
1. Destination Glasgow.
2. Destination London.
17-91-17 MIDLAND 1991
Red body, white . . ., destination Tamworth.
17-91-18 N C B 1991
Blue-black body, chassis and roof, cream windows, NCB logo.
1. Destination Calverton.
2. Destination Eastwood.
17-91-19 NORTHERN 1991
Yellow body, white . . .
1. Destination Portsmouth.
2. Destination Torbay.
17-91-20 NOTTINGHAM EVENING POST 1991
Green body . . ., destination Westdale.
17-91-21 NOTTINGHAM FOREST FOOTBALL CLUB 1991
Red body, roof and windows, white chassis, Nottingham Forest

Football Club logo, Littlewoods Cup Winners 1988/89, 1989/90.
1. Destination Nottingham.
2. Destination Wembley.
17-91-22 ROCHDALE CORPORATION 1991
Cream body, black . . .
1. Destination Bamford.
2. Destination Castleton.
17-91-23 ST. JOHN AMBULANCE 1991
Black body and chassis, white roof and windows, Radford Combined
Division Ambulance logo, 1925 St. John Ambulance Brigade 1991
on boards.
1. Destination Radford.
2. Destination Wollaton Park.
17-91-24 SCOTTISH YOUTH HOSTELS 1991
White body, black chassis, red roof and windows, S Y H A triangle
logo, same on rear, Scottish Youth Hostels on boards, destination
Broadmeadows.
17-91-25 SOUTH CAVE SCOUTS 1991
Green body, blue . . ., destination Luxembourg.
17-91-26 THAMES VALLEY 3 1991
Red body . . .
1. Destination Bracknell.
2. Destination Reading.
17-91-27 WALSALL CORPORATION 1991
Blue body, chassis and roof, light blue windows, Walsall Corporation
logo with stripe, destination Bloxwich.
17-91-28 WEST RIDING 1991
Green body . . .
1. Destination Castleford.
2. Destination Wakefield.
17-91-29 YORK PULLMAN BUS CO. 1991
Maroon body and chassis, cream roof and windows, York Pullman
Bus Co. emblem logo.
1. Destination Racecourse.
2. Destination York.
17-92-1 ALTONIAN 2 1992
Orange body . . .
1. Destination Bognor.
2. Destination Canvey.
17-92-2 BIRMINGHAM NEC 1992
Dark blue body, cream . . .
1. Destination Elmdon.
2. Destination NEC.
17-92-3 BTS COVENTRY 1992
Blue-black body, cream chassis, roof and windows, BTS emblem
logo, BTS Coventry on rear, destination Coventry.
17-92-4 BUDE SCOUTS 1992
Light blue body, yellow . . ., destination Stratton.
17-92-5 BUNTY COACHES 1992
Green body, chassis, roof and windows, Bunty Coaches emblem logo
with cream stripe, destination Coventry.

17-92-6 DEVON GENERAL 1992
Red body, cream . . ., destination Brixham.
17-92-7 EAST MIDLANDS (blue) 1992
Dark blue body . . .
1. Destination Chest[erfield?]
2. Destination Sheffield.
17-92-8 EAST MIDLANDS (yellow) 1992
Yellow body, brown . . ., destination Clowne.
17-92-9 EAST YORKSHIRE TRACTION 1992
Blue-black body and roof, black chassis, cream windows, East
Yorkshire logo, destination Scarborough.
17-92-10 EASTERN NATIONAL 1992
Green body . . .
1. Destination Chelmsford.
2. Destination Southend.
17-92-11 J. G. FINCH 1992
Green body, light green . . .
1. Destination Blackpool.
2. Destination Southport.
17-92-12 GWR HAMPTON LOADS 1992
Brown body, cream . . .
1. Destination Bewdley.
2. Destination Bridgnorth.
17-92-13 HALIFAX 1992
Orange body and chassis, green roof, cream windows, Halifax logo.
1. Destination Halifax.
2. Destination Queensbury.
17-92-14 HARPER BROTHERS 1992
Light green body, black chassis, cream roof and windows, HB
emblem logo.
1. Destination Cannock.
2. Destination Heath-Hayes.
17-92-15 HEBBLE/WEBSTERS BEER 1992
Yellow body and windows, dark red chassis and roof, Hebble logo,
Webster's Perfect Beer on boards, destination Halifax.
17-92-16 HEBBLE 1992
Dark red body, black chassis, brown roof, maroon windows, Hebble
logo, destination Burnley.
17-92-17 HEINZ/SOUTHERN VECTIS 1992
Light green body and roof, dark green chassis, cream windows,
Southern Vectis and Heinz Salad Cream logo, Enjoy your salad days
on boards, destination Newport.
17-92-18 HICK'S 1992
Blue body . . ., destination Braintree.
17-92-19 HILLCREST RADIO COACHES 1992
Gray body, cream . . .
1. Destination Alvechurch.
2. No destination?
17-92-20 ISLE OF WIGHT CREAMERIES 1992
Light green body and roof, dark green chassis, cream windows,
Southern Vectis logo, Isle of Wight Creameries Ltd. on boards,

destination Newport.
17-92-21 JANICK TRAVEL 1992
White body, blue . . .
1. Destination Mansfield.
2. Destination Nottingham.
17-92-22 LANCASHIRE CONSTABULARY 1992
Maroon body, navy blue . . .
17-92-23 MAIDSTONE & DISTRICT 1992
Green body and chassis, cream roof and windows, Maidstone &
District logo, Maidstone-Detling-Sittingbourne on boards, destination
Sittingbourne.
17-92-24 MANCHESTER UNITED F. C. 1992
Red body, black chassis and roof, cream? windows, Manchester
United F. C. logo with emblem, The Red Devils on boards,
destination Wembley.
17-92-25 MOORES 1992
Green body . . .
1. Destination Kelvedon.
2. Destination Tiptree.
17-92-26 NORWICH FOOTBALL CLUB 1992
Yellow body, green . . ., destination Carrow Road.
17-92-27 OSBORNES 1992
Red body, white . . .
1. Destination Maldon.
2. Destination Witham.
17-92-28 RED BUS SERVICES 1992
Red body, black . . ., white . . .
1. Destination Private.
2. Destination Swindon.
17-92-29 RED HOUSE MOTOR SERVICES 1992
Red body and roof, cream chassis and windows, R.H.M.S. logo,
emblem on rear, R.H.M.S. Radio Coach on boards, destination
Coventry.
17-92-30 RIDUNA BUSES 1992
Maroon body, cream . . .
1. Destination The Bays.
2. Destination The Boat.
17-92-31 SALFORD CORPORATION 1992
Red body, cream . . .
1. Destination Victoria.
2. Victoria Walkden.
17-92-32 SMITHS OF LISS 1992
White body, chassis, roof and windows, Smiths of Liss logo, same on
rear.
1. Destination Hawkley.
2. Destination Liss.
17-92-33 TAME VALLEY 1992
Yellow body, green . . .
1. Destination Earlswood.
2. Destination Solihull.

17-92-34 TRENT MOTOR TRACTION 1992
Red body and chassis, cream roof and windows, Trent logo.
1. Destination Buxton
2. Destination Derby.
17-92-35 W. WHITTAKER 1992
Light green body, red . . ., destination West Bromwich.
17-92-36 WILTSHIRE CONSTABULARY 1992
Black body, chassis and roof, blue-black windows, Wiltshire
Constabulary logo with emblem, Police Control on boards, Police on
front and rear.
17-92-37 YELLOWAY 1992
Orange body, cream . . .
1. Destination Rochdale.
2. Destination Torquay.
17-93-1 A G B TOURS 1993
Orange body, white . . .
1. Destination Amsterdam.
2. Destination Paris.
17-93-2 ALDERSHOT & DISTRICT 1993
Light green body, black chassis, dark green roof and windows,
Aldershot & District logo, To & From Farnham & London on boards.
1. Destination Farnham.
2. Destination London.
17-93-3 BOLTON CORPORATION 1993
No data; does it exist?
17-93-4 BRADFORD 1993
Navy blue body, gray . . ., Destination Private.
17-93-5 BRADFORD CITY 1993
Navy blue body, white . . .
1. Destination City.
2. Destination Thornbury.
17-93-6 BRAYBROOKES 1993
No data.
17-93-7 BRIDGEND & DISTRICT 1993
Black body, gold . . .
1. Destination Manchester.
2. Destination Swindon.
17-93-8 BUDE SCOUTS 1993
Orange body, green . . ., destination Kilkhampton.
17-93-9 EAST KENT 1993
Maroon body, black chassis, cream roof and windows, East Kent
logo, Daily Express Service and names of towns on boards,
destination Folkestone.
17-93-10 EASTERN COUNTIES 1993
Red body . . .
1. Destination Lowestoft.
2. Destination Norwich.
17-93-11 EASTERN NATIONAL 1993
Green body . . .
1. Destination Colchester.
2. Destination Tilbury.

17-93-12 J. G. FINCH 1993
Green body, dark green . . .
1. Destination Bower St.
2. Destination Newton Heath.
17-93-13 GELLIGAER U.D.C. 1993
Red body, gray . . .
1. Destination Aberfan.
2. Destination Ysradmynach.
17-93-14 GREEN BUS SERVICE 1993
Green body, cream . . .
1. Destination Landywood.
2. Destination Rugeley.
17-93-15 HUDDERSFIELD CORPORATION 1993
Red body . . .
1. Destination Holmfirth.
2. Destination Huddersfield.
17-93-16 LEEDS CITY TRANSPORT 1993
Blue body, dark blue . . .
1. Destination Gledhow.
2. Destination Leeds.
17-93-17 LEEDS UNITED FOOTBALL CLUB 1993
White body, yellow . . .
1. Destination Elland Road.
2. Destination Wembley.
17-93-18 MAPLINS HOLIDAY CAMP 1993
Yellow body and roof, green chassis and windows, Country Coach
Company emblem logo, Maplins Holiday Camp on boards.
17-93-19 MIDLAND 1993
Red body . . ., destination Birmingham.
17-93-20 PREMIER ALBANION 1993
Maroon body, cream . . .
1. Destination Excursion.
2. Destination Watford.
17-93-21 SALFORD CITY 1993
Green body . . .
1. Destination Peel Green.
2. Destination Victoria.
17-93-22 SALVATION ARMY (blue) 1993
Blue body . . .
17-93-23 SALVATION ARMY (maroon) 1993
Maroon body . . .
17-93-24 SHEFFIELD 1993
Cream body, navy blue . . .
1. Destination Gainsborough.
2. Destination Retford.
17-93-25 SILVER SERVICE 1993
Silver body, dark blue . . .
1. Destination Bakewell.
2. Destination Matlock.
17-93-26 SOUTHEND CORPORATION 1993
Light blue body, white . . .

1. Destination Central.
2. Destination Victoria.
17-93-27 STATE HOUSE, LAND'S END 1993
Cream body, green . . ., destination Lands End.
17-93-28 STEVLYN & CO. 1993
Gold body, green . . .
1. Destination Radlett.
2. Destination Watford.
17-93-29 TRAFALGAR TOURS 1993
White body . . .
17-93-30 VICEROY COACHES 1993
Blue body, dark blue . . .
1. Destination Dunmow.
2. Destination Saffron Walden.
17-93-31 WESTERN WELSH 1993
Red body, white . . .
1. Destination Cardiff.
2. Destination Newport.
17-93-32 YORKSHIRE TRACTION 1993
Red body, white . . ., destination Barnsley.
17-94-1 ATLANTIC BLUE 1994
Light blue body, navy blue . . .
1. Destination Barnstaple.
2. Destination Ilfracombe.
17-94-2 BUDE SCOUT GROUP 1994
Gray body, green . . ., destination Marham Church.
17-94-3 COURTESY COACH 1994
Red body, cream . . ., destination Crinkley Bottom.
17-94-4 DAIRY FARM 1994
No data.
17-94-5 EAST YORKSHIRE 1994
Navy blue body, white . . ., destination Thorngumbo.
17-94-6 G W R TODDINGTON 1994
Maroon body, roof . . ., destination Toddington.
17-94-7 KENT RELIANCE 1994
No data.
17-94-8 LINCOLNSHIRE 1994
Dark green body . . ., destination Boston.
17-94-9 ORTONA (CWS LTD.) 1994
Red body, cream . . .
17-94-10 PULHAMS TRAVEL 1994
Red body, roof . . .
1. Destination Cheltenham.
2. No destination?
17-94-11 RED IMPS TRAVEL 1994
Navy blue body, white . . ., destination Special.
17-94-12 RIBBLE 1994
Maroon body, cream . . .
1. Destination Blackpool.
2. Destination Southport.

17-94-13 STEVENSONS 1994
Yellow body, black . . ., destination Uttoxeter.
17-94-14 WESTCLIFFE ON SEA 1994
Red body, roof . . ., destination Great Wakering.
1. No side boards.
2. Side boards on roof.
17-94-15 WYCOMBE WANDERERS F C 1994
Green body, black chassis . . .
1. Destination Adams Park.
2. Destination Wembley.
18 PACKARD AMBULANCE/VAN 1986
18-86-1 BBC SERVICES 1986
White body, blue chassis . . .
18-86-2 JON ACC SERVICES 1986
Cream body and roof, black chassis, Jon Acc Services logo.
18-86-3 KENT COUNTY RED CROSS 1986
Dark blue body, black chassis, white roof . . .
18-86-4 MILK MARKETING BOARD 1986
Dark green body . . .
18-86-5 ST. JOHN AMBULANCE--PLYMOUTH 1986
Black body and chassis, white roof, St. John Ambulance Association
Plymouth Service logo.
18-86-6 ST. JOHN AMBULANCE--SURREY 1986
Black body and chassis, white roof, St. John Ambulance Service
Surrey Service logo.
18-86-7 WESTERN WOOLLENS 1986
Pinkish cream body, black chassis and roof, Western Woollens logo.
18-87-1 EXCHANGE & MART 1987
Dark blue body, black chassis, cream roof, The Exchange & Mart,
Over 6000 Bargains logo.
18-87-2 ST. JOHN--RADIO TRENT CARELINE 1987
White body, dark blue chassis . . .
18-88-1 4-TEL TELETEXT 1988
White body, blue chassis . . .
18-88-2 GERMAN UNDERGROUND HOSPITAL 1988
Dark blue body, black chassis . . .
18-88-3 MID-SUSSEX TIMES 1988
Cream body, blue chassis and roof, Mid Sussex Times Established
1881 logo.
18-88-4 STREPSILS 1988
Dark blue-green body and chassis, white roof, Strepsils Original
flavour and Crookes Healthcare logo.
18-88-5 WESTDEUTSCHER WACHDIENST 1988
White body, dark blue chassis . . .
18-89-1 3M WETORDRY 1989
Brown body, black chassis, cream roof, 3M Brand Wetordry logo.
18-89-2 COOK'S MATCHES 1989
Cream body and roof, black chassis, Cook's Matches logo.
18-89-3 VIKKI HARRIS LASER FUND 1989
White body, chassis and roof, The Vikki Harris Laser Fund logo.

18-89-4 WESTERN MORNING NEWS 1989
Cream body, blue chassis and roof, The Western Morning News logo.
18-89-5 WINDSOR WESTERN AMBULANCE 1989
White body, chassis and roof, Windsor Western logo with red cross
and green tree.
18-90-1 ADSCENE 1990
White body, red . . ., blue . . .
18-90-2 CHESHIRE COUNTY BRANCH 1990
White body and roof, black chassis, Cheshire County Branch, British
Red Cross Society logo.
18-90-3 COVENTRY & WARWICKSHIRE HOSPITAL 1990
Black body . . ., Coventry & Warwickshire Hospital Saturday Fund
logo.
18-90-4 M. J. DAVIS 1990
Cream body, green chassis and roof, M. J. Davis Decorating logo.
18-90-5 EASTER RALLY 1990, WAGGA WAGGA 1990
Yellow body, black . . .
18-90-6 G W R AMBULANCE 1990
Black body, chassis and roof, GWR Ambulance logo.
18-90-7 HARRY RAMSDEN 1990
Red body and chassis, black roof, Harry Ramsden's world famous
fish & chips logo.
18-90-8 PORTSMOUTH HOSPITAL LITHOTRIPTER 1990
White body, chassis and roof, Portsmouth Hospitals Lithotripter
Appeal logo, red crosses.
18-91-1 ATORA 1991
Yellow body, black chassis and roof, The Original Atora Shredded
Suit logo.
18-91-2 LEPROSY MISSION 1991
Cream body and roof, black chassis, The Leprosy Mission logo.
**18-91-3 RED CROSS NORTHAMPTONSHIRE JUBILEE
1991**
Cream body and roof, black chassis, British Red Cross
Northamptonshire Jubilee Appeal 1991 logo.
18-91-4 WALKERS CRISPS 1991
Gold body, green chassis and roof, Walkers Crisps logo.
18-92-1 SANDWELL HEALTH 1992
White body, black . . .
18-92-1 STANDARD OIL 1992
Red body, black chassis, dull red roof, Standard Oil Company of
California logo.
18-92-3 THERIAULTS 1992
Cream body, maroon . . .
18-92-4 VALOR HEARTBEAT 1992
Maroon body, white . . .
18-93-1 EXPRESS DAIRY 1993
Blue-black body, black chassis, white roof, Express Dairy logo.
18-93-2 GOTCHA VAN 1993
Red body, black . . .
18-93-3 LEWIS DMR 1993
White body, yellow . . .

18-93-4 J. C. PENNEY 1994
Cream body, black chassis and roof, J. C. Penney Co., 297 Stores
logo, Est. 1902 on roof.
18-94-1 HAUNTED HOUSE 1994
Black body, chassis and roof, The Haunted House logo, Alton Towers
emblem on rear.
18-94-2 ILKESTON CO-OP 1994
Yellow body, black chassis and roof, Co-Op Ilkeston logo.
18-94-3 KENT AMBULANCE SERVICE 1994
Tan body, black chassis . . .
18-94-4 SNICKERS 1994
Brown body and roof, black chassis, Snickers logo.
19 ROLLS-ROYCE PHANTOM II 1986
19-86-1 BLUE AND RED 1986
Dark blue body, red chassis and roof, blue seats and trunk.
19-86-2 ROYAL WEDDING 1986
White body, chassis and roof, blue seats and trunk, The Royal
Wedding 23 July 1986 on each side. H.R.H. Prince Andrew on left,
Miss Sarah Ferguson on right.
19-86-3 WHITE 1986
White body, chassis and roof, black seats and trunk. No logo.
19-87-1 BLACK (Franklin Diecast) 1987
Black body, chassis, roof, seats and trunk, red hubs, no logo.
19-87-2 CONGRATULATIONS 1987
Light blue body, darker blue chassis and roof, cream seats and trunk,
"Congratulations" logo.
19-87-3 MARILYN 1987
White body and chassis, black roof, tan seats and trunk, Happy 40th
Birthday Marilyn logo.
19-87-4 WHITE (Persil) 1987
White body, chassis, roof, seats and trunk, in Persil box. No logo.
Note: differs from 19-86-3 in having no black parts.
19-88-1 GOLD (Holland) 1988
Gold body, white . . .
19-88-2 TRACEY AND DAVID 1988
Metallic green body, black . . .
19-90-1 INSTITUTE SALES PROMOTION 1990
Dark blue body, tan
19-91-1 10TH WEDDING ANNIVERSARY 1991
Cream body, purple chassis, roof, seats and trunk, 19th July 1991
10th Wedding Anniversary logo.
19 91 2 POLYGONUM 1991
Red body, black . . .
19-92-1 GLADYS & RHYS GOLDEN WEDDING 1992
Gold body, chassis . . ., roof of LP 54.
19-93-1 DAMBUSTERS 1993
Black body, chassis, roof, seats and trunk, blue-white-red roundel on
left front fender.
20 MODEL A FORD STAKE TRUCK 1986

20-86-1 BBC (no logo) 1986
Dark green cab, rear and chassis, brown barrels, no logo; from BBC-Radio Times set.
20-86-2 BURT'S ALES 1986
Dark green cab and rear, red chassis, brown barrels, Burt's Ales, Ventnor, I.O.W. logo.
20-86-3 LAIRD'S APPLEJACK 1986
Tannish-yellow cab, dark tan rear, dark brown chassis, brown barrels, Laird's Blended Applejack logo.
20-86-4 LIONEL LINES 1986
Orange cab, blue rear and chassis, brown barrels, Lionel Track Repair logo, Nicholas Smith on front.
20-87-1 LOWCOCK'S LEMONADE 1987
Magenta cab and rear, black chassis, Lowcock's Lemonade logo; model comes with brown barrels and black bottle loads.
20-87-2 WATNEYS 1987
White cab, rear and chassis, red barrels, Watneys Imported Red Barrel Beer logo.
  1. Imported Barrel Red Beer logo.
  2. Imported Red Barrel Beer logo.
20-88-1 1905 1988
White cab? No other data.
20-88-2 BRANTH-CHEMIE 1988
Blue . . ., yellow . . .
20-88-3 CASTROL OIL 1988
Dark green cab and rear . . .
20-88-4 CLIFFORD'S DAIRIES 1988
Red cab, yellow rear, black chassis, no load, Clifford's Dairies logo.
20-88-5 EICHBAUM 1988
Green cab and rear . . .
20-88-6 GUERNSEY BREWERY/PONY ALES 1988
White cab, blue rear and chassis, brown barrels, Pony Ales, The Guernsey Brewery, Gold Medal Beers logo.
20-88-7 MOORE GREEN COLLIERY 1988
Dark blue cab and rear . . ., coal load?, Moore Green Colliery and NCB logo. (Should name be Moorgreen? See 28-88-7.)
20-88-8 SHELL FUEL SUPPLIES 1988
Yellow cab and rear, gray chassis, red barrels, Shell, emblem, Distributor for Shell U.K. Ltd. logo, Fuel Supplies (C.I.) Ltd. on doors.
20-89-1 ALLERTON BYWATER 1989
Navy blue cab and rear . . .
20-89-2 FORWARD CHEMICALS 1989
Blue cab and rear, black chassis, blue barrels, Forward Chemicals Ltd. logo, FC emblem on door.
20-89-3 K L M 1989
Light blue cab and rear, blue chassis, white barrels, KLM, The Reliable Airline logo.
20-89-4 RIDINGS BITTER 1989
Cream cab and rear . . .

20-90-1 ATLAS TYRES 1990
Red body, white rear, black chassis, tire load, Atlas Tires, Standard Oil Products logo.
20-90-2 GEDLING COLLIERY 1990
Black cab, rear, chassis and coal load, Gedling Colliery, Nottinghamshire and NCB logo.
20-90-3 TYRESERVICES 1990
White . . ., red . . .
  1. Action Line in red.
  2. Otherwise.
20-91-1 BROOKE BOND P G TIPS 1991
White cab, rear and chassis, light gray milk cans, Brooke Bond P G Tips logo.
20-91-2 CADBURYS 1991
Purple cab and rear . . .
20-91-3 DAIRY FARM 1991
Cream cab and rear, blue chassis, light gray milk cans, Dairy Farm logo.
20-91-4 HUCKNALL COLLIERIES 1991
Blue-black cab, rear and chassis, coal load, Hucknall Collieries Nos. 1 & 2 logo.
20-91-5 WALKERS CRISPS 1991
Maroon cab, rear and chassis, tan load, Walkers Crisps logo.
20-92-1 BILSTHORPE COLLIERY 1992
Blue-black cab, rear and chassis, coal load, Bilsthorpe Colliery, Nottinghamshire and NCB logo.
20-92-3 DUNLOP TYRES 1992
Blue cab and chassis, white rear, tire load, Dunlop, the world's master tyre logo with Union Jack.
20-92-3 LEWIS D M R 1992
White . . ., yellow . . .
20-92-4 SARSON'S MALT VINEGAR 1992
Maroon cab and rear, black chassis, black barrels, Sarson's logo.
20-92-5 WESTON BROS. DAIRIES 1992
Tan cab and chassis, white rear, light gray milk cans, Weston Bros. Dairies, Margate logo.
20-93-1 ABBOTT BROS. DAIRIES 1993
Cream cab and rear, maroon chassis, light gray milk cans, Abbott Bros. Dairies logo.
20-93-2 AMOCO 1993
Blue cab and rear . . .
20-93-3 BESTWOOD COALS 1993
Blue-black cab, rear and chassis, coal load, Bestwood Coals, Bestwood Colliery and Iron Company logo.
20-93-4 DOORSTEP FRESH 1993
Green . . ., white . . .
20-93-5 EXPRESS DAIRY 1993
Blue-black cab and rear, black chassis, cream load, Express Dairy Milk logo.

20-93-6 JOHNNIE WALKER RED LABEL 1993
Red body and rear, black chassis, brown barrels, Johnnie Walker Red Label logo.
20-93-7 LANG BROTHERS 1993
Red cab, rear and chassis, brown barrels, Lang Brothers Ltd. and Langs Supreme Scotch Whisky logo.
20-93-8 NORTHERN DAIRIES 1993
Cream cab and rear, green chassis, cream milk cans, Northern Dairies logo.
20-93-9 RIDINGS BITTER 1993
Orange cab and rear . . .
20-94-1 B O C GASES 1994
Gray cab and rear, black . . .
20-94-2 MARSTONS BREWERY 1994
Green cab and rear, black . . .
20-94-3 MORELLS OF OXFORD 1994
Blue cab, white . . .
20-94-4 NOTTS CENTRAL WASHERY 1994
Navy blue cab and rear, black . . .
20-94-5 PETERBOROUGH CO-OP COAL 1994
Maroon cab and rear . . .
20-94-6 RUFFORD COLLIERY 1994
Blue-black cab, rear, chassis and coal load, Rufford Colliery and NCB logo.
20-94-7 SHELL 1994
Red cab . . .
20-94-8 SOUTH STAFFS WATER 1994
Dark green cab and rear . . .
20-94-9 TYRESERVICES 1994
Blue cab, yellow . . .
21-86-1 ALLENBURYS DIET 1986
Magenta body, black chassis, pale tan roof, The Allenbury's Diet for Adults, Allen & Hanburys, Ltd. logo.
21-86-2 AUSTRALIAN MODEL SWAPMEETS 1986
Light orange body, green chassis and roof, Australian Model Swapmeets logo.
21-86-3 CANADA FRUIT AND VINE 1986
Cream body, maroon chassis and roof, Canada Fruit and Vine logo.
21-86-4 CITY MUSEUM AND ART GALLERY 1986
Cream body, brown chassis and roof, City museum & Art Gallery, Stoke-on-Trent logo.
21-86-5 DR. BARNARDO'S 1986
White body, black chassis, red roof, Dr Barnardo's, No destitute child ever refused admission logo.
21-86-6 FOX TALBOT 1986
Cream body, brown chassis and roof, Fox Talbot Quality Photographic Equipment logo.
21-86-7 EXCHANGE & MART 1986
Brown body, black chassis and roof, The Exchange & Mart and Collectors' Weekly, Thursdays, Bazaar logo.

189

21-86-8 EXPRESS & STAR 1986
Red body, black chassis, white roof . . .
21-86-9 LLEDO PROMOTIONAL 1986
Yellow-orange body, black chassis and roof, Your Own Promotional Car, Phone for Information logo.
21-86-10 OKTOBERFEST TOY SHOW 1986
Cream body, maroon chassis and roof, 2nd Annual Toy Show, Oct. 12, 1986 and Oktoberfest logo.
21-86-11 WEST POINT TOY SHOW 1986
Light orange body, blue chassis and roof, West Point Toy Show, June 22, 1986 logo.
21-87-1 A A C A NATIONAL FALL MEET 1987
White body, blue chassis, red roof, AACA National Fall Meet logo, Hershey Region on header.
21-87-2 ANC PARCEL SERVICE 1987
White body, blue chassis, ivory roof, The British Parcel Service, ANC, Next Day--Nationwide logo.
21-87-3 BRENMARK 1987
Cream body and roof, black chassis, Brenmark logo.
21-87-4 THE CITIZEN/GLOUCESTER JOURNAL 1987
Yellow body, black chassis and roof, The Citizen, Gloucester Journal logo.
21-87-5 CO-OPERATIVE MILK 1987
Light yellow body, brown chassis and roof, Co-operative Milk, Milk Service Dept., Pure Bottled Milk logo, brown tires.
21-87-6 DEANE'S 1987
Green body, dark green chassis and roof, Deane's Fresh Vegetables, Fresh Fruit, Flowers logo.
21-87-7 HOBBYCO 1987
White body, red chassis and roof, Hobbyco logo.
21-87-8 JERSEY EVENING POST 1987
White body, black chassis and roof, Jersey Evening Post, St. Savior, Jersey, Channel Islands logo, Part of Jersey Life on header.
21-87-9 RDP LLEDO COLLECTOR GUIDES 1987
Cream body, red chassis and roof, Lledo Collector Guides logo, RDP 1987 on doors.
21-88-1 BIRMINGHAM MAIL 1988
Blue body, black chassis, bright blue roof, Birmingham Mail, First with the News logo, Birmingham 236 3366 on header.
21-88-2 BRIAN ANDERSON PLANT HIRE 1988
Light tan body, brown chassis and roof, Brian Anderson Plant Hire & Civil Engineering Contractors logo, Brian Anderson on header.
21-88-3 BROOKE BOND TEA 1988
Red body, white . . .
21-88-4 EDINBURGH EVENING NEWS 1988
White body and roof, black chassis, Edinburgh Evening News, The Scotsman on header.
21-88-5 EVENING TIMES 1988
Pale red body, black chassis, red roof, Evening Times logo, same on header.

21-88-6 FIRST IMPRESSIONS 1988
Light gray body, maroon chassis and roof, First Impressions logo, Clothes for Work on header.
21-88-7 FUTURA MOTORS 1988
White body, black . . .
21-88-8 GREAT YARMOUTH MERCURY 1988
Blue body, cream chassis and roof, Great Yarmouth Mercury logo, Your Weekly Newspaper on header.
21-88-9 HARRY RAMSDEN'S 1988
Cream body, green chassis and roof, Harry Ramsden's logo.
21-88-10 HEIGHTS OF ABRAHAM 1988
White body and roof, green chassis . . .
21-88-11 HUNTLEY AND PALMER 1988
Maroon body, black chassis and roof, Huntley & Palmers logo, Delisious Biscuits on blade.
21-88-12 KENT COUNTY BRANCH 1988
Blue body, black chassis, white roof, Kent County Branch logo with red cross, Ambulance on header.
21-88-13 K L M AIR MAIL 1988
Light blue body, blue chassis, white roof, KLM Air Mail logo.
21-88-14 KRYSTIE'S OF KITCHENER 1988
Dark cream body, brown chassis . . .
21-88-15 LEISURE WORLD 1988
Light blue or white body, dark blue chassis, yellow roof, Leisure World 10th Anniversary logo, Leisure World on blade.
 1. Light blue body.
 2. White body.
21-88-16 LLEDO PROMOTIONAL (AUSTRALIA) 1988
Blue body, chassis and roof, Lledo Promotional Models logo with address.
21-88-17 LOWER DECK SEAFOOD RESTAURANT 1988
Green body, dark green chassis and roof, Lower Deck Sea Food Restaurant logo.
21-88-18 MORTEIN 1988
Red body, chassis and roof, When you're onto Mortein, stick to it! logo, model on plinth.
21-88-19 OXFORD MAIL 1988
White body and roof, red chassis, Oxford Mail logo.
21-88-20 OXO 1988
Red body, white . . .
21-88-21 PRESS & JOURNAL 1988
Blue body, black chassis, white roof, Press & Journal, Your first daily logo, Press & Journal on header.
21-88-22 SALVATION ARMY 1988
Dark green body, black chassis and roof, The Salvation Army Men's Social Services logo.
21-88-23 SOUTH WALES EVENING POST 1988
Red body, black chassis and roof, South Wales Evening Post logo.
21-88-24 SUNLIGHT WORKWEAR 1988
Dark blue body, black chassis and roof, Sunlight logo.

21-88-25 SWINDON EVENING ADVERTISER 1988
Yellow body, black chassis and roof . . .
21-88-26 TIMBERCRAFT 1988
Tan body, black chassis and roof, Timbercraft logo.
21-89-1 BATCHELOR'S CORDON BLUE SOUPS 1989
Maroon body, black chassis, white roof, Batchelors Cordon Bleu Soups logo, Batchelors on header.
21-89-2 BEDFORD BUILDING SOCIETY 1989
White body, pale blue . . .
21-89-3 BOOTS 1989
Blue body, white . . .
21-89-4 BROOKE BOND P G TIPS 1989
White body, red chassis and roof, Brooke Bond P G Tips logo.
21-89-5 CLAN DEW 1989
Light tan body, red-brown chassis, brown roof, The Original Clan Dew logo.
21-89-6 DERBY EVENING TELEGRAPH 1989
Red body and roof, black chassis, Derby Evening Telegraph logo, same on header.
21-89-7 EASTBOURNE NEWS 1989
Gray body, red chassis and roof, The Eastbourne News Series logo.
21-89-8 EASTER RALLY 89 1989
Red body, black . . .
21-89-9 EVENING ECHO (Basildon) 1989
Red body and chassis, white roof, Evening Echo Always ahead logo, Evening Echo on header.
21-89-10 EVENING ECHO (Dorset) 1989
Dark blue body, black chassis and roof, Evening Echo logo.
21-89-11 EVENING TELEGRAPH-CITIZEN 1989
White body and roof, blue chassis, Evening Telegraph logo, Citizen on doors.
21-89-12 FISHERMAN'S FRIEND 1989
White body, red chassis and roof, Fisherman's Friend logo.
21-89-13 FOX-TALBOT 150 YEARS 1989
White body, black chassis, green roof, 150 Years Fox Talbot logo.
21-89-14 GLASGOW HERALD 1989
Blue body, black chassis, white roof, The Glasgow Herald logo.
21-89-15 LINCOLNSHIRE ECHO 1989
Light red body, black chassis and roof, Lincolnshire Echo logo, Britain at war design. Lincolnshire Echo on header.
21-89-16 R. S. MALCOLM FAMILY BAKER 1989
Cream body, brown chassis and roof, R. S. Malcolm Family Baker Banbury Cakes logo.
21-89-17 MONO BAKERY EQUIPMENT 1989
Peach body, red chassis, black roof with header . . .
21-89-18 NATIONAL GARDEN FESTIVAL 1989
Cream body, black chassis, red roof, National Garden Festival, Gateshead 1990 logo.
21-89-19 NET WORTH 1989
Cream body, blue . . .

21-89-20 RUTLAND & STAMFORD MERCURY 1989
Blue body, white . . .
21-89-21 ST. JOHN AMBULANCE/YORKSHIRE 1989
Black body, white . . .
21-89-22 TORBAY HERALD AND EXPRESS 1989
Red body, black chassis and roof, Torbay Herald and Express Serving South Devon with the News logo.
21-89-23 VAN DIJK VERF 1989
White body and roof, black chassis, Van Dijk Verf, Almelo logo.
21-90-1 B. A. P. S. 1990
White body, black . . .
21-90-2 BASSETTS DOLLY MIXTURE 1990
Purple body and chassis, black roof, Bassetts Dolly Mixture logo.
21-90-3 BEWLEYS 1990
Maroon body, black . . .
21-90-4 BRANNIGANS 1990
Purple body, black . . .
21-90-5 CADBURYS TWIRL 1990
Yellow body and chassis, black roof, Cadbury's Twirl logo.
21-90-6 CLEANING SOLUTIONS 1990
Black body, chassis and roof, Cleaning Solutions logo.
21-90-7 DAILY HERALD 1990
Blue body, chassis and roof, Daily Herald logo, same on header.
21-90-8 EXCHANGE & MART 1990
Tan body, black chassis, red roof, Exchange & Mart logo.
21-90-9 EVENING WORLD 1990
Red body, black chassis and roof, Evening World, Bristol's Newspaper logo, The Latest News on header.
21-90-10 HAPPY EATER 1990
Yellow body, red chassis and roof, Happy Eater Family Restaurants logo, Happy Eater on header.
21-90-11 HORNBY'S DAIRIES 1990
Yellow body, black . . .
21-90-12 KENT & SUSSEX COURIER 1990
Blue body, black chassis and roof, Kent and Sussex Courier, same on header.
21-90-13 LANES HEALTHCARE PRODUCTS 1990
Tan body, green chassis and roof, Lanes Healthcare Products logo.
21-90-14 LIVERPOOL ECHO 1990
Red body, blue chassis, white roof, Liverpool Echo logo, Liverpool Daily Post & Echo on blade.
21-90-15 NEWS OF THE WORLD 1990
Red body, chassis and roof, Read the News of the World logo, Best Sunday Paper on header.
21-90-16 PREMIUM INCENTIVE SHOW 1990
White body, red . . ., blue . . .
21-90-17 SCHNEIDER MEATS 1990
Orange body, blue . . .
21-90-18 SHANNON DUTY FREE SHOP 1990
White body, red chassis and roof, Shannon Duty Free Shop logo.

21-90-19 TAMWORTH HERALD 1990
White body and roof, black chassis, Tamworth Herald logo, same on header.
21-90-20 TELEGRAPH AND ARGUS 1990
Yellow body, black chassis and roof, Telegraph & Argus and Craven Old Wheels Society logo, Telegraph & Argus on header.
21-90-21 THERIAULTS 1990
Lilac body, green . . .
21-90-22 WALKERS POTATO CRISPS 1990
Dark green body, red chassis and roof, Walkers Potato Crisps logo, Walkers on header.
21-90-23 ZEROLENE 1990
Blue body and chassis, white roof, Zerolene, the Standard Oil for Motor Cars logo, Zerolene on header.
21-91-1 BASSETTS ALLSORTS 1991
Black body, chassis and roof, Bassetts Liquorice Allsorts logo.
21-91-2 CABLE SERVICES 1991
Dark blue body, black . .
21-91-3 CADBURYS ECLAIRS 1991
Purple body and roof . . .
21-91-4 DESERT RATS AMBULANCE 1991
Cream body, chassis and roof, red cross logo.
21-91-5 DR. PEPPER 100TH ANNIVERSARY 1991
Red body, white . . .
21-91-6 GLOUCESTERSHIRE ECHO 1991
Red body and roof, black chassis, Gloucestershire Echo logo, same on rear.
21-91-7 LLEDO 1991
Cream body, green . . .
21-91-8 NORTHUMBERLAND GAZETTE 1991
Red body, black chassis, white roof, Northumberland Gazette logo, same on header.
21-91-9 NORWICH RED CROSS 1991
Cream body, black chassis, white roof, Norwich Red Cross Ambulance logo, Ambulance on header.
21-91-10 P D S A 1991
White body, blue . . .
21-91-11 SHEPSHED BUILDING SOCIETY 1991
Tan body, black chassis and roof, Shepshed Building Society logo.
21-91-12 SOMERSET COUNTY GAZETTE 1991
Yellow body, black . . .
21-92-1 4TH BRAMHALL SCOUT GROUP 1992
Green body, red . . .
21-92-2 BEKONSCOT MODEL VILLAGE 1992
Yellow body, green chassis and roof, Bekonscot Model Village logo.
21-92-3 BURTON MAIL 1992
Yellow body, black . . .
21-92-4 BURTONS FISH 'N' CHIPS 1992
Red body, black chassis and roof, Burton's Fish 'n' Chips, Chicken 'n' Chips logo, Burton's on header.

21-92-5 CORNISH GUARDIAN 1992
Red body and roof . . .
21-92-6 DURHAM AMBULANCE 1992
Ivory body, black chassis, cream roof, Durham Ambulance Service logo.
21-92-7 G & S ELECTRICAL 1992
Light blue body, black . . .
21-92-8 KENT COUNTY 1992
White body and roof . . .
21-92-9 LNER AMBULANCE 1992
No data.
21-92-10 QA & TB 1992
Light orange body, white . . .
21-92-11 ROYAL MAIL 1992
Red body, black chassis and roof, Royal Mail logo, Bypost box.
21-92-12 SOMERSET COUNTY GAZETTE 1992
Dark yellow body, black chassis and roof, Somerset County Gazette logo, same on header.
21-92-13 VALOR BLACK BEAUTY 1992
White body, dark green . . .
21-92-14 WESTERN GAZETTE 1992
Orange body, blue . . .
21-93-1 COURIER & PRESS 1993
White body, gray . . .
21-93-2 CREAMOLA CUSTARD 1993
Orange-yellow body, blue chassis and roof, Creamola Custard Powder logo.
21-93-3 KENT AMBULANCE SERVICE 1993
White body, black . . .
21-93-4 LEWIS DMR 1993
White body, yellow . . .
21-93-5 MARIAN VIAN 1993
White body . . .
　　1. Green . . .
　　2. Red . . .
21-93-6 MOTIVATION/LLEDO 1993
White body, maroon chassis and roof, Motivation, McCormick Place North, Chicago logo, 1993 on header.
21-93-7 ROYAL NATIONAL LIFE-BOAT INSTITUTION 1993
Red body and roof, black chassis, Saved design, Royal National Life-Boat Institution logo.
21-93-8 SHEFFIELD STAR 1993
White body, blue . . .
21-93-9 O. G. WELCH BUTCHER 1993
Brownish maroon body, black chassis, cream roof, Butcher O. G. Wwelch & Grazier logo.
21-94-1 AUTO TRADER 1994
Light blue body, red . . .

21-94-2 CO-OPERATIVE MILK 1994
Red body, black chassis and roof, Co-Operative Milk, Milk Service Dept., Pure Bottled milk logo.
21-94-3 LNER AMBULANCE 1994
White body, black . . .
21-94-4 MILWAUKEE JOURNAL 1994
Green body, black . . .
22 PACKARD TOWN DELIVERY VAN 1986
22-86-1 J. FRED JONES 1986
Blue body, navy blue chassis, cream roof, J. Fred Jones Packard Sales & Service logo.
22-86-2 JUST CONTINENTAL 1986
Blue body . . .
22-87-1 EXCHANGE AND MART 1987
White body, black chassis and roof, Exchange & Mart, 1987 Motoring News logo with emblem.
22-87-2 FELTON WORLDWIDE 1987
Light gray body, black chassis and roof, Felton Worldwide logo.
22-87-3 JOHN HARVEY COLLECTION 1987
Dark brown body and roof, cream chassis, The John Harvey Collection, Harvey House, Tring, Herts logo; in Fuji box.
22-87-4 TELEMEDIA SPORTS 1987
White body, blue chassis and roof, Telemedia Sports Radio Day, September 12, 1987 logo, Toronto Blue Jays emblem.
22-87-5 WEST POINT MILITARY ACADEMY/TOY SHOW 1987
Yellow-orange body, black chassis and roof, West Point Military Academy, Hotel Thayer logo.
    1. As above.
    2. Red "Toy Show, June 21, 1987" in logo.
22-88-1 BIRDWOOD MILL 1988
Black body, chassis and roof . . .
22-88-2 SHOWGARD MOUNTS 1988
Cream body, red chassis and roof, Showgard Mounts Est. 1960 logo.
22-89-1 3M STYLE 'N' STRIPE 1989
Black body and roof, red chassis, Style 'n' Stripe logo with 3M emblem on door and rear.
22-89-2 EVENING HERALD 1988
Cream body, blue chassisn red roof, Evening Herald logo.
22-89-3 LEICESTER MERCURY 1989
Blue body, black chassis and roof, Leicester Mercury logo.
22-90-1 KODAK T MAX FILM 1990
White body, black . . .
22-91-1 ELIZABETH SHAW 1991
Cream body, blue-black chassis and roof, Elizabeth Shaw logo.
22-91-2 LEWIS DMR 1991
White body, yellow . . .
22-91-3 PASCALL 1991
Cream body, green . . .
22-91-4 THERIAULTS 1991
Light yellow body . . .

22-91-5 WALKERS POTATO CRISPS 1991
Blue body and chassis, cream roof, Walkers Potato Crisps logo.
22-93-1 3M PROFESSIONAL 1993
Cream body, navy . . .
22-93-2 AUTO TRADER 1993
Light gray body, maroon chassis and roof, Auto Trader logo.
22-93-3 GLENGOYNE 1993
Black body, chassis and roof, Glengoyne emblem logo.
23 SCENICRUISER 1987
23-87-1 A.R.C. OF ALLEN COUNTY 1987
White body, black chassis, ARC Learning Living Guidance Industries of Allen County logo.
23-87-2 B & A TOP MARKS 1987
Rose pink body and chassis, B & A Top Marks logo.
23-87-3 TÖFF-TÖFF 1987
Pink or yellow body and chassis, To"*ff To"*ff logo.
    1. Pink body, Your Lledo Specialist in Essen, West Germany logo.
    2. Yellow body, Your Diecast Model Specialties logo.
23-88-1 BLUE CANADIAN 1988
Light blue body, unpainted chassis, logo types as below:
    1. Banville Milton Ontario.   6. Stagecoach.
    2. Emerald City Tours.   7. Thomas Tours.
    3. Fountainhead Raiders.   8. Toy Fair, Jan. 24-29, 1988.
    4. Frandello.   9. Victoriaville Viscounts.
    5. Niagara-on-the-Lake.
23-88-2 GREEN CANADIAN 1988
Green body, unpainted chassis, logo types as below:
    1. Banville Milton Ontario.   6. Stagecoach.
    2. Emerald City Tours.   7. Thomas Tours.
    3. Fountainhead Raiders.   8. Toy Fair, Jan. 24-29, 1988.
    4. Frandello.   9. Victoriaville Viscounts.
    5. Niagara-on-the-Lake.
23-88-3 YELLOW CANADIAN 1988
Yellow-orange body, black chassis, logo types as below:
    1. Banvil Milton Ontario.   4. Stagecoach.
    2. Frandello.   5. Thomas Tours.
    3. R.U.I.N. Wheeling, West Va. 6. Toy Fair, Jan. 24-29, 1988.
24 ROLLS-ROYCE PLAYBOY 1987
24-87-1 BLACK (Franklin) 1987
Black body, chassis, top and seats, red hubs.
24-87-2 RED-WHITE-GREEN (Fuji) 1987
Red body, white chassis, green top and seats.
24-89-1 K L M 1989
Light blue body, blue chassis, white top and seats, KLM logo.
24-91-1 10TH WEDDING ANNIVERSARY 1991
Cream body, purple chassis, top and seats, H.R.H. Princess Diana logo on left, 29th July 1991 10th Wedding Anniversary on right.
25 ROLLS-ROYCE SILVER GHOST 1987
25-87-1 BLACK (Franklin) 1987
Black body, chassis, top and seats, red hubs.

25-87-2 CONGRATULATIONS 1987
Rose pink body, white chassis, top and seats, Congratulations logo.
25-89-1 K L M 1989
Light blue body, blue chassis, white top and seats, KLM logo.
26 CHEVROLET DRINKS VAN 1988
26-88-1 CASTROL MOTOR OIL 1988
Green cab, rear, chassis and blade, tan load, Wakefield Castrol Motor Oil logo.
26-88-2 LOWCOCK'S LEMONADE 1988
Magenta cab, rear and chassis, brown blade, tan load, W. J. Lowcock logo, Drink Lowcock's Lemonade on doors.
26-89-1 K L M 1989
Light blue cab and rear, blue chassis, white blade and load, KLM logo.
26-89-2 UNIGATE 1989
Red cab, blade and rear, black chassis, white load, Unigate logo.
26-91-1 WALKERS CRISPS 1991
Dark green cab, rear and blade, black chassis, cream load, Walkers Crisps logo.
26-92-1 HEINZ 57 VARIETIES 1992
Dark green cab, rear and blade, black chassis, cream load, Heinz 57 Varieties logo, H. J. Heinz Co. Ltd. on doors.
26-92-2 J & B SCOTCH WHISKY 1992
Dark green cab and rear . . .
26-93-1 BERRY BROTHERS 1993
Black cab and rear . . .
26-93-2 FINCHES LEMONADE 1993
Blue cab, rear and blade, black chassis, tan load, Finches White Lemonade logo.
26-93-3 SCHWEPPES 1993
Yellow cab, rear and blade, black chassis, white load, Schweppes Refreschhhing! logo, emblem on doors.
26-94-1 FLYING FLOWERS 1994
Cream cab, rear and load, apple green chassis, no blade, Flying Flowers logo, flower figures on load.
26-94-2 ROLLING ROCK 1994
Green cab and rear . . .
27 MACK BREAKDOWN TRUCK 1988
27-88-1 BEAN STREET KIDS 1988
Orange body, chassis and boom, black bed, Bean St. Kids logo.
27-88-2 BOURNEMOUTH TRANSPORT MUSEUM 1988
Yellow body, black chassis, maroon boom, gray bed, Bournemouth Transport Museum logo.
27-88-3 K L M MAINTENANCE 1988
Light blue body and boom, blue chassis, white bed, KLM Maintenance logo.
27-90-1 NEWMAN-TIPPER TUBES 1990
Red body, black chassis . . .
27-92-1 BROOKLANDS A. R. C. 1992
Yellow body and boom, green chassis and bed, Brooklands Sutomobile Racing Club logo.

27-92-2 PANELCRAFT AMOCO SERVICE 1992
White body and boom, blue chassis, black? bed, Amoco Service Provider logo, Panelcraft emblem on doors.
27-93-1 AMOCO 1993
White body . . .
27-93-2 VOGON 1993
White body . . .
27-94-1 SUNOCO 1994
No data.
28 MACK CANVAS BACKED TRUCK 1988
28-88-1 BESTWOOD--BRITISH COAL 1988
Dark blue body and chassis, tan cover, Bestwood National Workshops logo, British Coal on doors.
28-88-2 ECONOFREIGHT 1988
Blue body and chassis, white cover, Econofreight emblem with arrow to front or back of lettering.
28-88-3 GWR EXPRESS CARTAGE 1988
Brown body and chassis, tan cover . . .
28-88-4 INDUSTRIAL EXCHANGE AND MART 1988
Blue body, black chassis, light tan cover, The Industrial Revolution is here and Industrial Exchange & Mart logo.
28-88-5 LMS EXPRESS PARCELS 1988
Maroon body and chassis, black cover, L.M.S. Express Parcels Traffic logo.
28-88-6 LNER EXPRESS PARCELS 1988
Dark blue body and chassis, black cover, L.N.E.R. Express Parcels Services logo.
28-88-7 MOORGREEN--BRITISH COAL 1988
Dark blue body and chassis, tan cover, Moorgreen National Workshops logo, British Coal on doors.
28-88-8 S.R. EXPRESS PARCELS 1988
Green body, chassis and cover, SR Express Parcel Service logo.
28-89-1 AUSTRALIAN CAR MODELLER 1989
Black body and chassis . . .
28-89-2 CASTROL 1989
Dark green body, cream cover . . .
28-89-3 CLAN DEW 1989
Red-brown body, black chassis, cream cover, Clan Dew and The Original logo.
28-89-4 LOCKHEED HYDRAULIC BRAKES 1989
Brown body, black . . .
28-89-5 TRELOARS 1989
Green body, cream cover . . .
28-89-6 ZEALLEY 1989
Blue body, gray cover . . .
28-90-1 ANCHOR STEAM BEER 1990
Dark blue body, tan cover . . .
28-90-2 ELM FARM CATERING 1990
White body, green . . .
28-90-3 EXCHANGE AND MART 1990

Red body, black chassis, tan cover, Exchange & Mart logo. Note difference between this and 28-88-4!
28-90-4 KLEENEX VELVET 1990
Light green body, white cover . . .
28-90-5 SCHNEIDER MEATS 1990
Orange body, blue cover . . .
28-90-6 TREBOR REFRESHERS 1990
White body and chassis, yellow cover, Trebor Refreshers logo.
28-90-7 UNITED DAIRIES 1990
Red body and cover . . .
28-91-1 ST. IVEL GOLD 1991
Blue body and cover . . .
28-91-2 SHOWGARD MOUNTS 1991
Red body, gold cover . . .
28-92-1 MIKE BIRCH LTD. 1992
Light blue body and cover . . .
28-92-2 NATIONAL PROVISIONING CENTRE 1992
Dark blue body, black chassis, tan cover, National Provisioning Centre Fence and British Coal logo.
28-92-3 POST OFFICE TELEPHONES 1992
Olive body, black chassis, cream cover, Post Office Telephones logo.
28-93-1 ARMY BROADCASTING STUDIO 1993
Olive body, chassis and cover, Mobile Army Broadcasting Studio logo.
28-93-2 CRINKLEY BOTTOM 1993
Blue body and chassis, cream cover, Lledo and Crinkley Bottom Collectors Club logo.
28-93-3 FINCHES DRY TONIC WATER 1993
Yellow body, tan cover, black chassis, Finches Dry Tonic Water logo.
28-93-4 HARRY RAMSDEN 1993
Red body, cream cover, Harry Ramsden's logo . . .
28-93-5 IT AIN'T HALF HOT MUM 1993
Tan body and chassis, cream cover, It ain't half hot mum, Concert Party and Union Jack logo.
28-93-6 JOHNNIE WALKER 1993
Black body, chassis and cover, Johnnie Walker Black Label logo.
28-93-7 LANGS SELECT 1993
Blue body, black chassis, blue-black cover, Langs Select 12 Years Old Scotch Whisky and Lang Brothers Ltd logo.
28-93-8 LEWIS DMR 1993
Yellow body, white cover . . .
28-93-9 MASSEY SHAW FIRE BOAT 1993
Green body and chassis, gray cover, L.C.C. Massey Shaw Fire Boat Support Vehicle and London Fire Brigade logo.
28-93-10 ROYAL NATIONAL LIFEBOAT INSTITUTION 1993
Navy blue body and cover . . .
28-94-1 N H S SUPPLIES 1994
Blue body and chassis, white cover, NHS Supplies, South East Division logo.

28-94-2 PORT OF LONDON POLICE 1994
Cream body . . .
29 DODGE 4 X 4 1988
29-90-1 CREW TRANSPORT/EXCHANGE & MART 1990
Blue body and chassis, Crew Transport logo with roundels and emblem, Exchange & Mart box.
29-90-2 CROYDON-SUTTON DISTRICT 1990
Red body and chassis, Croydon/Sutton Letters District serving you logo.
29-91-1 DESERT RATS 1991
Cream body and chassis, Desert Rats emblem and red crosses.
29-93-1 THE DARLING BUDS OF MAY 1993
Blue body and chassis, no logo, Darling Buds of May box.
29-93-2 GRAB A GRAND 1993
Dark blue body, red chassis . . .
29-93-3 LEWIS DMR 1993
White body, yellow chassis . . .
29-93-4 MOBILE TRANSMITTER 1993
Olive body and chassis, Mobile Transmitter logo, white star.
29-94-1 BOY SCOUTS AMBULANCE 1994
Olive green body and chassis, red cross, scout emblem and star.
29-94-2 KODAK EKTACHROME 1994
Black body, yellow chassis . . .
30 CHEVROLET PANEL VAN 1989
30-89-1 3M BODY TALK 1989
Orange body, black chassis, 3M Company Body Talk logo.
30-89-2 COWES TOY & MODEL MUSEUM 1989
Green body, black chassis, Cowes Toy & Model Museum logo.
30-89-3 FAMILY REUNION 1989
Red body, black chassis . . .
30-89-4 FARNHAM MALTINGS SEPT. 1989 1989
Red body, black chassis . . .
30-89-5 FUTURA AMBULANCE 1989
Tan body and chassis . . .
30-90-1 BIRDWOOD MILL 1990
Red body, black chassis . . .
30-90-2 EXCHANGE & MART 1990
Red body, black chassis, Exchange & Mart logo.
30-90-3 FOTORAMA 1990
White body and chassis, Fotorama, A World of Colour logo.
30-90-4 SCHNEIDER MEATS 1990
Orange body, blue chassis . . .
30-91-1 3M DE TREEPLANK 1991
Yellow body, black chassis, 3M on door, De Treeplank logo.
30-91-2 LEWIS DMR 1991
White body, yellow chassis . . .
30-91-3 SHIELDS GAZETTE 1991
Yellow body, black chassis, Shields Gazette logo.
30-92-1 EKTAPRO 1992
Gray body, yellow chassis . . .

30-30-1 BRANTHE-KORRUX 1993
Red body, blue chassis . . .
30-93-2 J. C. PENNEY 1993
Green body, black chassis, J. C. Penney Co, A Nation Wide
Institution logo, Est. 1902 on doors.
30-93-3 THERIAULTS 1993
Pink body, light blue chassis . . .
30-93-4 TOMS ROASTED PEANUTS 1993
Silver body and chassis . . .
30-94-1 AFTENPOSTEN 1994
Light blue body and chassis . . .
30-94-2 DULUX WEATHERSHIELD 1994
Yellow body and chassis . . .
30-94-3 KODAK EXPRESS 1994
White body . . .
31 HORSE DRAWN BRERER'S DRAY 1988
31-88-1 BURT'S ALES 1988
Green body, hitch and seat, Burt's Ales, Ventnor, Isle of Wight logo.
   1. Dark brown barrels and horses, gold wheels.
   2. Black barrels, horses and wheels.
31-89-1 EVERARDS 1989
Green body . . ., gold . . .
31-92-1 FREMLINS (brown horses) 1992
Black body, hitch and seat, brown barrles and horses, Fremlins
traditional beers and ales logo.
31-93-1 FREMLINS (gray horses) 1993
Black body, hitch and seat, gray horses . . .
31-93-2 MORLAND BREWERY 1993
Brown body . . .
31-93-3 RANDALL'S 1993
Black body, hitch and seat, Jersey's Original Brewers (?) logo.
31-94-1 BENSKINS BREWERY 1994
Blue body . . .
31-94-2 GUINNESS 1994
Black body . . .
31-94-3 HORSES AT WORK 1994
Green body . . .
32 ROLLS-ROYCE SILVER GHOST 1989
No promotional models yet.
33 MODEL T FORD 1989
33-89-1 DERBYSHIRE CONSTABULARY 1989
Navy blue body, black . . .
33-89-2 HOOLEY'S GARAGE 1989
Black body, chassis and roof . . .
33-90-1 CASTROL MOTOR OIL 1990
Red body and chassis, black roof, Wakefield Castrol Motor Oil logo.
33-90-2 ESSEX CONSTABULARY 1990
Dark blue body, black chassis and roof, Essex Constabulary logo.
33-91-1 SUN CHEMICAL 1991
Dark green body, black chassis . . .

33-91-2 WESSEX CLASSIC CAR SHOW 1991
Maroon body, black chassis and roof, Wessex Classic Car show logo.
33-92-1 LINCOLNSHIRE STANDARD 1992
Dark green body, black chassis . . .
33-93-1 CADBURYS 1993
Purple body, white . . .
33-94-1 DAYS GONE 1994
White body, green . . .
33-94-2 GRAND HOTEL 1994
Dark blue body and chassis, black roof, Grand Hotel at the Opera--
Paris logo, House of Eliott box.
33-94-3 HARRY RAMSDEN 1994
Cream body, maroon chassis and roof, Harry Ramsden's, the world's
most famous fish & chips logo.
34 DENNIS DELIVERY VAN 1989
34-89-1 3M FINESSE IT 1989
Red body and roof, black chassis, 3M Finesse It logo.
34-89-2 ADT LONDON MARATHON 1989
Blue body, red chassis, white roof, ADT London Marathon and
Fotorama Film for the Occasion logo.
34-89-3 BOOTS QUALITY PRODUCTS 1989
Blue body, chassis and roof, Boots Quality Products logo.
34-89-4 FOTORAMA 1989
Blue body, red chassis, gray roof . . . Note that 34-89-1 also has
Fotorama logo, but roof is white.
34-89-5 SHOWGARD MOUNTS 1989
Blue body, chassis and roof, Showgard Mounts logo.
34-89-6 TETLEY'S TEAS 1989
Dark blue body, black chassis, light blue roof, Tetley's Teas logo.
34-90-1 CASTROL 1990
Green body and roof . . .
34-90-2 CROYDON LETTERS 1990
Red body . . .
34-90-3 EXCHANGE AND MART 1990
Dark yellow body, black chassis, light yellow roof, Exchange & Mart
Bazaar logo.
34-90-4 ISLE OF MAN PENNY POST 1990
Red body, roof and chassis, 1840 1990 Isle of Man penny post logo.
34-90-5 SIMONIZ 1990
Yellow body and roof . . .
34-90-6 WALKERS POTATO CRISPS 1990
Black body and roof, red chassis, Walker's Potato Crisps logo.
34-91-1 BIRMINGHAM CITY POLICE 1991
Navy blue body . . .
34-91-2 DAIRY FARM BISCUITS 1991
Tan body, dark cream roof, Dairy Farm Traditional
Recipe Biscuits logo.
34-91-3 HARRY RAMSDEN 1991
Light tan body and chassis, pale tan roof, Harry Ramsden's, the
world's most famous fish & ships logo.

34-91-4 KENDAL MILNE & CO. 1991
Dark green body, cream roof . . .
34-92-1 DISABLED 1992
White body . . .
34-93-1 BLACK & DECKER 1993
Dark green body . . .
34-93-2 FINCHES PURE ORANGE JUICE 1993
Dark green body, chassis and roof, Finches Pure Orange Juice logo.
34-93-3 HADRIAN CRYSTAL 1993
Dark green body . . .
34-93-4 LEWIS DMR 1993
White body, yellow . . .
34=94=1 LILLIPUT LANE 1994
Yellow body, red . . .
34-94-2 MARSTONS BREWERY 1994
Green body, white . . .
35 DENNIS LIMOUSINE 1989
35-89-1 ISLE OF WIGHT FIRE BRIGADE 1989
White body and roof, red chassis and ladder, Isle of Wight Fire
Brigade logo.
35-91-1 BBC RECORDING VAN 1991
Olive green body, chassis and roof, black ladder, BBC Recording Van
logo.
35-91-2 CITY OF COVENTRY AUXILIARY 1991
Red body, white . . .
35-93-1 NTV INSIDE BROADCAST 1993
Olive green body, roof and chassis, tan ladder, NTV Inside Broadcast
logo. (Or is this 35-94-1?)
35-93-2 PORT OF LONDON POLICE 1993
Cream body and roof, black chassis, tan ladder, Port of London
Autoority Police, Tilbury Docks logo.
35-94-1 LONDON FIRE BRIGADE 1994
Red body and roof, black chassis, tan ladder, London Fire Brigade
Emergency Unit logo, L.F.B. on hood, London's Burning box.
35-94-2 NTV INSIDE BROADCAST 1994
Green body . . .
36 CHEVROLET PICK-UP TRUCK 1989
36-91-1 STANDARD OIL 1991
Green body, black chassis, barrel load . . .
36-92-1 CASTROL 1992
Green body, black chassis, green barrels, Wakefield Castrol Motor
Oil logo.
36-92-2 TYRE SERVICES 1992
White body, blue chassis . . .
36-93-1 BRANTHO-KORRUX 1993
Red body, blue chassis, barrel load, Brantho-Korrux Langzeit-
Rostschutz logo.
37 MODEL A FORD PANEL VAN 1990
37-90-1 HARTLEPOOL MAIL (green/black) 1990
Green body, black . . .

37-90-2 HARTLEPOOL MAIL (green/gray) 1990
Green body, gray . . .
37-90-3 SCHNEIDER MEATS 1990
Orange body, blue . . .
37-90-4 SUNDERLAND ECHO (red/black) 1990
Red body, black . . .
37-90-5 SUNDERLAND ECHO (maroon/gray) 1990
Maroon body, gray . . .
37-90-6 WESTERN EVENING HERALD 1990
Maroon body, black . . .
37-91-1 CHAMPION SPARK PLUGS 1991
Blue body, chassis and roof, Champion emblem and globe logo.
37-91-2 CHELTENHAM NEWS 1991
Blue body, chassis and roof, Cheltenham News logo, News on header.
37-91-3 GRIMSBY EVENING TELEGRAPH 1991
Red body, black . . .
37-91-4 HALIFAX EVENING COURIER 1991
Green body and roof, black chassis, Halifax Evening Courier logo,
phone number on header.
37-91-5 THE UNIVERSE 1991
Brown body and roof . . .
37-92-1 EXIDE BATTERIES 1992
Light cream body, green chassis, cream roof, Exide, the long life car
battery logo, Exide on header.
37-92-2 VALOR DREAM LPG 1992
Blue body and roof . . .
37-94-1 HAMMERITE KURUST 1994
Gray body, black . . .
38 ROLLS-ROYCE SILVER GHOST 1989
38-90-1 H.R.H. THE QUEEN MOTHER 1990
Purple body and chassis, lilac top, H.M. Queen Elizabeth The Queen
Mother logo.
38-90-2 P. & P. PROMOTIONS 1990
Maroon body, cream . . .
38-91-1 CHARLES & DIANA 10TH ANNIVERSARY 1991
Dark blue body and chassis, cream roof, Charles and Diana 10th
Wedding Anniversary logo.
38-91-2 PEGGY & KEN'S GOLDEN WEDDING 1991
Gold body, maroon . . .
38-91-3 ROYAL BIRTHDAYS 1991
Dark red body and chassis, cream roof, H.M. Queen Elizabeth II 65th
Birthday on left side, H.R.H. Prince Philip 70th Birthday on right.
38-91-4 SHARON & PAUL 1991
Green body, cream . . .
38-92-1 PREMIER 1992
Cream body and chassis, maroon top, Premier logo.
39 MACK SACK TRUCK 1989
39-89-1 YORKSHIRE MINING MUSEUM 1989
Dark green body, black chassis and load, Yorkshire Mining Museum
logo.

39-90-1 STAUFFER CHEMICALS 1990
Black body and chassis . . .
39-92-1 THWAITE MILLS 1992
Red body, black chassis, gray load, Thwaite Mills logo.
40 MACK CRANE TRUCK 1990
No promotional models yet.
41 KARRIER TROLLEY BUS 1990
41-90-1 BENTALLS/LONDON UNITED 1990
Red body, cream . . .
41-90-2 BOURNEMOUTH: MUSEUM/PIER 1990
Yellow body, brown . . .
　　1. Destination Museum.
　　2. Destination Pier.
41-90-3 BOURNEMOUTH CENTENARY 1990
Yellow body, cream . . ., lower logo: Corporation Transport.
　　1. Destination Iford.
　　2. Destination Square.
41-90-4 EVENING POST/NOTTINGHAM 1990
Dark green body . . ., Evening Post upper, Nottingham City lower
logo.
41-90-5 EVENING TELEGRAM/GRIMSBY 1990
Maroon body . . ., Evening Telegraph upper, Grimsby Corporation
lower logo.
41-90-6 EXPRESS & STAR/WOLVERHAMPTON 1990
Light green body and chassis, light orange roof and windows, first
with the news Express & Star upper, Wolverhampton Corporation
Transport lower logo, destination Dudley.
41-90-7 HULL DAILY MAIL/KINGSTON 1990
Dark blue body . . ., Hull Daily Mail upper, Kingston upon Hull
lower logo.
41-90-8 ROBIN HOOD/NOTTINGHAM CITY 1990
Dark green body and roof, black chassis, cream windows, Pork Farms
and Robin Hood Marathon upper, Nottingham City Transport lower
logo, destination 1990.
41-90-9 SALVATION ARMY/BIRMINGHAM 1990
Dark blue body, black chassis, cream roof and windows, Salvation
Army and Birmingham Citadel Centenary upper, Birmingham City
Transport lower logo, destination Saint Chads.
41-90-10 SHOWGARD MOUNTS/DONCASTER 1990
Maroon body, chassis and roof, cream windows, Showgard Mounts
for stamps of all nations upper, County Borough of Doncaster lower
logo.
41-90-11 TREBOR MINTS/COLCHESTER 1990
Dark green body, chassis, roof and windows, Trebor Extra Strong
Mints upper, Colchester District lower logo.
41-91-1 80 YEARS TROLLEYBUS/BRADFORD 1991
Navy blue body and windows, black chassis, gray roof, 80 Years of
the Trolleybus 1911-1991 upper, Bradford City Tramways lower
logo.
　　1. Destination Dudley Hill.
　　2. Destination Laisterdyke

41-91-2 ANADIN 1931-1991/WHITEHALL LAB 1991
Yellow body, green . . ., Anadin 1931-1991 upper, Whitehall
Laboratories lower logo, destination Chenies St.
41-92-3 BENTALLS/LONDON 1991
Red body, brown . . ., white . . ., Bentalls upper, London Transport
lower logo.
41-91-4 BIRMINGHAM MAIL 1991
Navy blue body and chassis, cream roof and windows, The
Birmingham Mail upper, Birmingham Corporation lower logo with
coat of arms.
41-91-5 BIRMINGHAM POST/WOLVERHAMPTON 1991
Green body, chassis, roof and windows, The Birmingham Post upper,
Wolverhampton Corporation Transport Dept. lower logo.
41-91-6 BOARDMANS/GORDON OMNIBUS 1991
Red body, white . . ., Boardmans upper, Gordon Omnibus Co. lower
logo.
　　1. Destination Chingford.
　　2. Destination Stratford.
41-91-7 BOURNEMOUTH HERITAGE 1991
Yellow body, cream . . ., Bournemouth Heritage upper, Bournemouth
lower logo.
　　1. Destination Centre.
　　2. Destination Pier.
41-91-8 BRETTS FURNITURE/IPSWICH 1991
Green body . . ., Bretts Furniture upper, Ipswich Corporation lower
logo.
　　1. Destination Airport.
　　2. Destination Electric House.
41-91-9 CACTI NURSERY/MAIDSTONE 1991
Light brown body, cream . . ., Cacti Nursery upper, Maidstone &
District lower logo.
　　1. Destination Loose.
　　2. Destination Maidstone.
41-91-10 CLEETHORPES BOROUGH COUNCIL 1991
Black body and chassis, cream roof and windows, Cleethorpes
Borough Council upper, Cleethorpes lowerr logo.
　　1. Destination Cleethorpes.
　　2. Destination Grimsby.
41-91-11 DERBYSHIRE CONSTABULARY 1991
Black body, chassis and roof, white windows, Derbyshire Police,
working with Derbyshire People upper, Derbyshire Constabulary
lower logo.
　　1. Destination Alfreton.
　　2. Destination Butterley.
41-91-12 DONCASTER STAR 1991
Maroon body, roof and windows, black chassis, The Doncaster Star
upper, gold coat of arms lower logo, destination Racecourse.
41-91-13 DONNINGTON 1991
Light blue body, dark blue . . . (is Donnington the correct spelling?)
　　1. Destination Donnington.
　　2. Destination 1991.

41-91-14 E F T U 1991
Silver body . . .
  1. Destination East St.
  2. Destination The Grove.
41-91-15 EVENING CHRONICLE/NEWCASTLE 1991
Yellow body, maroon chassis, cream roof and windows, Evening
Chronicle upper, Newcastle Transport lower logo.
41-91-16 EVENING TELEGRAPH/DERBY 1991
Dark green body, cream . . ., Evening Telegraph upper, Derby
Corporation lower logo.
41-91-17 G B MODELS/BRIDGEND 1991
Black body, gold . . ., GB Models upper, Bridgend & District lower
logo.
  1. Destination Bridgend.
  2. Destination Sandwell.
41-91-18 HARRY RAMSDEN 1991
Blue body, chassis and roof, cream windows, Harry Ramsden's, the
world's most famous fish & chips logo.
41-91-19 HIGHGATE ALE/WALSALL 1991
Dark blue body . . ., Highgate Ale upper, Walsall Corporation lower
logo.
  1. Destination Bloxwich.
  2. Destination Leamore.
41-91-20 LEEDS MERCURY DAILY 1991
Yellow body, maroon chassis, light gray roof, white windows, The
Leeds Mercury Daily upper, coat of arms on lower logo.
  1. Destination City Square.
  2. Destination Whitehall Road.
41-91-21 LLEDO PROMOTIONAL/LONDON 1991
Red body, chassis and roof, cream windows, Lledo Promotional,
Sandwell 1991 upper, London Transport lower logo.
  1. Destination Enfield.
  2. Destination Ponders End.
41-91-22 MULLION MODEL MUSEUM 1991
Blue body, red . . ., white . . .
  1. Destination Bay West City.
  2. Destination Mullion.
41-91-23 N. E. C. TOYFAIR/COVENTRY 1991
Maroon body, cream . . ., NEC Toyfair upper, Coventry lower logo,
destination Solihull.
41-91-24 NEWS OF THE WORLD/LONDON 1991
Red body, chassis and roof, cream windows, News of the World
upper, London Transport lower logo, destination Hampton Court.
41-91-25 A. E. REEDER/LONDON 1991
Red body . . ., A. E. Reeder's, London Transport lower logo.
  1. Destination Kingston.
  2. Destination Worcester Park.
41-91-26 ROTHERHAM STAR 1991
Dark blue body, chassis and roof, cream windows, The Rotherham
Star upper, Rotherham Corporation Transport logo, destination
Ickles.

41-91-27 ST. JULIANS/LLOYD? 1991
Maroon body, cream . . .
41-91-28 SANDOWN TOY/LONDON 1991
Red body, black . . ., Sandown Toy upper, London United lower logo.
  1. Destination Esher.
  2. Destination Sandown.
41-91-29 SPORTS ARGUS/WALSALL 1991
Blue body, chassis, roof and windows, Sports Argus upper, Walsall
Corporation lower logo.
41-91-30 STONELEIGH TOY/LEICESTER 1991
Cream body, red . . ., Stoneleigh Toy upper, Leicester lower logo.
41-91-31 TRITON SHOWERS 1991
Blue body . . .
  1. Destination Nuneaton.
  2. Destination Triton House.
41-91-32 TROLLEY BUS ASSOCIATION 1991
Blue body, gray . . .
41-91-33 V B MODELS 1991
White body, blue . . .
  1. Destination Sandwell.
  2. Destination Victoria
41-91-34 WALSALL ILLUMINATIONS (blue) 1991
Light blue body . . . (tampo-print).
41-91-35 WALSALL ILLUMINATIONS (green/red) 1991
Dark green body, red . . . (adhesive labels).
41-91-36 WALSALL MANOR HOSPITAL 1991
Dark green body . . ., H.R.H. Princess of Wales upper, Walsall Manor
Hospital lower logo, destination Manor Hospital.
41-92-1 3RD NEC 92 1992
Dark blue body, red . . . (See also NEC below.)
  1. Destination Bull Ring.
  2. Destination NEC.
41-92-2 ANADIN 1992
Green body, yellow . . ., destination Braydon Road.
41-92-3 BEAMISH MUSEUM 1992
Maroon body, black chassis, cream roof and windows, Beamish Open
Air Museum upper, Beamish Tramways lower logo.
41-92-4 BLACKPOOL BEACH 1992
White body . . .
41-92-5 BRITISH GAS 1992
Light blue body, cream . . ., British Gas upper, no lower logo.
  1. Destination Donington.
  2. Destination 1992.
41-92-6 CASTROL/DONCASTER 1992
Maroon body . . .
41-92-7 CLARENDON COLLEGE, NOTTINGHAM 1992
Dark green body and roof, black chassis, white windows, Clareodon,
Telelang, Bass Leisure, etc. upper, City of Nottingham lower logo.
  1. Destination Cinderhill.
  2. Destination Victoria Embankment.

41-92-8 DAILY ECHO/BOURNEMOUTH 1992
Yellow body, white . . ., Daily Echo upper, Bournemouth lower logo,
destination Bournemouth.
41-92-9 DOVE HOLES FESTIVAL 1992
Black body, gold chassis and roof, cream windows, Dove Holes
International Beer and Jazz Festival upper, North Western lower logo.
  1. Destination Buxton.
  2. Destination Dove.
41-92-10 ELAM SCHOOL 1992
Green body, yellow . . .
  1. Destination Canterbury.
  2. Destination Folkestone.
41-92-11 EVENING GAZETTE/TEESSIDE 1992
Dark green body . . ., Evening Gazette upper, Teesside Railless lower
logo.
41-92-12 EXCHANGE AND MART 1992
Red body. chassis, roof and windows, Exchange & Mart upper,
London Transport lower logo, destination Croydon.
41-92-13 FARNHAM SWAPMEET 1992
Red body . . ., Farnham (Maltings?) Swapmeet upper, London United
lower logo.
  1. Destination Maltings.
  2. Destination Square.
41-92-14 FISHERMAN'S FRIEND/FLEETWOOD 1992
White body, orange . . ., Fisherman's Friend upper, Fleetwood
Corporation lower logo.
  1. Destination Blackpool.
  2. Destination Festival.
41-92-15 HANCOCKS/CARDIFF 1992
Maroon body . . ., Hancocks upper, Cardiff lower logo.
  1. Destination Llandaff.
  2. Destination Victoria.
41-92-16 HEATHROW TOYFAIR 1992
Red body . . ., Heathrow Toyfair upper, London Transport lower logo.
  1. Destination Kempton.
  2. Destination Sunbury.
41-92-17 HEINZ TOMATO KETCHUP 1992
Red body and roof, black chassis, cream windows, there's no taste
like Heinz Tomato Ketchup upper, London Transport lower logo.
41-92-18 HUDDERSFIELD 1992
Red body and roof, black chassis, cream windows, no upper,
Huddersfield Corporation Transport lower logo.
  1. Destination Almondbury.
  2. Destination Waterloo.
41-92-19 KIDS ACROSS EUROPE 1992
Blue body, white . . ., red . . .
  1. Destination Chatham.
  2. Destination Peinze.
41-92-20 KLEENEX BOUTIQUE TISSUES 1992
Red body and roof, black chassis, white windows, Kleenex Boutique
Tissues upper, London Transport lower logo.

41-92-21 LAST TROLLEY/BRADFORD 1992
Light blue body . . ., Last Trolley upper, Bradford Corporation lower logo.
  1. Destination Duckworth.
  2. Destination Thornbury.
41-92-22 MAIDENHEAD S. M. C. 1992
Red body . . ., Maidenhead S.M.C. upper, London Transport lower logo, destination Tolworth.
41-92-23 MEXBOROUGH & SWINDON 85 YEARS 1992
Green body . . ., 85 Years upper, Mexborough & Swindon lower logo.
  1. Destination Mexborough.
  2. Destination Rawmarsh.
41-92-24 N E C 1992
Navy blue body, cream . . . (See also 3rd NEC above.)
  1. destination NEC.
  2. Destination Snow Hill.
41-92-25 NORTHAMPTON G. H. 1992
Maroon body . . .
41-92-26 NOTTINGHAM BATTALION 1992
Dark green body and roof, black chassis, cream windows, Nottingham Battalion upper, Nottingham coat of arms lower logo.
41-92-27 PILGRIM HOSPITAL 1992
White body, blue . . .
  1. Destination Boston.
  2. Destination Hospital.
41-92-28 PILKINGTON CYCLE 1992
Yellow body, black . . .
  1. Destination Milk Race.
  2. Destination Tour de France.
41-92-29 QUEEN ELIZABETH: 40 YEARS 1992
Maroon body, gold . . .
  1. Destination Const . . .
  2. Destination The Mall.
41-92-30 ST. DAVIDS FOUNDATION 1992
Red body . . .
41-92-31 ST. GEORGE'S SCANNER APPEAL 1992
White body, chassis, roof and windows, St. George's Scanner Appeal upper, 1992 and emblems lower logo.
  1. Destination St. George.
  2. Destination Tooting.
41-92-32 SALVATION ARMY/GRIMSBY 1992
Dark blue body, white . . ., Salvation Army upper, Grimsby lower logo.
  1. Destination Duncombe.
  2. Destination East Marsh.
41-92-33 SCALEXTRIC CLUB 1992
Black body, yellow . . .
  1. Destination Brands Hatch.
  2. Destination Silverstone.

41-92-34 SCOTTISH DAILY EXPRESS 1992
Orange body, black chassis, green roof and windows, Stay in front, Scottish Daily Express upper, Glasgow coat of arms lower logo.
  1. Destination Hampden.
  2. Destination Queens Cross.
41-92-35 SILVER QUEEN 1992
Silver body, black chassis, white roof and windows, no upper (just stripes), Silver Queen lower logo.
  1. Destination Brace Bridge.
  2. Destination Lincoln.
41-92-36 TELEGRAPH AND ARGUS/BRADFORD 1992
Light blue body, chassis and roof, white windows, 1992 Telegraph & Argus upper, Bradford lower logo.
  1. Destination Bradford.
  2. destination Morecambe.
41-92-37 TELEPHONE CARD CLUB 1992
White body and windows, black chassis, yellow roof, The Telephone Card Club upper, credit card design lower logo.
41-92-38 TOYTOWN MODELS 1992
Yellow body, red . . .
  1. Destination Bridlington.
  2. Destination Leeds.
41-92-39 WATSONS/NEWCASTLE 1992
Yellow body, cream . . ., Watsons upper, Newcastle lower logo.
  1. Destination Byker.
  2. Destination Parkside.
41-93-1 ABBEY LIGHT RAIL 1993
Navy blue body, gray . . ., two destinations?
41-93-2 BEAMISH TRAMWAYS 1993
Blue body, black chassis, cream roof and windows, Beamish upper, Beamish Tramways lower logo.
41-93-3 BRADFORD CORPORATION 1993
Dark blue body, white . . ., Parcel Department upper, Bradford Corporation lower logo.
  1. Destination Clayton.
  2. Destination Odsall.
41-93-4 DAIRY FARM/DONCASTER 1993
Dark blue body and roof, maroon chassis, cream windows, Dairy Farm Quality Hampers are Best upper, County Borough of Doncaster lower logo, destination Woolwich.
41-93-5 EXPRESS & STAR/BIRMINGHAM 1993
Dark blue body, cream . . ., Express & Star upper, Birmingham Corporation lower logo, destination Nechells.
41-93-6 HORNBY 1993
Red body, yellow . . ., destination Binns Road.
41-93-7 LANCASTER 800 1993
Tan body, maroon . . ., two destinations?
41-93-8 NEWS OF THE WORLD 1993
Red body and roof, black chassis, cream windows, News of the World upper, London Transport lower logo.

41-93-9 REVELL 1993
White body, yellow . . .
  1. Destination Kitts.
  2. Destination Revell.
41-93-10 SERVICE INTEG... 1993
Dark blue body, orange . . .
  1. Destination Broad Quay.
  2. Destination Harry Stone.
41-93-11 SOUTH WALES FESTIVAL
Maroon body, cream . . .
  1. Destination Abertillery.
  2. Destination Ebbw Vale.
41-94-1 BARCLAYS BANK 1994
Light blue body . . .
41-94-2 E R A PARTNERSHIP 1994
Navy blue body, light tan roof and windows, black chassis, ERA Partnership Against Crime, Neighborhood Watch upper, coat of arms lower logo.
  1. Destination Old Square.
  2. Destination Station Street.
41-94-3 MIAMI MODES 1994
Maroon body and roof, black chassis, cream windows, Miami Modes Department Store upper, Weatherfield & City lower logo.
41-94-4 RADIO TIMES 1994
Red body and chassis, cream roof and windows, Radio Times/BBC emblem upper, London United lower logo, House of Eliott box.
41-94-5 ST. DAVID'S 1994
Yellow body, light blue . . .
41-94-6 TOM COBLEIGH/MANSFIELD 1994
Green body, cream chassis, roof and windows, Tom Cobleigh upper, Mansfield & District lower logo.
41-94-7 WALSALL POLICE 1994
Light blue body . . .
  1. Destination Bloxwich.
  2. Destination Walsall.
42 MACK TANK TRUCK 1990
42-90-1 CASTROL 1990
Dark green body and tank, black chassis, Wakefield Castrol Motor Oils, The Masterpiece in Oils logo.
42-90-2 DAN-AIR 1990
Blue body and tank, white chassis, Dan-Air Scheduled Service logo.
42-90-3 RED CROWN 1990
Red body and tank, black chassis, RedCrown, The Gasoline Of Quality logo, emblem on door.
42-91-1 DOMINION 1991
Red body and chassis, blue tank, Dominion highly inflammable logo.
42-91-2 FOOD FLYING SQUAD 1991
Light gray body, chassis and tank, Food Flying Squad, Ministry of Food, U.S.A. to Britain logo, Allied Relief Fund emblem on doors.

42-91-3 UNIGATE 1991
Red body, white tank . . .
42-92-1 EXPRESS DAIRY 1992
Blue-black body and chassis, white tank, Express Dairy Milk logo.
42-92-2 SHELL FUEL OIL 1992
Red body and tank, black chassis, Shell Fuel Oil logo.
42-94-1 GUNGE TANKER MARK II 1994
Green cab, black chassis, cream tank, Crinkley Bottom Gunge Tanker logo, Crinkley Bottom box.
42-94-2 MARATHON OIL 1994
Dark blue body, red . . .
43 MORRIS 1937 VAN 1990
43-90-1 BROCK METAL 1990
White body, black . . .
43-90-2 DAIRY FARM 1990
Cream body, blue chassis and roof, Dairy Farm Rich Clean Milk logo.
43-90-3 DANEPAK 1990
White body, chassis and roof, Danepak logo, emblem on doors, Thetford 1965-1990 on rear.
43-90-4 EVENING SENTINEL 1990
Dark blue body, black . . .
43-90-5 LINCOLNSHIRE ECHO 1990
Red body, white roof, black chassis, Lincolnshire Echo logo.
43-90-6 ST. IVEL 1990
Yellow body, black . . .
43-90-7 SUNDERLAND STAR 1990
Red body, black . . .
43-91-1 ADVERTISER 1991
Red body, black chassis, white roof, Advertiser logo.
43-91-2 ANGLIAN WINDOW CENTRES 1991
White body, chassis and roof, Anglian window centres logo, emblem on doors.
43-91-3 ASDA BRITISH SAUSAGES 1991
Tan body, green . . .
43-91-4 BIRMINGHAM POLICE AMBULANCE 1991
Green body, white . . .
43-91-5 BRITISH RED CROSS, KENT BRANCH 1991
White body, roof and chassis, British Red Cross Society, Kent Branch Ambulance logo.
43-91-6 CAMBRIDGE MULTIMEDIA 1991
White body, dark blue . . .
43-91-7 CONWY TUNNEL OPENING 1991
Cream body, dark blue chassis and roof, Conwy Tunnel officially opened by HM Queen Elizabeth II logo in Welsh and English.
43-91-8 COVENTRY POLICE AMBULANCE 1991
Cream body, white . . .
43-91-9 HEMGLAS 1991
White body, blue chassis and roof, Hemglas logo.

43-91-10 INTERNATIONAL POLICE ASSOCIATION 1991
Green body, roof and chassis, The Kent Branch 25th Anniversary logo.
43-91-11 J. JONES FAMILY BUTCHER 1991
Dark blue body and chassis, cream roof, J. Jones Family Butcher, Waited on Daily logo.
43-91-12 NATIONAL ARMY MUSEUM 1991
Olive green body . . .
43-91-13 ROYAL MAIL--BYPOST 1991
Red body, black chassis and roof, Royal Mail logo, Post Office emblem, Bypost box.
43-91-14 SAXA TABLE SALT 1991
Red body, black chassis and roof, Saxa table salt logo.
43-91-15 S.R. EXPRESS PARCELS 1991
Dark green body, white . . .
43-91-16 TETLEY'S TEAS 1991
Blue body, black chassis, white roof, Tetley's Teas logo.
43-91-17 VALOR CALORFLAME 1991
Tan body, black . . .
43-92-1 ADAMS 1992
Cream body, green . . .
43-92-2 ARMLEY MILLS 1992
Pale yellow body, chassis and roof, Armley Mills Leeds logo.
43-92-3 BERRY BROTHERS AND RUDD 1992
Black body, white . . .
43-92-4 BRISTOW'S OF DEVON 1992
Dark blue body, blue . . .
43-92-5 CAITHNESS CRYSTAL 1992
White body, lilac . . .
43-92-6 CARNATION EVAPORATED MILK 1992
Red body, chassis and roof, Carnation Evaporated Milk, Since 1922 logo, Carnation from contented cows on rear.
43-92-7 ELIZABETH SHAW 1992
Cream body, dark blue chassis and roof, Elizabeth Shaw logo with coat of arms.
43-92-8 EXCHANGE AND MART 1992
Green body, black chassis and roof, Exchange and Mart Weekly Paper, The Bazaar logo, 2d every Thursday on doors.
43-92-9 EXPRESS DAIRY 1992
Blue-black body and chassis, white roof, Express Dairy non-combine logo.
43-92-10 HADRIAN CRYSTAL 1992
Blue body, black . . .
43-92-11 HARRY RAMSDEN 1992
No data.
43-92-12 HULL DAILY MAIL 1992
Red body . . .
43-92-13 JOSEPH LUCAS 1992
Dark green body, white . . .

43-92-14 KLEENEX FOR MEN 1992
Black body, chassis and roof, Kleenex Tissues for men logo.
43-92-15 KODAK 1992
White body, light blue . . .
43-92-16 LANCASHIRE CONSTABULARY 1992
Cream body, navy blue . . .
43-92-17 NORTH LONDON DISTRICT 1992
White body . . .
43-92-18 NORTHCLIFFE NEWSPAPERS 1992
White body, red . . .
43-92-19 PORK FARMS 1992
Creen body, black chassis and roof, Pork Farms, Much Prized Quality logo, gold medals on doors.
43-92-20 RINGTONS TEA 1992
Black body, yellow chassis and roof, Ringtons Tea logo, Ringtons Tea Merchants on rear.
43-92-21 ROYAL WORCESTER 1992
Blue body, white roof, black chassis, Royal Worcester Porcelain logo.
43-92-22 W. H. SMITH & SON 1992
Red body, black chassis, white roof, W. H. Smith & Son logo, emblem on roof and rear, 200 Years box.
43-92-23 SOUTH STAFFORDSHIRE WATER 1992
Dark green body, black . . .
43-92-24 WEETAFLAKES 1992
Red body, blue chassis and roof, Weetabix Weetaflakes logo.
43-92-25 WHEELSPIN 100TH EDITION 1992
Cream body, maroon chassis and roof, Wheelspin Magazine 100th Edition, House Journal of Coventry Diecast Model Club logo.
43-92-26 WILTSHIRE CONSTABULARY 1992
Green body, black chassis, white roof, Wiltshire Constabulary Ambulance logo.
43-92-27 WOLVERHAMPTON POLICE 1992
Dark blue body, black . . .
43-92-28 WORTH RAILWAY 1992
Maroon body, cream . . .
43-93-1 CAITHNESS CRYSTAL 1993
White body, green . . .
43-93-2 CASTROL 1993
Dark green body and roof . . .
43-93-3 CITY OF LONDON POLICE AMBULANCE 1993
Cream body, black chassis and roof, City of London Police ambulance, City Police Hospital, Bishopsgate logo.
43-93-4 DUNLOP TYRES 1993
Tan body, black . . .
43-93-5 GO GREAT WESTERN 1993
Brown body and roof . . .
43-93-6 GOD SAVE THE QUEEN 1993
Dark green body and roof, black chassis, Buckingham Palace and Coronation Souvenir logo, God Save The Queen box.

43-93-7 GWR COUNTRY CARTAGE 1993
Brown body, _____ chassis, cream roof, GWR emblem, Country Cartage Services and Shakespeare Express logo.
43-93-8 NORTHUMBRIA AMBULANCE 1993
Cream body and roof . . .
43-93-9 NSPCC/UNIGATE 1993
Blue body and roof, red chassis, Unigate emblem, NSPCC and working together to prevent cruelty to children logo.
43-93-10 PETERS ICE CREAM 1993
Dark green body, black . . .
43-93-11 PORT OF LONDON AUTHORITY 1993
Cream body and roof, black chassis, Port of London Autoority emblem and Ambulance logo.
43-93-12 PORTSEA ISLAND 1993
Dark blue body, cream . . .
43-93-13 ROYAL NATIONAL LIFE-BOAT INSTITUTION 1993
Yellow body and roof, black chassis, Free Lantern Lecture, Royal National Life-Boat Institution logo.
43-93-14 SOMERSET GAZETTE 1993
Blue body and roof . . .
43-93-15 TREBOR MINTS 1993
White body, silver . . .
43-93-16 WORCESTER CITY POLICE 1993
Navy blue body and roof . . .
43-93-17 YORKSHIRE TEA 1993
Orange body, black . . .
43-94-1 ABERCONWY CENTER 1994
Tan body, black . . .
43-94-2 ACTION 1994
Navy blue body, yellow . . .
43-94-3 ADAMS/SAVE THE CHILDREN 1994
Blue body, red . . ., yellow . . .
43-94-4 AUTO TRADER 1994
No data.
43-94-5 BARCLAYS BANK 1994
Light blue body . . .
43-94-6 BIRMINGHAM CO-OP BAKERY 1994
Dark green body, cream . . .
43-94-7 CHESSINGTON 1994
Blue body, cream . . .
43-94-8 CITY OF SHEFFIELD 1994
Black body, chassis and roof . . .
43-94-9 CRUMPSALL CREAM CRACKERS 1994
Green body, black chassis and roof, Crumpsall Cream Crackers logo.
43-94-10 ELECTROLUX 75TH 1994
White body, silver . . ., blue . . .
43-94-11 HAMMERITE RUST BEATER 1994
Brown body, white . . .

43-94-12 ILKESTON CO-OP 1994
Dark green body, black . . .
43-94-13 LEWIS D M R 1994
White body, yellow roof and chassis, Lewis DMR logo.
43-94-14 LILLIPUT LANE 1994
Brown body, cream . . .
43-94-15 PETERBOROUGH CO-OP GROCERY 1994
Maroon body, cream . . .
43-94-16 THE REPOSITORY 1994
Dark blue body, black . . .
43-94-17 SEA SALTER 1994
Cream body, brown . . .
43-94-18 STANLEY GIBBONS 1994
Blue body, white . . .
44 SCAMMELL SIX-WHEELER 1990
44-90-1 KLEENEX MAXI DRI 1990
White body and roof, black chassis, Kleenex Maxi Dri logo.
44-91-1 BISTO 1991
Dark brown body, black chassis, cream roof, Bisto for all Meat Dishes logo.
44-91-2 BRITISH COMMERCIAL VEHICLE 1991
Dark green body, black . . .
44-91-3 DAIRY FARM MILK 1991
Cream body, blue chassis and roof, Dairy Farm logo.
44-91-4 HUMBER BRIDGE 1991
White body, blue . . .
44-91-5 LOVE ROMANIA 1991
White body and roof . . .
44-91-6 R. S. MALCOLM BREAD 1991
Pale tan body, red chassis and roof, R. S. Malcolm Quality Bread, Banbury Cakes logo.
44-91-7 ROYAL MAIL/BYPOST 1991
Red body, black chassis and roof, Royal Mail logo, Bypost box.
44-91-8 TRANSPORT 91 1991
Tan body, brown . . .
44-91-9 VIMTO 1991
Black body and roof, red chassis, Vimto logo.
44-91-10 WINCANTON 1991
White body, light blue . . .
44-91-11 YOUNGS CASH & CARRY 1991
Light blue body and roof . . .
44-92-1 ALBANIA RELIEF 1992
Dark blue body, white . . .
44-92-2 CHRISTMAS CHILD 1992
White body, black . . .
44-92-3 DAVID SUMNER TRANSPORT 1992
Blue body, chassis and roof, David Sumner Transport logo.
44-92-4 ENFIELD PAGEANT OF MOTORING 1992
Cream body, dark green . . .

44-92-5 EXCHANGE AND MART 1992
Cream body, orange-brown chassis, light brown roof, Exchange & Mart, only 2d weekly logo.
44-92-6 JOHN AIREY DIE-CASTS 1992
Blue body, black . . .
44-92-7 LLEDO SHOW 92 1992
Cream body, green . . .
44-92-8 PRESTON GUILD 1992
White body, blue . . .
44-92-9 SHOWGARD MOUNTS 1992
Blue body and roof . . .
44-92-10 TOYMASTER 1992
Dark green body and roof . . .
44-92-11 WALSALL ILLUMINATIONS 1992
Cream body, green . . .
44-92-12 WEETAFLAKES 1992
Yellow body, red chassis and roof, Weetabix Weetaflakes, crunchy whole wheat flakes logo.
44-93-1 3M 1993
Red body and roof . . .
44-93-2 ABERCONWY-LLANDUDNO 1993
Tan body, black . . .
44-93-3 ALTON MOVES 1993
Orange body and roof . . .
44-93-4 BARTRUMS 1993
Blue body and roof . . .
44-93-5 B H B N 1993
Red body, white . . .
44-93-6 GEORGE NEWNES 1993
Red body and roof . . .
44-93-7 GO DUTCH 93 1993
Black body, white . . ., red . . .
44-93-8 GOD SAVE THE QUEEN 1993
Maroon body, black chassis and roof, Westminster Abbey and coronation souvenir logo, God Save the Queen box.
44-93-9 GREAT DORSET STEAM FAIR 1993
Maroon body and roof . . .
44-93-10 HARRY RAMSDEN 1993
Red body, white . . .
44-93-11 T. HUGHES 1993
Cream body, red . . .
44-93-12 HULL TRUCK THEATRE 1993
Light blue body, white . . .
44-93-13 IND COOPE BURTON 1993
Green body, black . . .
44-93-14 JOHNNIE WALKER 1993
Navy blue body, chassis? and roof, Johnnie Walker Established 1820 logo.
44-93-15 MORLAND BREWERY 1993
No data.

44-93-16 NETLEFOLDS 1993
White body and roof . . .
44-93-17 POLARINE--AMOCO 1993
Navy blue body and roof . . .
44-93-18 PUNJANA TEA 1993
Red body, cream . . .
44-93-19 TURNBULLS 1993
Green body, black . . .
44-93-20 WADDINGTONS PUZZLES 1993
Blue body, red . . .
44-94-1 BENSKINS BREWERY 1994
No data.
44-94-2 THE BIG PORK PIE 1994
Tan body, green chassis and roof, True False and The Big Pork Pie logo.
44-94-3 CARTERS STEAM FAIR 1994
Maroon body, cream . . .
44-94-4 EDDIE STOBART 1994
Green body, red . . .
44-94-5 EVANS TRANSPORT 1994
Green body, red chassis, Evans Transport Ltd. logo.
44-94-6 EXPERT PRODUCTS 1994
White body . . .
44-94-7 FREIGHT TRANSPORT ASSOCIATION 1994
Black body, chassis . . .
44-94-8 GARTH 1994
Light blue body and roof, dark blue chassis, Garth logo with figure.
44-94-9 I.A.D. 1994
White body, red . . .
44-94-10 LIONS CLUB OF NORTH WALES 1994
Silver body, yellow . . .
44-94-11 NOTTINGHAM GOOSE FAIR 1994
Green body, black . . .
44-94-12 PADDERS 1994
Cream body, navy blue . . .
44-94-13 PICKFORDS 1994
Navy blue body, white . . .
44-94-14 PULLMAN FOODS 1994
White body, green . . .
44-94-15 C. SALVESON 1994
White body, blue . . .
44-94-16 SOUTHPORT FLOWER SHOW 1994
Cream body, red . . .
44-94-17 TOYTOWN MODELS 1994
Yellow body, red . . .
44-94-18 UNITED DAIRIES 1994
Orange body, black . . .
44-94-19 WADDINGTONS PUZZLES 1994
Blue body, red . . .
45 ROLLS-ROYCE SILVER GHOST COUPE 199_

45-94-1 HOUSE OF ELIOTT 1994
Green body, chassis and windshield, no logo, House of Eliott box.
46 BENTLEY 4.5 LITRE 1991
46-91-1 SARAH AND MARK 1991
Dark green body and chassis . . .
46-92-1 BROOKLANDS 85 1992
Dark green body and chassis, cream seats, black #85 and Union Jack logo, Brooklands box.
46-94-1 CREAM AND TAN 1994
Cream body, tan chassis . . .
47 AUSTIN 1933 TAXI 1991
47-92-1 BLACKPOOL PLEASURE BEACH 1992
White body . . .
47-93-1 68-X 1993
Navy blue body, black chassis . . .
47-94-1 CRINKLEY BOTTOM TAXI 1994
Dark brown body and chassis, tan top, Wait till I get you home logo, Crinkley Bottom box.
47-94-2 MARS 1994
Black body, chassis and roof, Mars logo, in candy box.
47-94-3 TURTLE WAX 1994
Black body and chassis . . .
48 CHEVROLET 1939 CAR 1991
48-94-1 SNICKERS 1994
Red body, brown chassis . . .
49 AEC RENOWN DOUBLEDECK BUS 1991
49-91-1 CITY OF COVENTRY 1991
Maroon body, cream roof and windows, City of Coventry logo, destination 2 Radford.
49-91-2 EXPRESS & STAR/WOLVERHAMPTON 1991
Green body, yellow . . ., Express & Star and Wolverhampton Corporation logo.
49-92-1 2ND NEC TOY AND TRAIN 1992
Navy blue body, cream roof and windows, 2nd Toy and Train Extravaganza, National Exhibition Centre upper, Birmingham City Transport lower logo.
    1. Destination Bull Ring.
    2. Destination NEC.
49-92-2 ANADIN PARACETAMOL 1992
Blue body, light blue . . ., Anadin Paracetamol upper logo, destination Wrafton.
49-92-3 BEAULIEUFULL/GENERAL 1992
Red body, silver . . ., Beaulieufull upper, General lower logo, destination 1992.
49-92-4 BRIDLINGTON/EAST YORKSHIRE 1993
Blue-black body and roof, black chassis, cream windows, Bridlington frequent services to Hull upper, East Yorkshire lower logo, destination Hull.
49-92-5 BRITISH BUSES/DONCASTER 1992
Maroon body . . ., British Buses upper, Doncaster Corporation lower logo.

49-92-6 BROADLAND COLLECTION/EASTERN COUNTIES 1992
Red body, white . . ., Broadland Collection upper, Eastern Counties lower logo.
49-92-7 CAR CRIME/REGENT SCHOOL 1992
Red body . . ., Car Crime logo, destination Regent School.
49-92-8 CITY OF BIRMINGHAM POLICE 1992
Navy blue body, cream . . ., City of Birmingham Police upper, City of Birmingham lower logo.
    1. Destination Kitts Green.
    2. Destination Outer Circle.
49-92-9 CUCKOO FAYRE 1992
Yellow body . . ., Cuckoo Fayre upper logo.
    1. Destination Eastbourne.
    2. Destination Pevensey.
49-92-10 DAIRY FARM/LONDON 1992
Red body, black chassis, silver roof, cream windows, Dairy Farm quality hampers are best upper, London Transport lower logo, destination 7 Windsor Slough.
49-92-11 DERBYSHIRE CONSTABULARY 1992
Blue body and roof, black chassis, white windows, Griffith Laboratories & the Derbyshire Constabulary upper, Derbyshire Constabulary lower logo.
    1. Destination Langley.
    2. Destination Somercote.
49-92-12 EAST LANCASHIRE RAILWAY/BURY CORP. 1992
Light green body and roof, black chassis, cream windows. East Lancashire Railway upper, Bury Corporation lower logo.
    1. Destination Bury.
    2. Destination Jericho.
49-92-13 EPM/NOTTINGHAM CITY 1992
Dark green body . . ., EPM and Nottingham City logo.
49-92-14 EVENING SENTINEL/PMT 1992
Red body, cream . . ., Evening Sentinel upper, P M T lower logo.
    1. Destination Hanley.
    2. Destination Stoke.
49-92-15 G B MODELS/BRIDGEND 1992
Black body, gold . . ., G B Models upper, Bridgend & District lower logo.
    1. Destination Bridgend.
    2. Destination Swindon.
49-92-16 GRAY LINE TOURS/SAN FRANCISCO 1992
Red body . . ., San Francisco upper, Gray Line Tours lower logo, destination Gray Line.
49-92-17 JAX 1982-92-LONDON TRANSPORT 1992
Red body . . ., Jax 1982-92 upper, London Transport lower logo.
    1. Destination Harrow.
    2. Destination Picketts.
49-92-18 LEICESTER MERCURY/CITY OF LEICESTER 1992

Maroon body and chassis, cream roof and windows, Leicester Mercury largest circulation upper, City of Leicester Tramways lower logo, destination 31 Evington.

49-92-19 LIVERPOOL FOOTBALL CLUB 1992
Red body, silver . . ., destination Sunderland.

49-92-20 MANOR LEAS/LINCOLN 1992
Green body, cream . . ., Manor Leas School upper, Lincoln Transport lower logo.
1. Destination Lincoln.
2. Destination School.

49-92-21 MARS/LONDON TRANSPORT 1992
Red body and roof, black chassis, cream windows, Mars are marvelous upper, London Transport lower logo, destination Regent Street.

49-92-22 NORTH LONDON HOSPICE 1992
Red body and roof, North London Hospice upper, London Transport lower logo.

49-92-23 NOTTINGHAM CITY/NOTTS INTERNATIONAL 1992
Green body and roof, black chassis, cream windows, Notts International above, Nottingham City Transport below.
1. Destination Market Square.
2. Destination University.

49-92-24 P. & O. EUROPEAN/LONDON 1992
Red body, black chassis, silver roof, white windows, P & O European Ferries upper, London Transport lower logo, destination Liverpool St. 9.

49-92-25 PHOTOKINA 1992
Red body and roof . . ., Pkotokina logo, destination Ko"ln.

49-92-26 SILVER QUEEN 1992
Silver body, black chassis, white roof and windows, Silver queen lower and rear logo.
1. Destination Grantham.
2. Destination Sleaford.

49-92-27 SOUTHPORT 200 1992
Red body, cream . . ., Southport 200 upper, Southport Corporation lower logo.
1. Destination Pleasure.
2. Destination Scarisbri.

49-92-28 TRANSPORT 92 1992
Dark blue body, silver . . ., Transport 92 upper logo.

49-92-29 UNITED DAIRIES 1992
Red body and roof, black chassis, cream windows, A United Dairies milkman serves in every London street upper, London Transport lower logo, destination Liverpool Street.

49-92-30 WALSALL OBSERVER 1992
Light blue body . . ., Walsall Observer upper, Walsall Corporation lower logo, destination Aldridge.

49-92-31 YORKSHIRE EVENING POST/LEEDS 1992
Cream body, silver . . ., Yorkshire Evening Post and Leeds City Tramway logo.

1. Destination City.
2. Destination Cross Gate.

49-93-1 ANADIN (Portugal) 1993
Red body, yellow chassis, roof and windows?, Anadia 1962-1992 upper, 30 Years Brand Leader and Whitehall lower logo, destination Taplow.

49-93-2 BARCLAYS/OXFORD 1993
White body, black . . ., Barclays upper, Oxford Bus Co. lower logo.
1. Destination Botley.
2. Destination Carfax.

49-93-3 CASTROL/GREEN LINE 1993
Green body and roof, black chassis, cream windows, Castrol, the Masterpiece in Oils upper, Green Line lower logo.

49-93-4 EVENING TELEGRAPH/LINCOLNSHIRE 1993
Dark green body and roof . . ., Evening Telegraph upper, Lincolnshire lower logo.
1. Destination Grimsby.
2. Destination Scunthorpe.

49-93-5 EXCHANGE & MART/BIRMINGHAM 1993
Dark blue body, black chassis, cream roof and windows, The Exchange & Mart Every Thursday upper, Birmingham City Transport lower logo, destination Colmore Row.

49-93-6 GUIDE DOGS 1993
Yellow body, red . . ., Guide Dogs upper logo.
1. Destination Blackbrook.
2. Destination Clennon.

49-93-7 MILWALL FOOTBALL CLUB 1993
White body, yellow . . ., blue . . .

49-93-8 NORTHAMPTON CORPORATION 1993
Red body, black chassis, silver roof, white windows, Northampton Corporation logo.
1. Destination Abingdon.
2. Destination All Saints.

49-93-9 OXFORD MAIL 1993
White body and roof . . ., Oxford Mail upper, Oxford Bus Co. lower logo, destination Park Ride.

49-93-10 PRIMROSE HOSPICE 1993
Yellow body, green . . ., Primrose Hospice upper logo.
1. Destination 144.
2. Destination X15.

49-93-11 PUNJANA TEA/GENERAL 1993
Red body and roof . . ., Punjana Tea upper, General lower logo, destination High St. 72.

49-93-12 QUEEN ELIZABETH II 1993
Red body, silver . . ., Queen Elizabeth II upper, General lower logo, destination 399 Strand.

49-93-13 SANDWELL POLICE/WEST BROMWICH 1993
Navy blue body, cream . . ., destination Britannia.

49-93-14 WITHAM MODELS/LINCOLNSHIRE 1993
Dark green body and roof . . ., Witham Models upper, Lincolnshire lower logo, destination Lincoln 6.

49-94-1 ANTHONY NOLAN 1994
Blue body, black chassis, white roof and windows, The anthony Nolan Bone Marrow Trust upper, London Transport lower logo.

49-94-2 APPLE APPEAL/UNITED 1994
Dark green body . . .
1. Destination Belfast.
2. Destination Bristol.

49-94-3 BEAULIEU USA 1994
Red body . . ., destination Lymington.

49-94-4 BEAULIEUFUL UK 1994
Red body, silver . . ., destination 1994.

43-94-5 CHELSEA FOOTBALL CLUB 1994
Blue body . . ., The Blues lower logo, destination Stamford.

49-94-6 CHESSINGTON/LONDON 1994
Red body . . ., London Transport lower logo.

49-94-7 CHURCHILLS/LONDON 1994
Red body . . ., London Transport lower logo, destination London

49-94-8 EXAMINER/ISLE OF MAN 1994
Cream body, red . . ., destination Ramsey.

49-94-9 HELP LONDON CHILD 1994
Red body . . ., London Transport lower logo, destination Barbican.

49-94-10 HERTS MERCURY 1994
Blue body, white . . .

49-94-11 IPSWICH TOWN FOOTBALL CLUB 1994
Dark blue body, red . . ., Ipswich town lower logo.

49-94-12 MAKE AND MOVE/JMT 1994
Blue body, white . . .

49-94-13 MAN CITY FOOTBALL CLUB 1994
Light blue body, white . . .

49-94-14 MANCHESTER UNITED F.C. 1994
Red body, black . . .
1. Destination Old Traff.
2. Destination Wembley.

49-94-15 MUCH ADO TOYS/STRATFORD BLUE 1994
Light blue body . . .,
1. Destination Stratford.
2. Destination Warwick.

49-94-15 NEALS TOYS 1994
Cream body . . .

49-94-16 RDP 10TH ANNIVERSARY 1994
Red body, silver roof, cream chassis, RDP Publications 1984 1994 upper, Halesowen lower logo, destination Limited Edition.

49-94-17 SANDWELL POLICE/MIDLAND 1994
Red body, silver . . .
1. Destination Bearwood.
2. Destination Spon Croft.

49-94-18 WEST BROM POLICE 1994
Red body, silver . . ., Midland lower logo.
1. Destination Sandwell.
2. Destination S. Olympic.

50 MORRIS BULLNOSE VAN 1992
The second color listed may be that of the chassis, roof or both.
50-92-1 CANNES 1992 1992
White body, black . . .
50-92-2 CAPTAIN'S COLLECTION 1992
Black body, chassis and roof, Captain's Collection Toy & Model
Dealers logo.
50-92-3 COVENTRY POLICE 1992
Navy blue body, white . . .
50-92-4 DAIRY FARM MILK 1992
Dark blue body, dark red chassis, white roof, Dairy Farm logo with
milk can.
50-92-5 DORSET CONSTABULARY 1992
Black body, chassis and roof . . .
50-92-6 EAST YORKSHIRE ENGINEERING 1992
Blue-black body, black chassis, cream roof, East Yorkshire
Engineering Department logo with poster.
50-92-7 EVENING TELEGRAPH 1992
Red body, black chassis, white roof, Evening Telegraph Logo.
50-92-8 GAINSBOROUGH SCOUTS 1992
Yellow body, green . . .
50-92-9 HARRY RAMSDEN 1992
Maroon body, white . . .
50-92-10 MERSEY TUNNEL 1992
Red body, black . . .
50-92-11 NESTLE'S MILK 1992
White body, blue chassis and roof, Nestle's Milk logo.
50-92-12 NEWS OF THE WORLD 1992
White body, red chassis and roof, Read the News of the World logo.
50-92-13 OUTLOOK FOUNDATION 1992
White body, blue . . .
50-92-14 PUSSERS RUM 1992
Dark blue body, white . . .
50-92-15 H. SAMUEL JEWELLER 1992
Black body and roof, red chassis, H. Samuel, The Empire's Largest
Jeweller logo.
50-92-16 SOUTHPORT FLOWER SHOW 1992
Tan body, green . . .
50-92-17 SOUTHPORT MODEL RAIL 1992
Black body, yellow . . .
50-92-18 STANDARD FIREWORKS 1992
Dark blue body, light blue
50-93-1 3M SCOTCH BRITE 1993
Maroon body, cream . . .
50-93-2 ABACUS FROZEN FOODS 1993
White body, black . . .
50-93-3 ABBEY LIGHT RAILWAY 1993
Maroon body, black . . .
50-93-4 ABERDEEN FISH FESTIVAL 1993
White body, red . . .

50-93-5 AEROGRAMME 1993
Blue body, red chassis, white roof . . .
50-93-6 ALTON FIRE BRIGADE 1993
Red body and roof . . .
50-93-7 ANTHONY NOLAN 1993
White body, black . . ., blue . . .
50-93-8 AUTO TRADER 1993
Green body, red . . .
50-93-9 AYRSHIRE SECURITY ALARMS 1993
Green body and roof, black chassis, Ayrshire Security Alarms logo.
50-93-10 BARTON TIMBER 1993
Tan body, red . . .
50-93-11 BATTERSEA DOGS HOME 1993
Red body, black chassis, tan roof . . .
50-93-12 BERNI CLASSIC 1993
Cream body, green . . .
50-93-13 BEAULIEU 1993
Dark blue body, cream . . .
50-93-14 BIG BEN BAR 1993
White body, blue . . .
50-93-15 BILLYS 1993
Silver body and roof . . .
50-93-16 BILLYS 93 1993
Silver body, maroon . . .
50-93-17 BRADFORD SCOUTS 1993
Green body, gray . . .
50-93-18 BRIAN YEO & SON 1993
Cream body, green chassis and roof, Brian Yeo & Son logo.
50-93-19 BRITISH SAILORS SOCIETY 1993
White body, blue . . .
50-93-20 THE BUTTY BASKET 1993
White body, black . . .
50-93-21 CAITHNESS CRYSTAL 1993
White body, green . . ., magenta . . .
50-93-22 CANNON IRON FOUNDRIES 1993
Brown body, black . . .
50-93-23 CARBURETTOR HOSPITAL 1993
White body, black . . .
50-93-24 CASTROL 1993
Green body and roof . . .
50-93-25 CENTURION 1993
Pink body, black . . .
50-93-26 CHAPPIE 1993
Yellow body, brown chassis, red roof . . .
50-93-27 CHIPPERFIELDS 1993
Blue body, red . . .
50-93-28 F. COOKE EEL MERCHANTS 1993
Green body, tan . . .
50-93-29 COUGHLIN BUTCHERS 1993
White body, black . . .

50-93-30 CRAVEN OLD WHEELS 1993
Black body, chassis and roof . . .
50-93-31 CRAYFORD SCOUTS 1993
Green body, white . . .
50-93-32 CYCLE MUSEUM 1993
Dark green body, black . . .
50-93-33 DAYS GONE INTERNATIONAL SHOW 1993
Yellow body, green chassis and roof, Days Gone International Show
& Auction logo.
50-93-34 DENNIS FILM DELIVERY 1993
White body, light blue chassis and roof, Dennis Film Delivery
Service logo.
50-93-35 D R S HEATING 1993
White body, maroon . . .
50-93-36 DRUNK'N N DUCK 1993
Yellow body, blue . . ., white . . .
50-93-37 EAST ANGLIAN GUNNERS 1993
Blue body, red . . ., yellow . . .
50-93-38 EAST KENT GUNNERS 1993
Red body, black . . .
50-93-39 ELIZABETH SHAW 1993
Cream body, navy blue . . .
50-93-40 ESSEX FIRE BRIGADE 1993
Red body, white . . .
50-93-41 ESSEX RADIO 1993
White body, red . . .
50-93-42 EVENING POST 1993
Red body, white . . .
50-93-43 EXCHANGE AND MART 1993
Red body, black chassis and roof, Exchange and Mart logo, Since
1868 on doors.
50-93-44 FAIRFORD STEAM 1993
Black body, chassis and roof . . .
50-93-45 FATHER CHRISTMAS 1993
White body, black chassis, red roof . . .
50-93-46 FLOWERS BY AMANDA 1993
Reddish-brown body, cream . . .
50-93-47 FRED DIBNAH 1993
Dark green body, black . . .
50-93-48 GERRY COTTLES CIRCUS 1993
Yellow body, red . . .
50-93-49 GIRL GUIDES (LINCS-HUMBER) 1993
Blue body, yellow . . . (Healing District?)
50-93-50 GRIMEWATCH 1993
Blue body, red . . .
50-93-51 GUERNSEY POLICE 1994
Navy blue body and roof . . .
50-93-52 HAIR DESIGN 1993
No data.
50-93-53 HARLEQUIN CIRCUS 1993
Navy blue body and roof . . .

50-93-54 HAYES GARDEN WORLD 1993
Green body, white . . .
50-93-55 HENRY ADLAM 1993
Black body, white . . .
50-93-56 HIGHLAND SPRING 1993
Green body, tan . . .
50-93-57 HOPKINSON 1993
Maroon body, black . . .
50-93-58 HORNSEA FREEPORT 1993
Maroon body, white . . .
50-93-59 HUMBERSIDE COUNTY COUNCIL 1993
White body, black chassis and roof, Humberside County Council
1993 logo with coat of arms.
50-93-60 HUSH PUPPIES 1993
Cream body and roof . . .
50-93-61 INTERFLORA 70TH 1993
Yellow body, black . . .
50-93-62 ISLE OF MAN STEAM PACKET 1993
White body, red . . ., green . . .
50-93-63 JACOBS 1993
White body, black . . .
50-93-64 JOHNNIE WALKER 1993
Black body, chassis and roof, Johnnie Walker logo.
50-93-65 KINGSBURY CUB LACK 1993
White body, light blue . . .
50-93-66 KWIK FIT (Esher) 1993
White body and roof . . .
50-93-67 LANCASHIRE WILDLIFE TRUST 1993
Silver body, black . . .
50-93-68 LANCASTER 800 1993
Tan body, maroon . . .
50-93-69 LANGS SELECT SCOTCH 1993
Blue body and chassis, cream roof, Langs Select Since 1861 logo.
50-93-70 LEEDS TV EXPRESS 1993
Yellow body, blue . . ., red . . .
50-93-71 LEICESTER MERCURY 1993
Blue body, black chassis, white roof, Leicester Mercury, Largest
Circulation logo.
50-93-72 LEICESTERSHIRE CONSTABULARY 1993
Navy blue body, black . . .
50-93-73 LIDOS 1993
No data.
50-93-74 LILLIPUT LANE 1993
Purple body, cream . . .
50-93-75 LINCOLNSHIRE ECHO 1993
Red body, black . . .
50-93-76 LINCOLNSHIRE STANDARD 1993
Red body, black . . .
50-93-77 LIVERPOOL DAILY POST 1993
Red body, black . . .

50-93-78 LIVERPOOL FOOTBALL CLUB 1993
White body, red . . .
50-93-79 LIVERPOOL OVERHEAD RAIL 1993
Brown body, cream . . .
50-93-80 LIVERPOOL POLICE 1993
Blue body and roof . . .
50-93-81 LOCKFORD INN 1993
Green body, black chassis, red roof . . .
50-93-82 LOUND HALL BRITISH COAL 1993
Black body, chassis and roof, Lound Hall and British Coal logo.
50-93-83 MALLING ROTARY CLUB 1993
White body, blue . . .
50-93-84 MAMAS SECONDS 1993
Brown body and roof . . .
50-93-85 MANCHESTER UNITED F.C. 1993
Red body, white . . .
50-93-86 MATTHEW ALGIE 1993
Dark green body and roof . . .
50-93-87 MOLLYS FLORISTS 1993
Dark brown body, yellow . . .
50-93-88 MORAY SCANNER APPEAL 1993
No data.
50-93-89 MORLAND BREWERY 1993
Green body, black chassis, white roof . . .
50-93-90 MORRIS 80 YEARS 1993
Blue body, black chassis, white roof, 80 Years Morris 1913-1993
logo.
50-93-91 MR. BLOBBY 1993
White body, pink . . .
50-93-92 NATIONAL BENEVOLENT 1993
Black body, orange . . .
50-93-93 NEALS TOYS 1993
White body, black . . .
50-93-94 NEWARK AIR MUSEUM 1993
Navy blue body and roof . . .
50-93-95 NEWTON COURIER 1993
White body, black . . .
50-93-96 NOCTON SHEEP DOG TRIALS 1993
Yellow body, black . . .
50-93-97 NOS GALAN 1993
Black body, red . . .
50-93-98 OLD GLORY 1993
Gray body, black . . .
50-93-99 OMEGA CONTRACT CLEANING 1993
White body, dark blue . . .
50-93-100 P.A.A. SHOOTING CHAMPIONSHIPS 1993
White body, black chassis and roof, P.A.A. National Short-Range
Shooting Championships, East Kilbride 1993 logo.
50-93-101 PERKINS OF OXFORD 1993
White body, blue . . .

50-93-102 PET WORLD 1993
No data.
50-93-103 PETER UNDERWOOD 1993
Brown body, tan . . .
50-93-104 PHILEAS FOGG 1993
Tan body, blue . . ., red . . .
50-93-105 PILGRIM HEART AND LUNG 1993
White body and roof . . .
50-93-106 PIT STOP 1993
Yellow body, green . . .
50-93-107 POPEYE THE SAILOR 1993
White body, black chassis and roof, Popeye The Sailor logo.
50-93-108 PRETTIGE FEESTDAGEN 1993
Blue body, red . . .
50-93-109 QUICK FIT 1993
White body, black . . .
50-93-110 RAINBOW CHILDREN'S WARD 1993
White body, yellow . . .
50-93-111 RENTOKIL 1993
White body, black . . .
50-93-112 REVELL 1993
Blue body, yellow . . ., red . . .
50-93-113 RIBENA 1993
White body, plum . . .
50-93-114 RIPLEY SCHOOL 1993
Light blue body, black chassis and roof, Ripley School, Mill Hill
emblem logo.
50-93-115 ROBINSONS LEMON BARLEY 1993
Dark green body, tan . . .
50-93-116 ROSE RESTAURANT 1993
White body, pink . . .
50-93-117 ROUND TABLE 1993
Red body, black . . .
50-93-118 ROVER MODEL CAR CLUB 1993
Maroon body, cream . . .
50-93-119 ROYAL AIR FORCE 75 1993
Pale blue body, ? chassis and roof, Royal Air Force 1918-1993 logo
with roundel and 75.
50-93-120 ROYAL COLLEGE OF NURSING 1993
White body, blue . . ., red . . .
50-93-121 ST. GILES HOSPICE 1993
White body, orange . . .
50-93-122 ST. JOHN AMBULANCE 1993
White body and roof . . .
50-93-123 SAVE THE CHILDREN/ADAMS 1993
White body, blue . . ., red . . .
50-93-124 SAVONA PROVISIONS 1993
No data.
50-93-125 SEECO 1993
White body, maroon . . .

50-93-126 SHIRLEY TYRES 1993
Red body, black . . .
50-93-127 SOUTHAMPTON ECHO 1993
White body, black chassis, red roof?
50-93-128 STANLEY GIBBONS 1993
Green body and roof . . .
50-93-129 STEVELYN & COMPANY 1993
Gold body, green chassis and roof, Stevelyn & Company 1983-1993 logo with wreath.
50-93-130 F. STOKES COWKEEPER 1993
Blue body, tan chassis and roof, F. Stokes Cowkeeper logo.
50-93-131 STOKES TEA & COFFEE 1993
Tan body, black . . .
50-93-132 STURMINSTER MARSHALL 1993
Green body, black . . .
50-93-133 G. SWADDLING LIMITED 1993
Light blue body, white . . .
50-93-134 TAMWORTH HERALD 1993
White body, red . . .
50-93-135 THE TEAR FUND 1993
White body, red . . .
50-93-136 TEN 17 1993
White body, red . . .
50-93-137 TETLEY'S TEAS 1993
Blue body and roof, black chassis, Tetley's Teas logo.
50-93-138 TEXAS 21ST 1993
White body, red . . ., blue . . .
50-93-139 THAME SHOW 93 1993
Yellow body, green . . .
50-93-140 N. THURSTING 1993
White body, green . . .
50-93-141 TORQ THE JEWELLERS 1993
Black body, silver . . .
50-93-142 TOTS 2000 1993
Blue body, gold . . .
50-93-143 TOWN & COUNTRY 1993
Blue body, white . . .
50-93-144 TOYTOWN MODELS 1993
Yellow body, red . . .
50-93-145 TRAFFIC JAM 1993
White body, black . . .
50-93-146 TRANS-PENNINE FAIRS 1993
Black body, gold . . .
50-93-147 TROTTERS 1993
Black body, red . . .
50-93-148 UNIQUE ADVERTISING 1993
Red body, blue . . ., gray . . .
50-93-149 WADDINGTONS PLAYING CARDS 1993
Maroon body and roof . . .
50-93-150 WADDINGTONS PUZZLES 1993
Tan body, red . . .

50-93-151 WALSALL ILLUMINATIONS 1993
Blue body and roof . . .
50-93-152 WARWICKSHIRE CONSTABULARY 1993
Navy blue body, gray . . .
50-93-153 WEST YORKSHIRE GUNNERS 1993
Black body, chassis and roof . . .
50-93-154 WOOD GREEN SCOUTS 1993
Green body, white . . .
50-93-155 WORLD PILOT GIG 1993
Dark green body, tan . . .
50-93-156 WREXHAM LEADER 1993
Light red body, white . . .
50-93-157 WYCOMBE WANDERERS 1993
Dark blue body, light blue . . .
50-93-158 YORKSHIRE CHRONICLE 1993
Orange body, black . . .
50-94-1 3M 1994
Purple body, white . . .
50-94-2 A DAY AT THE RACES 1994
Navy blue body . . .
50-94-3 AMERICAN CIRCUS 1994
White body, blue . . .
50-94-4 ANTHONY NOLAN 1994
White body, blue chassis and roof, The Anthony Nolan Bone Marrow Trust Delivering the Gift of Life logo.
50-94-5 ARKELLS BEERS 1994
Blue body, red . . .
50-94-6 ATLANTIC MODELS 1994
Black body, chassis and roof . . .
50-94-7 AUTOMOBILE ASSOCIATION 1994
Yellow body, black chassis and roof, A.A. Through-Way and A.A. Loop-Way Road Signs logo with emblem.
50-94-8 BAIN HOGG 1994
White body, red . . ., black . . .
50-94-9 BATTLE OF BRITAIN FLIGHT 1994
Navy blue body and roof . . . (Is there a second issue?)
50-94-10 BENSKINS BREWERY 1994
No data.
50-94-11 BERTRAM MILLS CIRCUS 1994
Red body, gray . . .
50-94-12 BILLY SMARTS CIRCUS 1994
Gray body, green . . .
50-94-13 BIRMINGHAM SCOUTS 1994
White body, blue . . ., green . . .
50-94-14 THE BLACK WATCH 1994
Blue body, maroon . . .
50-94-15 BLACKPOOL TOWER CENTENARY 1994
White body, black chassis and roof?
50-94-16 BLACKPOOL TOWER CIRCUS 1994
White body, black chassis and roof?

50-94-17 BOBBY ROBERTS CIRCUS 1994
No data.
50-94-18 BRACHIS OF BARDI 1994
White body, green . ., red . . .
50-94-19 BRENTWOOD GAZETTE 1994
Black body, chassis and roof . . .
50-94-20 BRITISH DECORATORS ASSOCIATION 1994
White body, black chassis and roof . . .
50-94-21 BROGLIA PRESS 1994
White body, black chassis and roof?
50-94-22 B S A 1994
White body, blue . . .
50-94-23 BULMERS ORIGINAL 1994
Green body, black chassis, white roof, Bulmers Original logo.
50-94-24 BURTON MAIL 1994
Yellow body, black chassis and roof . . .
50-94-25 CANARIES OVER EUROPE 1994
Yellow body, blue chassis, green roof?
50-94-26 CHINESE STATE CIRCUS 1994
Black body, orange . . .
50-94-27 CIRCUS HOFFMAN 1994
White body, blue . . .
50-94-28 CIRCUS RISAIRE 1994
Maroon body, cream . . .
50-94-29 THE CORNISH CHALLENGE 1994
Black body, gold . . .
50-94-30 COVENTRY CITY FOOTBALL CLUB 1994
Light blue body, white chassis and roof, Coventry City Football Club shield logo, Sky Blues 1883 on doors.
50-94-31 D-DAY 1994
Gold body, green . . .
50-94-32 DEWSBURY RLFC 1994
Yellow body, red . . .
50-94-33 DISS TOWN FOOTBALL CLUB 1994
Orange-red body and roof . . .
50-94-34 DOLPHIN DIECASTS 1994
Light blue body, gray . . .
50-94-35 EDRADOUR DISTILLERY 1994
Cream body, red . . . (plus a second issue, no data)
50-94-36 EVENING TELEGRAPH 1994
No data.
50-94-37 EVERARDS BREWERY 1994
Green body, black . . .
50-94-38 EXPRESS & STAR 1994
Red body, white . . .
50-94-39 F. CHRISTMAS 1994
Red body, black chassis, white roof, F. Christmas Express Delivery Service logo.
50-94-40 FOREST PRIMARY SCHOOL 1994
No data.

50-94-41 GAINSBOROUGH SEA SCOUTS 1994
White body, blue . . .
50-94-42 GLASGOW RANGERS 1994
No data.
50-94-43 GOLDEN DAYS 1994
Blue body, cream . . .
50-94-44 GRIMWADES IPSWICH 1994
Dark blue body, black chassis and roof . . .
50-94-45 GUERNSEY FIRE BRIGADE 1994
Red body, black chassis . . .
50-94-46 G W R EXPRESS CARTAGE 1994
Cream body and roof, brown chassis, G W R Express Cartage
Services logo, House of Eliott box.
50-94-47 G W R SERVICES 1994
Brown body, cream chassis and roof?
50-94-48 GUINNESS BROS. GROUP 1994
Blue body, white . . ., black . . .
50-94-49 HAMMERITE 1994
Blue body and roof . . .
50-94-50 HMS BELFAST 1994
Gray body, navy blue . . .
50-94-51 HORNSEY & DISTRICT TRADING POST 1994
Red body, black chassis and roof?
50-94-52 ISLE OF WIGHT STEAM RAILWAY 1994
Dark green body, black chassis and roof?
50-94-53 JOHN BULL PUB 1994
Cream body, black chassis and roof . . .
50-94-54 JOHN ROBERTS CIRCUS 1994
Light blue body, black chassis and roof?
50-94-55 KEIGHLEY & WORTH LIGHT RAILWAY 1994
Blue body, cream . . ., red . . .
50-94-56 KENT COUNTY BRANCH, RED CROSS 1994
Navy blue body, cream . . .
50-94-57 KENT POLICE CHOIR 1994
White body, black chassis and roof, Kent Police Male Voice Choir
logo.
50-94-58 LANGHAM 1994
No data.
50-94-59 LEEDS UNITED FOOTBALL CLUB 1994
White body, blue . . ., yellow . . .
50-94-60 LONAN PARISH COMMISSIONERS 1994
Maroon body, cream . . .
50-94-61 R. S. MALCOLM 1994
Cream body, green chassis and roof? (Is there a second Malcolm
issue?)
50-94-62 MANCHESTER FOOTBALL CLUB 1994
No data.
50-94-63 MANCHESTER SHIP CANAL 1994
Black body, white . . .
50-94-64 MANX RADIO 1994
No data.

50-94-65 MELTONIAN POLISH 1994
No data.
50-94-66 MOSCOW STATE CIRCUS 1994
Red body, black chassis and roof . . .
50-94-67 NATIONAL TRUST 1994
Green body, black chassis and roof, The National Trust logo.
50-94-68 NEIGHBOURHOOD WATCH 1994
Yellow body, gray . . .
50-94-69 NEWARK AIR MUSEUM 1994
Green body and roof . . .
50-94-70 NEWCASTLE UNITED 1994
No data.
50-94-71 NIGHT AT THE OPERA 1994
White body and roof . . .
50-94-72 NOCTON SHEEPDOG TRIALS 1994
Red body, black chassis and roof . . .
50-94-73 NORWICH 800 1994
Black body, chassis and roof . . .
50-94-74 NORTON 1994
Black body, chassis and roof . . .
50-94-75 NOTTINGHAM CITY POLICE 1994
Navy blue body, gray . . .
50-94-76 NOTTINGHAM FOREST FOOTBALL CLUB 1994
Red body, black chassis and roof . . .
50-94-77 NOTTINGHAM STEAM FAIR 1994
Cream body, red . . .
50-94-78 NRG INTERNATIONAL 1994
White body, red . . .
50-94-79 OLD BLACKSMITHS SHOP 1994
Black body, white . . .
50-94-80 OXFORD AMBULANCE SERVICE 1994
Black body, cream chassis and roof?
50-94-81 THE PARACHUTE REGIMENT 1994
Light blue body, maroon . . .
50-94-82 PRESTON NORTH END F.C. 1994
White body, black chassis and roof . . .
50-94-83 PRESTIGE FEESTDAGEN 1994
1. Light blue body, dark blue . . .
2. Green body, dark blue . . .
50-94-84 PUTTING CHILDREN FIRST 1994
White body, red chassis, blue roof, Putting Children First and Adams,
the childrenswear specialist logo.
50-94-85 RDP 10TH ANNIVERSARY 1994
Red body, black chassis and roof?
50-94-86 ROYAL AIR FORCE 1994
Blue body and roof . . .
50-94-87 ROYAL ARTILLERY 1994
Dark blue body, yellow . . .
50-94-88 ROYAL ENFIELD 1994
Blue body, chassis and roof . . .

50-94-89 RUPERT BEAR 1994
Yellow-orange body, black chassis, red roof, Rupert logo.
50-94-90 ST JOHN'S, COUNTY OF SUSSEX 1994
White body, black chassis and roof, St. John Ambulance emblem and
County of Sussex logo, Youth 94 on doors, Ambulance on rear.
50-94-91 ST. JULIAN'S CHURCH/LLOYDS 1994
Green body, white . . .
50-94-92 ST. MARK'S SCHOOL 1994
Blue body, gray chassis, red roof?
50-94-93 ST. MARY'S CHURCH 1994
White body, blue . . .
50-94-94 SCUNTHORPE UNITED 1994
Maroon body, white . . .
50-94-95 SHEFFIELD UNITED F.C. 1994
Red body, black . . ., white . . .
50-94-96 SHEPHERD NEAME 1994
Red body, blue chassis, white roof?
50-94-97 SOUTHERN SUPPLIES 1994
Blue body, black chassis and roof?
50-94-98 SPARKYS 1994
White body, blue chassis, red roof . . .
50-94-99 STAFFORDSHIRE CONSTABULARY 1994
Navy blue body, black chassis and roof . . .
50-94-100 STANLEYS OF WINDSOR 1994
Navy blue body and roof . . .
50-94-101 STOKES HIGH BRIDGE 1994
Black body, chassis and roof . . .
50-94-102 S T P 1994
White body, black chassis and roof . . .
50-94-103 SUPERDROME CIRCUS 1994
Black body, chassis and roof . . .
50-94-104 T-CUT 1994
Red body, yellow . . .
50-94-105 THERIAULTS 25TH ANNIVERSARY 1994
Dark green body, cream . . .
50-94-106 TOWER BRIDGE 1994
Black body, gold . . ., red . . .
50-94-107 TOWER COLLIERY 1994
Silver body, black chassis and roof?
50-94-108 TOY TRADER 1994
White body, green . . ., red . . .
50-94-109 TOYS BEE USED 1994
Yellow body, black chassis and roof . . .
50-94-110 TREORCHY CHOIR 1994
Green body, white . . .
50-94-111 TUCKERS RADIO & TV 1994
Blue body, white chassis and roof?
50-94-112 TURTLE WAX 1994
Green body, white . . .
50-94-113 VELOCETTE 1994
Silver body, black chassis and roof . . .

50-94-114 VICTOR ARTS 1994
Red body, cream . . ., black . . .
50-94-115 VINCENT 1994
Gray body and roof . . .
50-94-116 VINTAGE DAD 1994
Cream body, black chassis and roof . . .
50-94-117 WADDINGTONS GET SET 1994
White body, blue . . .
50-94-118 WARRINGTON RLFC 1994
Yellow body, blue . . .
50-94-119 WATSONS OF SALISBURY 1994
Green body, black . . .
50-94-120 WEST BROMWICH F.C. 1994
White body, navy blue . . .
50-94-121 WIDNES R L F C 1994
White body, black chassis and roof . . .
50-94-122 WOLVES 1994
Orange body, black chassis and roof . . .
50-94-123 WORLD PILOT GIG 1994
Maroon body, cream . . .
50-94-124 WYCOMBE WANDERERS 1994
No data.
51 CHEVROLET BOX VAN 1992
In many cases the cab and box are one color, the chassis and roof
another.
51-92-1 LLEDO/PR 1 1992
White cab and box, black chassis and roof?
51-92-2 SWAN VESTAS 1992
Yellow cab and box, green chassis and roof, Swan Vestas logo,
Bryant & May Ltd. on door.
51-93-1 GLENGOYNE SCOTCH WHISKY 1993
Green cab, box and roof, black chassis, Glengoyne Single Highland
Malt Scotch Whisky logo.
51-93-2 HARRY RAMSDEN 1993
Black cab, box, chassis and roof . . .
51-93-3 HENRY COLBECK 1993
Yellow cab and box, red chassis and roof?
**51-93-4 ROYAL NATIONAL LIFE-BOAT INSTITUTION
1993**
Blue-black cab, box, chassis and roof, To The Rescue and Royal
National Life-Boat Institution logo.
51-93-5 TETLEY TEA 1993
Blue cab and box, black chassis and roof, Tetley Tea tastes better
logo.
51-93-6 TYRONE CRYSTAL (first) 1993
No data.
51-93-7 TYRONE CRYSTAL (second) 1993
Green cab and box . . .
51-93-8 YORKSHIRE CAR COLLECTION 1993
White cab and box, green chassis and roof, Yorkshire Car Collection,
Grange Street, Keighley logo.

51-94-1 GLENGOYNE 1994
Green cab and box . . .
51-94-2 HARRY RAMSDEN 1994
Black cab, box, chassis and roof . . .
51-94-3 HENRY COLBECK 1994
Yellow cab and box, red chassis . . .
51-94-4 P. B. D. 1994
Dark blue cab and box, black chassis . . .
51-94-5 P D PRINTING 1994
Gray cab and box, black chassis . . .
51-94-6 PRESCRIPTION TEA/CO-OP 1994
Cream cab and box, light blue chassis and roof, Prescription Tea
logo.
51-94-7 STANLEY GIBBONS 1994
No data.
52 MORRIS PARCELS VAN 1992
Here too, the cab and body are usually the same color, though it is not
easy to generalize beyond that.
52-92-1 THE MODERN PRINTERS 1992
White cab, body and roof, black chassis, The Modern Printers logo.
52-92-2 WOLVERHAMPTON POLICE 1992
Dark green and white . . .
52-93-1 ANADIN 1993
Blue cab, box and roof, light blue chassis, Anadin and Whitehall
logo.
52-93-2 DAILY EXPRESS/SICILY 1993
Black cab, box, chassis and roof . . .
52-93-3 DENNIS FILM DELIVERY 1993
White cab and box, light blue chassis and roof, Dennis Film Delivery
logo.
52-93-4 EXCHANGE AND MART 1993
Dark green cab and box, black chassis and roof, The Exchange &
Mart logo.
52-93-5 GOD SAVE THE QUEEN 1993
Black cab, box, chassis and roof, Marble Arch and Coronation
souvenir logo.
52-93-6 LEEDS CITY POLICE 1993
Navy blue cab, box, chassis and roof?
52-93-7 NSPCC-UNIGATE 1993
White cab and box, light green chassis and roof, NSPCC for the sake
of the children logo.
52-93-8 ROWNTREES 1993
Light green cab, box and roof, black chassis, Rowntrees table jellies
logo, since 1923 on door.
**52-93-9 ROYAL NATIONAL LIFE-BOAT INSTITUTION
1993**
Green cab, box and roof, black chassis, Launching the Lifeboat and
Royal National Life-Boat Institution logo.
52-93-10 ROYAL WORCESTER 1993
Blue cab, box and roof, black chassis, The Worcester Royal Porcelain
Co., Ltd. logo.

52-93-11 STRATHMORE VINTAGE VEHICLE 1993
Black cab, box, chassis and roof . . .
52-93-12 UNWINS WINE MERCHANTS 1993
Dark green cab, box and roof, black chassis, Unwins Family Wine
Merchants logo.
52-94-1 ANADIN 1994
Blue cab . . ., light blue . . .
52-94-2 BLACKPOOL PLEASURE BEACH 1994
White cab and box . . .
52-94-3 DAD'S MY BEST FRIEND 1994
White . . ., red . . .
52-94-4 EVENING SENTINEL 120TH 1994
Navy blue body . . .
52-94-5 NEWS OF THE WORLD 1994
Cream cab and box, black chassis and roof, News of the World and
Battle Joined in Normandy logo.
52-94-6 RAOB GLE 1994
Olive green cab and box . . .
52-94-7 ROUND TABLE 1994
Dark green . . ., red . . .
52-94-8 RUPERT BEAR 1994
White cab and box, green chassis and roof, logo includes Rupert,
butterflies and clouds.
52-94-9 SUNDAY EXPRESS 1994
Black cab and box . . .
52-94-10 TESCO EGGS 1994
Cream cab, box and roof, black chassis, Tesco Fresh British Eggs
Delivered Daily logo, Tesco on roof.
53 ROLLS ROYCE LANDAULET 1992
53-92-1 ANADIN EXTRA 1992
Red body, yellow . . .
53-92-2 DARLING BUDS OF MAY 1992
Yellow body, black chassis and roof, L monogram on doors.
53-92-3 QUEEN ELIZABETH 1992
Green body, black chassis, cream roof, H.M. Queen Elizabeth II
1952-1992 logo.
53-93-1 BLUE/BLACK 1993
Light blue body, black chassis and roof, no logo.
53-93-2 GOD SAVE THE QUEEN 1993
Gold body and chassis, maroon roof, no logo.
53-94-1 HOUSE OF ELIOTT 1993
Light gray body, black chassis and roof, black stripe, no logo, House
of Eliott box.
54 ROLLS ROYCE D BACK 1992
54-92-1 BADEN-POWELL JAM ROLL 1992
Green body, black chassis and roof, gold stripes, no logo.
54-92-2 QUEEN ELIZABETH 1992
Maroon body, black chassis and roof, H.M. Queen Elizabeth II, 1952-
1992 logo.
55 HORSE DRAWN TANKER 1992

55-92-1 POLARINE 1992
Dark green body, chassis and hitch, light gray tank on red bed, Polarine for Motor Cars and Standard Oil Company logo.
56 MODEL A FORD VAN 1992
56-92-1 ATLAS TIRES 1992
Blue body, black chassis and roof, Atlas Tires logo.
56-93-1 SANDRIDGE 1993
Tan body, black chassis and roof, Sandridge Window Blind Manufacturers logo, SWB emblem on doors.
56-93-2 WHAT'S ON TV 1993
Blue body, black chassis and roof . . ., Crinkley Bottom box.
57 FORD TANKER 1993
57-93-1 STANDARD OIL 1993
Blue cab and rear, white tank, Standard Oil logo on tank and emblem on doors.
57-94-1 LONDON FIRE BRIGADE 1994
Red cab, rear and tank, L.C.C. London Fire Brigade Water Tender logo, Blackwall Division emblem on doors, London's Burning box.
57-94-2 SUNOCO 1994
No data.
58 MORRIS Z VAN 1993
58-93-1 AUTO MODELS 1993
No data.
58-93-2 BILLY & SON 1993
No data.
58-93-3 COLLECTORS GAZETTE 1993
White body, red chassis . . ., Collectors Gazette logo.
58-93-4 THE CORNISHMAN 1993
No data.
58-93-5 DAIRY FARM MILK 1993
Cream body, light blue chassis, black roof, Dairy Farm Rich Clean Milk logo.
58-93-6 FRED DIBNAH 1993
Maroon body, green chassis . . .
58-93-7 HULL DAILY MAIL 1993
Red body, black chassis and roof, Hull Daily Mail logo.
58-93-8 LEEDS MODEL CENTRE 1993
Yellow body, red chassis . . .
58-93-9 LONDON MOTOR SHOW 1993
Cream body . . .
58-93-10 MR. BLOBBY 1993
Yellow body, pink chassis, Mr. Blobby logo, Crinkley Bottom box.
58-93-11 OLD GLORY 1993
Gray body, navy blue chassis . . .
58-93-12 PROMOTORS 1993
Red body, black chassis and roof . . .
58-93-13 SENTINEL 1993
Navy blue body, black chassis and roof . . .
58-93-14 SHOWGARD MOUNTS 1993
Navy blue body and chassis

58-93-15 TRANS PENNINE FAIRS 1993
No data.
58-93-16 WADDINGTONS PLAYING CARDS 1993
No data.
58-94-1 AIDENSFIELD STORES 1994
Maroon body, black chassis and roof, Aidensfield Stores logo, Heartbeat box.
58-94-2 AIRBORNE FORCES MUSEUM 1994
Maroon body, light blue chassis and panels, Airborne Forces Museum Shop logo.
58-94-3 ALTON TOWERS 1994
White body, green . . .
58-94-4 ANADIN 1994
Yellow body, green chassis . . .
58-94-5 B.P.M.A. 1994
Cream body, blue chassis . . .
58-94-6 C & H WINDOW SYSTEMS 1994
White body, blue chassis . . .
58-94-7 CAMBRIDGE EVENING NEWS 1994
No data.
58-94-8 CAMBRIDGESHIRE CONSTABULARY 1994
Black body and chassis . . .
58-94-9 CHESTERFIELD ADVERTISER 1994
White body, black chassis . . .
58-94-10 CHESTERFIELD CO-OP 1994
Blue body, black chassis . . .
58-94-11 COLCHESTER BOYS' HIGH SCHOOL 1994
Blue body and chassis . . .
58-94-12 CORNISHMAN 1994
White body, navy blue chassis . . .
58-94-13 CORNWALL CONSTABULARY 1994
Black body and chassis . . .
58-94-14 CUMBRIA CLASSIC 1994
Gray body, black chassis . . .
58-94-15 DEVON CONSTABULARY 1994
Dark blue body and chassis, black roof, Devon Constabulary logo with emblem.
58-94-16 DULUX LOWBUILD 1994
Red body and chassis . . .
58-94-17 EPWORTH BELLS 1994
Yellow body, black chassis . . .
58-94-18 EXPRESS DAIRY 1994
Navy blue body and chassis . . .
58-94-19 GAMMA GARMENTS 1994
Cream body, brown chassis and roof, Gamma Garments logo.
58-94-20 GRIMSBY TELEGRAPH 1994
No data.
58-94-21 GUINNESS 1994
Black body and chassis . . ., Guinness logo with harp.

58-94-22 HARRY RAMSDEN 1994
Dark green body, black chassis and roof, Harry Ramsden's logo, HR monogram on doors.
58-94-23 ISLE OF MAN POST OFFICE 1994
Red body and chassis . . .
58-94-24 KINGSTON TELEPHONES 1994
No data.
58-94-25 LAGADU'S 1994
White body, black chassis . . .
58-94-26 LINCOLN CITY F. C. 1994
Red body, black chassis . . .
58-94-27 LINCOLNSHIRE CONSTABULARY 1994
Navy blue body and chassis . . .
58-94-28 LINCOLNSHIRE ECHO 1994
No data.
58-94-29 MANCHESTER UNITED F. C. 1994
Black body, yellow chassis . . .
58-94-30 MODEL & COLLECTORS MART 1994
Red body and chassis . . .
58-94-31 MORRIS GOLDEN GATE 1994
Yellow body, red chassis . . .
58-94-32 MUSCULAR DYSTROPHY 1994
Red body, black chassis . . .
58-94-33 PANASONIC 1994
Black body, gold chassis, Panasonic Batteries logo, in cylindrical box.
58-94-34 PICKFORDS 1994
Navy blue body and chassis . . .
58-94-35 PRETTIGE FEESTDAGEN 1994
Light blue body, red chassis . . .
58-94-36 PROMOTORS MORRIS 1994
Red body, black chassis . . .
58-94-37 PROMOTORS-TEL (49) 1994
Red body, black chassis . . .
58-94-38 ROVER MODEL CAR CLUB 1994
Orange body, green chassis . . .
58-94-39 R S P C A 1994
White body, blue chassis, black roof, RSPCA logo and box.
58-94-40 SERNEELS 1994
Dark green body, black chassis . . .
58-94-41 SHETLAND CLASSIC MOTORSHOW 1994
Maroon body, black chassis . . .
58-94-42 SHIELDS GAZETTE 1994
Yellow body, black chassis . . .
58-94-43 SPORTS MERCURY 1994
Pinkish tan body, body, black chassis and roof panel, Sports Mercury logo, City's League Cup Win! on doors, Great Stuff This Buff on rear.
58-94-44 TEDDY GRAY 1994
White body, green chassis . . .

58-94-45 THUNDERBIRD FREIGHT 1994
Light blue body, black chassis . . .
58-94-46 TOWN & COUNTRY FESTIVAL 1994
White body, dark blue chassis . . .
58-94-47 TUNNEL POLICE 1994
Navy blue body, black chassis . . .
58-94-48 WALSALL ILLUMINATIONS 1994
Black body and chassis . . .
58-94-49 WINNIE WILTS 1994
Cream yellow body,,red chassis and roof panel, Winnie Wilts Rice Pudding logo with cow figure, diploma on rear.
58-94-50 WORDSLEY PRINT 1994
Tan body, black chassis and roof panel, Wordsley Print Ltd. logo, 20 Years wreath.
58-94-51 WORTH VALLEY 1994
Maroon body and chassis . . .
58-94-52 WYCOMBE WANDERERS 1994
Navy blue body, yellow chassis . . .
58-94-53 YORKSHIRE POST 1994
No data.
59 BEDFORD 30 CWT TRUCK 1993
59-93-1 A. A. 1993
Yellow cab and rear, black chassis and cover, gray tires, AA emblem.
59-93-2 CANNES 93 1993
White cab and rear, black . . .
59-93-3 CARRINGTON VIYELLA 1993
No data.
59-93-4 DEVENISH BREWERY 1993
Dark green cab and rear, white . . .
59-93-5 EXPRESS DAIRY 1993
Blue-black cab and rear, black chassis, white cover, Express Dairy Milk logo
59-93-6 W. HODGES GREENGROCER 1993
Olive cab and rear, black chassis, green cover, W. Hodges logo.
59-93-7 JOHN RAMSEYS 1993
Navy blue cab and rear . . .
59-93-8 KLEENEX FOR MEN 1993
Red cab, white box, black chassis, light gray cover, Kleenex For Men logo.
59-93-9 KLEENEX TISSUES (gray) 1993
Gray cab, white rear and cover, pink chassis, Kleenex Tissues, soft, strong, pops up too logo.
59-93-10 KLEENEX TISSUES (blue) 1993
Dark blue cab, white rear and cover, pale blue chassis, Super Softness Kleenex Tissues with wet strength logo.
59-93-11 MAC TOOLS 1993
Yellow cab and rear, black chassis . . .
59-93-12 MACHINE MART 1993
White cab and rear . . .

59-93-13 MUSEUM OF BRITISH ROAD TRANSPORT 1993
White cab, rear and cover, blue chassis, Museum of British Road Transport logo.
59-93-14 NEWS OF THE WORLD 1993
Maroon cab and rear, black chassis and cover, News of the World logo.
59-93-15 QUEENS THEATRE 1993
Blue cab and rear, black chassis . . .
59-93-16 H. SAMUEL 1993
Black, chassis and cover, blue rear, H. Samuel, the Empire's largest Jeweller logo.
59-93-17 S.G.S. 1993
White cab and rear, black . . .
59-93-18 STOKE ADVERTISER 1993
Red cab and rear . . .
59-93-19 UNIGATE FRESH MILK 1993
Red cab and cover, white rear, black chassis, Unigate emblem and Fresh Milk logo.
59-94-1 COMPASS THEATRE 1994
White cab and rear, black chassis . . .
59-94-2 DAIRY FARM MILK 1994
Dark blue cab and rear, cream chassis and cover, Dairy Farm Rich Clean Milk logo, emblem on door, lettering on rear.
59-94-3 DEVON FIRE BRIGADE 1994
Red cab, roof, rear and chassis, Devon Fire Brigade logo with checkered stripe.
59-94-4 DOVE HOLES BEER & JAZZ 1994
Dark green cab and rear . . .
59-94-5 ENFIELD PAGEANT OF MOTORING 1994
Cream cab and rear, brown chassis . . .
59-94-6 EPAC 1994
No data.
59-94-7 FAST TRACKS 1994
Black cab and rear, white . . .
59-94-8 GILES 1994
White cab and rear, red chassis and roof, Santa Claus picture logo, Giles box.
59-94-9 ISLE OF MAN TT 1995 1994
Blue cab and rear, red chassis and roof, Isle of Man TT 1995 29th May-9th June logo with Manx emblem.
59-94-10 JANE IN THE MIRROR 1994
Green cab and rear . . .
59-94-11 LONDON FIRE BRIGADE 1994
Red cab, chassis, rear and roof, London Fire Brigade Mobile Control Unit logo, Blackwall Division emblem on doors, London's Burning box.
59-94-12 MAC TOOLS 1994
Yellow cab and rear, black chassis . . .
59-94-13 MILLBROOK 1994
White cab and rear . . .

59-94-14 NORTH RIDING POLICE 1994
Blue-black cab, chassis, rear and roof, North Riding Police Control logo, Heartbeat box.
59-94-15 PRETTIGE FEESTDAGEN 1994
Blue cab and rear, red . . .
59-94-16 ROYAL NATIONAL LIFE-BOAT INSTITUTION 1994
No data.
59-94-17 RUPERT BEAR 1994
Green cab and rear, red chassis and cover, Adventures of Rupert logo.
59-94-18 SCOTTISH TRANSPORT EX... 1994
Maroon cab and rear, cream chassis . . .
59-94-19 TV TIMES 1994
Yellow cab and rear, red chassis, TV Times, Britains best family TV guide logo.
59-94-20 YOUNGSTERS 25TH ANNIVERSARY 1994
Silver cab and rear . . .
60 DENNIS F8 FIRE ENGINE 1993
60-93-1 NEW ZEALAND FIRE SERVICE 1993
Red body and chassis, black roof, New Zealand Fire Service logo with coat of arms.
60-94-1 CITY OF LINCOLN 1994
Red body, black chassis . . .
60-94-2 CITY OF NOTTINGHAM 1994
Red body, black chassis and roof, City of Nottingham logo with coat of arms.
60-94-3 CITY OF SHEFFIELD 1994
Red body, black chassis and roof . . .
60-94-4 CORNWALL COUNTY FIRE BRIGADE 1994
Red body, black chassis and roof . . .
60-94-5 COVENTRY 1994
Yellow body . . .
60-94-6 ESSEX FIRE BRIGADE 1994
Red body, white chassis and roof, Essex County Fire Brigade logo with coat of arms.
60-94-7 FIRE SERVICE PRESERVATION 1994
Red body, black chassis and roof . . .
60-94-8 KENT FIRE BRIGADE 1994
Red body, chassis and roof, Kent Fire Brigade logo with coat of arms.
60-94-9 LONDON FIRE BRIGADE 1994
Red body and roof, black chassis, London Fire Brigade logo, L.C.C. emblem, London's Burning box.
60-94-10 NORTH RIDING OF YORKSHIRE 1994
Red body, black chassis and roof, North Riding of Yorkshire County Fire Brigade logo, Heartbeat box.
60-94-11 PETERBOROUGH VOLUNTEER F.B. 1994
Red body, black chassis and roof . . .
60-94-12 RUPERT BEAR/NUTWOOD 1994
Red body, black chassis and roof, Nutwood Fire Brigade logo.

60-94-13 SMETHWICK & WEST BROMWICH 1994
Red body, black chassis and roof . . .
60-94-14 STATES OF JERSEY F. B. 1994
Red body, black chassis and roof . . .
61 PONTIAC DELIVERY VAN 1993
No promotional models yet.
62 FORD ARTICULATED TANKER 1994
62-94-1 CHEVRON 1994
Dark green cab and semi . . .
62-94-2 DAD'S BEER 1994
Red cab and chassis, white tank, Dad's Beer and "Super Dad" logo.
62-94-3 DAIRY FARM 1994
Blue cab and both chassis, cream tank, Dairy farm logo on tank and cab, Bulk Delivery and Fresh Rich Clean Milk on semi chassis.
62-94-4 FINA 1994
Blue cab and semi . . .
62-94-5 UNITED MOLASSES 1994
Navy blue . . ., maroon . . .
63 BEDFORD 30 CWT DELIVERY VAN 1994
63-94-1 ANTHONY NOLAN 1994
White body, blue chassis, The Anthony Nolan Bone Marrow Trust logo with emblem. two emblems on rear.
63-94-2 ASHFORDLY BREWERY 1994
Green body and chassis, Ashfordly Brewery logo, Heartbeat box.
63-94-3 BIRMINGHAM POST 1994
No data.
63-94-4 DUXFORD LLEDO SHOW 1994
Black body, gold chassis, Lledo Show 1994 at Duxford logo, Imperial War Museum emblem on doors.
63-94-5 EMERGENCY VEHICLE RESTORATION 1994
Dark green body, black chassis, Emergency Vehicle Restoration Project logo with coat of arms.
63-94-6 EXPRESS DAIRY 1994
Navy blue body . . .
63-94-7 HULLS NEWS 1994
No data.
63-94-8 RDP 10TH ANNIVERSARY 1994
Red body, black chassis . . .
63-94-9 ROYAL MAIL 1994
Red body . . .
63-94-10 SHOWGARD 1994
Green body, black chassis . . .
64 BEDFORD AMBULANCE 1994
64-94-1 CHESHIRE RED CROSS 1994
Cream body, black chassis. British Red Cross, Cheshire Braqnch logo.
64-94-2 CORNWALL COUNTY COUNCIL 1994
Tan body, black chassis . . .
64-94-3 LEPROSY MISSION 1994
Cream body . . .

64-94-4 LINCOLN CITY AMBULANCE 1994
White body . . .
64-94-5 NORTH RIDING AMBULANCE SERVICE 1994
Cream body and chassis, North Riding Ambulance Service logo, Heartbeat box.
64-94-6 NOTTINGHAM--ST. JOHN 1994
Black body and chassis . . .
64-94-7 ST. JOHN AMBULANCE BRIGADE 1994
White body, black chassis . . .
65 MORRIS MINOR TRAVELLER 1994
65-94-1 DAIRY FARM 1994
Cream body, tan woodwork, red interior, Dairy Farm logo.
65-94-2 FIRE PREVENTION OFFICER 1994
Red body, tan woodwork, black interior, Fire Prevention Officer logo, Blackwall Division emblem, London's Burning box.
65-94-3 LLEDO CANNES 94 1994
White body . . .
65-94-4 VECTIS MODELS 1994
Tan woodwork, gold stripe on doors, VM monogram on rear.
   1. Blue body.
   2. Black body.
   3. Cream body.
   4. Gray body.
   5. Green body.
   6. Maroon body.
   7. Rosy tan body.
   8. Turquoise body.
65-94-5 VOTE FOR SWINLEY 1994
Cream body, tan woodwork, red interior, Vote for Swinley logo.
66 DENNIS DELIVERY VAN 1994
66-94-1 BOY SCOUTS 1994
Olive green body, chassis, roof and rear, The Boy Scouts Association logo with emblem.
66-94-2 CHILDREN IN NEED 1994
White body and rear, red roof, black chassis, We're supporting BBC Children In Need logo and box.
66-94-3 HAVEN SUPPLIES 1994
White body and rear, green . . .
66-94-4 PETER UNDERWOOD 1994
Maroon body and rear, cream . . .
66-94-5 R S P C A 1994
Dark blue body and rear, black chassis, cream roof, Royal Society for the Prevention of Cruelty to Animals logo, RSPCA box.
66-94-6 H. SAMUEL JEWELLER 1994
Maroon body and rear, black chassis, cream roof, H. Samuel, The Empire's Largest Jeweller logo; in special box.
67 FORD 3 TON ARTICULATED TRUCK 1994
67-94-1 EDDIE STOBART 1994
Green . . ., red . . .
67-94-2 EXPRESS DAIRY 1994

Navy blue . . ., white . . .
68 AEC REGAL OPEN TOP BUS 1994
68-94-1 STRATFORD BLUE 1994
Light blue body . . .
PM 100 FORD TRANSIT BUS 1991
Minibus with cast body, plastic windows, interior, lights, base and wheels.
100-91-1 TETLEY VARIETY CLUB 1991
White body, black interior, Tetley Variety Club Sunshine Coach logo with figures and emblem. Special Tetley box.
100-93-1 223RD SQUADRON, HALESOWEN 1993
White body . . .
100-93-2 CHILDREN IN HOSPITAL 1993
White body, black interior, Children in Hospital logo on sides, H Hospitals on roof, Kleenex on nose, special Kleenex box.
100-94-1 AMBULANCE SERVICE 1994
White body . . .
100-94-2 BUTLINS VARIETY COACH 1994
White body . . .
100-94-3 POLICE MINI BUS 1994
Dark blue body . . .
PM 101 MG MAGNETTE 1992
Cast body, plastic chassis-grille, exhaust pipe, driver, 20-spoke hubs (matching body color). White box.
101-92-1 BLUE 1992
Blue body, silver gray chassis and pipe, tan driver, #5 labels.
PM 102 ASTON MARTIN 1992
Cast body, plastic chassis-grille, exhaust pipe, driver, 20-spoke hubs (matching body color) and tires.
102-92-1 GREEN 1992
Green body, silver gray chassis and pipe, tan driver, #21 labels.
PM 103 SUNBEAM 1992
Cast body, plastic chassis-grille, exhaust pipe, driver, 20-spoke hubs (matching body color) and tires. White box.
103-92-1 CREAM 1992
Cream body, silver gray chassis and pipe, gray driver, #2 labels.
PM 104 ALFA ROMEO 1992
Cast body, plastic chassis-grille, exhaust pipe, driver, 20-spoke hubs (matching body color) and tires. White box.
104-92-1 RED 1992
Red body, silver gray chassis and pipe, gray driver, #14 labels.
PM 105 FORD TRANSIT VAN 1992
Components as PM 100, but no side windows.
105-92-1 BOTHAM GOES SOUTH 1992
White body, black interior, Leukaemia Research Fund and Botham Goes South logo, What's On TV emblem on nose. Special box.
105-93-1 RACAL DATACOM 1993
White body . . .
105-94-1 A A 1994
Yellow body . . .

105-94-2 BRITISH TELECOM 1994
Gray body . . .
105-94-3 LONDON FIRE SERVICE 1994
Red body . . .
105-94-4 PANIC LINK 1994
No data.
105-94-5 RYDER TRUCK RENTAL 1994
Yellow body, Ryder Truck Rental logo.
PM 106 CHAIN DRIVE TANK TRUCK 1993
Cast front body and chassis, plastic tank, racks, steering wheel, grille and base, 10-spoke hubs and tires.
106-93-1 ZEROLENE 1993
Red open cab, light gray tank, black chassis and racks, silver grille, Zerolene, The Standard Oil for Motor Cars logo, Red Crown Gasoline emblem on rear of tank, "Chevron No. 11" on base.
PM 107 1927 GASOLINE TRUCK 1993
Cast cab and chassis, plastic tank, rear, cans, steering wheel, base and grille, 12-spoke hubs, tires.
107-93-1 STANDARD GASOLINE 1993
Black cab and chassis, red tank and rear, silver grille, Standard, the Gasoline of Quality logo, Red Crown Gasoline emblem on rear, "Chevron No. 10" on base.
107-94-1 LINCO GASOLINE 1994
Black cabm chassis and tank . . .
PM 108 HORSE DRAWN DELIVERY VAN 1993
Cast body and dashboard, plastic roof, seat and horse, spoked wheels.
108-93-1 NEWS OF THE WORLD 1993
Black body and dash, white roof and seat, brown horse, News of the World logo, also on rear. Special News of the World box.
108-93-2 RINGTONS TEA 1993
Black body, yellow dash, roof and seat, black horse, Ringtons Tea logo.
PM 109 SPIRIT OF AMERICA 1993
Cast upper body (with fin) and chassis, plastic lower body, small black wheels. White box.
109-93-1 METALLIC PURPLE 1993
Metallic purple upper body and chassis, white lower body, Spirit of America, emblems on lower body, American flag and name of Craig Breedlove on upper body.
PM 110 RAILTON MOBIL SPECIAL 1993
Cast body, black plastic chassis and small wheels White box.
110-93-1 SILVER 1993
Silver body, Railton "Mobil" Special and flying red horse logo.
PM 111 BLUEBIRD 1993
Cast body, black plastic chassis and seat, silver gray hubs, black tires. White box.
111-93-1 BLUE
Blue body, Union Jack on fin, crossed flags on nose.
PM 112 THRUST 2 1993
Cast body, plastic chassis, fins, windows, silver gray rear and wheels. White box.

112-93-1 GOLD 1993
Gold body, white fins, Thrust 2 logo with many sponsor emblems, blue IS monogram on fins.
PM 113 HORSE AND CART 1993
Cast flatbed, chassis, hitch and axle mount, plastic driver, horse, 20-spoke hubs and tires.
113-93-1 STEPTOE AND SON 1993
Navy blue bed, chassis, hitch and mount, red hubs, broan horse, tan driver, Steptoe & Son logo. BBC Vintage Comedy Classics box.
PM 114 STREAMLINE TANK TRUCK 1994
114-94-1 STANDARD OIL
Red lower, gray upper body, Standard Oil logo, Chevron base.
PM 115 HORSE DRAWN TANK WAGON 1994
115-94-1 STANDARD OIL
Black body, red tank, Standard Oil Company Kerosene logo, Chevron base.
PM 116 TYNE CLASS LIFEBOAT 1994
Cast upper and lower hull, plastic superstructure, rails, parts and plinth. The many variations of this model are listed in the RDP catalogs.
116-94-1 MARINERS FRIEND 1994
White lower hull, Mariners Friend logo, Lledo on plinth.
116-94-2 RNLB JAMES BURROUGH 1994
White lower hull, #47-003, RNLB James Burrough logo, Padstow on plinth.
116-94-3 RNLI FLAG 1994
    1. White lower hulll, no number, three names on plinth to date.
    2. Red lower hull, no number, Fishguard Goodwick on plinth.
116-94-3 RNLI GARSIDE 1994
Navy blue upper, white lower hull, orange superstructure, black rails and parts, R.N.L.S. Garside logo, #47-026, Kleenex Products logo on plinth, Royal National Lifeboat Institution/Kleenex box. This model also exists with, to date, 15 other names on the plinth, listed in the RDP catalogs.
116-94-4 SAM & JOAN WOODS 1994
Red lower hull, #47-002, seven names on plinth to date.
116-94-5 SIR WILLIAM HILLARY 1994
White lower hull, #47-032, RAOB GLE on plinth.
PM 117 STEP TRUCK 1995
To be issued in 1995.
PM 118 KENWORTH SEMI 1994
(Only one 1995 issue--the one I have--is listed here.)
118-94-1 SIMMONDS 1994
Black cab and semi, Simmonds logo.
118-95-1 PROMOVERS 1995
Green cab and semi chassis, white semi box, black wheels, Promovers emblem, Fuelling Your Promotion lettering.
PM 119 VOLVO SEMI 1994
(1995 issues are not listed.)
119-94-1 PROMOVERS 1994
No data.

119-94-2 RDP PUBLICATIONS 1994
Red cab and semi, black semi chassis, RdP Publications logo.
PM 120 MORRIS DROPSIDE TRUCK 1994
120-94-1 HEARTBEAT 1994
Brick red body, black chassis and grille, no logo, Heartbeat box.
120-95-1 FAIRCLOUGH AND BOOTH 1995
Blue body and rear, black chassis, silver grille, blue 6-bolt hubs, black tires. Logo: white "Fairclough and Booth Builders" etc. Special Coronation Street box.
PM 122 THRUST SSC 1995
122-95-1 THRUST SSC 1995
Black body, fin and chassis, multicolored logo, red stripes. In special box.
PM 123 MERCEDES SPECIAL EVENTS VAN 1995
123-95-1 DR. OETKER
Yellow body, brown chassis, silver grille and hubs. Dr. Oetker logo. In set of three Dr. Oetker models.
PM 124 SIX WHEEL OIL TANKER 1995
124-95-1 CHEVRON GASOLINE 1995
Red cab and chassis, white tank, Supreme Chevron Gasoline logo.
PM 125 FORD FLAT BED 1995
125-95-1 STANDARD OIL ROOF PAINT 1995
Blue cab and body, Standard Oil Roof Paint logo.

MARATHON

PROMOTIONALS

MP1 LEYLAND OLYMPIAN 1987
MP1-88-1 BOLTON EVENING NEWS 1988
Red body, roof and interior, Bolton Evening News upper logo.
MP1-88-2 BOURNEMOUTH/YELLOW CARS 1988
Yellow body and roof . . .
MP1-88-3 COUNTY PRESS/SOUTHERN VECTIS 1988
Green body, white . . .
MP1-88-4 EXPRESS LINK/NORTHERN 1988
White body and roof, black windows . . .
MP1-88-5 GLOUCESTER CITIZEN 1988
Yellow body and roof . . .
MP1-88-6 HEINZ BEAN STREET KIDS 1988
Red body and roof . . .
MP1-88-7 HUDDERSFIELD EXAMINER 1988
White body, orange . . .
MP1-88-8 PAN AM/LONDON TRANSPORT 1988
Red body and roof . . .
MP1-88-9 PEOPLE/EAST KENT 1988
Maroon body, cream roof and windows, Read Ashford People Every Week upper, East Kent lower logo.

MP1-88-10 YORKSHIRE RIDER 1988
Yellow body, green . . .
MP1-89-1 BBC SOLENT/ SOLENT BUS LINE 1989
Dark blue body, blue . . .
MP1-89-2 EASTERN EVENING NEWS 1989
White body, dark blue . . .
MP1-89-3 HOLIDAYS/STEVENSONS 1989
Yellow body, black . . .
MP1-89-4 HULL DAILY MAIL/EAST YORKSHIRE 1989
Red body and roof . . .
MP1-89-5 INVICTAWAY/MAIDSTONE 1989
Cream body, roof and windows, Invictaway upper, Maidstone &
District lower logo.
MP1-89-6 NOTTINGHAMSHIRE CC 1989
White body, roof and windows . . .
MP1-89-7 ROYAL BRITISH LEGION 1989
Dark blue body and roof . . .
MP1-89-8 SURREY CC 1989
Silver body and roof . . .
MP1-90-1 BLACKPOOL PLEASURE BEACH 1990
White body and roof, blue roof, Blackpool Pleasure Beach
upper, B P B lower logo.
MP1-90-2 DELAINE CENTENARY 1990
Dull blue body, black roof and windows, Delaine Centenary 1890-
1990 upper, The Delaine lower logo.
MP1-90-3 CHRONICLE & ECHO 1990
Yellow body, roof and windows, Chronicle & Echo, Your Local
Evening Newspaper logo.
MP1-90-4 GUIDE DOGS/DEVON GENERAL 1990
Cream body and roof . . .
    1. Destination Taunton.
    2. Destination Torquay.
MP1-90-5 MERSEYBUS 1990
Maroon body and roof . . .
MP1-91-1 ALLIED/EAST KENT 1991
Red body, cream . . .
    1. Destination Guildford.
    2. Destination Horsham.
MP1-91-2 PRESTON GUILD 1991
Grayish-blue body and roof, cream windows, Preston Guild 92 upper,
Preston Bus lower logo.
MP1-91-3 SURREY ADVERTISER/ALDER VALLEY 1991
Green body and roof, black windows, Surrey Advertiser upper, AV
Alder Valley lower logo.
MP1-92-1 EAST YORKSHIRE 1992
White body, roof and windows, East Yorkshire Motor Services logo.
    1. Destination Hedon.
    2. Destination Hull.

MP1-92-2 PRESTON GUILD 92 1992
White body, dark blue roof . . .
    1. Destination Avenham Park.
    2. Destination Deepdale.
MP1-92-3 YORKSHIRE 90 YEARS 1992
Red body and roof . . .
    1. Destination Barnsley.
    2. Destination Leeds.
MP1-94-1 NUTRASWEET/LONDON TRANSPORT 1994
Red body and roof . . .
MP2 SETRA COACH 1987
MP2-88-1 PAN-AM CREW BUS 1988
White body, blue roof . . . (How does this differ from the regular
issue?)
MP2-90-1 CROYDON ADVERTISER 1990
Yellow body and roof, ? windows, Croydon Advertiser logo.
MP3 NEOPLAN SPACELINER 1987
MP3-88-1 PAN AM HOLIDAYS 1988
Blue body, white roof . . .
MP3-88-2 SCOTTISH CITYLINK 1988
Blue body, yellow roof . . .
MP3-89-1 LONDON LINK/ALDER VALLEY 1989
White body and roof . . .
MP3-90-1 AIR RIANTA 1990
White body, red roof . . .
MP4 LEYLAND RIGID TRUCK 1988
MP4-88-1 BEAN STREET KIDS 1988
Green . . ., yellow . . .
MP4-89-1 GCM OF LEICESTER 1989
Blue . . ., white . . .
MP4-90-1 MK CABLE MANAGEMENT 1990
White . . .
MP4-90-2 TRANSPORT WEEK 1990
White . . .
MP4-92-1 BEANZ MEANZ HEINZ 1992
Turquoise cab, box and top, white chassis, Beanz Meanz Heinz logo,
Heinz emblem on rear.
MP4-93-1 TETLEY TEA FOLK 1993
Blue cab, box and top, black chassis, Tetley logo with figures.
MP4-94-1 CHESTERFIELD CO-OP 1994
White . . ., gray . . .
MP4-94-2 CUISINE FOOD SERVICE 1994
White . . .
MP4-94-3 NESCAFE 1994
White . . .
MP4-94-4 ROCHDALE PIONEERS 1994
White cab, chassis, box and top, blue and gold emblem, blue 150
Years of Co-operation, Co-op emblem on doors.

VIEW VANS

View Vans and their companion
Souvenir Buses first appeared in 1987
and 1989 respectively. They were com-
missioned by a renowned giftware firm,
Stevelyn & Co., primarily for sale to
tourists and participants in special
events.

Each of the five Lledo models used
in this way has been prepared in three
basic colors by Lledo, while Stevelyn
applies the logo details. Early in 1991
the lettering on the View Vans boxes
was changed to Souvenir Vans, but the
models are so well known by their earlier name that it is worth retaining here.

As I write this, my information on
View Vans and Souvenir Buses extends
only to the end of 1990. RDP Publications offer a catalog of all of these models, and my data come from the 1991
RDP catalog as well as from the models in my own collection. The RDP
catalog is well worth obtaining, as it
offers much more information than we
can provide here, and lists the models
by the type of locality or event they rep-
resent. They are listed here according

to which Lledo model casting they utilize.

View Van 6

The Model T Ford Van has been used as a view van in three color forms: maroon, green and blue, with the same basic color generally being used for both the body and roof, though the first blue-bodied models had black roofs and the green models had light green roofs for a time in 1988-89. Each model may be available in all three basic colors. All the models have a gold camera on the door, gold coach lines, and (with few exceptions) a gold name on the header, plus a gold-rimmed circular scene on each side. The models, like all View Vans, have LP baseplates.

VV06-87-1 BECKEY FALLS 1987
View of Beckey Falls.
VV06-87-2 BLACKPOOL 1987
View of Blackpool Tower.
VV06-87-3 CAMBRIDGE 1987
View of Kings College.
VV06-87-4 CARLISLE 1987
View of Carlisle Cathedral.
VV06-87-5 CHESTER 1987
View of Eastgate Clock.
VV06-87-6 LICHFIELD 1987
Front view of Lichfield Cathedral.
VV06-87-7 LONDON 1987
  1. View of Big Ben tower.
  2. View of Horseguards.
  3. View of Tower of London.

VV06-87-8 LONDON/FARNHAM 1987
View of Farnham Maltings.
VV06-87-9 SCARBOROUGH 1987
View of seashore.
VV06-87-10 VICTORIAN TRADITIONS 1987
View of brass bell.
VV06-87-11 THE WAREHAM BEARS 1987
View of . . .
VV06-87-12 WINDSOR 1987
  1. View of Windsor Castle.
  2. View of Windsor Tower.
VV06-88-1 BANBURY 1988
View of Banbury Cross.
VV06-88-2 BATH 1988
View of Roman baths.
VV06-88-3 BATTLE ABBEY 1988
View of Battle Abbey.
VV06-88-4 BEAULIEU 1988
View of Rolls-Royce and open-top bus.
VV06-88-5 BURY ST. EDMUNDS 1988
View of Abbeygate.
VV06-88-6 CANTERBURY CATHEDRAL 1988
View of Canterbury Cathedral from town.
VV06-88-7 CORFE CASTLE 1988
View of Corfe Castle ruins.
VV06-88-8 EASTENDERS 1988
View of Old Vic Theatre.
VV06-88-9 GREAT YARMOUTH 1988
View of docks.
VV06-88-10 IPSWICH TOWN FOOTBALL CLUB 1988
Emblem of football club.
VV06-88-11 JERSEY 1988
View of Beauport Bay.
VV06-88-12 LEEDS 1988
View of Harewood House.
VV06-88-13 LEIGH ON SEA 1988
View of seashore.
VV06-88-14 LINCOLN 1988
  1. View of Lincoln Cathedral.
  2. View of imp?
VV06-88-15 NEWMARKET 1988
View of clock tower.
VV06-88-16 NORTH NORWICH RAILWAY 1988
View of saddle tank locomotive.
VV06-88-17 NORWICH 1988
View of Norwich?
VV06-88-18 PETERBOROUGH 1988
View of Peterborough?
VV06-88-19 SALISBURY 1988
View of Salisbury from river.

VV06-88-20 TOAD HALL 1988
View of . . .
VV06-88-21 VICTORIA HOSPITAL 1988
Canford School coat of arms.
VV06-88-22 WEYMOUTH 1988
View of clock tower.
VV06-88-22 WOBURN ABBEY 1988
View of . . .
VV06-88-23 WORCESTER 1988
View of Worcester from river.
VV06-89-1 BERKELEY CASTLE 1989
View of Berkeley Castle from air.
VV06-89-2 BOSTON WEST END 1989
View of church and bridge.
VV06-89-3 BRADFORD 1989
View of church tower.
VV06-89-4 BRIGHTON 1989
View of Royal Pavilion.
VV06-89-5 BRISTOL 1989
View of Clifton Suspension Bridge.
VV06 89 6 BURNHAM 1989
View of old lighthouse.
VV06-89-7 CAERPHILLY 1989
View of Caerphilly riverside.
VV06-89-8 CLIFTON 1989
View of Clifton Suspension Bridge over Avon Gorge.
VV06-89-9 COVENTRY 1989
View of Daimler doubledeck bus.
VV06-89-10 GAILEY WHARF 1989
View of canal.
VV06-89-11 GREAT YARMOUTH 1989
View of pier.
VV06-89-12 GWR DIDCOT OXON 1989
GWR coat of arms.
VV06-89-13 GUILDFORD 1989
View of Guildford Cathedral.
VV06-89-14 HALESOWEN 1989
View of parish church.
VV06-89-15 IPSWICH 1989
View of Arch Lloyds Avenue.
VV06-89-16 ISLE OF WIGHT 1989
View of Needles Lighthouse.
VV06-89-17 NOTTINGHAM 1989
View of Robin Hood.
VV06-89-18 THE OTTER TRUST 1989
View of otter.
VV06-89-19 OXFORD 1989
View of tower.
VV06-89-20 PLYMOUTH 1989
View of Plymouth Hoe.

VV06-89-21 ST. ALBANS 1989
View of ?
VV06-89-22 ST. IVES 1989
View of harbor.
VV06-89-23 SHERINGHAM 1989
View of Market Tower.
VV06-89-24 TRURO 1989
View of Cathedral.
VV06-89-25 WELCOME BREAK 1989
View of Welcome Break.
VV06-89-26 WINCHESTER 1989
View of Winchester from air.
VV06-90-1 BIRXHAM 1990
View of harbor.
VV06-90-2 BURLEY 1990
View of village cross.
VV06-90-3 CHRISTMAS (Xmas) 1990
View of Father Christmas (Santa Claus).
VV06-90-4 FELIXSTOWE 1990
View of beach promenade.
VV06-90-5 GREAT YARMOUTH 1990
View of tower.
VV06-90-6 G.T.M. ALFORD 1990
View of oldtime racing car at Grampian Transport Museum.
VV06-90-7 JERSEY 1990
View of Corbiere Lighthouse.
VV06-90-8 LOWESTOFT 1990
   1. View of beach and pier.
   2. View of lighthouse.
VV06-90-9 LYME REGIS 1990
View of harbor.
VV06-90-10 MERLEY HOUSE & MODEL MUSEUM 1990
View of Merley House.
VV06-90-11 OBAN 1990
View of monument.
VV06-90-12 POOLE WATERFRONT 1990
View of . . .
VV06-90-13 PORTMINIAN 1990
View of Italian village.
VV06-90-14 PRESTON 1990
View of church.
VV06-90-15 SHEFFIELD 1990
View of church.
VV06-90-16 STUDELEY 1990
View of woodlands.
VV06-90-17 SUNKEN GARDENS, FLORIDA 1990
View of flamingos in garden.
VV06-90-18 WALL HEATH 1990
View of kingfisher.
VV06-90-19 WISBECH 1990
View of memorial.

VV06-91-1 SANDWELL HISTORIC VEHICLE PARADE 1991
   1991
View of West Bromwich bus.
VV06-91-2 WROXHAM 1991
View of Roys Stores.

View Van 13

The Model A Ford View Van has been made with green body and roof, brown body and roof, and cream body with brown roof, all three versions having black chassis. The roof casting with the blade angled from left front to right rear has been used for all the View Van issues. The lettering on the blade is in gold, as are the camera design on the doors and the coach lines. The nature of this model affords more room for both view and lettering than was available on the Model T van, though without the latter's antique styling. Once again, the LP base is used.

VV13-87-1 ALBERT DOCK, LIVERPOOL 1987
View of Albert Dock.
VV13-87-2 BATTLE SHOP MUSEUM 1987
View of guns on ramparts.
VV13-87-3 BERRY POMEROY CASTLE 1987
View of Berry Pomeroy Castle.
VV13-87-4 BLACKPOOL 1987
View of Blackpool Tower.
VV13-87-5 CHESTER 1987
   1. View of cathedral.
   2. View of The Rows.
   3. View of Eastgate.
VV13-87-6 DUNSTER 1987
View of Yarn Market.
VV13-87-7 EDINBURGH 1987
View of Edinburgh Castle.

VV13-87-8 FAIRFORD 1987
View of church.
VV13-87-9 FLAG OFFICER, ROYAL MARINES 1987
   1. View of Royal Marines.
   2. View of Royal Marine Band (may not be VV13).
VV13-87-10 GUERNSEY 1987
View of St. Peter Port.
VV13-87-11 ISLE OF WIGHT 1987
   1. View of Godshill Church.
   2. View of Shanklin village.
VV13-87-12 JERSEY 1987
   1. View of Corbiere Lighthouse.
   2. View of Mont Orgeuil by day.
   3. View of Mont Orgeuil by night.
VV13-87-13 LINCOLN 1987
View of city.
VV13-87-14 LLANGOLLEN 1987
View of bridge.
VV13-87-15 LONDON 1987
   1. View of Tower Bridge.
   2. View of Westminster Abbey.
VV13-87-16 MARGATE 1987
View of beach.
VV13-87-17 THE PEAKS 1987
View of Peak District scenery.
VV13-87-18 P.M.C.C. 1987 1987
View of Civil War cannon.
VV13-87-19 ROMSEY 1987
View of abbey.
VV13-87-20 SHREWSBURY 1987
View of Town Hall.
VV13-87-21 SOUTHPORT 1987
View of shops.
VV13-87-22 STIRLING 1987
View of Stirling Castle.
VV13-87-23 STRATFORD UPON AVON 1987
   1. View of Anne Hathaway's Cottage.
   2. View of Shakespeare's birthplace.
VV13-87-24 VICTORIAN TRADITIONS 1987
   1. View of brass cannon.
   2. View of brass heater.
VV13-87-25 WINDERMERE 1987
View of Lake Windermere.
VV13-87-26 WINDSOR 1987
View of Windsor Castle.
VV13-87-27 WYE COLLEGE 1987
View of Wye College.
VV13-87-28 YORK (Memories of York) 1987
View of York Minster (not same as 1989 issue).

VV13-88-1 ASHBY DE LA ZOUCH 1988
View of castle ruins.
VV13-88-2 ATTLEBOROUGH 1988
View of Defiant DIY plane.
VV13-88-3 AXBRIDGE 1988
View of half-timbered house.
VV13-88-4 BARROW IN FURNESS 1988
View of old buildings.
VV13-88-5 BEAULIEU 1988
View of antique cars.
VV13-88-6 CANTERBURY 1988
View of city.
VV13-88-7 CHEDDAR CAVES 1988
View inside cave.
VV13-88-8 CHEDDAR GORGE 1988
View of Cheddar Gorge.
VV13-88-9 CORFE CASTLE 1988
View of castle ruins.
VV13-88-10 EASTENDERS 1988
View of Albert Square.
VV13-88-11 EXETER 1988
View of cathedral by night.
VV13-88-12 HALESOWEN 1988
View of half-timbered cottages.
VV13-88-13 HAPPY HARMONIST 1988
View of Pell Continental Organ.
VV13-88-14 HAPPY WANDERER 1988
View of Pell Mini Showmans Organ.
VV13-88-15 HAREWOOD HOUSE 1988
View of Harewood House?
VV13-88-16 HIGH CLARE 1988
No data.
VV13-88-17 HUNSTANTON 1988
View of beach. (No name on blade?)
VV13-88-18 KENT & EAST SUSSEX 1988
View of locomotive. (No name on blade?)
VV13-88-19 KRISTEN POTTERY 1988
View of Beaulieu village.
VV13-88-20 LONGLEAT 1988
View of Longleat.
VV13-88-21 LOWESTOFT 1988
View of harbor.
VV13-88-22 LYME REGIS 1988
View of The Cobb.
VV13-88-23 MAMMOTH GAVIOLI 1988
View of fairground organ.
VV13-88-24 MERLEY HOUSE & MODEL MUSEUM 1988
View of Merley House.
VV13-88-25 MODEL VILLAGE 1988
   1. View of Model Village.
   2. View of suspension bridge.

VV13-88-26 NORFOLK BROADS 1988
View of Horning.
VV13-88-27 NORTH NORFOLK RAILWAY 1988
View of BR Eastern locomotive.
VV13-88-28 PETERBOROUGH 1988
View of town.
VV13-88-29 POOLE HARBOUR 1988
View of sailboats.
VV13-88-30 ROCKINGHAM 1988
No data.
VV13-88-31 ROMAN BATHS, BATH 1988
View of Roman baths.
VV13-88-32 RYE 1988
View of Penny Royal. (No name on blade?)
VV13-88-33 ST. ALBANS 1988
View of town?
VV13-88-34 SANDBANKS POOLE 1988
View of seashore.
VV13-88-35 SWANAGE 1988
View of seashore.
VV13-89-1 ALTON TOWERS 1989
View of Corkscrew.
VV13-89-2 ARUNDEL 1989
View of Arundel from the air.
VV13-89-3 ASTON HALL 1989
View of Aston Hall.
VV13-89-4 BENTLEY WILDFOWL & MOTOR MUSEUM 1989
View of mandarin duck.
VV13-89-5 BLACK COUNTRY MUSEUM 1989
View of oldtime village.
VV13-89-6 BOURNEMOUTH 1989
View of old square.
VV13-89-7 BOURTON ON THE WATER 1989
View of bridge over river.
VV13-89-8 BURLEY, NEW FOREST 1989
View of village cross.
VV13-89-9 BURY ST. EDMUNDS 1989
View of Bury in bloom.
VV13-89-10 CARDIFF 1989
   1. View of city wall.
   2. View of red dragon. (No name on blade?)
VV13-89-11 CHASEWATER LIGHT RAILWAY 1989
View of saddle tank locomotive.
VV13-89-12 CHATSWORTH HOUSE 1989
View of Chatsworth House from air.
VV13-89-13 COCKINGTON 1989
View of village.
VV13-89-14 COVENTRY 1989
View of old and new cathedrals.

VV13-89-15 CROMER 1989
View of pier.
VV13-89-16 DARTMOUTH 1989
View across bay.
VV13-89-17 DEFIANT DIY CENTRE 1989
View of Defiant DIY plane.
VV13-89-18 DOVER 1989
View of White Cliffs of Dover.
VV13-89-19 EXMOOR 1989
View of Lorna Doone Farm. (No name on blade?)
VV13-89-20 FESTIVAL OF TRANSPORT, WESTON PARK 1989
View of oldtime vehicles.
VV13-89-21 GLAMIS 1989
View of Glamis Castle.
VV13-89-22 GRANGE OVER SANDS 1989
No data.
VV13-89-23 HENLEY IN ARDEN 1989
View of High Street.
VV13-89-24 IPSWICH 1989
View of street scene.
VV13-89-25 JOHN O' GROATS 1989
View of rocky seacoast
VV13-89-26 KING OF SALTBURN 1989
View of seashore.
VV13-89-27 KIRKLEES HISTORIC VEHICLE PARADE 1989
View of doubledeck bus.
VV13-89-28 LANDS END 1989
View of rocky seacoast.
VV13-89-29 LEICESTER TRANSPORT PAGEANT 1989
View of Mercury van.
VV13-89-30 LIVERPOOL 1989
View of new cathedral.
VV13-89-31 LYNDHURST, NEW FOREST 1989
View of cottages.
VV13-89-32 LONDON 1989
View of Buckingham Palace.
VV13-89-33 M.A. ARTS (Birmingham) 1989
View of Bull Ring.
VV13-89-34 MATLOCK BATH AND RIVER DERWENT 1989
View of Matlock river scene.
VV13-89-35 MOOR STREET 1948 1989
View of GWR locomotive in station.
VV13-89-36 MUSEUM OF BRITISH ROAD TRANSPORT 1989
View of car (not same as 1990 issue).
VV13-89-37 NORTH NORFOLK RAILWAY 1989
View of saddle tank locomotive.

VV13-89-38 OUTER CIRCLE RALLY 1989 1989
View of four West Midland doubledeck buses.
VV13-89-39 PORT ISAAC 1989
View of harbor.
VV13-89-40 RINGWOOD 1989
View across river.
VV13-89-41 SALCOMBE 1989
View of harbor.
**VV13-89-42 SANDWELL HISTORIC VEHICLE PARADE
      1989**
View of two oldtime cars.
VV13-89-43 SEVERN BRIDGE 1989
View of Severn Bridge.
VV13-89-44 SOUTHEND ON SEA 1989
View of pier.
VV13-89-45 SPROWSTON 1989
View of St. Cuthbert's Church.
VV13-89-46 STONEHENGE 1989
      1. View of Stonehenge from air.
      2. View of Stonehenge from ground.
VV13-89-47 TORQUAY 1989
View of harbor.
VV13-89-48 VALLEY ANGLESEY 1989
View of Menai Straits bridge.
VV13-89-49 WARWICK 1989
View of Warwick Castle.
VV13-89-50 WYTHALL 1989
      1. View of Routemaster and BMMO D9 buses.
      2. View of Bristol MW singledeck bus.
VV13-89-51 YORK 1989
View of York Minster.
VV13-90-1 BEESTON HALL 1990
View of Beeston Hall.
VV13-90-2 BERWICK ON TWEED 1990
View of bridge.
VV13-90-3 CANNOCK 1990
View of downtown area.
VV13-90-4 COVENTRY 1990
      1. View of City Centre in thirties.
      2. View of buses in wartime.
VV13-90-5 DUNDEE 1990
View of ship MS Discovery.
VV13-90-6 EPCOT CENTER 1990
View of street scene.
VV13-90-7 THE FEW 1990
View of Supermarine Spitfire plane.
VV13-90-8 FLATFORD 1990
View of Willy Lotts Cottage.
VV13-90-9 FORGE MUSEUM 1990
View of Forge Museum.

VV13-90-10 FORT WILLIAM 1990
View of ski lift.
VV13-90-11 GOLD HILL, SHAFTESBURY 1990
View of Gold Hill.
VV13-90-12 GREAT YARMOUTH 1990
View of beach promenade.
VV13-90-13 INVERNESS 1990
View of castle and River Ness.
VV13-90-14 J. W. STRINGER LTD. 1990
No data.
VV13-90-15 KIRRIEMUIR 1990
No data.
VV13-90-16 LINCOLN 1990
View inside cathedral.
VV13-90-17 LITTLEPORT 1990
View of parish church.
VV13-90-18 LOWESTOFT 1990
View of Sparrows Nest Pavilion.
VV13-90-19 MANCHESTER 1990
View of bus station.
VV13-90-20 MOSQUITO AIRCRAFT MUSEUM 1990
View of DH Mosquito plane.
VV13-90-21 MULLION COVE, CORNWALL 1990
View of harbor.
**VV13-90-22 MUSEUM OF BRITISH ROAD TRANSPORT
      1990**
View of Model T Ford.
VV13-90-23 NEEDLES, ISLE OF WIGHT 1990
View of Pleasure Park.
VV13-90-24 OUTER CIRCLE RALLY 1990 1990
View of Outer Circle buses.
VV13-90-24 PRESTON 1990
View of Town Hall.
VV13-90-25 ST. DAVIDS 1990
View of cathedral.
VV13-90-26 ST. IVES 1990
View of harbor.
VV13-90-27 ST. JOHNS GATE 1990
View of historic scene.
VV13-90-28 SHETLAND 1990
View of puffins.
VV13-90-29 SUNKEN GARDENS, FLORIDA 1990
View of flamingos in garden.
VV13-90-30 SWINDON & CRICKLADE RAILWAY 1990
View of passenger train.
VV13-90-31 TAUNTON 1990
View of castle.
VV13-90-32 TORQUAY 1990
View of Model Village. No name on blade?
VV13-90-33 WIDECOMBE IN THE MOOR 1990

View of countryside.
VV13-90-34 WIMBORNE 1990
View of Model Village. No name on blade?
VV13-90-35 WROXHAM 1990
View of Norfolk Broads.
VV13-91-36 TEMPLE GROVE SCHOOL, UCKFIELD 1991
View of Temple Grove School.
VV13-??-1 CHARTWELL year?
No data.
VV13-??-2 KINGSBRIDGE year?
No data.
VV13-??-3 YE OLDE CHOCOLATE BOX year?
No data.
VV13-??-4 WATFORD F C year?
View of football team.

Souvenir Bus 15

   The AEC Regent doubledeck bus
was first used as a souvenir model in
1989. It exists in the usual three versions, all with cream windows and interior. One type has a red body and roof
and black chassis, the second has a
green body with darker green roof and
chassis, and the third has a light blue
body, dark blue chassis and silver roof.
The upper logo shows the name of the
place flanked by "The Place" and "To
Visit", the lower logo is the familiar
"General" livery, and there are no pictures; thus we can only list the buses
by name.

SB15-89-1 BATH SPA 1989
SB15-89-2 BRISTOL 1989
SB15-89-3 CHESTER 1989
SB15-89-4 COWES WEEK 1989 1989
SB15-89-5 DEFIANT DIY CENTRE 1989

215

SB15-89-6 GREAT YARMOUTH 1989
SB15-89-7 HALESOWEN 1989
SB15-89-8 HENLEY IN ARDEN 1989
SB15-89-9 LITTLECOTE TOYFAIR 1989
SB15-89-10 MERLEY HOUSE & MODEL MUSEUM 1989
SB15-89-11 NORTH NORFOLK RAILWAY 1989
SB15-89-12 NORWICH 1989
SB15-89-13 REDDITCH 1989
SB15-89-14 SWANAGE 1989
SB15-89-15 THE WAREHAM BEARS 1989
SB15-89-16 WEST END OF BOSTON 1989
SB15-90-1 ASTON HALL 1990
SB15-90-2 BENTLEY WILDFOWL & MOTOR MUSEUM
     1990
SB15-90-3 BROCKENHURST 1990
SB15-90-4 BURLEY, NEW FOREST 1990
SB15-90-5 DUNDEE 1990
SB15-90-6 GLEN CLOVA 1990
SB15-90-7 GLEN PROSSEN 1990
SB15-90-8 HAPPY WANDERER 1990
SB15-90-9 ISLE OF WIGHT 1990
sb15-90-10 LEATHERLAND, JERSEY 1990
SB15-90-11 LYNDHURST 1990
SB15-90-12 MOSQUITO AIRCRAFT MUSEUM 1990
SB15-90-13 MULLION COVE, CORNWALL 1990
SB15-90-14 PORTMINIAN 1990
SB15-90-15 PRESTON 1990
SB15-90-16 ST. DAVIDS 1990
SB15-90-17 SUNKEN GARDENS, FLORIDA 1990
SB15-90-18 TAUNTON 1990
SB15-90-19 TINTAGEL 1990
SB15-90-20 WISBECH 1990
SB15-91-21 MANCHESTER 1991
SB15-91-22 SHERINGHAM WEYBOURNE 1991

Souvenir Bus 17

The A.E.C. Regal singledeck bus was first used as a souvenir model in 1990. Like the doubledecker, it bears the name of the place, flanked by "The Place" and "To Visit", on its boards; unlike it, it has room for a picture below the windows. The three color com-binations are: Maroon body and roof, black chassis, ivory windows and seats; green body and roof, otherwise as the first type; and tan body, windows and seats, with dark brown chassis and roof.

SB17-90-1 EAST LANCASHIRE RAILWAY 1990
View of East Lancashire Railway emblem.
SB17-90-2 FELIXSTOWE 1990
View of beach promenade.
SB17-90-3 ISLE OF WIGHT 1990
No data.
SB17-90-4 LOWESTOFT 1990
View of marina.
SB17-90-5 MATLOCK BATH 1990
View of Matlock River.
SB17-90-6 MERLEY HOUSE & MODEL MUSEUM 1990
View of Merley House.
SB17-90-7 NORWICH 1990
View of Norwich Castle.
SB17-90-8 PITLOCHRY 1990
View of Main Street.
SB17-90-9 POLPERRO 1990
View of harbor.
SB17-90-10 THE POPPY LINE 1990
View of passenger train.
SB17-90-11 STIRLING 1990
View of Stirling Castle.
SB17-90-12 TAMWORTH 1990
View of castle, bridge and river.
SB17-90-13 WISBECH 1990
View of Peckover House.
SB17-91-1 ASHFORD IN THE WATER 1991
View of river.
SB17-91-2 SHERINGHAM HOLT 1991
View of saddle-tank locomotive.

View Van 21

The #21 Chevrolet Van was also first used as a View Van in 1990. The name of the place appears in gold on a longitudinal roof blade, with the pic-ture in a large oval on the body sides. The three color combinations are: Maroon body and roof, gold chassis; gold body, maroon roof, black chassis; and navy blue body and roof, black chassis.

VV21-90-1 1ST LLEDO SHOW 1990
View of #17 AEC singledeck bus.
VV21-90-2 BOURNEMOUTH CENTENARY 1990
No data.
VV21-90-3 EDRADOUR DISTILLERY 1990
View of distillery.
VV21-90-4 LINCOLN 1990
View inside cathedral.
VV21-90-4 LONGLEAT 1990
View of Longleat House.
VV21-90-5 MERLEY HOUSE & MODEL COLLECTION
     1990
View of Merley House.
VV21-90-6 PORT ISAAC 1990
View of harbor.
VV21-90-7 SANDOWN I-o-W 1990
View of cliffs.
VV21-90-8 SANDWELL HISTORIC VEHICLE PARADE
     1990
View of doubledeck bus.
VV21-90-9 TINTAGEL 1990
View of castle ruins.
VV21-90-10 WIMBORNE 1990
     1. View of Wimborne Minster.
     2. Different view of Minster.
VV21-91-1 BROADLAND COLLECTION 1991
View of Beeston Hall.
VV21-91-2 SHERINGHAM WEYBOURNE 1991
View of Great Eastern passenger train.
VV21-??-1 NORTH YORKSHIRE MOORS RAILWAY year?
No data.

PRICE GUIDE

I never enjoy compiling price guides, and my readers hardly ever enjoy reading them. Unless a model is current and sells for a more or less standardized price, the value of a model depends on such factors as how much the seller wants to receive and how much the buyer wants to pay—which can vary extremely from one buyer or seller to another. Then too, the value of obsolete models has a way of going up, particularly between the time I compile the price guide and the time the book is printed!

We can only approximate values, and as usual in my books, I'll state two prices, the lower one for a garden-variety collector buying from an easygoing dealer, the higher for a collector who absolutely has to have that model or a dealer who has to double what he paid for the model. The prices stated are for mint boxed models; mint unboxed specimens will be at least 10% less, and the more damage a model has, the more the value will drop.

The Days Gone models are fairly easy to list; current issues will sell for current prices, common obsolete models will usually go for $6 to $12, so our only problems are the few foreign-market or otherwise limited issues, which I'll try to list separately.

As for the Lledo Promotionals, anything is possible. Some of them can be had for as low as $10, some will demand three-figure prices, and in most cases I have no idea what range a given promotional model will fall into. Our only guides are dealers' sales lists and the prices we see at toy shows.

DAYS GONE

1   Horse Drawn Tram: all obsolete, $6-12.
2   Milk Float: all obsolete, $6-12.
3   Delivery Van: all obsolete, $6-12.
4   Omnibus, all but 017 obsolete, $6-12 except
    000: some varieties may be $12-20.
    002: some varieties may be $12-20.
    005: reverse tampo, $25-40.
    010: A Million Copies: $40-60.

5   Fire Engine: all but 010 obsolete, $6-12 except
    001: gold wheels, cream horses, $100-?
    002: black boiler, $100-125.
    003: red boiler, $100-125.
6   Ford Van: all but last few obsolete, $6-12, except
    002, 003, 006, 016, 033, 034, 036, 042: some varieties may be worth two or more times the usual price.
    050: Toy Fair issues may be worth $20-40.
7   Woody Wagon: all obsolete, $6-12.
8   Ford Tanker: all obsolete, $6-12 except

000: "Inflamable" misspelling, $20-30.
003: white roof, $40-50.
010: $30-45.

9 Model A Ford: all obsolete, $6-12 except
000: some varieties may be worth ⁻20-35.

10 Dennis Coach: all obsolete, $6-12 except
000, 002, 004, 005, 008, 014: some varieties may be $20-40.

11 Horse Drawn Van: all but 025 obsolete, $6-12.

12 Fire Engine: all but last few obsolete, $6-12 except
000, 003, 005: some varieties may be worth $20-30.

13 Ford A Van: all but 061 obsolete, $6-12 except
021: yellow chassis, $40-60?
053, 054: German issues, $40-60.

14 Model A Ford: all obsolete, $6-12 except
000, 004: some varieties may be worth $12-25.

15 AEC Doubledecker: all but last few obsolete, $6-12 except
005: some varieties may be worth $12-25.
007: unpainted model $30-45.

16 Dennis Van: all but last few obsolete, $6-12 except
014, 021: some varieties may be worth $12-25.

17 AEC Singledecker: all but last obsolete, $6-12 except
001: model with filler cap $100 and up; red body $30-45.

18 Packard: all but last obsolete, $6-12 except
No# Camperdown: $50-75.

19 Rolls-Royce: all obsolete, $6-12 except
000: $15-25.
002: some varieties may be worth $12-20.
003: undrilled base, $50 and up?
011: German issue, $40-60.
No#: cream, $35-50.

20 Stake Truck: all but last few obsolete, $6-12, except
001: red barrels, $25-40.

21 Chevrolet Van: all but last few obsolete, $6-12 except
000, 001: some varieties may be worth $12-20.
033: Scribbans $30-45?

040: German issue, $40-60.

22 Town Van: all obsolete, $6-12.

23 Scenicruiser: all obsolete, $6-12.

24 Rolls-Royce Playboy, all obsolete, $6-12 except
002: undrilled base, $50 and up?

25 Rolls-Royce Ghost: all obsolete, $6-12, except
002: undrilled base, $50 and up?

26 Bottle Truck: all but 015 obsolete, $6-12 except
000, 007: some varieties may be worth $12-25.
011: reversed tampo, $25-35?

27 Breakdown Truck: all obsolete, $6-12, except
003: French issue, $12-20.

28 Canvasback Truck: all but last few obsolete, $6-12 except
012, 018: $20-35 each.

29 Dodge 4x4, all but last few obsolete, $6-12.

30 Chevrolet Van, all but last few obsolete, $6-12.

31 Brewers Dray, all but 008 obsolete, $6-12 each, except
001: limited, $12-20.
002, 003: reverse tampo, $20-35 each.

32 Rolls-Royce, all obsolete, $6-12, except
006, 007: $35-50 each.

33 Model T Ford, all but last few obsolete, $6-12, except
008: not sure.

34 Dennis Van, all obsolete, $6-12.

35 Dennis Limousine, all obsolete, $6-12.

36 Chevrolet Pickup, all but last few obsolete, $6-12 except
006: German issue, $45-60.

37 Model A Ford Van, all obsolete, $6-12.

38 Rolls-Royce, only issue obsolete, $8-12.

39 Mack Truck, all obsolete, $6-12.

40 Crane Truck, all obsolete, $6-12.

41 Trolley, all but last few obsolete, $8-12.

42 Mack Tanker, all but last obsolete, $6-12 except
006: German issue, $40-60.

43 Morris Van, all but last few obsolete, $8-12 except

	009: Toy Fairs model, $20-30.
	016: German issue, $40-60.
44	Scammell 6-Wheeler, all but last few obsolete, $8-12 except 009: German issue, $40-60.
45	Rolls-Royce, all but last obsolete, $6-12.
46	Bentley, all but last obsolete, $6-12.
47	Austin Taxi, all but last obsolete, $8-12.
48	Chevrolet, all but last few obsolete, $6-12.
49	AEC Renown, all but last few obsolete, $8-12.
50	Morris Van, all but last few obsolete, $6-12 except 007: not sure.
51	Chevrolet Box Van, all but last few obsolete, $6-12 except 006: German issue, $40-60.
52	Morris Van, all but last obsolete, $8-12 except 008: Toy Fair issue, $20-35.
53	Rolls-Royce, 000 $8-12, 001 German issue, $40-60.
54	Rolls-Royce D, both obsolete, $8-12.
56	Ford Van, 000 obsolete, $8-12.
57	Ford Tanker, current or recently obsolete, $6-12.
58	Morris Z Van, current or recently obsolete, $6-12.
59	Bedford 30cwt, currnet or recently obsolete, $6-12 except 009, 010: Toy Fair models, $20-35.
60	Fire Engine, current or newly obsolete, $6-12.
61	Pontiac Van, current or newly obsolete, $6-12.
62	Ford Tanker, 000 current.
63	Bedford Van, all more or less current.
64	Ambulance, all more or less current.
65	Morris Traveller, all current.
66	Dennis Van, all current.
67	Ford Semi, all current.
68	Open Top Bus, all current.
69-75	all current.

Gray Series	$25-50 each, or maybe more.
Fantastic Set o' Wheels	$6-12 each.
Edocar Series	$10-16 each.
Marathons	$6-12 each.

Lledo Promotionals

As stated above, the values of these can vary from less than $10 to more- sometimes much more—than $100, and I have no way of evaluating them. This includes Marathon promotionals.

PM Series

$8-16 each. Some may be worth more.

View Vans and Souvenir Buses

I have no way of knowing.

In closing, let me say that Lledo models in general offer more collecting for less money than most brands on the market today.

NOTES

NOTES

NOTES

NOTES

NOTES